THE PARTICULAR
ASSESSMENT LISTS

FOR
BALTIMORE AND CARROLL COUNTIES,
MARYLAND

1798

George J. Horvath, Jr.

HERITAGE BOOKS
2015

HERITAGE BOOKS
AN IMPRINT OF HERITAGE BOOKS, INC.

Books, CDs, and more—Worldwide

For our listing of thousands of titles see our website
at
www.HeritageBooks.com

Published 2015 by
HERITAGE BOOKS, INC.
Publishing Division
5810 Ruatan Street
Berwyn Heights, Md. 20740

International Standard Book Numbers
Paperbound: 978-1-58549-092-9
Clothbound: 978-0-7884-6248-1

CONTENTS

PREFACE

Early in July, 1798, Congress passed a tax law which came to be known as the "window tax." Commissioners in each state were to divide the state into districts, and collect data on the valuation of lands and dwelling houses and the counting of slaves. For dwelling houses the commissioners were to specify "their situation, their number of stories, the number and dimensions of the windows (hence the nick-name)," and the materials of which the houses were built.[1]

When the commissioners for Maryland had completed their task they had compiled a three part record series. The first was a general assessment list giving names of owners of dwelling houses, lands, wharfs, and slaves on 1 October 1798. The first list also contained property subjected to valuation, property that the chief assessor had determined should be exempt from valuation, and the revisions made by the Tax Commissioners. The second part of the list was a "Particular Assessment List" giving dimensions of dwellings, outbuildings, and land as of 1 October 1798. The third list was a general tax list giving the names of persons who were to pay the tax, the amount of valuation, the rate per sentum, and the amount of tax due. The original papers are available on microfilm at the Maryland Historical Society.[2]

This volume contains the information found in the second part of the tax list, the Particular Assessment List, for Baltimore County (exclusive of Baltimore Town, plus the information for the three hundreds in Frederick County that later made up Carroll County. In addition, names from the "precincts" surrounding Baltimore Town were garnered from an 1804 Tax list. In some cases when the Particular list was missing, names were drawn from the General List.

Although the names in the tax list for Baltimore Town have not been included, researchers have a number of sources available for determining who lived in Baltimore Town. First of all, of course, is the 1800 Census of Baltimore Town. Then there is Richard J. Cox''s Name Index to the Baltimore City Tax Records, 1798-1808, of the Baltimore City Archives, published in 1981 by the Baltimore City Archives and Records Management Office: Department of Legislative Reference. Finally there are the Baltimore City Directories, which first appeared in 1796. City directories for 1796, 1799 and 1807 have been republished by Family Line Publications.

The value of this work to genealogists and historians lies in the informatin found in the entries. Not only are the names of property owners of Baltimore County given, but also the acreage, the name of the tract (in many cases), a description of the buildings on the property and a comment on the quality of the property. If the property was actually occupied by someone other than the owner, the name(s) of the occupant(s) is also given. Since the 1800 Census for Baltimore County is largely non-existent, this work becomes even more important.

Robert Barnes

NOTES

1. Harry Marlin Tinkom, The Republicans and Federalists in Pennsylvania, 1790-1801 (Harrisburg: Pennsylvania Historical and Museum Commission, 1950), p. 215.

2. Mary K. Meyer, Genealogical Research in Maryland: A Guide (Baltimore: Maryland Historical Society, 1983), p. 16.

ABBREVIATIONS

The following abbreviations have been used in this volume to conserve space.

A - acres (A+ signifies acreage slightly more than given figure, by less than an acrea.)

add. - additional (added to a earlier structure)

adj - adjoining

brk - brick

dwlg - dwelling

fr - frame

ft - feet (All dimensions are given in feet, whether indicated or not.)

Hd - Hundred (A subsection of the county)

hse - house

indiff - indifferent

kn - kitchen

out repair - out of repair; in need of repair

pt - part or part of

rd - road

stble - stable

stry - story

tol - tolerable

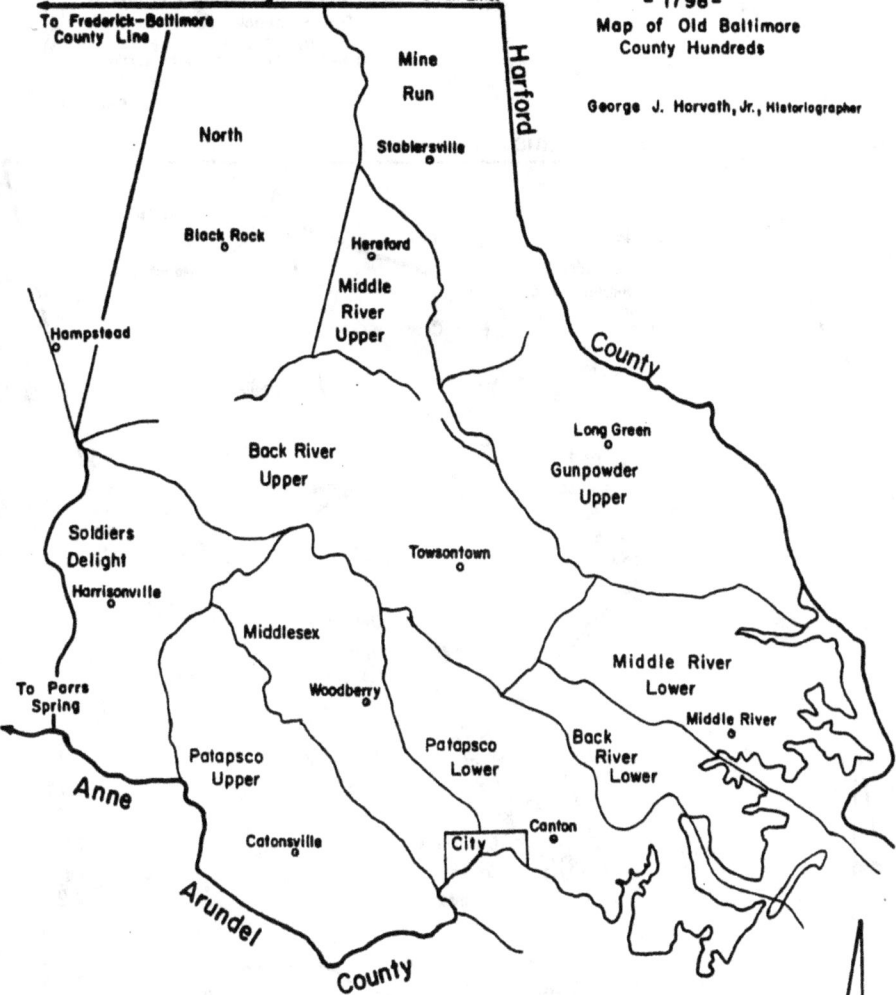

Pennsylvania (Mason-Dixon Line)

To Frederick-Baltimore
County Line

Mine
Run

– 1798 –
Map of Old Baltimore
County Hundreds

George J. Horvath, Jr., Historiographer

North

Stablersville

Harford

Black Rock

Hereford

Middle
River
Upper

Hampstead

County

Back River
Upper

Long Green

Gunpowder
Upper

Soldiers
Delight

Towsontown

Harrisonville

Middlesex

Middle River
Lower

Middle River

To Parrs
Spring

Woodberry

Patapsco
Upper

Anne

Patapsco
Lower

Back
River
Lower

Canton

Catonsville

City

Arundel

County

Drawn by:

Robert Wilkinson
3030 Woodside Ave.
Baltimore, MD. 21234

vii

To Baltimore-
Harford County
Line

Pennsylvania   (Mason - Dixon Line)

North
Hundred

Taneytown *and*   Piney Creek

Hundreds
District No. 6

o Manchester

Pipe Creek
and

Westminster

Hundreds
District No.3

Snydersburg
o

Unity *and*

Burnt House

Hundreds
District
No. I

Pipe
Creek
Hundred

Westminster

LINE
LINE 1837

Delaware

Upper

Hundred

Finksburg
o

FREDERICK COUNTY

BALTIMORE COUNTY

Falls

Delaware

Lower

Hundred

Eldersburg
o

North Branch Patapsco

Parrs
Spring

Anne

Arundel

County

↑

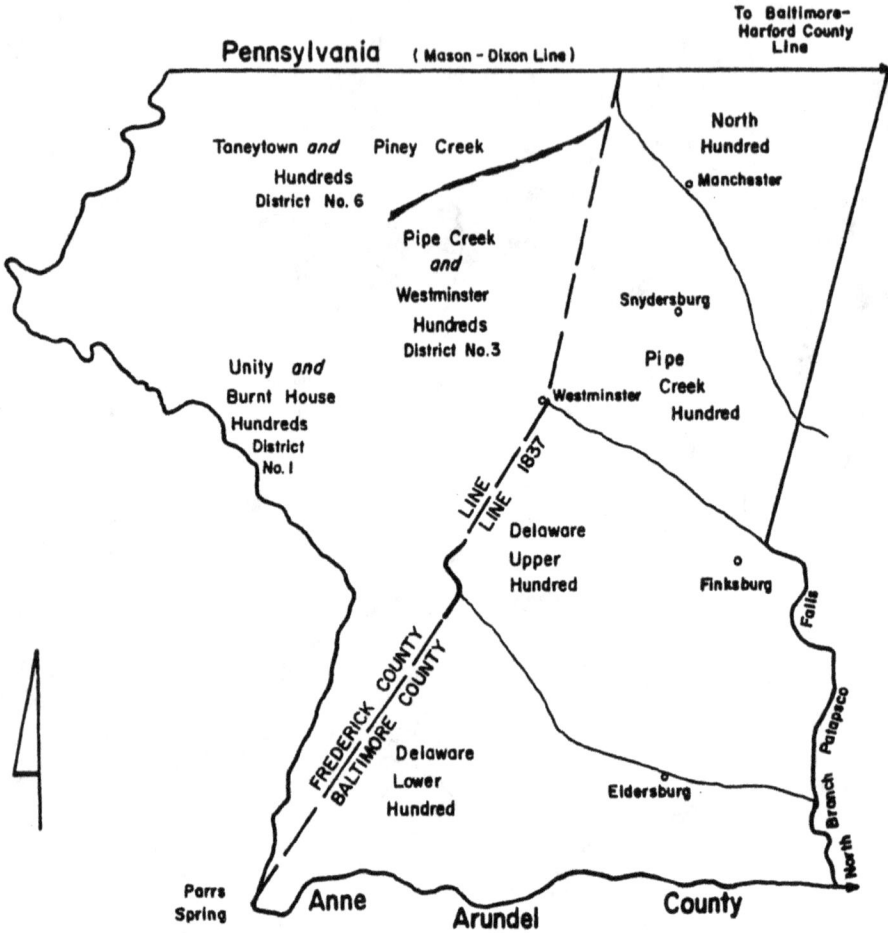

Drawn by:

Robert Wilkinson
3030 Woodside Ave.
Baltimore, MD. 21234

ANDERSON, Thomas; 228 1/2 A; dwlg hse of hewn log, 1 stry, 39x18, piazza, 6x39; old kn, 16x16, log; meat hse, 8x8; log stbles, 24x12; land adj Carroll Manor, Temperance BACON and others

ALMANY, Mary (6 slaves); Mine Run Hd; 522A; log dwlg hse, 53x14, 1 stry, in tol repair; old log kn, 16x12; new log meat hse, 10x12; old log hen hse & spring hse, both 10x12, tol repair; log barn 64x18; old log stbles, 16x12 & 10x12; new log corn hse, 24x14; old corn hse, 22x12; land adj Harford Co line, Jacob DALEY and others

ANDERSON, Benj. Sr (5 slaves); Mine Run Hd; 522A; Lot 60; dwlg hse, pt log, pt fr, 24x16, 1 stry; fr hse, 16x16, much out repair; old log kn, 12x12; meat hse 10x12; barn of hewd logs thatched with straw not quite finished, 48x24; land adj John MERRYMAN, Esq., Walter PERDUE and James BOSLEY

ANSEL, Benj. 14A; log dwlg hse, 16x14, old and indiff; land adj John SOWERS & Daniel SHAW

ARMSTRONG, Solomon - On the Manor - 46A (20 acres sold for taxes - 1805); log dwlg hse, 1 stry, 18x16; land adj Joseph McCLUNG, Abraham NORRIS

ARMS, Thomas; 54A; log dwlg hse, 16x18; log stble, 12x14; land adj Christian CROUSE

ANDERSON, Joshua (6 slaves); 829A; Mine Run Hd; (Manor); Occupants: Thomas ANDERSON (6 slaves), Benj. ANDERSON, Jr. (5 slaves); Anderson Retreat; log dwlg hse, 16x16; kn 14x12; log meat hse 12x10; spring hse 8x8 each, very old, indiff; log granary 12x10; log stble 20x12; stble 16x12; land adj Joseph SUTTON & Samuel MERRYDITH

ALLEN, William (1 slave); 126 1/4 A; Land Promise; log dwlg hse 20x16; log kn, 16 ft; log hen hse, 10x10; log corn hse 18x18, stble under it; occuant: Wm. GROVER; old dwlg hse, 20x16, out of repairs - adj land of Charles RIDGLEY and others

AMOSS, Benjamin; 55A; Hills Camp & Mill tract; adj Little falls of Gunpowder

ALLENDER, Wm. (1 slave); Up Gunpwdr Hd; 140A; log dwlg hse, 20x16, 1 stry; adj Edw. ALLENDER, Geo. HOLLAND & others

ALLENDER, Edw'd; 150A; old fr dwlg hse, 26x16, out repair; barn, 26x26, old, out of repair; adj Underwood GUITON & Mary HOLLAND, &C

BURKE, Mary (1 slave); Mine Run Hd; 131A; old log dwlg hse, 32x14, out repair; log stble 16x12; log stble 20x18; adj John JONES & others

BOSLEY, James (5 slaves); Mine Run Hd; 344 3/4 A; dwlg hse, 42x22, fr, hypt roof, a little out of repair; kn, logs, 20x18, old out repair; new log meat hse, 10x10; stble, logs, thatched with straw; adj Benj. MERRYDITH, John SOWERS

BACON, Temperance (3 slaves); Mine Run Hd; 148 1/4 A; Lot 53; dwlg hse, 26x26, fr, 1 stry, old much out repair; old fr kn, 20x16, indiff; meat hse, 12x12; barn, 40x20, shingle roof, 1 stry, not quite finished; adj Edmond STANSBURY & Thomas ANDERSON

BOSLEY, Elijah (23 slaves); Mine Run Hd; dwlg hse, stone, 2 stry, 46x24, new, in good repair; kn, stone, 1 stry, 45x24, in good repair; quarter hse, 20x16, in bad repair; spring hse, stone, 12x12; hen hse, stone, 15x15, very much out repair; old quarter hse, logs, 20x16, not repaired; barn, stone, 60x30, 1 1/3 stry, good repair; stble, 42x27, stone, 2 stry, tol good repair; old stble, fr, 24x24; old log stble, 22x12, adj Carrolls Manor; Occupant: John CUDDY; dwlg hse, fr, hipt roof, 30x20, very old, out repair - adj Elijah MERRYMAN

No land (Renters): Benjamin BOYCE (2 slaves); Up Gunpwdr Hd
John BRADFORD (2 slaves); Up Gunpwdr Hd

Asael BARTON (8 slaves); Up Gunpwdr Hd

Richard BIDDLE (1 slave); Mine Run Hd

BOND, Thomas, Esq.; 15A; land adj little falls & Elijah BOSLEY

BURNS, Michael; 46A; dwlg hse, logs, 18x24, 1 stry, out repair; shed, 10x18, _us shop; barn, 36x15, logs, thatcht with straw, tol good

BULL, Jacob; 136A (100 acres sold for taxes - 1805); ; dwlg hse, stone, 27x18, 1 stry, tol repair; old meat hse, logs, 10x10; spring hse, 6x8; stble 24x12, logs; shop, 16x12, logs; adj Wm. SINCLAR and Ezekiel BOSLEY

BOSLEY, Ezekiel (5 slaves); Mine Run Hd; Manor Green; 599A; dwlg hse, 20x26, fr, hip roof, with add. 1 stry, 28x16; log kn, 16x14, 1 stry; stone milk hse, 8x10; old meat hse, logs, 12x12, hen hse, 8x10 logs; dwlg hse, logs, 12x16; cabin 10x12; cabin 12x16; old corn hse, log, 30x10; log barn 70x20, log, in good repair; adj John MERRYMAN & Wm. KLAINE(?); property at Little Falls & Jarrettsville Pike

BURNS, John; 71A; log hse, 16x16, log kn, 10x12; old spring hse, log, 10x12d; log barn, 50x22, very indiff; adj George ELLIOTT & Gist VAUGHAN

BULL, William and VAUGHAN, Gist; Occupant: Arthur RYLAND; 285A; dwlg hse, logs, 18x18, out repair; stble, 17x9, indiff; log still hse, 10x10, indiff built; grist mill, 24x24, hewn logs, 2 stry; saw mill, 24x24, hewn logs, much out repair; adj Jacob SPLITSTONE & George ELLIOTT

BELL, John; Occupant: Joshua SUTTON; 148A; dwlg hse, hewd logs, 33x14, 1 stry, tol repair; hen hse, 10x12, logs; old log barn, 34x18, indiff; adj Joseph SUTTON, Wm. COULSON

BOND, Edward; 168 1/2 A; old dwlg hse, 20x18, logs; hen hse, logs, 8x8; barn, 46x14, logs, indiff; adj Thomas MARSHAL, Chas. BOND

BOND, Charles; 369A; dwlg hse, hewd logs, 20x20, 1 stry; meat hse, logs, 10x10; old kn, logs, 19x14, indiff; stble 20x14; barn 58x20, not quite finished; adj Jacob ROCKHOLD, Edw. BOND

BAKER, John; 51A; old log hse, 16x18, cabin built; barn, 24x15, logs

BAKER, Margaret; 92 1/2 A; old log dwlg hse, 30x18, 1 stry; barn, logs, 48x12, indiff; old log stble, 14x10, indiff; adj John BAKER, Elizabeth ROSIER

BURNES, Adam (Possibly at White Hall); 140A; dwlg hse, logs, 35x18, old, indiff; spring hse, cabin built, 12x14; good barn, logs, 51x20; adj Jacob SPLITSTONE, Jr. and Jonathan PLOWMAN

BUCHANAN, George (1 slave); Up Gunpwdr Hd; Occupant: Nicholas FULLER (supt.); next to "Clynmalira"; 861 3/4 A; dwlg hse, fr & weatherboard, 2 stry, well finished inside, 30x18; kn, hewd log, 1 stry, 30x16; stbles out repair, 36x14; barn out repair, 30x24, fr; quarter hse hewd log, 1 stry, 16x26; meat hse, logs, 12x12; adj Carrolls Manor

BUSSEY, Edward B.; Occupant: Jesse BUSSEY (4 slaves); Up Gunpwdr Hd; 301 1/2 A; dwlg hse, fr, 26x26, hipt roof, very out of repair; kn, log, 20x15, very indiff; old fr barn, 40x24, much out repair; old corn hse, 20x12, logs; old corn hse, 15x10, logs; stble, 24x12, much out repair; quarter hse, logs, 18x15, old; meat hse, logs, 10x12, old; out hse, 24x15, logs, tol good; adj George BUCHANAN, Christopher DIVERS

BUSSEY, Bennet; Occupant: Francis COSKERY; 140A; old fr dwlg hse, 45x18, very indiff; adj Edward B. BUSSEY & Sutton GUDGEON

BAKER, Nathan (11 slaves); Up Gunpwdr Hd; 188A; new dwlg hse, fr & weather boarded but only board supposed to be only 1/2 finished; dwlg hse, logs, 16x18, weatherboard, out repair; kn, logs, 16x12; meat hse 10x12; corn hse, stbles, 10x16; adj Mathew JOHNSON and Charles GORSUCH

2

Upper Gunpowder Hundred and Mine Run Hundred

BRITTON, Richard (24 slaves); Up Gunpwdr Hd; 498A; dwlg hse, stone, 2 low
   stry high, 20x30, much out repair; kn adj 12x16, stone, 1 stry; meat hse,
   15x15, stone; barn, 60x20, pt fr, pt logs, a little out repair and shed
   20x10; stone mill, 36x36, 2 stry; 2 pair stones, good repair; hse adj
   mill, 16x16, stone, 1 stry; quarter hse, 25x18, stone, old, out of
   repair; lying on the Great falls; (Merryman Mill Rd & Gunpowder Falls)
BARTLESON, Rachael; 84A (80 acres sold for taxes - 1805); dwlg hse, logs,
   16x14, out repair; adj Richard BRITTON
BUTLER, Mary; 87A; dwlg hse, logs, 20x18; kn, logs, 24x14; old barn, 20x20,
   very indiff; adj Wm. BALDWIN and John WATKINS
BOSLEY, James of Wm. (1 slave); Up Gunpwdr Hd; 107A; dwlg hse, logs, 18x20,
   1 stry; stble, 10x12, logs; corn hse, 10x18, logs, stbles under; adj
   Sarah SMITH & John NICHOLSON
BELT, Catharine (20 slaves); Up Gunpwdr Hd; 568A; dwlg hse, fr, 50x30, add.
   50x18, hip roof, 10 window above; fr kn; meat hse, hewd log, 12x12, very
   good; barn fr, 50x18, in good repair; old log stlbes, 40x18; smiths shop
   12x10; quarter hse 18x24, old, out of repair; overseers hse, 18x24, logs,
   out repairs; old hen hse, logs, 12x12; old lumber hse, logs, 18x20, very
   indiff; adj Wm. GOODWIN & Edwd PIERCE
BELT, James; 128A (80 acres sold for taxes - 1805); 2 old dwlg hses, very
   much out repair; adj Aquila HALL and Henry WILSON
BALDWIN, Wm.; 216A+; (Long Green?); dwlg hse, logs, 18x20, old, out repair;
   log barn 20x16; adj James GITTINGS and John & Sam. WATKINS
CURTIS, Joseph (1 slave); Mine Run Hd; 133A; dwlg hse, logs, 40x18, 1 stry,
   but indifferently finished; stbles, 12x16, logs; fr shed, 16x8, old,
   indiff; adj George ELLIOTT and Ezekiel BOSLEY
CURTIS, William (2 slaves); Mine Run Hd; 132A+; dwlg hse, 24x24, old and out
   repair; adj Edw'd STANSBURY and Gabriel HOLMES
CARLON, James; 110A; adj Thomas LYTLE and Harford Co line
CUNYER, Wm.; 150A; log dwlg hse, 16x16, 1 stry; log dwlg hse, 16x16, 1 stry,
   not finished; old barn 38x18, out repair; adj Abraham SLADE, Mary ALMANY
CARKWOOD, Wm.; 70A; adj Benjamin SHIPLEY & Jacob DALEY
COULSON, Wm.; 139A; dwlg hse, logs, 18x20, 1 stry; meat hse, 10x10; stble
   10x20; spring hse, 10x10, old; adj Samuel MERRYDITH & Joseph SUTTON
CURFMAN, George; (at Walker Rd on N.C.R.R.); 140A; dwlg hse, logs, 12x14;
   adj Capt. CALDER & Daniel WALKER
COLTRIDER, George; (near Parkton); 67 1/2 A; dwlg hse, logs, 16x18, old;
   stble 10x12; adj Capt. CALDER
CROUSE, Christian; (near Parkton); 100A; dwlg hse 18x16 & stble 18x14; adj
   George COLTRIDER, Capt. CALDER
CALDER, James (2 slaves); (York Rd. N. of Dairy Rd., Parkton); Mine Run Hd;
   3836 3/4 A; 4 dwlg hses, logs, 14x16; dwlg hse, stone chimney, 14x16;
   dwlg hse, logs, out of repair, 14x16; dwlg hse, logs, 16x20; old log
   cabin, wood chimney, 16x14; 2 log cabins 16x14; hse, shingle roof, 16x16;
   log cabins: 16x16, 12x14, 14x16, 12x14
CHANCE, John; 60A; dwlg hse and kn under one roof, 39x14, old, out of
   repair, logs; spring hse, logs, 10x8; hse, logs, 16x12, indiff; adj
   Aquilla HALL, Chas. GORSUCH
CUPPER, Nicholas; 389A; dwlg hse, logs, much out of repair; kn, log, 12x16;
   stble, 12x20, old; adj Wm. GOODWIN's land
CARROLL, Henry H.; (19 slaves); Up Gunpwdr Hd: (names of tenants
   unreadable); 5791A+; (Sweet Air Rd., east of Manor Rd.); brk dwlg hse, 2

3

stry, 53x22, in good repair, well finished; piazza 8x53, brk, 2 stry; brk wing, 1 stry, 22x22, in good repair; kn, brk, 16x16, 1 stry; quarter hse, logs, 40x20, 1 stry; meat hse, logs, 12x14, 1 stry; poultry hse, logs, 16x12, 1 stry; stone spring hse; 1 row of stbles and corn hses of log, 42x12; fr stble 18x12; fr barn 18x16; sheds around in tol repair

CHAMBERLAIN, Philip; (near Hartley Mill) (1 Slave); Up Gunpwdr Hd; 146A; dwlg hse, logs, 20x16, old, out of repair; kn 16x14; meat hse, 18x20; shop, log, 16x14; stble, 20x12 and corn hse; adj Aquila HALL & James GITTINGS

CROMWELL, William and Thomas CROMWELL (2 slaves); Occupants: John WILMOTT, Elijah MERRYMAN (supt.); Mine Run Hd; 178A; (Exclusion of the dwlg); dwlg hse, pt log, pt fr, 1 stry, 50x18, very much out repair; hen hse, old fr, 12x12; corn hse, 20x12, logs, out of repair; old stble, 20x20, old & worthless; adj Chas. RIDGLEY & Great Falls

DIXON, John; 165A; log dwlg hse, 18x20, out of repair; old barn, 30x22, indiff; adj John MERRYMAN, James ELLIOTT

DAYLEY, Jacob; 270A+; dwlg hse, logs, 1 stry, 28x14, tol good repair, porch 6x28; old log hse, 10x12; meat hse 8x10; barn, logs & stone under, 50x24; corn hse, log & stables under, 26x12; spring hse, log, 8x10; adj Mary ALMANY, Joseph SUTTON

DUNNOCK, John, Sr.; Occupant: John DUNNOCK, Jr; 448A; dwlg hse, logs, 16x18; dwlg, 12x16, cabin built; stble, logs, 20x14; adj Capt John RUTLEDGE, Thomas HUNT

DIXON, Jacob; 53A; old dwlg hse, 14x12; adj Edmond STANSBURY

DAWS, Francis; (probably on Little Gr. Falls?); 94A; mill, logs, 22x26, very old, out of repair, two pairs of stones, one tol good, other country stone very indiff; adj Joshua MERRYDITH, Wm. GWYNN

DIVERS, Christopher (2 slaves); Up Gunpwdr Hd; 150A (125 acres sold for taxes - 1805); dwlg hse, logs, 30x18, old, out of repair; meat hse, 10x12, log; barn, 25x20, log, tol good

DELAVET, Peter (4 slaves); Up Gunpwdr Hd; 138A; dwlg hse, fr, 32x20, hip roof, 4 dormer windows above old, very much out repair; log kn, 16x14, tol good; adj Nathan BAKER & Thomas G. HOWARD

DARNELL, Francis (4 slaves); Up Gunpwdr Hd; Occupant: Asael WILSON; (near Hartley Mill?); 282A; dwlg hse, logs, 22x14, logs up, chimney up; old log stbles, very much out repair; dwlg hse, pt fr, pt stone, 1 stry, most out of repair; old fr kn, much out of repair; adj Aquilla HALL, Chas. RIDGLEY

DIVERS, Ananias (Little Gunpowder near Md. 7) (9 slaves); Up Gunpwdr Hd; 349A+; dwlg hse, logs, 20x18 weather boarded, in good repair, 1 stry, 2 dormer windows above, porch 6x19; barn, logs, 50x20, in good repair; stone mill, 2 stry, 4 pairs of stones, new, in good repair; kn, stone, 16x18, 1 stry, 2 dormer windows above and adj this dwlg; meat hse, stone, 14x14; hen hse, log, 14x14; old quarter hse, log, 15x20; adj FORD & PAXON, Wm. ONION

DEMMITT, William; (near Franklinville & Jericho); 240A; dwlg hse, stone, 30x20, 1 stry, windows above in good repair; barn, logs, and cow hse underneath of stone, 45x20; stble, old, out repair, 30x14; kn, logs, 1 stry, 16x20; meat hse, logs, 12x12; hen hse, logs, 12x12; adj Jesse TYSON, Thomas G. HOWARD

DUBURY, Joseph; 12A+; log dwlg hse, 12x14, old, indiff; adj Thomas G. HOWARD & Howard Englehard YEISER

DAY, Doctor William F. (near Upper Falls?) (3 slaves); Up Gunpwdr Hd; 11A+; dwlg hse, fr & weather board, 32x14, 1 stry, 3/4 finished; stble 18x25, logs; shop, 18x12, logs; hen hse, 10x10, logs; spring hse, 8x8, logs; adj Thomas G. HOWARD

DANNALLY, Cornelius (3 slaves); Up Gunpwdr Hd; 131A; dwlg hse, 16x20, fr, 1 stry, new, good repair; kn, logs, 16x20, old, out of repair; stble, logs, 16x18

DEMMITT, William of James (4 slaves); Up Gunpwdr Hd

DIMMITT, William Senr (4 slaves); Up Gunpwdr Hd

ELLIOTT, James (1 slave); Up Gunpwdr Hd; 115A; dwlg hse, logs, 20x24, old, most out repair; shed, 18x19, old; kn, logs, 15x18, very old, indiff; meat hse, 9x9; barn, logs, 20x32, very old, but lately board with shingles; corn hse, stble under, 16x12; adj My Ladys Manor

ELLIOTT, Wm.; Mine Run Hd; (on the Manor near Hunter's Mills); 219A; dwlg hse, log, 16x20, old; old kn, 12x12, log; meat hse, 10x10, log; barn, 56x20, in good repair; stble, 16x16, pt in good repair; adj Gist VAUGHAN

ELLIOTT, George (1 slave); Mine Run Hd; (on the Manor); 135A+; dwlg hse, 20x22, hewd, 1 1/2 stry, tol repair; kn, log, 20x16, adj the above; 2 old stbles, 10x16; meat hse, log, 10x10; spring hse, log, 8x10; adj Gist VAUGHAN & Joseph CURTIS

ELLIOTT, Arthur; 182A; dwlg hse, log, 16x18, in good repair; old kn, 16x16, very indiff; meat hse, 10x10; new log barn, 65x20, very good; corn hse & stble, very good, 16x12; adj Jacob SPLITSTONE & Wm. ELLIOTT

EINSEL, Henry; 225A+; dwlg hse, logs, 32x12, very old, out of repair; log barn, stble under, 40x16, tol good repair, shed 10x16 add.; adj Jesse POCOCK & Francis SPARKS

ELLIOTT, James of James; 198A; dwlg hse, hewd log and weather boarded, 1 1/2 stry, 22x15, new, well finished; corn hse & shop under it, 16x13; barn & stble, 24x16, out repair; adj Henry H. CARROLL & John ELLIOTT

ELLIOTT, John; 90A; dwlg hse,log, 18x16, 1 stry, good repair; old hse, log, 18x16, out of repair; stble, log, 16x10; adj James ELLIOTT & Solomon WRIGHT

ELLIOTT, Benjamin; 57 1/2 A; dwlg hse, logs, 20x18; in good repair

ELLIOTT, Thomas (1 slave); Up Gunpwdr Hd

FOSTER, George (1 slave); Mine Run Hd; 74A; dwlg hse, 22x20, out of repair; dwlg,old, indiff, 18x16; old spring hse, 12x10, log; adj the Great Falls & Joshua MERRYDITH

FUGATE, Elizabeth; (My Lady's Manor); 98A; dwlg hse, stone, 24x18, 1 stry, out repair; kn, logs, 20x16, tol repair; adj Joseph McCLUNG & Christopher MUCHNER

FUGATE, Martin; (on the Manor lots, 84, 97, 51); 102A; dwlg hse, log, 16x20, 1 stry; barn, logs, 49x20, not finished; old smith shop, logs, 22x16; adj Joseph McCLUNG, Solomon ARMSTRONG

FRANCES, Jonathan; 192a; dwlg hse, 16x16, logs; adj John FREE

FREE, John (probably near Freeland on N.C.R.R. near Penna Line; 14aA+; dwlg hse, stone, 2 stry, 26x20; tol good repair; barn, logs, 36x18, good repair; old log kn, 12x16; adj Jonathan & Solomon FLOWERS

FREELAND, Moses; 123A+; dwlg hse, logs, 16x18; stble, logs, 12x16; adj Solomon FLOWERS

FREELAND, John; 142A; log dwlg hse, 16x18; stble, logs, 12x14; adj John FREE, Moses FREELAND

FISHER, Christian; 153A; dwlg hse, logs, 18x20, good repair; barn, logs, 20x16,good repair; adj John & Moses FREELAND

FLOWERS, Solomon; 334A; log dwlg hse, 18x20; stble 12x16; adj Jonathan FLOWERS & John FREE

FULLER, Nicholas; Occupant: Wm. WATSON; 97A; old dwlg hse, 19x16, log, out repair; barn, logs, 2 stry, 24x19; adj Dixon STANSBURY, Sr.

FORD, Isaac (3 slaves); Occupant: Jereimiah FORD (5 slaves); 127A; dwlg hse, hewd logs, hip roof, 4 dormer, 28x8; log hse, made in as shop, 22x16; old stble, logs, 16x14; log old kn, 18x16, very indiff; adj James GITTINGS & Michael JENKINS

FITZHUGH, George (24 slaves); Up Gunpwdr Hd; 678A; dwlg hse, pt fr, pt logs, fr pt 36x24, hip roof, 9 ft pitch, log pt 36x20, hip roof 9 ft pitch; log kn & wash hse, 40x20, __ars much out of repair; barn, log & stble, under, stone 60x40, good repair; log stble and carriage hse, 50x20; log corn hse, 30x15; stble, 12x12, log, stble, 12x12, log; grist mill 50x26 & saw mill adj, each in good repair, but of little value from the quantity of water; adj Wm. GOODWIN & the Great Falls

FORD & PAXON (4 slaves); Up Gunpwdr Hd; 643A+; dwlg hse, brk, 2 stry; has been a good hse but at present the wall much broken and inside out repair; old corn hse, 20x12 old, out of repair; stble, 18x16, old & out of repair; large stone mill, 2 stry, 3 pairs of stones, but considered of not so much value as the description merits from the scarcity of grain; saw mill adj in tol repair; ressage of brk, 13x18, 1 stry; kn, brk, 2 stry, 34x18, out of repair; meat hse, 16x18, out of repair; adj A. DIVERS & the Great Falls

FELL, Elijah (1 slave); Up Gunpwdr Hd; 284A+; dwlg hse, logs, old, out of repair, 20x16; mill, logs, hull very old, out of repair, 24x20; 1 pair of stones and stream very good, tol; saw mill, good stream, just out repair; adj little falls & Edw. ALLENDER

GREEN, Isaac (5 slaves); Occupant: Abednego GREEN; Mine Run Hd; 83A; dwlg hses, logs, 24x18, 1 stry, tol good repair, public hse on the public road; old dwlg hse, logs, 18x16; corn hse, 12x14; stble, 24x10, logs; old barn, 16x20, indiff; kn, logs, 1 stry, 26x14, old and very much out repair; adj Elijah MERRYMAN

GIVENS, John (1 slave); Mine Run Hd; 130A; dwlg hse, log (20x16), pt stone (16x15), 1 stry, tol repair; barn, logs, 40x20, out repair; mill, logs, 26x20, 2 pairs of stone, indiff, scarcity of water; adj Ezekiel SLADE & Joseph McCLUNG

GALLOWAY, Thomas; Occupant: Salathiel GALLOWAY (1 slave); Up Gunpwdr Hd; 178A+; log dwlg hse, 20x17, old; spring hse, 8x10, old; barn, 20x16, logs; stble, 26x13, logs, indiff; corn hse, 14x10; adj Joshua & Nicholas HUTCHINS

GIST, Joshua, Heirs; Occupant: Archey WATSON; 133A+; small log hse, 14x16, indiff; adj Joshua MERRYDITH, James BOSLEY

GILLIS, Robert; 240A; log dwlg hse, 2 stry, 24x20, old, much out repair; old log kn, 16x14; ship 14x14, logs; 2 old log stbles, 15x18; old barn, 50x15, out repair; adj Jean WILSON, Mary ALMANY

GORSUCH, Elisha; 397A; dwlg hse, logs, 16x16; old, out repair; old hse, 20x18, logs; stble, 20x18, logs; adj Penna. Line & Thomas IRUSE(?)

GORSUCH, David; 321A+; dwlg hse, logs, 16x18, old; log kn, 12x14; old meat hse, 10x12; barn, 50x18, logs, thatched; stone mill, 30x36, 2 stry, one pair stones, not finished; adj Elisha GORSUCH and Penna. Line

6

GILBERT, Eleazer; 51A+; adj Penna Line and Jesse POCOCK
GUNDY, Peter; 132A+; dwlg hse, logs, 14x16; barn, logs, 60x20, good repair; adj Capt. James CALDER
GREENFIELD, Nathan; 16A; old dwlg, logs, 18x20; barn 20x18; stble 10x12; adj the Great falls
GOODWIN, Rachael (1 slave); Mine Run Hd; 206A+; dwlg hse, 34x16, fr, 2 dormer windows, much out repair, 1 stry; barn, logs, 50x20, good repair; stil hse, logs, 20x20; dwlg adj logs up, 1 stry, 16x16; kn, logs, 16x16; meat hse, log, 12x14; adj Gabriel HOLMES & Thomas ANDERSON
GOODWIN, Wm. (53 slaves); 2073A; Up Gunpwdr Hd; Occupant: Geo. BOND; dwlg, hse, stone, 30x30, 2 stry, tol good repair; 2 dwlg, 30x18, much out repair; dwlg hse, fr, 32x20; 1 stry, in midling repair; Occupant: Richard JONES; 3 hses for servants, logs, apple hse, stble, corn hse, smith's shop, waggon hse, and barn of logs, stble of stone, 3 log hses for servant; an old stble; fr barn; 2 log hses and an old fr hse out of repair and not used; 3 log hses for servant; meat hse & milk hse; log stble; hen hse; fr barn; 2 old hses for servant; meat hse; milk all logs; fr barn and stone stable; kn, logs; 2 old hen hses, log; milk hse, stone, 13x12; meat hse, logs
GUDGEON, Sutton (6 slaves); Up Gunpwdr Hd; 371A+; dwlg hse, old, out repair, 20x16; dwlg hse, logs, out repair, 18x16; dwlg, 24x16, old, out repair; dwlg hse, old, out repair, 12x16; old stble and corn hse, logs, 10x16
GREEN Shadrach (6 slaves); Up Gunpwdr Hd; Occupant: James GIVENS; Mine Run Hd; 94A+; dwlg hse, stone, 22 1/2x16, 1 stry, new, good repair; hen hse, 10x12, logs; hen hse, logs, 10x12; row of stables, 32x12, old and much out repair adj to Isaac GREEN, Elijah MERRYMAN
GRAY, Thomas, living in Calvert Co; 20A (20 acres sold for taxes - 1805); adj Wm. BALDWIN & Benj. AMOSS
GOTT, Henrietta; Occupant: Jeremiah CULLUM; 98A (90 acres sold for taxes - 1805); dwlg hse, logs, 22x22, 1 stry, situated on public road; 2 small dwlg hses, logs, cabin built; kn, logs, 18x14; adj Sutton GUDGEON, GITTINGS
GUYTON, Benj. Sr. (2 slaves); Up Gunpwdr Hd; 157A+; log dwlg hse, 22x18, 1 stry; kn, log, 18x14, 1 stry; barn, logs, 20x18, out of repair; adj Wm. BALDIN, Benj. AMOSS
GUYTON, Benj., Jr.; 100A; dwlg hse, logs, 18x20; kn, logs, 16x14; meat hse, 18x12; barn, logs, 14x22, shingle roof; adj Benj. GUYTON, SR. 7 Cornelius DANNALLY
GORSUCH, Charles (2 slaves); Mine Run Hd; 543A; dwlg hse, fr, 26x18, 1 stry, tol good repair; porch 8x26; old kn, 18X16, very indiff; corn hse, logs, 12x18; stble 30x10; shop, logs, 20x18, old, out of repair; old fr shop, 18x12; stble, 12x14, add. 10x10; Occupant: Thomas McLAUGHLIN (5 slaves); Up Gunpwdr Hd; dwlg hse, logs and weatherboards, 2 stry, 20x18, in midlin repair; adj Aquila HALL, John CHANCE
GUYTON, John; occupant: Doctor John BRADFORD (10 slaves); Up Gunpwdr Hd; 98A; dwlg hse, fr, 22x16, weather boarded, little out repair; add. 9x12; kn, logs, 12x14; adj Henry GUITON & Chas. GORSUCH
GUYTON, Henry (4 slaves); Up Gunpwdr Hd; 340A; dwlg hse, 22x18, fr, 1 stry; porch, 8x22, add. to dwlg 14x12; log kn, 20x16; stone hse, 14x16, fr; barn 22x22, logs; loom hse, 12x16, logs; meat hse, 10x12, logs; adj Clement GREEN, John CHANCE; Occupant: Joshua TUDER; dwlg hse, stone,

30x20, 2 stry, much out repair, add. 30x18; kn, stone, 30x20, out repair; 1 meat hse and 1 spring hse, 10x10, stone

GROVER, William; 59A; dwlg hse, logs, 20x16; kn under same roof, 12x16; indifferently built but in good repair; barn, logs, 20x16, earthin floors; meat hse 10x10; adj Thomas STONE & Edw. PIERCE

GREEN, Clement (2 slaves); Up Gunpwdr Hd; 224A; dwlg hse, 32x18, pt fr, pt logs, 1 stry, midling repair, piazza 5x32; kn, logs, 18x24; kn, 16x20, out repair; corn hse & stble under, 22x12, logs; barn, 24x20, fr, out of repair; corn hse, 10x20, logs; hatters shop & bow room, 28x15, logs, good repair; hen hse 10x12; meat hse, 12x12; adj the little falls & Henry GUITON

GUITON, Underwood (4 slaves); Up Gunpwdr Hd; 258A; meat hse, logs, 12x12; hen hse, logs, 12x12; dwlg hse, fr, hipt roof, 24x20, old and much out repair, porch 8x24, tol condition; old kn, 16x18, out repair; land adj John HATTAN, Matthew JOHNSON

GALLOWAY, Aquilla (8 slaves); Up Gunpwdr Hd; 184A; dwlg hse, logs, 20x15; old log kn, 18x15, out repair; meat hse & stble under, 18x9; barn, logs, shingle roof, 40x20; cutting room, 10x10, logs; adj Charles RIDGLEY

GITTINGS, Thomas, Esq. (11 slaves); Up Gunpwdr Hd; 729A; dwlg hse, stone, 2 stry, 46x26, midling ggod repair; kn, 30x26, 1 stry, stone; meat hse, 15x12; hen hse 14x12; spring hse 10x12; 2 stone hses not occupied, 20x14, 2 stry, out repair; 2 fr barns 56x18, stbles under; corn hse, logs & stble 22x16; stble, logs, 14x12; dwlg hse, logs, 20x14, new; hen hse, 10x12, logs; adj Aquila HALL, Joseph SLEE

GITTINGS, James of Thos. (7 slaves); Up Gunpwdr Hd; 158A; dwlg hse, logs, 1 stry, 26x24, out repair; kn hewd logs, 18x14, in good repair; meat hse, logs, 10x14, hen hse, 16x16; corn hse, logs 28x14; barn 24x16, logs; 2 add. 10x16, out repair; adj Thomas GITTINGS, Esq. & Martha RIDGLEY

GITTINGS, Hannah (4 slaves); Up Gunpwdr Hd; 264A+; dwlg hse, stone, 38x18, 1 stry, old, much out repair; kn, brk, 12x10; meat hse, 12x10, logs; corn hse, out repair; adj James GITTINGS of Thomas

GITTINGS, James, Sr., Esq. (50 slaves); Up Gunpwdr Hd; 2003A; dwlg hse, pt stone & fr, stone pt 30x37; kn new & wash hse unfinished, 2 stry, good repair, fr pt 37x17, 1 stry, in tol repair; old store hse, logs, 34x15; fr barn & stone under, 60x30, good repair; granary, fr, 35x25, good repair; barn, fr 35x25, good repair; stone mill, 2 stry, 50x25, much out of repair; negro hse, logs, 25x20, 1 stry; spring hse, logs, 12x12; spring hse, logs, 12x12; poultry hse, 25x15; dwlg hse, stone, walls up and not quite finished, covered in 35x20, passage & kn 35x20, 2 low stry same as above; James GITTINGS, Jr. (5 slaves): dwlg hse, fr, 30x16, 1 stry; spring hse, logs, 12x12; poultry hse, 25x15

GITTINGS, Benj. (1 slave); Up Gunpwdr Hd; 261A; dwlg hse, logs, 20x18, out repair; adj Hannah GITTINGS, Harry GOUGH

GWYNN, Wm.; Occupant: George BOND; 64A; stone mill, 36x28, 2 stry, inside work much out repair and lying idle; adj Jesse TYSON, Little Falls

GOUGH, Harry Dorsey (11 slaves); Up Gunpwdr Hd; Occupant: Joshua TUDOR (superinden- dent); 947A+; dwlg hse, stone, 30x20, 2 stry, much out repair, add. 30x18; kn, stone, 30x20, out repair; barn, 54x20, logs, good repair; barn, fr, 35x20, good repair; stble, 10x12, fr; stble and corn hse, 22x20, logs; meat hse, log, 16x12; spring hse, 10x10, stone; adj Thomas TODD

GIVEN, James (1 slave); Mine Run Hd

8

HOLMES, Gabriel (3 slaves); Mine Run Hd; 82A; dwlg hse, pt fr, pt logs, 40x16, 1 stry, fr add. 10x20; piazza, 6x40, in midling repair and situated on the public road; stble, logs, 29x11, shingle roof; adj Edmond STANSBURY & Rachel GOODWIN

HUTCHINS, Wm. (6 slaves); Mine Run Hd; 91A; dwlg hse, fr, 26x22, 1 stry, in midling repair; kn, logs, 22x15; meat hse, logs, 10x12; stble, 12x18, logs, indiff; barn, logs, 18x18, old, out repair; add. 10x18, very indiff; adj Joshua HUTCHINS, Thomas BOND

HAW, Francis (1 slave); 122A+; dwlg hse, logs, old, out repair, 18x14; meat hse, 10x8, logs; spring hse, stone, 10x8; adj John MEGAW, Thomas GALLOWAY

HUTCHINS, Joshua (1 slave); Mine Run Hd; 171A; dwlg hse, logs & weatherboarded, 26x24, in midling repair; kn, 18x15, logs; corn hse, logs, 10x16; meat hse, 12x10, logs; adj Wm. HUTCHINS & Ezekiel SLADE

HUTCHINS, Nicholas (10 slaves); Mine Run Hd; Lady's Manor; 200A; dwlg hse, 20x22, hewd logs, 1 stry, add. 20x18; kn, 18x14, logs; barn, 20x27, logs, shingle roof; stbles: 12x12, 10x12, 18x12, 10x9; meat hse, 14x12, log; spring hse, 10x9; adj Josias & Wm. SLADE & Edmond STANSBURY

HUTCHINS, James; 199A+; dwlg hse, logs, 14x16, very old; old fr hse, almost rotten, down over; corn hse & stble under, 10x16, logs; adj Nicholas HUTCHINS & John MEGAW

HUNT, Thomas; 254A; dwl hse, hewd logs, 1 1/2 stry, 23x19, tol well finished; corn hse, logs, 12x16; old barn, logs, 35x18, out repair; adj Jacob ROCKWELL & John Rutledge

HUGHES, Samuel; 164A; old fr dwlg hse, 18x20; old kn, logs, 16x18; barn, logs, shingle roof, 20x24; stble, 12x20; meat hse, 10x12; adj Abraham NORRIS & Abraham RYSTON

HUGHES, James (3 slaves); Mine Run Hd; 184A (60 acres sold for taxes - 1805); 2 dwlg hse, logs, old & out repair, 36x16; old barn, 18x18, logs; stble 28x12, very old, logs; adj Thomas LYTLE & Sam'l HUGHES

HURST, Benedict; 40A; adj Gist VAUGHAN

HOOVER, John; 314A+; dwlg hse, logs, 16x18; new barn, logs, 56x20, good repair; adj Capt. James CALDER

HUTCHINS, Thomas (10 slaves); 130A+; land only; adj John Stewart, Jr.

HAIN, Andrew; 86A; dwlg hse, logs, 18x20; barn; 32x14, logs; adj Capt. CALDER & John HOOVER

HAMILTON, Susanna; 86A; dwlg hse, log, 14x12; adj Capt. James CALDER &c.

HINDLE, Michael; 109A; log dwlg hse, log, 16x16, old; old barn, log, 40x16; adj Peter GUNDY &c.

HENDRICKS, Adam; Occupant: Nathan EVANS; 138A; dwlg hse, log, 14x16; adj Peter GUNDY, Michael HINDLE

HOLLAND, Mary; 76A; old dwlg, 14x18, very indiff; corn hse & stbles under, 10x16, old; adj Clement GREEN, Wm. ALLENDER &c

HATTAN, John; 65A; dwlg hse, log 16x24, old, out of repair; meat hse, 10x16, old; stble, 10x12, out repair; adj Mary HOLLAND, Underwood GUITON

HOLLAND, George; 65A; old dwlg, log, 14x14, old, indiff; barn, log, 15x15, old & old out hse, very old, 14x14; adj Edw. ALLENDER, Underwood GUITON

HOPKINS, Ezekiel (3 slaves); Up Gunpwdr Hd; 100A; very old dwlg hse, 16x20, indiff; the wall up of a new hse of stone, not quite covered, 20x22; meat hse, 10x10, old and out repair; adj Joshua MARSH & Thomas MARSH, &c

HATTAN, Aquilla; Occupant: Jacob FULKS; 122A; dwlg hse, fr, hipt roof, 20x18, much out repair; add. stone, 1 stry, 18x18, out repair; adj Hannah GITTINGS, Henry D. GOUGH &c

9

HALL, Aquilla (39 slaves); Up Gunpwdr Hd; 1421A; dwlg hse, pt stone, pt fr, stone pt 24x22, 2 stry, good repair; fr pt 27x24, 2 stry, midling repair; kn, 20x35, logs; hse for negroes, 20x18, logs; hse for negroes, 18x26; stone spring hse, 12x12; log milk hse, 18x14; meat hse, log, 20x16; hen hse, log, 12x16; Occupants: John MOPHETT, Robt. HOWARD; dwlg hse, fr, 20x18, old and out repair; dwlg hse, log 22x18, old, indiff; log kn, 12x10, old, indiff; carriage hse, fr, 24x18; corn hse, 20x10, fr, logs, & granary, log, 16x8; log stble, 10x12; barn, fr, shed around, 35x18, much out repair; log stbles, 22x18, old; stble, logs, 20x16, indiff; smith shop, 18x14, log; quarter hse, 18x14, log; work shop, stone, 14x14; quarter hse, logs, 35x18, out repair; barn fr, 30x20, out repair; old log hse, 12x12; stone mill with one country (?) stone, 40x32, lately repaired and not quite finished

HALL, Francis; 28A (15 acres sold for taxes - 1805); Land of Promise; adj to Aquilla HALL, Francis DARNELL

HOWARD, A. Edward (12 slaves); Up Gunpwdr Hd; 235A; dwlg hse, fr, 32x16, hipt roof, 2 windows above, 1 stry, add. 16x14, midling repair; meat hse, 14x18; corn hse, logs, 16x18, out repair; stble, logs, 16x18, out repair; adj Thomas G. HOWARD &c.

HOWARD, Thomas G. (13 slaves); Up Gunpwdr Hd; Occupant: William ASQUITH; 1778A; dwlg hse, fr, 26x26, hipt roof, 4 windows above an old old hse, but newly repaired; log kn, 16x16; dwlg hse, fr, 60x24, hipt roof; 10 windows above in midling repair; old kn, logs, 16x18; meat hse, 12x12; barn, stone, 1 stry, little out repair; store hse, fr, 16x18; old log hse, 16x16; stble, 16x16, logs

HUNTER, Peter (7 slaves); Up Gunpwdr Hd; 102a; dwlg hse, pt fr, pt logs, kn under same roof, 45x20, an old hse but newly repaired, 1 stry; meat hse, logs, 12x10; adj James GITTINGS, Esq., Thomas RINGOLD

HALL, John (erroneously recorded as John NAU on land assessment listing) (3 slaves); Up Gunpwdr Hd

JOHNSON, David (2 slaves); 1779 1/2 A; dwlg hse, logs, 20x20, out repair; kn, logs, 16x12, old, out repair; meat hse, log, 12x10; 2 stbles, log, 12x12; adj Dixon STANSBURY Senr and John STANDIFORD &c.

JONES, Richard; Occupant: John ANDERSON; 264A; dwlg hse, fr and weather boarded, 24x18, tol good repair; log kn, 14x12, good repair; corn hse, log, 10x18; barn, log 24x84, out repair; adj Wm. ELLIOTT, Daniel SHAW

JOHNSON, Wm.; 220A; dwlg hse, logs, 22x20, 1 stry; kn, log, 12x14, 1 stry; spring hse, log, 8x10; corn hse, log, 12x14; barn, 44x22, not quite finished; stble, 34x32, out repair; adj Edw. PARISH, Jean WILSON &c.

JOHNSON, Edward, actor for Jonathan PLOWMAN; 350A; log dwlg hse, 16x18; stble, log, 20x10; adj David SAMPSON, James POCOCK &c.

JARRETT, Abraham; 60A; old log dwlg hse, 30x12, very indiff; adj Harford line, Thomas LYTLE

JENKINS, Michael (13 slaves); Up Gunpwdr Hd; 489A; fr dwlg hse, hipt roof, 3 dormer windows, 38x16, piazza, 10x38, an old hse, but in midling repair; kn, brk, 20x16; log hen hse, 10x10; quarter hse, 16x15, stone, 2 log hses, 12x14, each, stble, stone, 15x15; old fr barn, 24x32, out repair; 2 sheds, 10x24 each, add. to barn; adj James GITTINGS, Rebecka RIDGLEY

JOHNSON, Matthew (1 slave); Up Gunpwdr Hd; 123A; dwlg hse, log, 36x16, 1 stry, tol repair, weather boarded; barn, log, 20x16; corn hse, log, 16x12; adj Underwood GUYTON, Nathan BAKER

JENKINS, Walter (9 slaves); Up Gunpwdr Hd; 236A; 2 quarter hses, logs, each 12x16; corn hse, 12x18, logs; barn 18x26, good repair; adj Geo. FITZHUGH, Wm. GOODWIN

JONES, John (5 slaves); Up Gunpwdr Hd; dwlg hse, logs, 20x18, tol repair; kn, log, 16x14; hen hse 12x14, log; meat hse, 12x12, log; spring hse 10x10; barn, logs, 50x22, covered shingles; corn hse, 24x10, log; old log hse, 15x18, out repair; adj Chas. RIDGLEY land, Rich'd BRITTAIN land

KELSO, James; Occupant: Wm KELSO (1 slave); Mine Run Hd; 100A; dwlg hse, logs, 16x16; stble, logs, 16x14; adj Capt. James CALDER &c.

KING, Susannah (5 slaves); Up Gunpwdr Hd; 150A; dwlg hse, log, 20x16, indiff; Occupant: John WELSH; dwlg hse, log, 18x16, indifferently finished; old kn, log, 12x14; adj Chas. RIDGLEY, Francis DARNELL

LOVE, Thomas and Phillip (2 slaves); Mine Run Hd; Occupant: Elijah SPARKS (supt.); 275A; dwlg hse, log, 14x16, indiff; adj John RIDGLEY &c.

LUX, William; Mine Run Hd; Occupant: Amos OGDEN (6 slaves); 555A; old dwlg hse, logs, very different; old corn hse; old barn, very indiff; adj John RIDGLEY, Thomas LOVE

LYTLE, Thomas; Mine Run Hd; Occupant: Wm. LYTLE (2 slaves); 100A; old dlg, logs, 16x14; dwlg hse, new and not finished, 12x16, log; meat hse, 10x10, logs; stble, 40x12, old, indiff; adj land of James CARTER, James HUGHES

LYTLE, James; 15A; adj Harford Co line, Thomas LYTLE

LESOURD, John; 112A; log dwlg, weather boarded, 16 1/2 sq.; old dwlg adj, 12x16 1/2; barn, logs, almost new, 45x20; adj properties of Robt. GILLIS & James POCOCK

LOW, John; log dwlg hse, 16x14; stble, 16x18, log; adj Joseph MORRIS, Thomas WANTLING

LOW, Joshua; Occupant: Jesse LOW (2 slaves); Mine Run Hd; 600A; dwlg hse, hewn log, 1 1/2 stry, 24x19, tol well finished; meat hse, 10x10, hewn log; barn, log, 47x21, good repair; stble, 14x16, log; corn hse & stbles under, 14x18; old stble, 14x16, indiff; adj Penna. line, Thomas HUNT

LEACH, Clement; 100A; dwlg hse, log, 20x16; log stble, 12x14; adj STANDIFORD & James CALDER

LINSEY, John (1 slave); Up Gunpwdr Hd; 334A; dwlg hse, fr, 24x20; hipt roof, 3 windows above, midling repair; old log kn, 16x16; stone meat hse, 13x10, very good; granary, logs, 16x18, indiff; stble, log, 20x10; stble 14x14; barn, 30x20, logs, stble under, shed add. 10x30, good repair; barn, log, 18x33, midling repair; spring hse, 10x13, logs; adj Michael JENKINS, Rebecka RIDGLEY

LYNCH, Cornelius & Bernard; Up Gunpwdr Hd; 122A; dwlg hse, log, 16x20, out repair; stble, log, 16x10, indiff; adj John LYNSEY, Bennet BUSSEY land

LYNCH, Patrick (10 slaves); 284A; dwlg hse, fr, 24x16, hipt roof, very much out repair; kn, logs, 12x12, old out repair; fr barn, 30x26, midling; corn hse, log 18x10; stble, 16x12, log

LEE, David; Occupant: Samuel YOUNG; 50A; log dwlg hse, 18x16, old, out repair; adj little fawls, Jesse TYSON

LIEDLEY, Isaac; 101A (50 acres sold for taxes - 1805); dwlg hse, log 18x18; stble, 16x18, log; adj Englehard YEISER

LYTLE, William (2 slaves); Mine Run Hd

LOWE, Jesse (2 slaves); Mine Run Hd

MERRYMAN, Elijah (9 slaves); Mine Run Hd; dwlg hse, fr, 27x15, weather board, hipt roof, a dormer window, add. of stone, 27x16, 1 stry, much out repair; dwlg hse, 30x15, log old and out repair; old barn, 30x20; stone mill 50x40, 1 stry, 2 pair of stones, wall very much out repair, inside works in tol repair; meat hse, & hse adj 30x15, stone, 1 stry; hen hse, 14x12, fr; 2 out hses, log, 15x16, each indiff; hse, 15x16, log; hse 12x14, log; hse, stone, 15x18, out repair; adj Wm. GOODWIN, the Great falls

MERRYDITH, Benj.; 140A (all 140 acres sold for taxes - 1805); dwlg hse, log 22x16, 1 stry, out repair; kn, log, 14x16; meat hse, 9x9; spring hse, 8x9, log; adj Joshua MERRYDITH &c.

MERRYDITH, Joshua (1 slave); Mine Run Hd; dwlg hse, pt fr, pt logs, fr pt 22x28, 1 stry and weatherboarded, log pt 24x22, hewd, 1 stry, midling repair, add. 28x6 of stone; fr barn, 34x24, 1 stry, stble, 24x14, logs, small hse, 8x12, coopers shop, 14x16, log, out repair, old; meat hse,log,12x12; adj land of Francis DAWS, William GWYNN & the Great Falls

McCLUNG, Joseph (5 slaves); Up Gunpwdr Hd; Mine Run Hd; 375A+; dwlg hse, log 20x16, 2 stry, tol repair; kn, logs, 20x16, 1 stry; barn, log, 20x18, shingle roof; stble, log, 12x18; dwlg hse, log 16x20, very old, indiff; old hse, 30x15, 1 stry, indiff; meat hse, 10x10, logs; spring hse, log, 8x10; adj John GIVENS, Walter PERDUE

MUCHNER, Christopher (1 slave); Mine Run Hd); 318a; dwlg hse, hewd logs and kn underneath, 38x15, add., logs, 15x10, midling repair; barn, log, 40x20, indiff; old dwlg hse, log, 30x20, very indiff; old spring hse, 8x10; meat hse, 8x9, stone; stone milk hse, 8x8; adj John GIVENS, John MEGAW

MORTON, Benj.; 100A; dwlg hse, log, 1 stry, 20x22, indifferently built; old kn, 12x10, log; spring hse, 8x8; barn, log, 40x18, old, out of repair, adj John MEGAW, Christopher MUCHNER

MEGAW, John (5 slaves); Mine Run Hd; 306A+; dwlg hse, 26x22, logs, weather boarded, 2 stry, lower stry well finished, upper stry not quite finished; barn, log, 34x20, midling repair; 2 stble, 32x12; granary, log 12x12; old fr kn, 16x14; meat hse, 10x9, log; spring hse, 13x11, stone; adj James HUTCHINS, Christopher MUCHNER

MERRYDITH, Sam'l; 235A; dwlg hse, log, 16x20, 1 stry; hen hse, 10x8; stble, 16x12, log; adj Thomas Merrydith &c.

MERRYDITH, Thomas (2 slaves); 349A; Mine Run Hd; dwlg hse, log, 16x16; kn, 16x18, log; meat hse, 10x10; barn, log, 40x20, thatched roof, stables of stone underneath in good repair; adj Samuel MERRYDITH & Joseph SUTTON &c.

MARSHEL, Thomas; 190A; dwlg hse, log, 14x818, old and indiff; meat hse, log 9x10; old stble, indiff; barn 42x14, indiff; adj Edw. BOND, Jesse POCOCK

MILLER, Matthias; Occupant: Wm. Tyson; 33A; dwlg hse, log, 14x16, old, indiff; stble, 12x14, log cabin built; adj Penna line & Jesse POCOCK

McCASLIN, Jacob; 269A; dwlg hse, hewd logs, 32x16, 1 stry, tol repair; kn, logs, 18x16, old, indiff; corn hse, stble, under, 10x14; spring hse, 10x8, log; adj John WILSON, Jr. & Sutton GUDGEON

MORRIS, Israel; 20A; tract adj Edw. A. HOWARD & the little falls

McCUBBIN, Wm.; 30A; dwlg hse, 20x16, tol good; adj Edward A. HOWARD &c.

MARSH, Joshua (11 slaves); Up Gunpwdr Hd; Occupant: John HAMILTON; 639A; dwlg hse, logs, 1 stry, 20x16; kn, logs, 16x16; meat hse, 16x16, very good; spring hse, 12x12; dwlg hse, logs, 16x22, old, much out repair; old meat hse, 12x12, log; log stble, 30x12, old, out repair; corn hse above; corn hse, log, 20x28, good repair; fr barn, 40x22, newly repaired, tol good; adj Geo. FITZHUGH, Thomas MARSH

MARSH, Thomas (18 slaves); Up Gunpwdr Hd; 280A; dwlg hse, stone, 1 stry, new
and well finished, 20x18; kn 20x18, logs, old and indiff; meat hse,
12x12; old dwl, out repair, log; corn hse, 36x12, log, much out repair;
barn, log, 30x20, midling repair; adj George FITZHUGH, Larkin SMITH
McCLEARY, John; 80P; dwlg hse,log, 16x14; adj Cornelius DANNALLY, Mary
BUTLER
MUMMY & HUSHEY; 99A; small dwlg hse; barn, log, 20x30; adj Samuel MORRIS
MORRIS, John & Edward; 179A; dwlg hse, log, 16x18; dwlg hse, log, 14x16,
adj; 2 old stble, cabin built; adj Edw. MATHEW and pt of tract adj to
land of Richard RIDGLEY
MATHEWS, Edw.; 241A; dwlg hse, log, 16x12; barn, log, 18x24; adj Geo.
CURFMAN; Dan'l WALKER
MATTHEWS, Wm.; 171A+; dwlg hse, log, 1 stry, 18x20; stble, 16x12; adj Edw.
MATHEWS
MORRIS, Sam'l; 260A; dwlg hse, log, 16x14; stble, 14x12; adj James CALDER
MORRIS, Joseph; 188A; dwlg, 16x18, log; barn 14x32, thatched; adj Penna line
MERRYMAN, John, son of Benjamin (8 slaves); dwlg hse, logs, 1 stry, 28x30, a
little out repair; spring hse, 8x8, log, old; Occupant: Nathaniel BELL;
dwlg hse, old, out repair; hipt roof, old kn, 14x16; old stble, 10x12;
old corn hse & stable under, 15x10; adj Benj. ANDERSON, Ezekiel BOSLEY
MERRYMAN, Benj'm (0 slaves); Mine Run Hd; 147A+; tract of land adj John
MERRYMAN and Ezekiel BOSLEY
MERRYMAN, John, Senr 1 house, value $50.
MERRYMAN, John (3 slaves); Mine Run Hd
NORRIS, Charlotte & SHACK, Peter; 122A; old dwlg hse, log, 15x10; old stble,
very indiff; adj Abraham RYSTON & Samuel HUGHES
NORRIS, William; 60A; dwlg hse, log, 17x15; stble, log, 15x12; adj Adam
BURNS, Abraham SLADE
NORRIS, Abraham; 190A; Occupant: Solomon WADLEY; dwlg hse, log, old, indiff,
15x20; stble, log, 10x15; adj Samuel HUGHES, James HUGHES
NUMAKER, Solomon; 68A; tract adj Penna line
NIGHT, Benjamin; 81A; old dwlg hse, log, 12x14; adj Clement GREEN & Michael
JENKINS
NICHOLSON, Doct. John (13 slaves); Up Gunpwdr Hd; 358A; dwlg hse, pt stone
and pt logs, stone pt, 1 stry, 24x20, 3 dormer windows above in good
repair, log pt, 20x20, 1 stry, 2 dormer windows not quite finished; meat
hse, 20x16, logs; corn hse & stble underneath, 24x14, good repair;
quarter hse, logs, 24x16, 1 stry, good repair; poultry hse, 24x16, well
built; adj Sarah SMITH, Geo. FITZHUGH
NAU, John (6 Slaves.); Up Gunpwdr Hd; 243A; dwlg hse, fr, 30x30, 1 stry, old,
out repair; kn, logs, 12x16, indiff; old barn, log, 20x18, indiff; adj
Jacob McCASLIN, James ELLIOTT
ONION, William (5 slaves); Up Gunpwdr Hd; 248A; dwlg hse, pt fr and pt logs,
fr pt 18x16, 1/2 stry, not quite finished, log pt 20x16, 1 1/2 stry, good
repair; log barn, 30x20, not quite finished; stble,logs, 16x12, very
indiff; kn, log, 16x14; meat hse, log, 12x12; adj Thomas G. HOWARD &
Little Falls
OSBURN, Elizabeth; 155A; stone hse, old, much out repair, 1 stry; old log
hse, adj, 12x10; adj Elijah MERRYMAN, Elijah BOSLEY
OGDEN, Amos (6 slaves); Mine Run Hd

13

PRICE, Thomas; 89A+; dwlg hse, log, 20x16, indiff; kn adj, 16x16; barn 30x18, log, old, out repair; old hse 10x12; old hse 8x10; adj land of Wm. GOODWIN

PARISH, Edward; 180A; dwlg hse, log, 18x25, 1 stry; dwlg hse, adj, 30x15, out repair; kn, logs, 12x12; barn, log, 28x18; stble 18x9; adj Wm. JOHNSON, Rich'd JONES

PEARCE, Wm.; 30A; tract adj Lydys Manor

PEARCE, Thomas; 205A; dwlg hse, hewd logs, 24x13; 1 1/2 stry, add. 20x16, log, 1 1/2, midling repair; stble, 14x14, log; spring hse, logs, 8x10; adj Joshua ANDERSON

POCOCK, Jesse (3 slaves); Mine Run Hd; 210A; dwlg hse, log 18x20, out repair; old kn, 10x12; old hen hse, 12x14, log; barn, log, 50x22, logs, not quite finished; adj Henry EINSEL, Francis SPARKS

POCOCK, James; 106a; 2 dwlg hse, adj 30x14, indifferently built; meat hse, 12x12; old spring hse, 10x10; stble, log, 18x12; adj David SAMPSON, Jonathan PLOWMAN

PERDUE, Walter (3 slaves); Mine Run Hd; 508A; dwlg hse, fr, out repair, 20x18, add. 10x12; spring hse, 8x10, stone; corn hse, stble under; dwlg hse, fr, much out repair, 25x25; log kn, 12x12; spring hse, stone, 12x12; stble, log, 20 ft, good repair; dwlg hse, log, 14x16; adj Joseph McCLUNG

PAUL, John (12 slaves); Up Gunpwdr Hd; 604A; dwlg hse, stone, 30x21; 2 stry, good repair, add. of stone, 20x18, 1 stry; barn, stone, 40x40, 2/5 finished; corn hse, fr, 20x8; stble, fr, 12x12; cow hse, 12x20, out repair; meat hse, fr, 12x12, out repair; hen hse, 16x10; adj Thomas G. HOWARD, Rebecka YOUNG

PIERCE, Edward (9 slaves); Up Gunpwdr Hd; 532A; dwlg hse, logs, 50x24, large stone chimney in the middle under same roof, tol good repair, 1 stry; stble, log, 45x16, much out repair; barn, log,70x30, 1 stry, midling repair; meat hse, log, 16x16; spring hse, log 10x10; adj Catharine BELT, John NICHOLSON

RIDGLEY, John; Occupant: Shadrach GREEN; 641A; dwl hse, pt log, pt fr, log pt 20x18 weatherboarded, 1 stry, midling repair, fr pt 18x14, 1 stry, indiff; stble, old, indiff, 16x12; old barn 60x28, much out repair; meat hse, 10x10, logs; adj Wm. LUX, Great Falls

REED, Joseph 3 slaves); Mine Run Hd; 130A; dwlg hse, hewd logs, 1 stry, 18x15, in good repair; old hse, 22x15, logs, used as kn; meat hse, log,10x12; corn hse, log, 12x14, out repair; barn, log, 24x24, indiff; stble, 20x10, indiff; adj CARROLLs Manor, John STEWART

RYSTON, Sarah; Occupant: Thomas RICHARDSON; 110A; log dwlg hse, 16x14; meat hse, 10x12, log; corn hse, log, 12x16, stable under; adj John MERRYMAN, Jacob BULL

RUTLEDGE, John of Ephraim; 240A; dwlg hse, logs, 20x18, not quite finished, 1 stry; old hse, logs, 16x18, 1 stry, under for a kn; barn, log, 42x16, thatched; adj Jacob ROCKHOLD, John DUNNOCKS land

ROCKHOLD, Jacob, Sr.; 270A; dwlg hse, log, 34x16, old, out repair; old hen hse; Occupant: Jacob ROCKHOLD, Jr.; dwlg hse, 14x16, log; shed 8x14; barn, 14x14, log, newly thatched; stble, log, 8x14; barn, 16x16, log; stble, 8x12, under one roof; adj Charles ROSD(?), John RUTLEGE

RYSTON, Abraham; Occupant: Robt. ANDERSON; 79A; dwlg hse, logs, 22x15, out repair, new add. of logs, 15x15, 1 stry, good repair; old kn, log, 10x15; barn, logs, 22x16, good repair; old smith shop, 12x12; adj Samuel HUGHES, Edw'd PARRISH

ROSIER Elizabeth; 142A+; dwlg hse, 18x16, log, 1 stry; old kn, cabin built; old barn, 36x18, thatched; adj James CALDER, Jacob SPLITSTONE

RUTLEDGE, Thomas; 196A+; dwlg hse, log, 18x16; stble, 14x16; adj James CALAN, John RUTLEDGE

RUTLEDGE, Cottral John; 198A+; dwlg hse, 16x16, log; stble, log, 12x16; adj James CALDER

RICE, James; 93A; dwlg hse, log, 20x16, out repair; shop, 18x14,log; adj John ELLIOTT, John LUNEY

RINGOLD, Thomas (12 slaves); Up Gunpwdr Hd; 258A; brk dwlg hse, 2 large stry, 45x35, new and well finished; barn, log, 45x18, old, somewhat out repair; stble, 20x16, indiff, log; negro hse on kn and out repair, 32x20, fr; adj James GITTINGS

RUSSEL, William; Occupant: Thomas PAUL; 190A; dwlg hse, log, 16x18, out repair; dwlg old hse, log, 16x18; adj W___, England(?)

RIDGLEY, Martha, widow of Edward; 1862A; Occupant: Wm. LUX for Martha RIDGLEY (1 slave); dwlg hse, fr, 48x22, 1 stry, 3 windows above, in midling repair; porch 18x22, passage 10x16; kn, logs, 15x15; meat hse, 15x15, logs

RIDGLEY ___; 4A

RIDGLEY, Rebecca (10 slaves); Up Gunpwder Hd; 35A; dwlg hse, fr, 28x18, 2 stry, in good repair; log kn, 18x14

ROGERS, Phillip; 126A; old dwlg hse, log, indiff; adj Sam'l GITTINGS & Michael JENKINS

RIDGLEY, General Charles (22 slaves); Up Gunpwder Hd; 1877A+; Occupant: Aguila HATTAN: dwlg hse, hewd log, 2 stry, 44x18, a little out repair; log kn, 18x18; meat hse, 16x10; barn, log, 20x20, in good repair; barn, log, 40x18, good repair; Occupant: Joshua MILES: dwlg hse, fr, 30x16, 1 stry, indifferently built; a public hse; log kn, 14x12, hse, 10x10; Occupant: Thomas WATTS: dwlg hse, logs, 20x18; kn, 16x14, logs

RUTLEDGE, Abraham (8 slaves); Mine Run Hd; 1 hse, 36x18, 4 out hses, value $170

RYSTON, John (3 slaves); Mine Run Hd

RIDGELY, Martha and Wm. GOODWIN; 1 hse, value - $50

STANDIFORD, John; dwlghse, logs, 20x16, 1 stry, in good repair

STANDIFORD, John of Skelton (11 slaves); Mine Run Hd; dwlg hse, logs 24x18, 1 stry, midling repair; kn, logs, 21x17; meat hse, 10x12, logs

SPARKS, Elijah; dwlg hse, logs, 16x14, 1 stry, add. 15x15, stry, tol repair; meat hse, hewd log, 18x818

SLADE, Ezekiel; Occupant: Abraham SLADE; dwlg hse, log, 36x16; 1 stry, midling repair; meat hse, 8x10; hen hse, 8x10, log

SLADE, Ezekiel (1 slave); Occupant: Thomas SLADE (1 slave); Mine Run Hd; dwlg hse, logs, porch, 34x16, hewn, 1 stry, good repair; hen hse, 10x10; spring hse, 10x12

SMITH, Joshua (6 slaves); Up Gunpwdr Hd

SMITH, Robert; dwlg hse, log, 18x18, 1 stry; kn, logs, 19x18; meat hse, logs, 8x10

SPARKS, Josias; dwlg hse, logs, 16x18, 1 stry, add. 16x8, add. 16x18, 1 stry, tol repair; meat hse, logs, 12x12; spring hse, logs, 6x8

STEWART, John; dwlg hse, hewd logs, 22x20, 1 stry, add. 10x22, midling repair; kn, logs, 20x14, indiff; meat hse, 14x10, logs; spring hse, stone, 15x13

SLADE, Josias (2 slaves) & Wm.; Mine Run Hd; dwlg hse, pt stone, pt fr, 2
stry, 40x28, in a public hse, well situated, good repair, piazza, 7x40;
kn, fr, 1 stry, 21x16, old, out repair; meat hse, logs, 10x12; spring
hse, stone, 10x10

SHIPLEY, Benjamin; dwlg hse, fr, 24x16, 1 stry; kn, 16x18, fr, 1 stry; meat
hse, 10x10, logs

SUTTON, Joseph (7 slaves); Mine Run Hd; dwlg hse, log, 2 stry, 27x14, add.
32x20, 1 stry, an old hse, much out repair; stone spring hse, 12x12; meat
hse, 20x10, logs; hen hse, 12x10

SPARKS, Francis; 257A+; dwlg hse, pt stone, pt logs, stone 24x14, 1 stry,
log pt 14x12, midling repair; spring hse, 8x8; barn, logs, 40x16, stone
stble, under; corn hse, 16x10; adj Matthews SPARKS, Henry E.

STANSBURY, Dixon, Jr. (3 slaves); Mine Run Hd; 232A; dwlg hse, 28x28, hipt
roof, midling repair, fr; kn, logs, 20x16, 1 stry; hen hse, 8x12, logs;
stble 34x10, shingle roof, out repair; adj _

STANSBURY, Dixon, Sr. (11 slaves); Mine Run Hd; 170A; dwlg hse, 38x20, fr; 1
stry, very much out repair; kn, 28x16, fr, old, out repair; barn 25x20,
out repair; stble 40x12, old and much out repair; adj Dixon STANSBURY,
Jr. & Nich. FULLER

SMITH, Larkin (13 slaves); Up Gunpwdr Hd; 805A; dwlg hse, logs,
weatherboarded, 1 stry, newly repaired; kn, log, 18x21, 1 stry; spring
hse, hewd logs, 12x12k; corn hse, logs; stble under, 40x12; barn, 40x20,
out repair; adj Sarah SMITH, John STARDEON

STONE, Thomas (6 slaves); Up Gunpwdr Hd; 438A (30 acres sold for taxes -
1805); dwlg hse, fr, hipt roof, 6 windows above, 50x16, midling repair;
fr kn, 16x20, old, out repair; fr meat hse, 8x8; corn hse, logs, stble
under, 18x12; barn, log, 40x20, out repair; shed add. 10x20; adj Francis
DARNELL, Henry WILSON

SLEE, Joseph (11 slaves); Up Gunpwdr Hd; 198A; dwlg hse, stone, 2 stry,
36x21, good repair; old log kn, 18x16, log; meat hse, 12x16, log; hen
hse, 10x12, log; stone spring hse, 10x12; old lumber hse, 24x16, logs;
barn 16-20 shed, 3 sides, good repair; row hse for tann__, 54x20; adj
Aquilla HALL & Thomas GITTINGS

STEVENSON, John (6 slaves); Mine Run Hd; dwlg hse, fr, 24x24; kn 14x12; meat
hse 10x8

SMITH, Sarah (44 slaves); 826A+; Up Gunpwdr Hd; brk dwlg hse, 2 stry, wall
much cracked, but inside in tol repair, 36x22; fr add. 32x18, 1 stry,
newly repaired; kn, log, 26x16, add. 8x16, fr, good repair; meat hse,
16x16, log; hen hse 10x8; corn hse, 30x14, logs; stble, under, in good
repair; out hse 14x16; corn hse, 26x12, old, out repair; stable of logs,
16x12; barn, 30x40, fr, a little out repair; granary 12x16, 2 stry, good
repair; adj John NICHOLSON, Larkin SMITH

SPARKS, Matthew; 36A+; pt tract adj to Penna line and Joshua LOWE

SPLITSTONE, Jacob; Occupant: Stephen SPLITSTONE; 56A; log dwlg hse, 16x22;
log dwlg hse, 30x17; new spring hse, 30x15; old barn 22x38; adj VAUGHN,
ELLIOTT

SPLITSTONE, John; pt tract adj Jacob SPLITSTONE

SPLITSTONE, Jacob, Jr.; 285A; dwlg hse, log, 31x18, indiff; spring hse
16x14; barn, log, 64x24, good repair, 10 ft add.

SUMWAULT, Godfrey; Occupant: Wm. MARSH; 262A; dwlg hse 16x14; adj Michael
HINDLE

SAMPSON, Isaac, Junior; 180a; dwlg, 16x18, logs; stble 12x16; adj James CALDER &c.

STANDIFORD, Vincent; 172A; dwlg hse, logs, 18x20; stble 14x16; stble 12x20; adj Capt. CALDER

SHOCK, Peter; 444A; dwlg hse, logs, not finished, 16x20; adj to Great Falls

SHARP, George; 104A+; adj John M___

SPARKS, Thomas (4 slaves); Mine Run Hd; 1 hse, value $70

SHEPHERD, John (5 slaves); Mine Run Hd; 2 hses, value $50; occupant: Nathaniel SHEPHERD (1 slave); Mine Run Hd

SHAW, Daniel (10 slaves); Mine Run Hd; 1 hse, value $50

SINCLAIR, William (2 slaves); Mine Run Hd; 1 hse, value $40

SHEPHERD, Mary (5 slaves); Mine Run Hd; 1 hse, $16

SAMPSON, Elijah; 1 hse, $30

SOWERS, John; 1 hse, value $60

SELLMAN, Jonathan; Occupants: John WILSON, Charles RANDALL; 250A (80 acres sold for taxes - 1805); dwlg hse, 20x50, indiff built; old dwlg hse, 14x18, out repair; adj James ELLIOTT

SHANLEY, Doct. Jeffry; 120P; tract adj James ELLIOTT

SHAW, David (4 slaves); Up Gunpwdr Hd; 173A; dwlg hse, log, 22x18, old; kn, 1 stry, 16x12; meat hse, 12x16,old; stble 16x12; adj ___ RIDGELY & James

SKINNER, John; Occupant: Wm. YEARLY; 138A; dwlg hse, stone, 30x24, 1 stry, indiff repair

SHAW, Henry; 1 hse, value $20 ... (10 acres sold for taxes - 1805).....

SHAW, Samuel; 30A

TODD, Heirs of Thomas; Occupant: Thomas NICHOLSON; 498A; pt Gasaway's Ridge; dwlg hse, pt stone, pt fr, 26x24, 1 stry, add. of stone, 10x24, 1 stry, tol repair; meat hse, fr, 8x10; adj Henry D. GOUGH's land

STANSBURY, Edmond (7 slaves); Mine Run Hd; 328A; dwlg hse, fr, 26x20, 1 stry, very much out repair, add. 12x26, fr, out repair; _hse, stble under 12x18; spinning hse, 18x14, fr; barn, log, 18x16, out repair; kn, fr, 28x16; meat hse, log 12x14; adj Josia and William SLADE & Temperance BACON

SAMPSON, Abraham; 1 hse, value $20

SAMPSON, David; 1 hse, value $30

TYSON, Jesse; Occupants: James ARMITAGE, Jacob TYSON; 119A; dwlg hse, stone, 2 stry, 30x25, midling repair; kn, stone, 18x18; barn, stone, 2 stry, 50x40, good repair; stone hse, 1 1/2 stry, 25x25, good repair; mill, stone, 70x38, tol repair, but not made use of(?) come time for want of grain; adj to Little Falls and David LEE

TALBOT, Henry (1 slave); Mine Run Hd

TRAPNALL, Vincent (6 slaves); Mine Run Hd

VAUGHAN, Gist (2 slaves); Mine Run Hd; dwlg hse, stone, 2 stry, 24x26, new and not quite finished; 2 old kns each 16x12; spring hse, stone, 16x12; meat hse, 12x10, logs; hen hse, logs, 10x10; very old barn, 20x16, log; stbles, 33x14; old cooper shop, 16x12; still hse 20x20; grist mill, stone, good repair; saw mill, stone, but two small a stream of water; adj George ELLIOTTS, John BARNS

WILEY, Greenbury (8 slaves); Mine Run Hd

WILEY, Vincent (2 slaves); Mine Run Hd

WILMOT, John (9 slaves); Up Gunpwdr Hd

WILMOT, Ruth (1 slave); Mine Run Hd

WATTS, Thomas (2 slaves); Up Gunpwdr Hd

WIDENER, Susannah; Occupant: Job RICHARDS; 20A; stble; mill, logs, 20x32, much out of repair, 2 pair of stones; meat hse

WILSON, Jean; 202A; dwlg hse, log, 20x18; ___ shop, 20x12; stble, 15x16

WHEELER, Wasan; 50A; dwlg hse, log, 15x15, old, out repair; stble, 20x12; adj ___ ELLIOTT

WALKER, Daniel (2 slaves); Mine Run Hd; 709A; old dwlg hse; log, 25 1/2x18; old meat hse, 10x10; store hse 16x20; mill, logs, 2 pairs of stone, mill much out of repair; saw mill, log, ___ repair; adj Capt James CALDER and Great Falls

WANTLING, Isaac; 100A; old dwlg hse, log, cabin built, 14x16; adj Thomas WANTLING and John LOW

WANTLING, Thomas; 232A+; dwlg hse, log, 20x16; log kn, 16x18, indiff, 50x20; ___ John LOW

WILLIAMS, Thomas; 48A; dwlg hse, 14x16; stble 10x12

WILLIAMS, Reese; 63A; dwlg hse, log, 10x14; stble 12x12

WILLIAMS, Wm.; 63A; dwlg hse 16x__, cabin built; stble 12x14

WRIGHT, Solomon (5 slaves); Up Gunpwdr Hd; 150A; dwlg hse, log, 20x16, much out repair; kn 16x16; meat hse, 8x10; adj John ELLIOTT

WILSON, Gittings; (8 slaves); Mine Run Hd; 159A; dwlg hse, hewd logs, hipt roof, 20x16, midling repair, add. fr 12x20, 1 stry; kn, hewd logs, 26x16, 1 stry; meat hse, 12x10, logs; hen hse, 12x10, logs

WILSON, Andrew; 98A; dwlg hse, hewd logs, 26x20, 2 stry, tol good repair, situated on public road and a public hse

GOLDSMITH & WEATHEREL; 118A; dwlg hse, fr, 25x15, 1 stry, add. stone 12x14, 1 stry

WEATHRAL, William (2 slaves); Up Gunpwdr Hd

WILSON, John, Sr. (11 slaves); Up Gunpwdr Hd; 271A+; dwlg hse, fr, 44x16, 1 stry, old, much out repair; kn, log, 30x16, old, out repair; meat hse 8x10; meat hse 16x12; hen hse 8x10, log

WILSON, John, Jr.; 122A; dwlg hse, fr, 24x26, 1 stry, tol well finished; log spring hse, 10x10; adj John NICHOLSON & Edward PIERCE

WALL, Nicholas of Philadelphia; Occupant: Gabriel STEILL; 145A+; dwlg hse, stone, 1 1/2 intended for good hse but not quiite finished, 24x20; adj to Thomas G. HOWARD

WILSON, Benj. (11 slaves); 198A+; dwlg hse, 26x18, hipt roof, 4 windows above in good repair; kn, logs, 18x14, indiff; adj Aquilla HALL & Francis DARNELL

WOLFE, James (6 slaves); Up Gunpwdr Hd; 69A+ (60 acres sold for taxes - 1805); dwlg hse, log, 24x16, 1 stry; kn, logs, 16x16; sun porch, 12x10, logs; adj to David SHAW, Martha RIDGLEY

WILSON, Henry of John; 40A; dwlg hse, fr, 28x26, 1 stry, much out repair; kn, log, 16x18; hen hse, 10x10; adj John WILSON & Edw. PEIRCE

WALKER, John; 379A+; dwlg hse, log, 22x18, out repair; dwlg, old, much out repair, 18x20; kn ?x20; hse, log, 14x20; corn hse, 20x12, stble under, log, out repair; adj James GITTINGS

WILSON, Robt; 164A; old dwlg hse, log, 20x13, out repair; adj Thomas PRICE, John JONES

WILSON, Henry of Kid (22 slaves); Up Gunpwdr Hd; 481a; quarter hse, log, 18x16; stble & corn hse, 30x10; lumber hse, 14x14; barn, log, 18x30; 2 stbles each 10x10

WILSON, Asael (2 slaves); Up Gunpwdr Hd; 50A; adj to John NICHOLSON & Sarah SMITH

WATKINS, Jno. & Sam'l (7 slaves; Up Gunpwdr Hd; 2 hses, value $60 and $50

YOUNG, Rebecca (4 slaves); 758A; Occupant: Asael BARTON; dwlg hse, fr, 2 stry, 32x22, much out repair; kn, fr, 12x16, old, out repair; adj land of Henry D. GOUGH

YEISER, Englehard; Actor for Fred McCOMAS; Occupant: Nathan EVERET; 228A; dwl hse, stone, hipt roof, 22x18, 2 windows above, good repair, porch 6x22; kn, logs, 16x14; meat hse, 12x12, log; adj Edw. HOWARD

Glebe lands in Gun Powder Hd - 1 acre of land and fr hse, 10x30 for public worship called the Methodist fork Meeting adj to land of Charles GORSUCH

Glebe land in Mine Run Hd - 2 acres of land and a large brk hse for public worship called St. Pauls Church adj to Edward STANSBURY

North Hundred

ADRON, Christian; Occupants: Jacob ANTHORDON, Joshua CROSS; 327A; Christian's Chance; log dwlg hse, 1 stry, 30x20; log dwlg hse 24x17; old log dwlg hse 24x20

ARMEGOSTH, John; 140A; pt Stoddards Delight and other tracts; log dwlg hse, 1 stry, 18x16; log barn 50x16

ARCHHEART, Nich'l; 150A; Kill A Man

ARMEGOSTH, Mich'l; 95A; Addition to Timber Ridge; hewd log dwlg hse, 1 stry, 18x16; log barn 30x16

ARMEGOSTH, Christop.; 45A; pt Borings Choice; hewd log dwlg hse, 1 stry, 18x16

BOND, Denis; Occupant: Benj. TRACY; 333A; Absoloms Choice; log dwlg hse, 1 stry, 24x18; log corn hse, 20x12; log barn 36x20

BAUSLEY, Nicholas; 800A; Bacon Hall; log dwlg hse, 1 stry, 32x16; log kn 16x12; log barn 60x20; log hse 20x12; log corn hse 30x16

BAUSLEY, Nancy; Occupant: Johnson TIMOTHY; 82A; Anns Pleasant Ridge; log dwlg hse, 1 stry, 20x18; log smoke hse 12x10; log barn 20x20

BOND, John of John; John SKIPPER; 100A; name of land not known; log dwlg hse, 1 1/2 stry, 24x20

BOSSOM, Charles; 143A; Bossoms Spott; old log dwlg hse, 1 stry, 20x16; old log barn 24x20

BUSBY, Eddithy; 250A; pt Deer Park; hewd log dwlg hse, 1 stry, 24x12; log smoke hse 10x18

BUSBY, John; 100A; pt Deer Park

BORING, Absolom; 208A; pt Rogers Resurvey; hewd log dwlg hse, 1 stry, 18x16; log corn hse 12x10; log barn 20x16

BYRAM, John; 190A; Byrams Fancy; hewd log dwlg hse, 1 stry, 30x16

BULL, John; 136A; Bulls Fancy; log dwlg hse, 1 stry, 16x14

BULL, William; 314A; Bulls Bottom; log dwlg hse, 2 stry, 20x18; log corn hse 14x12

BOWERS, John; 265A; pt Bears Rock & Rocky Hills; log dwlg hse, 1 1/2 stry, 22x20

BOLINGER, Joseph; 332A; Bolingers Contrivance; log dwlg hse *, 2 stry, 26x24; log h___; log barn 40x20

BRANUMAN, Sam'l; 100A; Deercreek Park; hewd log dwlg hse 20x18; log barn 24x20

BROTHER, Richard; Occupant: Nathan COE; 300A; name of land not known; log dwlg hse, 1 stry, 18x16

BORING, Joshua; 183A; New Germany; log dwlg hse, 1 stry, 20x18

BICELINE, Abraham; 78A; Long Hill; log dwlg hse, 1 stry, 18x16

BORING, Thomas; Occupant: Samuel TIPTON; 178A (80 acres sold for taxes - 1805); Transylvania; log dwlg hse, 1 stry, 18x18 *; log kn 16x__; log barn 40x16

BOLINGER, Matthias; 147A; pt Stony Hills; hewd log dwlg hse, 1 1/2 stry, 26x __*

BARE, Jacob; 33A; pt Troy

BURNS, John; 170A; Two Brothers

BARE, John; 17A (1 acre sold for taxes - 1805); name of land not known; hewd log dwlg hse, 1 stry, 30x16

BAKER, William; 20A; Stony Mountain; hewd log dwlg hse, 1 stry, 20x16; hewd log mill hse 20x20; log barn 30x18

BAKER, Christian; 30A; name of land not known; log dwlg hse, 1 stry, 18x16; log barn 20x16

BORING, Ezekiel; 922A; Three Elbows; stone dwlg hse*, 2 stry, 30x24; log corn hse 20x16; log barn 40x18

BORING, Absolom; 219A+; Pearsons & Benjamins Lot; fr dwlg hse, 1 stry, 24x16; log kn 16x16; log hse 16x16; log barn 30x16

BORING, Pliles'r; 65A; Boring Struggle

BORING, James; 300A; pt Greens Desire; log dwlg hse, 1 stry, 30x18

BORING, Joshua of James; 100A; pt Greens Desire; log dwlg hse, 20x16, 1 stry

BARNEY, Thomas; 240A; Osburns Struggle

COLE, Joseph; 100A; Black Patch; log dwlg hse, 2 stry, 26x16; log kn 18x16

CAPLES, Robert; 410A+; Caples Habitation; log dwlg hse, 1 stry, 46x20*; row kn, 18x15; log barn 24x20; log smoke hse 12x10

CHANDLER, Joseph; 20A+; Addition to Brotherhood; log dwlg hse, 1 stry, 20x18; stone mill hse 40x35

COLE, Abraham; 163A+; Abraham's Prospect; log dwlg hse, 1 stry, 48x16; log barn 60x20

COLE, Christopher; 148A; Painters Hill; log dwlg hse, 1 stry, 22x18

CHENWORTH, Rich'd; 2A+; pt Elledges Farm; log dwlg hse, 1 stry, 20x16; log kn 12x12; log shop 30x18

COCKEY, Frederick; 945a; pt Stodards Delight; hewd log dwlg hse, 24x20, log add. 18x15; log smoke hse 10x10; log barn 30x18

CHILCOAT, Richard; 50A (4 acres sold for taxes - 1805); Chilcoat Lot; hewd log dwlg hse, 1 stry, 18x16

COLE, Thomas of Christopher; 145A; pt Preachers Policy; log dwlg hse, 1 stry, 20x18

CRATON, Mary; 48A (10 acres sold for taxes - 1805); Peggys Delight; log dwlg hse, 1 stry, 12x10

COLLET, Wm. __Sheph._; 307A; Blue Mountain Enlarged; old log dwlg 18x16

CAULDER, James; Castle Caulder

COLLET, Moses; 247A+; Collets Habitation; log dwlg hse, 1 stry, 18x16; log barn 20x16

COX, John; 100A; Coxes Ketch; log dwlg hse, 1 stry, 16x14; log barn 30x20

COX, Wm. 102A; Pleasant Meadows; fr dwlg hse, 20x18 *; ___ 18x16; log barn 40x20

COX, Jacob; 91A; Coxes Ketch; hewd log dwlg, 1 stry, 27x16

COX, Zebediah; 150A; pt Coxes Ketch; log dwlg hse, 1 stry, 16x14; log barn 30x20

CARLINGER, George; 293A; pt Plymoth; stone dwlg hse, 2 stry, 35x35*; stone mill hse, 2 stry, 40x40; log barn 40x20

CARLINGER, Conrod; 200A; no name for land; log dwlg hse, 1 stry, 18x16

CARLINGER, John; 200A; pt Plymoth; log dwlg hse, 2 stry, 18x16

CROMRINE, Abra'm; 223A; pt Epstone & pt other tracts; stone dwlg, 2 stry, 40x30; stone kn 18x18; stone milk hse, 16x12; barn, 2 stry, 1 stone, other logs, 100x10

COLTRITER, Davalt; 205A+; Heidellary and pt of other tracts; Heidlebury, Nightone; log dwlg hse, 2 stry, 45x24 *; log barn 20x20; log stble 30x12

COUTZ, Michael; 320A; Coutz Lot; hewd log dwlg hse, 2 stry, 24x20 (stone & logs); mill hse, 2 stry, 40x40; barn, 2 stry, 1 of stone, other of logs, 100x24

CATEAR, Henry; 201A; Milover; hewd log dwlg hse, 1 stry, 24x20*; log milk hse, 12x10; log barn 40x20

CATEAR, Peter; 16A+; Bowers Delight

COLTRITER, John; 213A; Porings Meadows & Fosters Chance; log fr dwlg hse, 2 stry, 32x28*; log kn 16x12; log milk hse 14x10; log barn 40x20

CULLASON, Wm.; 124A; Sportsmans Hall; log dwlg hse, 1 stry, 16x16

COLE, Ezekiel; Occupant: Henry HALE; 122A; pt Ezekiel's Lot; log dwlg hse, 20x16

CULLINGS, Jon.; 111A; Walls of Deary; log dwl hse 18x16

CULLINGS, Thos.; 128A; Cullings Lot; log dwlg hse, 1 stry, 16x14; log barn 30x18

CULLINGS, Isaac; 50A; Cammels Trouble; log dwlg hse, 16x12

CAMBEL, Moses; 266A; Holly Run (or Hilly Run); dwlg hse, 2 stry, 1 of stone, other fr, 30x20 *; log milk hse 10x8; log barn 50x18

CAPONHAVER, Conrod; 130A; name of land not known; log dwlg hse, 1 stry, 18x16; log barn 24x16

CAMPBEL, John; 98A; pt Foster's Hunting Ground; dwlg hse, 2 stry, 24x18*; stone milk hse 12x10; stone mill hse, 2 stry, 28x28

CAMPBEL, Aaron; 157A+; Campbels Pursuit; log dwlg hse, 1 stry, 16x14; log barn 48x16

CROSS, John of Benjamin; 100A; pt of Pitt; log dwlg hse, 1 stry, 14x12

CROSS, John; 100A; Bucks Range; log dwlg hse, 14x12

COOPER, John; 140A; Betsys Choice; log dwlg hse, 14x12

COLE, Elizabeth; 210A; pt Roger's Resurvey; hewd log dwlg hse, 1 stry, 22x16; log kn 16x16; log corn hse 14x12

COLE, Mordecai; 116A; pt Roger's Resurvey; hewd log dwlg hse, 1 stry, 20x18; log corn hse 16x12

COX, Kezia; 1A+; hewd log dwlg hse, 1 stry, 14x10

COX, Elisha; 148A; Merrymans Choice; log dwlg hse, 1 stry, 14x14; log corn hse 18x11

DAVIS, Samuel; 83A; pt Addition to Brotherhood; stone dwlg hse, 2 stry, 20x18 *; log hse 20x18; log shop 24x12; log barn 30x20

DAVIS, Francis; Occupant: Thos. ALMACH; 370A; pt Davis's Chance; log dwlg hse, 16x14

DAVIS, Benjamin; 198A; pt Davis's Chance; hewd log dwlg hse, 1 stry, 20x16 *; log kn 20x16

DAVIS, James; 200A; pt Davis's Chance; hewd log dwlg hse, 1 stry, 24x20; log kn 20x16; log barn 50x20

21

DORSEY, Elisha; 120A; Dorsey's Plains; log dwlg hse, 1 1/2 stry, 24x20; log kn 16x16

DICK, Jacob; 50A; hewd log dwlg hse, 1 1/2 stry, 18x16; log barn 30x16

DICK, Frederick; 50A; Huck Lot; log dwlg hse, 1 stry, 16x14; log barn 30x16

DEEDS, Philip; 61A; Fair Play; log dwlg hse, 1 stry, 16x14; log barn 20x16

DOWNEY, Thomas; 149A; pt Stansberry Grove; log dwlg hse, 1 stry, 18x16; log shop 18x16

DOWNEY, George; 131A+; pt Stansberry Grove; log dwlg hse 16x16

DOWNEY, Walter; 50A; pt Stansberry Grove; log dwlg hse, 1 1/2 stry, 18x16

DEAHOOF, John; 200A; pt Shillings Folly; log dwlg hse, 1 stry, 15x14; log barn 30x20

COCKEY, Thomas Dye; Occupant: Geo. HARRIS; 2562A+; Penelopes & Thos. Cockey Dye Resurv. and pt other tracts; log dwlg hse, 1 stry, 30x16

ENSOR, Darby; 368A+; Regulated Vineyard Resurveyed and pt of other tracts; log dwl hse, 1 1/2 stry, 24x16; log kn 16x14; log corn hse 16x10

ENSOR, George; 100A; Addition to Hit or Miss; log dwlg hse, 18x14

ENSOR, Nathan of George; Occupant: Elijah SKIPPER; 271A+; Orasia Lot; log dwlg hse, 1 1/2 stry, 18x16

ELSRODE, Freder'k; 90A+; Elsrode Forrest; log dwlg hse 18x16

EDWARD, Henry; 100A; Edwards Choice; log dwlg hse, 1 stry, 16x16; log kn 14x12

EDWARD, Edmon; 19A+; pt Tuckers Range; log dwlg hse, 1 1/2 stry, 16x16

FOSTER, Nicholas; 583A+; pt Ramble; log dwlg hse, 1 stry, 22x16; log kn 14x12

FOSTER, John; 840A+; pt Hunting Ground and pt of other tracts

FORD, Joshua; 193A; pt Quartermans Choice; hewd log dwlg hse, 1 1/2 stry, 34x18; log kn 19x15; log barn 24x16

FREELAND, Uriah, Sr.; 90A+; Crosse's Beginning; hewd log dwlg hse, 1 stry, 25x20, log barn 15x12

FREELAND, Uriah; 50A; name of land not known

FITZ, Ulerich; 153A; pt Vances Enlargement; log dwlg hse, 1 stry, 16x12; log barn 20x16

FAIR, George; 94A; Fredericks Conquest; log dwlg 16x14

FRAUNK, Peter; 120P; pt Spring Garden Enlarged; hewd log dwlg hse *, 2 stry, 24x18; log kn 16x10; log stble 16x16

FORD, Mordecai, Jr.; 99A+; pt Fords choice

FORD, Barney; 159A; pt Fords Choice; hewd log dwlg hse, 1 stry, 25x23

FOSTER, Absolom; 300A; pt Hunting Ground; hewd log dwlg hse, 1 1/2 stry, 25x17

FOSTER, George; Occupant: John SHOVER; 300A; Tiptons Fancy; log dwlg hse 18x16

FEATHER, Adam; 200A+; pt Three Brothers; hewd log dwlg hse, 24x20, 1 stry *; log barn 24x18; log stble 22x20

FOUBLE, Peter; 826A; Foubles Tract; hewd log dwlg hse, 2 stry, 30x26 *; log barn 30x20; log smoke hse, 1 stry, 10x9

FARE, Christopher; 134A+; Wallet; hewd log dwlg hse, 2 stry, 28x25 *; log barn 50x20

FARE, Jacob; 140A; Woolory's Folly; log dwlg hse 16x14

FELTS, John; 2A; hewd log dwlg hse, 2 stry, 18x16

GILL, Stephen; 542A+; pt Nicholsons Manor and other tracts; fr dwlg hse, 1 stry, 20x18; log kn 20x18; fr barn 40x24

GILL, Edward; 131A; pt Nicholson Manor; fr dwlg hse, 1 stry, 24x18 *; log kn, 24x18; log corn hse 24x12; fr barn 44x24; log smoke hse 14x12

GILL, Elizabeth; 113A; pt Nicholsons Manor; fr dwlg hse *, 1 stry, 24x20; log kn 16x16; log smoke hse 10x10; log corn hse 16x10; log barn 16x12; log poultry hse 10x10

GOODFELLOW, Wm.; 110A; pt Poormans Struggle; log dwlg hse, 21x17

GENT, Thomas; Occupant: Wm. ALMACK; 145A; log dwlg hse, 1 stry, 16x14

GAUL, Michael; 267A+; Shrewsbury; hewd log dwlg hse, 1 stry, 30x18; log corn hse 14x12; log barn 30x20

GIST, George; 427A+; Mary's Delight; hewd log dwlg hse, 2 stry, 24x18; log barn 26x20

GROG, Jacob; 50A; Youngman's Delight; hewd log dwlg hse, 1 stry, 18x16; log milk hse 12x10; log barn 30x18

GORE, Christian; 230A; Pitt; hewd log dwlg hse, 1 stry, 32x16; log kn 16x16

GRICE, Henry; 68A+; Bowers Delight; hewd log dwg hse, 1 stry, 21x17; log kn 12x10; log barn 24x20

GAIN, Wm.; 50A; Gain's Delight

GIST, Col. Thos.; 1405A+; Deer Park and pt of other tracts

HALE, Henry; 110A; Thomas's Lot; log dwlg hse 26x20

HARE, John; 216A (216 acres sold for taxes - 1805); Hare's Level; stone dwlg hse, 2 stry, 34x18 *; log kn 16x16; stone barn 40x24; stone milk hse 16x12

HUST, Benedick; 168A+; pt Hustes Hills log dwlg hse, not finished, 1 stry, 28x26; log barn 50x18

HURST, Bazzel; 81A+; pt Hurst's Hills; log dwlg hse 16x16

HURST, Shadrack; 55A; pt Hurst's Hills

HOSHEL, Jesse; 75A; pt Hurst's Hills; log dwlg hse, 18x16; log kn 14x12

HUBER, Frederick; 64A; name of land not known

HADLY, John; 75A; Chesnut Ridge; log dwlg hse, 16x12

HOOFMAN, Wm.; 826A; Paper Mill Hills and pt of other tracts; hewd log dwlg hse, 1 stry, 24x20, stone add. 20x12; stone paper mill, 4 stry, not finished, 80x44; barn, 2 stry, 1 of stone, other fr, 50x24; corn hse, 2 stry, 1 of stone, other logs, 20x12; log hse 16x16; fr mill hse, 2 stry, 28x22; saw mill flutter wheel 36x12

HALE, Tilly; 214A; Hales Hackle; log dwlg hse 16x16

HICKMAN, Boston; 122A; Poplar Run; log dwlg hse 18x16; log barn 24x16

HARNESS, Sam'l and Co.; Occupant: Warnell TRACY; 539A; log dwlg hse, 1 stry, 20x16

HARE, Jacob; 215A; Hares Retirement; hewd log dwlg hse, 24x20; log barn 30x20

HARE (HAIR), Christopher; 298A; name of land not known; hewd log dwlg hse, 1 1/2 stry, 26x22 *; log barn 40x20

JOHNSON, Jeremiah; 234A; pt Nicholson's; stone dwlg hse, 2 stry, 28x20; log hse, 1 stry, 52x18 *; log barn

JOHNSON, Timothy; 392A+; Bosmans Pleasant Ridges; log dwlg hse, 1 stry, 21x18; log hse 20x18; log hse 16x14

JOHNS, Richard E.; 635A+; pt Millers Delight; Occupant: Benjamin PRICE; stone cooper shop, 2 stry, 33x22; stone dwlg hse, 2 stry, 66x22, stone kn, 18x12 *; log barn 30x20; log smoke hse 12x12

KEMP, John; 228A; Second Cost; fr dwlg hse, 1 stry, 24x18

KIDD, John; 224A+; Dinah's Delight; log dwlg hse 18x16

KIDD, Joshua; 119A+; Ridd Wilderness; log dwlg hse 18x16

23

KEETH, Wm. Jr(?); 154A; hewd log dwlg hse, 1 stry, 18x16
KILBAUGH, Chris.; 60A; Tiptons Fancy; log dwlg 14x13; log barn 24x20
KILBAUGH, Henry; 50A; pt Spring Garden; log dwlg 16x14; log barn 24x12
KROFT, Jacob; 257A+; Fouble Lot; hewd log dwlg hse, 2 stry, 26x24; log mill
    hse, 1 stry, 30x26; saw mill 40x10
KILTER, Abraham; 280A; name of land not known
KROFT, Michael; 100A; name of land not known
KELLER, Jacob; 75A; name of land not known
LEMMON, Jacob; 770A+; pt Spring Field; stone mill hse, 2 stry, 24x30; hewd
    log dwlg hse, 2 stry, 30x20 *; log kn 20x16; hewd log milk hse 16x10; log
    barn 25x16
LEMMON, Thos.; 312A; Pleasant Meadows; log dwlg hse, 1 stry, 13x15; log corn
    hse 12x10
LEMMON, John; 300A; pt Hunting Ground; log dwlg hse 18x16; log corn hse
    12x10
LETSINGER, Henry; 64A; Addition to Slapbang Town; log dwlg hse, 1 stry,
    16x16
LEMMON, Alexis; 485A+; John's Adventure; log dwlg hse, 1 1/2 stry, 20x18;
    log barn 40x22
LAMMOT, Barbara; 277A; Fox's Range and other tracts; stone dwlg hse, 1 1/2
    stry, 30x26; hewd log hse, 26x24, shed add. 26x24 *; log barn 60x24
MALONEE, Wm.; 25A; Malonee's Habitation; log dwlg hse 25x14; log barn 24x16
MILLER, Eliz'th; 237A; pt Hard lot; log dwlg hse, 1 stry, 23x16; log kn
    12x12; log smoke hse 12x12; log barn 30x20
MATTHEWS, Susanah; 221A; Matthews Forrest; log dwlg hse, 1 stry, 18x16; log
    barn 20x16
McCOMESKY, Jno.; 450A; McComesky Folly; fr dwlg hse, 1 stry, 24x20, log add.
    20x16; log barn 20x16
MERRYMAN, Jno. (Baltimore); Occupant: Frederick BAUGHAN; 330A; Merryman's
    Look Out; log dwlg hse, 1 stry, 18x16
MERRYMAN, John; Occupants: Chas. CONWAY, Sam'l McAFFE, Sam'l BORING; 460A;
    Bush Cabbin Track; log dwlg hse, 1 stry, 20x16; log dwlg hse, 1 stry,
    20x16; log dwlg hse, 1 stry, 22x20
MILLER, Thomas; 167A; pt Hard Lot; log dwlg hse, 1 stry, 20x16
MORGAN, Nich's; 118A; Butlers Dependance; log dwlg hse, 1 stry, 16x14; log
    kn 16x12; log barn 16x13
MORGAN, Thos.; 42A; name of land not known; log dwlg hse, 1 stry, 14x13
MATTHEWS, Wm.; 302A; Matthews Choice; hewd log dwlg hse, 1 stry, 20x16; log
    kn 16x12; log barn 40x20
MERRYMAN Wm.; 160A; Merryman's Beginning; hewd log dwlg hse, 1 stry, 22x18;
    log kn 20x12; log barn 20x12
MURRAY, Wheeler; 159A; Murray's Ridge; hewd log dwlg hse, 1 stry, 16x16 *;
    log kn 20x16; log corn hse 15x9
MESSMORE, Henry; 150A; Yoeders Part; hewd log dwlg hse, 1 stry, 26x18; log
    milk hse 16x10; log barn 20x16
MARSHALL, Jacob; 270A; Crosse's Grove; hewd log dwlg hse, 1 stry, 22x18; log
    kn 16x12
MARSHALL, Wm.; 122A+; name of land not known; log dwlg hse, 1 stry, 20x18;
    log barn 39x18
MARSHALL, Thos.; 340A; Marshals Folly; hewd log dwlg hse, 2 stry, 17x17,
    stone shed add. 17x10 *; log barn 50x20
MATTHEWS, And'w; 80A; Grubby Thicket; log dwlg hse, 16x12

MARKE, Jacob; 298A; Crosses Boot Enlarged; hewd log dwlg hse, 1 stry,   28x20
   *; log kn, 20x20; log corn hse 14x12; log barn 60x20
MARSH, James; 79A; name of land not known; hewd log dwlg hse, 16x14
MARKE, Sam'l; 162A+; pt Walnut Hills; hewd log dwlg hse, 18x16; log barn
   20x16
MATTHEWS, Jesse; 110A+; Matthews Forrest; hewd log dwlg hse, 1 stry, 18x16;
   log barn 30x16; log corn hse 12x10
McCOMMESKY, Moses; 402A+; Medlicoats Adventure; log dwlg hse, 1 stry, 18x16;
   log barn 20x11
MERRYMAN, Geo.; 159A+; Merryman's Lot; log dwlg hse, 1 stry, 22x18; log kn
   14x14; log barn 40x20
MURRY, John; 183A+; Pleasant Meadows; hewd log dwlg hse, 18x16; log kn,
   18x10; log barn 40x20
MYERS, Philip; 160A; Borings Meadows; log dwlg hse 18x16
MARKEE, Henry; 166A+; Stansberry Ramble; hewd log dwlg hse, 18x16; log barn
   20x16
MILLER, John; 235A+; pt Little Meadow Resurveyed; hewd log dwlg hse, 1 1/2
   stry, 25x20 *; log barn 40x20
MINKY, Eliz'th; 218A; pt Ipstone; hewd log dwlg hse, 1 1/2 stry, 30x24 *;
   log milk hse, 12x10; log shop 14x12; log barn 50x24
MIRES, Peter; 128A; Belfast; hewd log dwlg hse, 1 1/2 stry, 30x26; log milk
   hse 12x10 *; barn, 2 stry, 1 of stone, other logs
MORTER, Mary; 448A; Morters Choice; hewd log dwlg hse, 2 stry, 30x26 *; log
   barn 40x24, shed add. 60x12
NAILOR, Sam'l; 63A; pt Mount Hazzard; hewd log dwlg hse, 1 1/2 stry, 24x16;
   log kn 12x10
NACE, Barnet; 108A; Higles Burgh; hewd log dwlg hse, 1 1/2 stry, 27x25 *;
   log milk hse 16x14; log barn 30x20; log shop 16x16
NULL, Anthony; 25A; Worms; hewd log dwlg hse, 20x18; log stble 16x14
NACE, William; 57A; pt Naces Tavern; hewd log dwlg hse, 2 stry, 26x22 *; log
   kn 16x16; log barn 50x20; bark shed 75x30
OSBORN, Daniel; 125A; Bosley's Range; hewd log dwlg hse, 18x16; log corn hse
   18x11
PRICE, John; 361A+; Prices Hunting Ground; log dwlg hse, 26x21; log kn
   26x15; log corn hse 12x10; log smoke hse 12x8; stone barn 30x20; stone
   shop 20x16; Occupant: Wm. PRICE: fr dwlg hse, 20x16; log kn 15x12; log
   barn 30x20; log shop 18x15; Occupant: John BARNET: log dwlg hse, 20x16
PETERS, Jacob; 117A; Jacobs Folly; stone dwlg hse, 1 stry, 28x20, stone shed
   add. 28x10 *
PARRISH, Mordecai; 75A; Price's Hunting Ground; log dwlg hse 24x16; log kn
   14x12; log smoke hse 10x10
PARRISH, Aquila; 48A; Millers Meadow; fr dwlg hse 50x18; corn hse 12x12
PRICE, Wm. 104A; Peggys Delight
PROSER, Isaac; 50A; log dwlg hse 18x16; log barn 24x24
PRICE, Joshua; 296A; Scarce of Timber; hewd log dwlg hse 18x18; log shed
   18x10; log corn hse 18x10
PRICE, Thomas of Gunpowder; 134A; name of land not known; hewd log dwlg hse,
   1 1/2 stry, 24x20 *; log kn 16x14; log corn hse 20x12; log smoke hse
   14x12
PRICE, Thomas, 110A+; Price's Chance; hewd log dwlg hse 18x18; log kn 18x12
PEREGOY, Henry; 70A (30 acres sold for taxes - 1805); Henry's Chance; hewd
   log dwlg hse, 1 stry, 20x16

PEREGOY, John; 82A+; Addition to Forest Level; log dwlg hse 16x16
POPLETS, Peter; 159A+; Poplets Delight; log dwlg hse 20x18; log barn 20x14
POPLETS, Charles; 164A; pt Henry's Hope; log dwlg hse 16x16; log barn 16x12
POBLETS, Charles; 149A; pt Henry's Hope; hewd log dwlg hse, 2 stry, 28x22
POBLETS, Michael; 47A; Sideling Hill; log dwlg hse 18x16
POBLETS, Chris'r; 152A+; Sideling Hill and others; hewd log dwlg hse 24x20; log barn 20x23
PLUCKER, Jacob; 112A+ (40 acres sold for taxes - 1805); pt Three Brothers; log dwlg hse, 14x12, logs add. 12x10; log barn 40x20
PLUCKER, John; 78A (70 acres sold for taxes - 1805); Cuckele's Point; log dwlg hse 16x14; log barn 40x20
PERKIPILE, Jacob; 80A; pt Boring Range; log dwlg hse 20x18
PLUCHOR, Abra'm; 47A+; pt Stoney Hills
PEACHY, Martin; 50A; Sportsman Hall
RICHARD, Rich'd; Occupant: Sam'l RICHARD; 100A; pt Corn Hill Resurveyed; hewd log dwlg hse, 1 1/2 stry, 16x16; log barn 18x15
RANDALL, Nicholas Beal; 132A; pt Fayett's Camp; fr dwlg hse 12x10
RISTON, Sarah; 355A; Riston's Folly; hewd log dwlg hse, 20x16; log kn 14x12
RANDALL, Chris.; 69A+; pt Fayett's Camp
RUBY, Thomas; 77A; Gib's Folly; hewd log dwlg hse, 1 stry, 20x16; log kn 17x16
RIBLE, Nicholas; 200A; name of land not known; hewd log dwlg hse, 1 1/2 stry, 24x20
RULE, George; 310A; United Friendship Enlarged; log dwlg hse, 1 stry, 20x18; barn, 2 stry, 1 of stone, other logs
STANSBURY, Joseph; 441A; Addition to Hobsons Choice; log dwlg hse 22x18; log kn 18x16; log barn 40x20; log corn hse 20x10
SPINDLER, George; 130A; Spindlers Chance; log dwlg hse, 1 stry, 20x16; log barn 43x20
SPINDLER, Nich's; 90A+; Jacobs New Design; log dwlg hse, 1 stry, 20x16; log barn 20x12
SPINDLER, Jacob; 134A; pt Candle; log dwlg hse, 1 stry, 26x18; log corn hse 40x25
SPINDLER, John; 134A; pt Candle; log dwlg hse, 1 stry, 23x18; log barn 40x18
STILTS, John; 65A; pt Low's Range; log dwlg hse, 1 stry, 30x16; log shop 16x14
FITZ SIMMONS, Pierce; 77A; name of land not known
STORMS, George; 365A+; Carthergena and George's Beginning; hewd log dwlg hse, 1 stry, 24x20; log barn 40x20; log barn 20x16
SHAUL, Joseph; 796A+; Mount Pleasant; hewd log dwlg hse, 1 stry, 24x18; log smoke hse 10x8; log corn hse 12x10; log barn 30x16
SNIDER, Abra'm; 100A; Greens Desire; hewd log hse, 1 stry, 24x18; log milk hse 10x10
STEVENSON, David; 225A; pt Rogers Resurvey; hewd log dwlg hse, 1 stry, 16x14; log smoke hse 12x9; log corn hse 20x12
STEFLAR, Jacob; 40A; Stony Bottom; log dwlg hse, 1 stry, 14x12
STANSBURY, Edwin (or Edmond); Occupant: Thos. TALBOT; 315A+; Archibals Level and others; hewd log dwlg hse, 1 stry, 18x16 *; log kn 18x16; log barn 50x18; log smoke hse 12x8
SMITH, Adam; 64A; Gains Rest; log dwlg hse, 1 stry, 24x20; log kn 18x16; log barn 40x20

STILTZ, Philip, Sr.; 198A; Shiltz's Park; hewd log dwlg hse, 2 stry, 30x26 *; log barn 26x20
STILTZ, Philip, Jr.; 100A; Shiltz's Deer Park; log dwlg hse, 1 stry, 20x18
SIMMERMAN, Jno.; 270A; pt Beaver Tract; log dwlg hse, 1 stry, 18x16; lob garn 20x18
SHAUK, John; 345A; Bite the Biter
SMITH, Joshua; 38A+; Joshua's Trust; hewd log dwlg hse, 1 stry, 18x16
SHEW, Henry; 132A+; Hardest's Chance; log dwlg hse, 1 stry, 16x14; log barn 30x20
SHAVER, M. George; 300A; Ground Wisinburgh; hewd log dwlg hse, 1 stry, 14x14; log kn 18x14; log barn 20x18; mill hse, 2 stry, 1 of stone, other logs, 28x28
SINGARY, Chris.; 1702A; Singary Trouting Streams; hewd log dwlg hse, 1 1/2 stry, 24x20 *; log barn 18x20
STEVENSON, Joshua; 74A+ (30 acres sold for taxes - 1805); Stevenson Wolf Den
SHAVER, Abraham; 286A; Piney Hills; dwlg hse, 2 stry, 1 of stone, other logs, 30x22 *; stone mill hse, 2 stry, 35x30; barn, 2 stry, 1 of stone, other logs; stone milk hse 20x16
SHARY, Daniel; 91A; Locust Bottom; hewd log dwlg hse, 1 1/2 stry, 20x20
SATER, Hannah; 205A; pt Stoney Hills
SHITEHOOF, John; 22A+; Spring Run; hewd log dwlg hse, 1 stry, 18x18; log mill hse, 2 stry, 28x24; saw mill 36x9
SHULS, Philip; 60A; name of land not known; log dwlg hse, 1 stry, 18x16; log barn 30x18
SEBB, Francis; 169A; Prusia and others; hewd log dwlg hse, 1 1/2 stry, 30x26 *; log barn 64x25
SAUBLE, Michael; 146A; Pomerania and Johns Burgh and others; hewd log dwlg hse, 1 stry, 30x20 *; log barn 40x20; log barn 30x20
SHAREMAN, John; 282A; Little Britain Enlarged; log dwlg hse, 1 stry, 20x16; stone milk hse, 14x12; barn, 2 stry, 1 of stone, other logs, 100x20
SWATZPAUGH, Geo.; 320A; Little Briton; hewd log dwlg hse, 2 stry, 30x26 *; log still hse 16x12; log barn 24x20
SHADE, John; 100A; Foubles Tract; log dwlg hse, 1 stry, 18x16; log barn 40x20
STANSBERRY, Rich'd; 259A+ (80 acres sold for taxes - 1805); Stony Hill; hewd log dwlg hse, 2 stry, 30x20 *; log barn 40x20; log corn hse 12x10
SHAPE, Peter; 135A; pt Callefurna; hewd log dwlg hse, 1 1/2 stry, 26x24
STANSBERRY, Charles; 350A; Stansberry's Groves
TRACY, Joshua; 90A; pt Poor Mans Strugle; log dwlg hse, 1 stry, 22x16
TRACY, P. of John; 254A+; Tracy's Beginning; log dwl hse, 1 stry, 16x14; log kn 10x10; log barn 18x18
TRACY, Rebecca; 84A; Hard Scuffle and Fare Play
TRACY, Bazzel; 199A+; Tracy's Pleasant Ridge; log dwlg hse, 1 stry, 16x12; log barn 32x28
TIPTON, Jonathan; 239A+; Cold Bottom; log dwlg hse, 1 stry, 16x14; log barn 20x18
TIPTON, Brian; 200A; Prospect and others; log dwlg hse, 1 stry, 20x16
TIPTON, Jerard; 318A; pt Boring Range; log dwl hse, 1 stry, 16x16
THOMAS, Benja'n; 149A; Little Prospect and others; log dwlg hse, 1 stry, 20x18; log kn 14x12
VAUGAN; Christ'r; 215A; Spring Garden Enlarged; fr dwlg hse, 1 stry, 24x24; log kn 20x16

WHISNER, Mathias; 468A; Whisner's Prospect; hewd log dwlg hse, 1 stry, 20x20, fr shed add. 20x14; stone milk hse 9x9

WOODCOCK, Robt.; 198A+; pt Springfield Enlarged; hewd log dwlg hse, 1 stry, 28x20

WOODING, Will'm; Occupant: Wm. MILLER; 200A; name of land not known; hewd log dwlg hse, 1 stry, 16x12

WARNER, Jacob; 119A; name of land not known; hewd log dwlg hse, 2 stry, 24x20 *; log barn 30x20

WALKER, John; 40A; pt Beavers New Invention; log dwlg hse, 1 stry, 16x14

WALKER, George; 85A+; pt Beavers New Invention; log dwlg hse, 1 stry, 16x14

WILLHELM, Henry; 122A; name of land not known; log dwlg hse, 1 stry, 16x14

WOOLF, Valentine; 82A+; pt Bucks Range; hewd log dwlg hse, 1 stry, 14x12

WHEELER, Mordecai; 223A; Barney's Timber Ridge; hewd log dwlg hse, 1 1/2 stry, 23x22 *; log barn 35x20

WHEELER, Brian; 131A; pt Cox's Catch; hewd log dwlg hse, 1 stry, 32x14 *; log barn 30x18

WHEELER, Richard; 227A+; Wheeler's Purchase; hewd log dwlg hse, 1 stry, 27x18; log kn 16x12 *; log barn 33x18

WILLHELM, John; 173A+; Braves Range; log dwlg hse, 1 stry, 16x16

WHEELER, Greenberry; 65A; Slapbang Town; log dwlg hse, 1 stry, 16x16

WARNER, Melchak; 220A+; Corpi and others; stone dwlg hse, 1 stry, 25x24; log barn 30x20

WEANT, Nicholas; 193A; pt Troy and Dughill; stone dwlg hse, 2 stry, 31x25 *; log barn 40x18

WALTER, William; 192A; Sring Run; log dwlg hse, 1 stry, 16x16; log milk hse 14x12; log barn 30x18

WANTZ, Adam; 169A; Smithfield; hewd log dwlg hse, 1 1/2 stry, 31x28 *; log barn 34x28

WARNER, Philip; 139A; Nothings Lot; stone dwlg hse, 2 stry, 30x24; stone hse, 2 stry, 25x20 *; log barn 40x18

WYMER, Barnet; 98A; pt Calleformer; hewd log dwlg hse, 2 stry, 28x24 *; log still hse 16x16; log barn 40x20

WEBLING, Charles; 148A; pt Calleformer

WAREHAM, Henry; 267A; pt Borings Range; hewd log dwlg hse, 2 stry, 26x24; hewd log kn 16x14 *; log barn 50x24, log add. 24x20; log corn hse 10x10; log shop 14x12

WOODCOCK, Robt.; 86A; pt Addition to Brotherhood; hewd log dwlg hse, 1 stry, 20x16

BINNIS, Barney; 72A; Full Bottle; 3 old hses
BOSLEY, Caleb (5 slaves); 116A; Bosley's Inheritance; log hse, 1 stry; log kn; barn & stables
BOSLEY, Greenbury (7 slaves); Occupant: Ann BOSLEY (5 slaves); 164A; Bosley's Good Luck; stone dwlg hse, 2 stry, 20x32; old log hse for negro 14x16; meat hse 10x12; 2 old log & stable & fr barn
BROOKS, Ch's; 120A; Hairs Meadows; 3 old log hses
COLE, Thomas (8 slaves); pt Conclusion, 386 1/2 A, pt Prices Good Will, 28A; 6 old hses
COLE, Abr'm (7 slaves); Abrahams Delight, 200 1/4 A; dwlg hse, 3 old hses; Pleasant Groves, 83A; 2 old hses
ENSOR, Geo. (4 slaves); 164 1/2 A; Spring Garden & Addition to Spring Garden; log dwlg hse, 1 stry, 16x20; log dwlg hse 14x14; barn & old stble; log dwlg hse, 1 1/2 stry, 14x20; hen hse
ENSOR, Nathan; 99 1/2 A; Nathans Prospect; log hse 16x20
ENSOR, Eliza., widow (6 slaves); 67A; Spring Garden & pt Vineyard; 5 old hses
ENSOR, Abr'm (3 slaves); Olivers Lott, 29 3/4 A; Marster's Care, 29A; Young Jacobs Chance, 122 A; 3 old log hses
ENSOR, John (5 slaves); 372 3/4 A; Cold Bottom
FOSTER, John (7 slaves); 570 1/2 A; pt Inclosure; stone dwlg hse, 2 stry, 20x30; stble & barn, both built of logs; 2 log hses for negroes, 14x20 each; log hse for negroes, 12x12
GOODWIN, Wm, GOODWIN, Lyde; Occupant: Mary BOSLEY; 987 3/4 A; St. Dennis Resurveyed; log dwlg hse, 2 stry, 18x25; log dwlg hse, 1 stry, 20x20; 2 log hses, 12x12, each; log hse 16x16; 1 out hse, 8x10; stble 10x18
GREEN, Abr'm (1 slave); 102 3/4 A; pt Susanah & Mary; 4 old hses
GRIFFITH Abrm.; 198 A; Pleasant Prospect & Red Oak Ridge; log dwlg hse, 1 stry, 15x25; stone barn 22x35; old log stble; log dwlg hse, 14x16
GWYNN, Wm. (1 slave); 97A; Monkton; stone barn, 22x46; stone hse; stone mill hse; stone dwlg hse, 2 stry, 26x30; stone kn 15x30; stone meat hse 12x16
GORSUCH, Ch's of Jno. (11 slaves); Gorsuchs Inclosure, 352A, 4 old hses; Coles Chance, 80A; Gorsuch's Adventure, 33 A; Green's Search, 16A, 2 old hses; Green's Hill, 9A; Gorsuch's Pleasant, 3A; Gorsuch Stony Barr, 1 A; stone dwlg hse, 2 stry, 24x36, old kn
GORSUCH, Jno., Jr. (1 slave); 250 1/2 A; pt Gorsuchs Enclosure; 3 old hses
GORSUCH, Thos.; Gorsuch Hills & Dales, 199 1/2 A; Lott #67, Lady's Manor, 50 1/4 A; 3 log hses
GORSUCH, Dickenson (6 slaves); Mill Seat, 7 1/4 A; Addition to Gorsuch's Retirement, 40A; Cold Bottom, 17 1/4
GORSUCH, Thos. of Thos; Gorsuch's Retirement, 346A; Sign of the Painter, 100A; log dwlg hse, 18x20; log dwlg hse, 16x18; Mattie: log hse 16x20; stone shop for blacksmith, 16x30; stone barn 27x40; stone stble 16x50
HICKS, Abr'm (2 slaves); Occupant: Jacob HICKS; 230A; Hales Forest, 100A; pt Hicks Forest, 10A; Wm. Folly, 40A; John's Lott, 80A
HARRYMAN, Geo. H. (14 slaves); 341A, pt Cumberland, pt Talbots Slavery, Harryman's Best Way, Addition to Lemmons Enlargment, pt Blath and Camb. 107 1/2 A, pt Cumberland & Brians Addition 50A, Wood & Stone, old fr dwlg hse, 1 stry, hip roof, 18x32; 4 old stbles; old barn 20x60; old hse 14x16; log hse for negroes, 14x16; hse 14x16; milk hse 13x15
HALL, Edward (7 slaves); 121A; pt Taylors String & Halls First Design; Small Wood & Addition to Small Wood; 4 old hses

29

HOOKER, Benj'm (1 slave); 147 1/2 A; pt Wheelers Chance; 4 old hses, out of repair

HAINES, Isaac; 109A; Samuels Meadow & others; 4 old hses out of repair

HICKS, Jacob (4 slaves); 105A; Hicks forest; 2 old hses

HALL, Wm (6 slaves); 114A; pt Taylors String & Halls First Design; Halls Discovery; stone dwlg hse, 1 stry, 17x28; stone kn 12x12; stone meat hse 10x10

JONES, Jacob; 117 1/2 A; Hookers Ridge; 3 old hses

LEMON (Lemmon), Hannah; Occupant: Jas. SCHRADER: 33A; pt Battle Abbey; old hse

LEMON, (Lemmon) Jno, Jr.; Lemmons Enlargement, 219A; Lemmons Patch, 26A; Lemmons Choice, 33 1/4 A; 4 old hses

LOVE, Thomas (12 slaves); Cromwells Chance & Cromwell Additon, 169A; St. Thomas Adventure, 72A; pt Coles Search Amended, 5 1/4 A; 5 old hses out of repair

MERRYMAN, Micajah (18 slaves); 375 1/2 A; pt Blathana Cambridge; pt Cumberland; pt the Valley of Jehosaphat; Merrymans Delight; log dwlg hse, 1 stry, 16x20; 2 log dwlg hses, 16x20 & 14x16; 2 old hses; stone mill hse; 2 log hses, 12x14 each; milk hse 14x16; hen hse 14x18

MERRYMAN, Elijah; pt Cromwells Chance & Addition to same, 298A; pt Coles Search Amended, 253A; 6A land; stone dwlg, 1 stry, 20x40; log kn, 16x20; old fr hse; old log barn; stble; stone stble, 28x32; old fr barn

MASON, James; 154A; Belle Haven; log barn; log dwlg hse, ready to fall down, 18x20; log kn; stble

MATHEWS, Mordecai; 120A; Taylors String; Taylors Discovery; pt Halls Design; log dwlg hse, 1 stry, 18x30; 2 out hses, 10x12 & 12x16; barn

MALONEE, John; 91 1/4 A; Malonee's Habitation; 5 old hses

MERRYMAN, Nic., Sr. (26 slaves); 1374A+; Bacon Hall Enlarged, 1272 3/4 A; Pine Ridge, 80A; pt Ells Grove, 7 1/4 A; Better Saved Than Lost, 3 1/2 A; Little Account 3/4 A+; Merryman's Slipe, 3 3/4 A; stone dwlg hse, 2 stry, 23x46; stone kn, 23x36; stone milk hse, 12x12; stone meat hse, 14x16; 2 log out hses, stble & stone barn 30x50

MERRYMAN, Benj'm (10 slaves); 663A; Inclosure Rectified; stone dwlg hse, 1 stry, 23x36; log dwlg hse, 1 stry for negroes, 15x20; stone stble; stone barn, 23x33; meat hse, 10x12

MERRYMAN, Nicholas of Benj. (2 slaves); 148A; pt Inclosure Rectified; log dwlg hse, 2 stry, 18x23; log dwlg hse, 12x20

MATHEWS, Rachel, widow; Price's Delight, 100A; Rachel Pleasant Hill, 69A; 5 old hses

MATHEWS, Eli; Olivers Lott Resurveyed, 103A; pt Samuels Meadows, 36 1/2 A

MATHEWS, Thos., 103A; pt Olivers Lott, 3 log hses

MERRYMAN, John, Sr.; Merrymans Mount, 47A; pt Eljies Grove, 43A; Herefort Resurveyed, 1035 3/4 A; Hobb Hall Enlarged Rectified, 121A; Holland Commission, 129 1/4 A; Mount Pleasant, 67 1/2 A; Buffalo, 40A; 3 log stbles; 2 stone barns; 2 log dwlg hses; Occupant: John GILLINGHAM; stone dwlg hse, 1 stry, 21x40; stone kn, 22x26; stone hse for negro; stone dwlg hse, 21x40, 2 stry high; log meat hse 12x14; hen hse 12x14; stone milk hse 10x10

NICHOLSON, Mary, widow (8 slaves); 392A; Benjamins Hills & Valleys; stone dwlg hse, 2 stry, 18x20; log hse 18x30; log hse 18x18; old barn; log stble; log hse, 1 1/2 stry, 18x18; log hse for negroes, 15x18; hen hse

ORRICK, John (8 slaves); 332A; Cromwell's Park; log dwlg hse, 2 stry, 20x24; stone add. 12x30; stone kn, 16x16; log negro hse, 20x24; hen & meat hse of log each 12x12; log milk hse 10x10; log barn 22x22; log stble

OGDEN, Amos; 130A; pt Taylors Discovery; 2 old hses

PERRIGO, Elisha; Occupant: John CHILDS (1 slave); 93A; pt Cold Friday & Elenor Look Out; 3 old hses

PERRIGO, William; 144 1/2 A; Union; 5 old hses out of repair

PRICE, Daniel; 98A; Samuel Meadows; stone dwlg hse, 2 stry, 12x30; stone hse, 1 stry, 12x18; meat hse, 10x18; old barn; stble

PRICE, James; 183 3/4 A; Benjamin Choice; fr dwlg hse, 1 stry, 12x30; stone hse, 1 stry, 12x18; 2 log stbles, 8x10 & 9x30; meat hse 10x12; barn 20x30

TOWSON, Francis (6 slaves); 181 1/2 A; pt Gays Inspection; Small Valley & Talbots Slavery; fr dwlg hse, 1 stry, 18x24; fr dwlg hse, 18x20; 2 old stbles; log hse 10x10; hse 20x20; 2 hse 16x20; hse 10x10

TALBOTT, Edward (15 slaves); 108A; Long Crandon on the Hill; Talbots Purchase; stone dwlg hse, 2 stry, 14x20; log hse, 1 stry, 14x20; stble & log barn, 20x30; old log hse, 14x20; meat hse 10x12; meat hse 12x12

TIPTON, Samuel, Sr. (7 slaves); 148A; pt Cromwells Park; stone dwlg hse, 2 stry, 28x28; log hse for negroes, 1 stry, 12x28; old stble of logs; meat hse 10x14

THOMAS, John, Sr.; 100A; pt Olivers Lott; 5 old hses ready to fall

TIPTON, Samuel, Jr.; 150A; pt Cromwells Park; 3 old log hses

WELSH, William (11 slaves); 236 1/2 A; pt Valley of Jehosaphat and pt St. Dennis; log dwlg hse, 1 stry, 16x12; barn; old stble; log hse 16x20; stone hse for negros, 12x42; 2 old hses

WHELAN, Joseph; 120A; Tiptons Adventure & Whelans Chance; old log hse

WHEELER, Amelia (6 slaves); 48A; Bachelors Neck; 4 old log & fr hses

WHEELER, Benj'm, Sr. (1 slave); 180A; Spring Garden; old fr & log hse

WHEELER, Benj'm, Jr. (2 slaves); 153A; Wheelers Chance; 3 old fr & log hses

WHEELER, James (1 slave); Taylors String and others, 142A; pt Nicholsons Manor, 107 1/2 A; 6 old log hses

WOODCOCK, Robt; 183A; Bachelors Choice; 4 old log hses

WHEELER, Wm., Jr. (4 slaves); 173A; Belle-air; 5 old log hses

WALKER, Joseph; 260A; Martins Mistake; 3 old hses

WHEELER, Stephen; fr dwlg hse, 2 stry, 15x30; log hse, 1 stry, 16x16; 2 hses, 16x16 & 16x20

AMOS, James (5 slaves); pt Fellowship Res. 100A; log dwlg 14x15; log dwlg 16x18; log dwlg 14x15; log dwlg 18x10; log dwlg 18x22; stone stble 18x24

BOSLEY, Wm. of Joseph (2 slaves) pt Nicholson Manor 150A; 4 old log hses

BOWEN, Solomon, Jr.; pt Samuels Hope 98A; log dwlg hses, 2 stry, 12x26; 1 stone hse, 1 stry, 12x12; 1 log meat hse, 12x12; log hen hse, 8x10; log stable 12x32; fr barn 24x32; log dwlg hse, 2 stry, 18x26; dwlg stone, 1 stry, 12x12; log meat hse 12x12; log hen hse 8x10

BOWEN, Nathaniel (6 slaves); pt Samuel's Hope 148A; log stable 12x12; stone barn 24x32; old fr dwlg hse, 1 stry, 20x24; old fr kn, 14x16; log meat hse, 10x12

BROWN, Abraham (3 slaves); pt Fellowship 4A+; log dwlg hse, 1 stry, 16x34; log dwlg hse, 1 stry, 16x18

BOWEN, Wm. (4 slaves); pt James Meadows 10 1/4 A; log dwlg hse, 1 stry, 14x18; log meat hse, 12x12; log meat hse, 20x20; blacksmith's shop, 14x26

BUSH, John; 1A; stone dwlg hse, 14x16

BOWEN, Josias (8 slaves); pt Sam's Hope 150A, Morgan's Delight 110A; old fr dwlg hse, 1 stry, 20x28; fr kn, 16x18; stone smoke hse, 12x12; fr hen hse, 8x10; stone barn 30x48

BOND, John (6 slaves); Occupant: Norman GORSUCH; Bond's Industry 450A, pt Friendship 100A; fr hse, 18x20, log hse, 16x18; fr barn, 22x28; log stble 12x26; log stble 20x20; log stble 12x14; fr dwlg hse, 1 stry, 18x20; log hse 16x10; fr dwlg hse, 1 stry, 16x22; fr dwlg hse, 12x28; log kn, 16x20, old and out repair; meat hse 10x12; hen hse 8x10

BOND, Edward (1 slave); pt Gists Search 25A; fr dwlg hse

BURNHAM, Jno. (1 slave); pt Gists Search 100A; log hse 14x16; log hse 14x16; stble 16x18

BOND, Nicodemus; pt Gist's Search, Middle Ridge, total: 215A; old fr dwlg hse, 1 stry, 18x30, log dwlg 18x20; smoke hse 12x14; hen hse 12x12; milk hse 12x12; log granary 12x16; log stble 20x20; log barn 20x38

BOND, Benj.; 110A; Middle Ridge, Bond's Industry, total: 110A; log hse 16x18

BUCHANAN, Andw., STONE & DORSEY, Trustees; Bank's Delight, Kings Adv., pt Chevy Chase, total: 1194A; fr dwlg hse, 1 stry, hip roof, 20x30; fr dwlg hse, 1 stry, 20x48; 4 log hses, 20x20, 16x20, 16x20, 14x15; log stble 20x50; log stble 20x30; granary 20x30; fr barn 20x40; log barn 20x30

BOSLEY, Ann, widow of John; pt Bosley's Adventure, pt Nicholsons Manor, Taylor's String, total: 147 1/2 A; several old hses fit for fuel

BOND, Col. Thos. of Harford Co; Stones Adventure 300A; dwlg hse, barn & stble fit for fuel

BOND, Solo'm, Sr. (2 slaves); Occupant: Solo'm BOWEN, Jr. (4 slaves); pt Samuel's Hope 126A; old fr dwlg hse, 20x39; log kn, 18x24; meat house; fr stble, 14x20; old fr barn fit for fuel; stone mill (milk?) hse

BLATCHLEY, Thos.; pt Mathews Forest, pt Bite Bit the Biter, total: 70A; log dwlg hse 18x30; meat hse 10x12; corn hse 12x18

BELT, Kitturah; pt Wms. Chance 117A; old log hse, 1 stry, 16x24; hse 12x16; 2 old stbles fit for fuel

CARROLL, Nicho. (37 slaves); Occupant: Christopher TURNPAUC; Coles Caves 2450A; fr dwlg hse, octagon, 24x24; old fr 16x21; stone kn, 13x30; old fr dwlg hse, 18x27; 2 old Negro hses, log, 16x20, 20x36; log smith shop; old fr warehse; log warehse; fr barn 30x50; log barn 20x50; fr mill hse, 2 stry, 28x28; log stble, 20x40; log corn hse, 20x30; fr meat hse 20x36; stone milk hse 10x12; log wash hse 15x20

COCKEY, C. Charcila; pt Bosley's Palace, Welch's Addition, total: 58A

COCKEY, Caleb (6 slaves); Young Richard Spring Garden, pt Addition to Poor Jamaicaman's Plague, Addition to Bite Upon the Biter Sulood(?), pt Poor Jamaicaman's Plague, total: 384A; Addition to Cockey's Delight 60A; stone dwlg hse, 2 stry, 22x48; stone kn, 1 stry 20x22; stone meat hse, 16x16; log hen hse, 16x20; log stble, 18x20; stble 22x32; fr barn 24x44; corn hse 10x16; 2 old fr and 1 log, lumber hses, each 10x10; log dwlg hse 14x16; 2 old dwlgs 16x20; log granary 10x16; log barn 22x36; "These houses are on the lands called above by the name of Poor Jamaicaman's Plague late the property of Stephen COCKEY, deceas'd. 3-old houses each 16x18 on Add. to Cockey Delight."

COWAN, Alex. Assco. of ___; pt Groves 200A

COCKEY, Capt. John (6 slaves); pt Hellmore, pt Hellmore Addition, pt Cockey's Trust, total: 360A; brk dwlg hse, 2 stry, 24x44; fr hse, 1 stry, 18x24; fr kn, 16x20; brk meat hse, 16x17; brk milk hse, 13x13 and 16x24; fr Negro hse, 16x20; log dwlg hse, 2 stry, 20x32, add. of log 20x24, 12x16, 12x12; brk barn 28x48; log stble 14x30; corn hse 12x16

COCKEY, John, Jr. (1 slave); Occupant: Jno. COCKEY of Thomas; brk dwlg hse, 2 stry, 20x40; fr kn, 12x16; log barn, 16x40; stble 16x16

COLE, Stephen (1 slave); pt Taylors Discovery; pt Prospect, total: 100A; fr dwlg hse, 1 stry, 18x30; log milk hse,, 8x10; log meat hse, 8x10; log stble, 12x20

COLE, Samuel of Christopher; Christopher's Lott, Coles Addition, Thomas Lott, total: 133A

CROMWELL, Thos.; pt Shawan Hunting Ground, 320A

COCKEY, Thomas of Edw. (7 slaves); pt Cockey's Delight, of Swern, pt Friendship, total: 102A; fr hse, 20x30; log hse, 16x38; log corn hse, 12x20; 2 old stbles; log milk hse, 12x12; log meat hse, 12x16

CARNAN, Col'l Charles (28 slaves); Greenspring 743A, Bring Me Home 117A, pt Harrisons Meadows 44A; fr hse, 60x20, 1 stry; log dwlg hse, 24x18 - kn & Quarter; meat hse, 15x20; stone barn 34x64; log stble & corn hse; log barn 50x18

COLE, Mordecai (4 slaves); pt Price's Good Will, pt Conclusion, total: 310A; log hse, 1 stry, 18x22; log hse 18x18; smoke hse 12x12; stble 12x16; log barn 20x40

COCKEY, Charles (4 slaves); pt Melinda 148A, pt Prospect 570A, pt Sulsed 60A; log barn 18x36; log stble 12x20; log stble 14x16; fr dwlg hse, 1 stry, 18x24; log hse 16x18; old log kn, 16x18; log meat hse 14x16; log hen hse 12x14; log barn, 18x36; log stble, 12x20; log stble, 14x16

CROMWELL, Nat. (Nathan) (14 slaves); Joshua's Lott 500A, pt Nicholsons Manor 151A, pt Eliza. Farm 50A; fr dwlg hse, 1 stry, 24x28; log hse 18x24; log kn 12x18; hse for Negros, 26x20; log meat hse 12x20; fr barn 24x39 with stbles at each end; corn hse 12x30

CRADOCK, Ann (2 slaves); pt Nicholsons Manor 336A; brk dwlg hse, 2 stry, 24x48; stone kn, 1 stry, 18x30; log hse 14x16; old fr 14x14

CROMWELL, Philemon (1 slave); pt Nicholsons Manor 290A; log stble, 18x24; fr barn, 20x20; old corn hse 10x20; 3 old tobacco hses, useless; log dwlg hse, 18x20, add. to hse; fr kn 16x18; log kn 16x18; log meat hse 12x14; stone milk hse 8x10

COCKEY, Thos. Deye (6 slaves); Antony's Delight 75A, Tye's Delight 75A, Cow hill & pt of Cockey Delight 175A; log dwlg hse, 1 stry, 16x20; log hse 16x16; meat hse, 14x16; hen hse 8x10; milk hse 12x12; old log barn 16x25

COLE, Giles; Nancy's Palace 121A; old fr hse 18x28; old log hse 10x18; old stble 12x14

COCKEY, Thos. of Thos. (8 slaves); pt Melindea 250A, Addition to Melindea 12A, Prospect 430A; log dwlg hse, 16x36; hse 14x14; hse 14x14; hse 10x14; hen hse 10x12; stble 12x20; log barn 18x34; fr barn 18x30

COLE, William of Briton Ridge (6 slaves); Young Man's Adventure 200A, Coles Discovery 30A; fr dwlg hse, 1 stry, 25x28; hse 16x20; barn 24x40; stble 12x24

COCKEY, John of Thos. (6 slaves); pt Sulsed 191A, Kings Evil & Pleasant Green 60A, Stansbury Plains 350A, Addition to Cockey's Delight 59A; barn 22x42; 2 stbles each 12x20

COALE, Philip (6 slaves); pt Martinton 50A, Benjamin Addition 48A; ; stone dwlg hse, 2 stry, 20x26; stone kn, 1 stry, 20x20; stble 10x20; barn 16x20

COALE, Sam'l (6 slaves); pt Martintons Addition 40A, Martinton Addition 100A, Britons Meadows 8A, Cole's Good Luck 32A, Samuel's Addition 8A; old fr hse, 1 stry, 15x25; hse log, 16x20; old log hse 16x16; log barn 24x30; stone stble 12x32; Occupant: William COLE; log hse 16x20; hse 16x20

CATON, Richard (13 slaves); pt Cockey's Forest 530A; 1 brk barn 32x52; 1 brk stble 32x32; smoke hse 13x15; 1 fr hen hse 13x16

DILLON, Moses; pt Nicholson Manor 224 1/2 A; stone dwlg hse, 2 stry, 20x36; stone hse, 16x20; 2 old out houses; 2 old hses, 1 barn

DAUGHADY, Rich'd; 145A; pt Taylors Discovery; 4 old hses

DAUGHADY, Jno. (14 slaves); Bachelors Habitation 195A, Taylors Direction 96A, Knights Addition 50A; old fr dwlg hse, 1 stry, 17x40; old kn, 18x25; log meat hse, 12x16; 2 old barns, fit for fuel

DEYE, Thomas Cockey (41 slaves); Taylors Hall 1022A, Thos. & John Cockey's Medow 1532 1/4 A, Gerah 280A, pt Welches Meadows 10A, pt Wilmotts Grange 4A, Hales Adventure 8A, Addition to Jno. & Thos. Cockey's Meadow 22 1/2 A, Lancaster, clear of Elder survey, Norfold & Steep Rockey Ivy Hill -80A, pt Broad Meadows 100A, Good Luck 125A, Addition to Good Luck 20A, Round about Neighbours 61A, Jack's Double Purchase 203 1/4 A, pt Welch's Hopeful Pallace 82A; old fr dwlg hse supported with props inside and out 33x39, hse 14x16 fortified with puncheons, log corn hses: 10x40, 10x30, 10x24, 14x18, 10x24, 12x15; log stbles 10x18 and 10x20; hse 14x20; hse supported, 14x16; meat hse 12x15; log hse, 1 stry, 20x30; old kn; log dwlg hse, 2 stry, 20x30; Occupants: Jn. SMITH: old log hse; Chs HART: old log hse 12x18; Sam'll TUDOR: log dwlg hse, 1 stry, 20x30, old kn, 3 log stbles 14x16; Wm. CARTER: log hse, 2 stry, 20x30, old kn, log stble 12x42; Jos. DICKSON: old log hse & old log hse 16x20 & log hse 14x20

EDWARDS, James (5 slaves); pt John & Thomas Forest 612A; log dwlg hse, 1 stry, 12x18; log dwlg, 1 stry, 12x18; old barn & stbles with other old hses fit for fuel; stone coopers shop, 15x22; stone distillery, 27x30; stone milk hse, 30x36

FISHPAUGH, Jno. (1 slave); pt Hop Yard 114A; 2 fr dwlg hses, 1 stry, 20x28 and 16x20; 2 log out hses, 10x12 each; log stble 14x16; fr barn 22x30

FORD, Loyd of Jno. (7 slaves); Occupant: Thos. C. FORD (1 slave); pt Gists Search & Loddy 107 1/2 A; old fr hse, 1 stry, 16x30; log hse 12x15; old log stble

FORT, Elizabeth; pt Friendship & Addition to Friendship 113A; old fr hse; 2 log hses fit for fuel

FORT, John; pt Friendship, Gists Search, pt Kindals Search, total: 39A; fr dwlg hse, 2 stry, 16x35

FREY, Andrew; pt Friendship 19A; old log hse, 12x16
GOTT, Edward (1 slave); pt Gunners Range 225A; fr dwlg, 1 stry, 16x20; log
hse, 14x14; log stable 12x24
GILL, John (4 slaves); Hiccory bottom Corrected 183 1/4; brk dwlg hse, 2
stry, 20x30; brk kn, 1 stry, 20x24; log meat hse 12x16; log hse for
Negroes, 16x20; fr barn 24x25; add. to barn 24x50
GIST, Col. Thos. (6 slaves); pt Nicholson's Manor 360A, Final Settlement 3
1/2 A; stone hse, 2 stry, 24x53; stone hse, 1 stry, 24x34; 2 old fr barns
each 24x40; old log stble 16x24; log hse, 17x32; hen hse 16x20
GOTT, Richard of Sam'l (7 slaves); pt Gunners Range, Gotts Hope, total:
225A; fr dwlg hse, 1 stry, 22x32; log kn 16x20; log Negro quarter 12x16;
stone milk hse 12x12; hen hse 12x12; stone and log stble 24x34
GORSUCH, Jeremiah; Occupant: Norman GORSUCH (5 slaves); pt Mathews Forest,
pt Bite bit the Biter, total: 40A; log dwlg hse 12x18; old hse 10x16
GILL, Stephen G. (3 slaves); Price's Favour 44 1/2 A, Addition to same 54A;
fr dwl hse, 1 stry, 18x12; old hse for Negros, 10x24; log meat hse 10x12
GENT, Thomas (6 slaves); Molly and Sally's Delight 200A; old log dwlg hse, 1
stry, 18x20; old kn, 16x18; old log meat hse, 10x12; 2 old log stbles
GILL, John of Stephen(?); pt Baton Forest 128A; old fr dwlg hse, 10x20
GORE, George (8 slaves); pt Murray's Plains 134 1/2 A; log dwlg hse, 22x30;
log milk hse, 16x16
GORE, Michael; pt Murray's Plains 84 1/2; log dwlg hse, 2 stry, 18x26; log
barn 22x38
GILL, Joshua; pt Murray's Plains 111A
GOTT, Richard of Rich. (2 slaves); pt Gotts Hope 155A; log dwlg hse, 1 stry,
18x30; meat hse 12x12; log stble 15x20
GORSUCH, Charles (5 slaves); Carraan 120A; log dwlg hse, 16x24; log kn
16x24; log meat hse 10x12; log stbles 10x20; log barn 20x30; all old hses
GRIFFITH, Abr'm; pt Shawan Hunting Ground 210A; fr dwlg hse 20x28; log dwlg
hse 18x20; log dwlg hse 12x15
GILL, Joshua of Jno.; pt Baton Forest 248A; brk dwlg hse, 1 stry, 24x24; fr
hse 16x24; old log stble 10x20; old fr barn; stble 14x18; stble 10x20;
stble 14x18; log hse 16x16; hen hse 8x10; all out of repair; stble 10x30;
old log barn 20x30 in bad repair
HALES, Charles; pt The Forest 119A, Good Luck 25A; 2 log old hses
HUNT Phineas (7 slaves); Beals Discovery, Addition to Poor Jamaica- man's
Plauge, total: 194A; old fr barn 30x50; 2 log hses & log barn; tract
called the Groves 166 1/2 A; fr dwlg hse, 2 stry, 18x26, add. to hse, 1
stry, 15x21; old fr Negro quarter; stone meat hse 12x16; stone milk hse
10x12
HUNT, Job (11 slaves); pt Smith's Plains, pt Beals Discovery, total: 180A;
fr dwlg hse, 2 stry, 16x20, add. to hse 12x24; old log kn; 2 old log
hses; brk milk hse; stble, 12 x16; old barn, 16x40; warehse 12x20; tract
called pt The Groves, 166A, Smith's Addition, 137A, pt of Parks Deathnot,
40A; Jno. TAYLOR, occupant: old fr hse, 18x30, log barn, 18x30
HOPKINS, Nich's (1 slave); pt Friends Discovery 155 1/2 A; stble 14x20; log
barn 16x24; fr dwlg hse, hip roof, 18x24; log hse 16x20; log hse 12x12
HALE, Nicholas of George; pt Tracey Park 7A; old log hse
HUNT, Sam'l (6 slaves); pt Groves, pt Sulsed, total: 314A; fr dwlg hse, 1
stry, hip roof, 15x18; hse, 1 stry, 18x20; log kn, 12x18; log stble,
10x18; log barn, 18x35; log Negro hse, 16x20; milk hse 8x15; hen hse 8x10

35

HOPKINS, Jos'l (Joseph) (4 slaves); pt Friends Discovery 155 1/2 A; fr dwlg hse, 1 stry, 20x40; old hse 18x18; log hse 12x12; fr barn 24x36; log stble 18x20

HOPKINS, John (7 slaves); pt Friends Discovery 158A; fr dwlg hse, 1 stry, hip roof, 18x30; log barn 15x40; dwlg hse, fr, 16x20; log hse 16x16; 2 log hses, 10x10 and 10x12

HOPKINS, Johnsy; pt Friends Discovery 158A; fr dwlg hse, 20x40; old fr dwlg hse, 16x18; log stble, 12x26, fr barn, 24x36; log dwlg hse, 10x10

HUGHS, Sam'l and Comp.; Tracey's park 5A, Crosses Choice 22A, Bucks purchase 70A; log hse, 18x35

HARVEY, Wm. (16 slaves); pt Nicholsons Manor 112A; Prices Goodwill 60A; The Groves 12 1/4 A; Biddleton 2A; Fords Choice 101A; Benjamins Beginning 50A; log dwlg hse 16x24; log kn 18x22; log smoke hse 10x12; log smoke hse 12x16; milk hse; hen hse

HOSS, Michael; pt Harrisons Meadows 143A; log dwlg hse 18x20; log old hse 10x14; log milk hse 10x14; log barn 28x38

HOLLIDAY, John R. (29 slaves); Goshen Resurveyed 470A; log dlwg hse, 12x12; 2 log Negro hse, 16x24 each; log hen hse 12x12; log barn 20x30; pt Northampton, 470A; 2 log stables 16x24 each; log stble 16x16; fr barn 16x20; log still hse 16x24; pt Fords Choice, 101A; log hse 12x12; log barn 20x30; stone hse, 2 stry, 24x53; stone kn, 2 stry, 24x40; stone hse, 16x16; log hse, 16x16; 2 old log & fr hses 16x20 each; fr meat hse 16x16; 2 log hen hses 12x12

JOHNS, Rich'd (7 slaves); pt Nicholsons Manor; pt Chevy Chase, pt Friendship, total: 456A+; brk dwlg hse, 1 stry, 24x40; brk kn, 12x15; stone meat hse, 10x10; old fr barn 27x45

JACKSON, Thos. (1 slave); pt Hales Fellowship and James' Meadows 151A; old fr dwlg hse, 18x20

JONES, Joshua (3 slaves); Stanes Discovery Corr. 179A+; log dwlg hse, 1 stry, 16x20; log kn, 16x24; lumber hse, 10x16; very old granary 8x16; old barn 20x24 and 20x24

KELLY, Thos. Deye (1 slave); Kelly's Delight 60A, Friendship 50A, Gist's Search 65A; old fr hse, 1 stry, 16x20; log hse, 16x20; log meat hse 12x14; log stble, 16x20, out of repairs

KING, Wm.; King's Evil 40A; old log hse 12x16

LYNCH, Roebuck (5 slaves); LYNCH, Wm. (1 slave); pt Stansbury's plains 346A; log hse, 1 stry, 18x28; log hse, 1 stry, 16x20; meat hse 10x12; old log barn 18x30; old stable 18x22

LUX, Rachel (12 slaves); Occupant: Darby LUX (4 slaves); Lanes Triangle 338A; fr dwlg hse, 16x30, 1 stry; stone hse 2 stry, 20x22; log stble old, 16x24; lumber hse 16x16; log Negro quarters, 14x20; hen hse 10x12; 2 hen hses, 10x12, 14x14

MOOR, Nich's Ruxton (5 slaves); Nich. R. MOOR, supt. for Anna MOOR (1 slave); pt Bosleys Adventure 314A; fr dwlg hse, 1 stry, 16x32; fr log hse 16x30; old log barn 18x30; log stble 10x16; log corn hse 10x16; stone milk hse 12x12; stone meat hse 12x12

MATHEWS, John; Mary's Meadows 280A; old fr & log hse, 1 stry, 16x30; meat hse 12x12; hen hse 10x10; old fr barn 18x35; log stble 12x16

MATHEWS, Oliver; pt Nicholsons Manor 278A; old fr dwlg hse, 1 stry, 24x24; log kn, 18x18; log milk hse 10 ft; log milk hse 11 ft; old log stble 12x18; log barn 24x45

MORFOOT, John; pt Gists Search 30A; log hse 12x14

36

METHLAND (Mothland), Sam'l; Coles Choice 165A; stone dwlg hse, 1 stry, 20x26; log kn 16x18; old log barn 20x40

McNUBIN, Wm. (11 slaves); pt Robert's Forest 250A; old fr dwlg hse, 1 stry 16x20; log hse for Negroes, 16x10; stone meat hse 10x10; stone milk hse 10x10; log hen hse 18x12, stble 12x20; old fr barn 22x40

MERRYMAN, Nich., Jr.; (14 slaves); pt Shawan Hunting Ground 335A, Merryman's Lott and others 160A; fr dwlg hse, 1 stry, 26x30; 3 old hses fit for fuel; log barn 20x40; log stble 10x22; log hse 18x18; log hse 12x18; stone mill hse

MOALE, Ellen (3 slaves); MOALE, John (4 slaves); MOALE, Robert (7 slaves); pt Shawan Hunting Ground 290A; old fr hse, 1 stry, 16x26; log kn 12x15; pt Green Spring Forest 743A; log stble, 12x20; stone barn 34x64(?); fr dwlg hse, 1 stry, 18x30; old hse, 20x24; log hse, 18x30; hen hse 10x12; meat hse 12x12; stble 14x26

MALES, John; 50A; old log dwlg hse, 12x20

McMACKIN, David; Prishels Prospect & Litchfield, City of Jeopoardy, total 778A; stone dwlg hse, 2 stry, 22x30, stone kn, 1 stry, 22x36; old log hen hse & fr meat hse each 12x12; log meat hse 12x14; milk hse 8x10; log barn 20x35; very old stble; log dwlg hse, 2 stry, 18x30; old log kn, 14x20

NAILOR, John; pt Nicholsons Manor 184A; log dwlg hse, 1 stry, 20x26; log dwlg hse, 1 stry, 12x16

OWINGS, Sam'l of Stephen; Drumqercastle & Hannah Lott 910A; stone dwlg hse, 1 stry, 14x16; log dwlg hse, 12x14; log barn 18x30

OWINGS, Jno; (COC)KEY, John (18 slaves); pt Haskers Addition 60A, Hookers farm and pt Gerah 180A, Addition to Addition 21A, pt John & Thos. Forest 837A; Harmony Hall 9A; log dwlg hse, 2 stry, 20x30; 3 old hses; stone barn

OWINGS, Richard (2 slaves); pt Cockeys Delight 1A; old log hse 16x20; old log hse 20x24

OWINGS, Dr. Beal (4 slaves); pt Urith's Fancy, Come by Chance & Severn, total: 133 1/4 A; brk dwlg hse, 1 stry, 16x36; log hse 10x12; log stble 10x30; old fr barn 24x36

OWINGS, Sam'l of Sam'l; Green Spring Punch 286A, Urith's fancy, Come by Chance & Severn - 133 1/4 A, Cockey's Folly, Cockey's Trust, pt Hale Resurv. - 480A; old fr dwlg, 1 stry, 16x40; log kn 16x20; hen hse 10x12; meat hse 10x12; negro hse 16x18; old log stble 22x28; fr stble 12x16; corn hse 12x30; fr granary 20x52; stone barn 40x80; Occupant: Jno. MARSH; brk dwlg hse, 2 stry, 24x40

OWINGS, Edw., heirs of; pt Tracey Park 1A; fr dwlg hse, 1 stry, 18x24; log kn, 18x24 (This entry is lined out.)

PHILPOT, Brian (14 slaves); Philpots Enquiry 425 1/4 A; Tiptons Puzzle & Addition to same 70A; Hamford 405 A; Cockey's Race 21A; fr dwlg hse, 1 stry, 15x16; log Negro hse 16x40; hen hse 12x14; meat hse 10x12; old fr barn 20x30; log barn 20x35; log stable 16x22

PARKS, Benj'm (4 slaves); pt Mathews Meadows 40A, pt Merrymans Adventure 19A; log dwlg hse, 18x24, 1 stry; hen hse 10x12; log barn 16x30

PARKS, David; pt Merrymans Adventure 69 3/4 A; fr dwlg hse, 1 stry, 16x20; meat hse 10x12; barn 16x24

PARKS, Wm.; pt Parks Deathnot 124A; log dwlg hse 10x20; corn hse 10x20; old barn 20x24

PRICE, Wm. (5 slaves); pt John & Thos. Forest 200A, Land belonging to the Mill 9A; fr dwlg hse, 2 stry, 16x38, unfinished; old log hse, 1 stry,

18x22; log kn 16x20; log meat hse 12x16; run hse 12x16; old log stble 22x22; log barn 22x50

PRICE, Mordecai; pt Sepatia Town 250A; brk dwlg hse, 2 stry, 24x36; log hse 16x20; meat hse 10x12; log barn 22x30; log stble 22x20; log work hse 16x40

PRICE, Benj'm (3 slaves); Sepatia Town and others 289A; fr barn 18x20; log stble 14x20; stone granary 10x20

PRICE, Stephen (12 slaves); Long Track 150A, Long Look 103A, James' Meadow 100A; brk dwlg hse (decayed), 2 stry, 30x30; stone kn 16x24; log barn 20x50; log corn hse 16x20; log hse 16x20

RIDGELEY, Charles of Hampton (92 slaves); North Hampton, South Hampton, Oak Hampton, Bolds Adventure, Sheridine Search, Drunkards Hall, Anna Spike, Fellowship Resurveyed - 3292 1/2 A; Little Maeth, Tillys Beginning and others - 228A; 1 stone dwlg hse; 2 stry 56x80; 2 wings to hse 23x25 each; 1 fr dwlg hse, 1 stry, 20x30; 1 hse 16x20; 1 fr kn 12x16; Negro hse 22x32; 8 Negro hses, some fr & log 15x23, 16x16, 12x12, 16x18, 16x18, 16x18, 10x12, 16x18; stone milk hse 16x23; 1 log hen hse; 2 fr hen hses; log wash hse 16x50; 2 meat hse; Occupants: Dick'n ANDERSON: log hse, 1 stry, 18x26; log hse 1 stry, 16x18; log hse, 1 stry, 12x12; Wm. COE: log hse, 1 stry, 18x26; log hsee 16x18; log hse 12x12; Dan'l BARBER: log dwlg hse, 1 stry, 12x15; Nat. CORBIN: log hse, 1 stry, 18x24; 2 log hses, 1 stry, 12x12 & 8x12; barn; Wm. ENSOR: log dwlg hse, 1 stry, 16x20; Tho. BURTON: log dwlg hse, 1 stry, 14x18; Jn. GORSUCH: 2 log hses 16x20; log hse 12x16; Occupant: James GRIFFITH; stone dwlg hse, 2 stry, 30x33; stone kn, 2 stry, 20x30; all unfinished; stone hse, 1 stry, 18x30; stone meat hse 14x14; stone hen hse, 12x12

ROLAND, Thos.; Long Valley 93 1/2 A; log hse

RIDGELY, Charles of Wm. (8 slaves); 150A; pt Sulsed; old fr dwlg hse, 16x20; fr stble, 12x30; fr barn 25x35

RIDGELY, Rebecca (16 slaves); 169A; pt Tracey's Park & others; stone dwlg hse, 2 stry, 24x50; fr kn, 16x33; barn 18x30; stble & out-hses 16x20; old log Negro hse 10x16; log meat hse 8x10; 2 old log stbles each 16x20

RIDGELY, LUX and Co. (26 slaves); 3580A; Furnace Land; stone dwlg hse, 1 stry, 20x50; log hse 18x18; log hse 16x20; 3 log hses: 14x14, 12x12, 16x20; 2 log stbles each 16x20; 2 log stbles each 12x16; log stble 12x12; log barn 18x30; stone granary 16x20; stone col hse 40x100; stone furnace 20x20; hse 20x20

STANSBURY, Jesse; in Middle River Upper Hundred; pt Gays Inspection 51 1/4 A; log dwlg hse, 1 stry, 16x20; stble

STANSBURY, Wm. of Jn.; in Middle River Upper Hundred; Cockey's Prospect 92A; fr dwlg hse, 1 stry, 16x24; log kn, 12x16; stble

STANSBURY, Wm. of Thos. (7 slaves); pt Long Crandon, Harvey Lott, Henry's Delight & others 196A; brk dwlg hse, 1 stry, hip roof, 27x37; stone kn, 15x27; stone meat hses, 12x14 and 16x18; stone stble, 12x50; old fr barn, stone barn

STONE, Capt. Wm.; Friendship 117A; Remtha Fancy & Severa 170A, pt Hellermore 198A; old fr dwlg hse, 1 stry, 16x45; log hse 16x28; 4 old hses

STEVENSON, Henry (7 slaves); pt Friendship 98A; fr dwlg hse, 1 stry, 20x30; log kn, 16x20; 2 log hses, 10x10 each; old barn 20x20

STEVENSON, Jno. of Henry (1 slave); Addition to Fellowship 100A; log hse, 2 stry, 18x20; log kn, 1 stry, 18x20

STANSBURY, Richardson (6 slaves); pt of Poor Jamaicamans Plague 100A; log dwlg hse, 1 stry, 12x16; old log dwlg hse, 15x20; stble 12x16
STEVENSON, Josia (7 slaves); Addition to Fellowship 98A; fr dwlg hse, 2 stry, 16x32; log & fr dwlg 16x40; old barn 24x44; log stble 12x12; stone milk hse, 11x11; log hen hse, 12x12
STANSBURY, Thos. of John (11 slaves); Daniel's Gift 127A, Carrs Lott 152A, pt Tracey's Park 23 1/2 A; fr dwlg hse, 1 stry, 16x40; log kn 16x30; log smoke hse 18x18; old barn, log stble 11x20; stble 12x12; log granary 11x15; old log hse 14x14
SATER, Joseph (1 slave); pt Sater Addition 99A, Egypt 30A, Egypt Enlarged 26A; log dwlg hse, 2 stry, 16x18; log kn, 11x18; meat hse, 10x12; hen hse, 10x11; milk hse 6x8; old stble 10x12
SATER, HANNAH (9 slaves); White Hall & Saters addition 150A; old fr dwlg hse, 1 stry, 18x30; add. to hse 10x18; log corn hse 10x16; log barn 16x30
TALBOTT, Benj'm (9 slaves); pt Barrets Delight & Barrets Addition 125A; fr dwlg hse, 1 stry, 18x38; stone kn, 3 out houses; 1 barn, 2 stbles
TRAPNELL, Vin.; Occupant: Jn. SMITH; pt Taylors Palace, pt Vularnia, total: 199A; 2 old hses
WALLACE, John; fr dwlg hse, 2 stry, 24x28
TOWSON, Wm. (4 slaves); Molly's Industry 78A(88A?); fr hse, 1 stry, hip roof, 25x25; log kn, 20x22; log hse, 14x20; log stble 14x20; log stble 14x14
TIPTON, Aquila (5 slaves); Tipton's Puzzle & Addition to same 100A; fr dwlg hse, 1 stry, 16x24; log dwlg hse, 16x20; log dwlg hse 15x16; smoke hse 10x12; old stble, old barn useless
TIPTON Angelico; pt Wm. Pasture, pt Bonds Industry, total: 19 1/2A; fr dwlg hse 16x24; 3 small log hses
TIGART, John (8 slaves); The Lions Den 220A, Elizabeth Meadows 400A, pt Gists Lime Pitts 36A, Harrisons Meadows 369A, Well Prospect 30A; brk dwl hse, 2 stry, 16x35; log hse for Negro 18x38; brk milk hse 12x12; log hen hse 16x24; brk barn 30x60; log stble 10x12
TIPTON, Joshua; Joseph Favour 107A; log dwlg hse 18x22; meat hse 18x8
USHER, Thos. (6 slaves); pt Fellowship 98A; fr dwlg hse, hip roof, 20x30; 2 hses 16x45 & 16x38; stone meat hse 12x12; fr hen hse 8x26; fr barn 20x38
TOWSON, Ezek's (2 slaves); Gunners Range 71A, Pierces Security to Molly's Industry 2A; stone dwlg hse, 1 stry, 16x22; fr dwlg hse, 16x40; log kn, 14x14; log stble 24x36; log smoke hse 14x14; log hse 14x20
TIPTON, Hyter; pt Williams Pasture, pt Bond Industry, total: 60A; log dwlg
TRUMBULL, Sarah; Timonium 330A; brk dwlg hse, 2 stry, 24x50; hse 24x50; hse 20x30; fr barn 30x50; log stble 20x24; log stble 12x20; milk hse 14x14; meat hse 14x14; log dwlg hse, 2 stry, 16x20; old dwlg & fr hse 12x12
TYE, George; pt Broad Mead 100A; log dwlg hse, 1 stry, 12x14; log dwlg hse, 1 stry, 12x16
TUDOR, Ialashiel (4 slaves); Lemmons Lott enlarged 153A; old log dwlg hse, 18x20; old log dwlg hse, 18x20
WORTHINGTON, Sam'l (31 slaves); pt Welchs Cradle and pt Long Discovery 1202 1/2A, pt Badsons Forest 125A, Ease Bolts Delight and pt of Fany's Plains 187 1/2 A; Geo. Improvements & Fair Dealing clear of elder survey 30A, Worthington's Bottom 9A; States Reversion 45A, pt Welchs Cradle 509A, pt Nicholsons manor and pt Chevy Chase 25 1/2, Calf Pasture 106A; brk dwlg hse, 2 stry, 30x50; old fr hse, 1 stry, 18x24; old fr kn, 16x24; brk meat hse 16x14; brk milk hse 8x12; log hse for Negro 16x24; old fr barn 16x36;

log stble 16x20; log stble 12x24; old fr lumber hse; log stble 14x16; log stble 12x16; log stble 12x16; Occupant: Charles WORTHINGTON (4 slaves): brk dwlg, 2 stry, 30x34; brk kn, 1 stry, 16x18; log for negro 16x24; old fr barn 16x30

WHEELER, Joseph of Sol'm (1 slave); Hookers Prospect 66 1/2 A; fr dwlg hse, 1 stry, 18x24; kn 16x16; hen hse 10x10; log barn 16x16; old stble

WORTHINGTON, John T. (19 slaves); pt Welch's Cradle, Long Discovery & others 300A, Mountain 83A, Todds Forest 500A, pt Nicholsons Manor 47A, pt Murray's Plains Regulated 41A; stone dwlg hse, 2 stry, 36x38, add. to hse 18x21; stone kn, 1 stry, 18x26; stone meat hse, 10x12; milk hse 12x14; log dwlg hse, 1 stry, 18x24; negro house 16x18; stone stble 16x16; log stble 18x40; log stble 24x28; milk hse 12x24; Occupants: Wm. WORTHINGTON (1 slave); log dwlg hse, 2 stry, 20x24; 2 hses, 12x14 & 12x12; milk hse, 12x12; log hse 16x20; Geo. BISS: log dwlg hse 16x35; Jos'h CLARK: log dwlg hse 16x20; Jn. McLANARAR; log dwlg hse 16x40

WOODCOCK, Thos.; pt Dusty Miller & others 106A; log hse 16x18; log stble 14x28; an old bark hut

WHEELER, Nat. of Wason; pt Turkey Cock Alley 8 1/4 A; log dwlg hse 14x16; log dwlg hse 10x12; log stble 10x12

WHITFORD, John; Water Oak Ridge & Tiptons Puzzle 125A; unfinished log hse

WINCHESTER, James (5 slaves); pt Shawan Hunting Ground 344A, Reparation 186A; an old barn; 2 small log hses

WRIGHT, Jonathan; Christopher Lott, Coles Addition to Greenspring, the Spring, total: 73A; log dwlg 16x20; log meat hse 10x10

YOUNG, Jno. T. (4 slaves); Tully's Adventure 30A; old dwlg hse; old log & fr hse

YOWN, John (4 slaves); pt Harrisons Meadows 240A; log hse, 1 stry, 25x30; log meat hse 12x16; hen hse 11x11; milk hse 10x12; log barn 28x38

Middle River Lower Hundred

"General List of all Dwelling Houses which, with the Out houses appurtenant thereto, and the Lots on which the same are erected, not exceeding two acres in any case, were owned, possessed or occupied on the 1st day of October 1798, within the 8th assessment District in the State of Maryland exceeding in value the sum of one hundred dollars."

ABRAHAM, Ashia; dwlg hse

ALLENDER, Sophia; Occupant: Thos LIDDARD; dwlg hse

ARNOLD, Joshua; dwlg hse

ARMITAGE, William; dwlg hse

BOSLEY, Wm.; dwlg hse, 45A (4A sold for taxes - 1805)

BRITTON, Richard; Occupant: Samuel FULLER; dwlg hse

BRITTON, Richard; Occupant: Wm. HENDERSON; dwlg hse

BRITTON, Richard; Occupant: James COO; dwlg hse

BURNETT, Joseph; dwlg hse

BRYAN, Nicholas; dwlg hse

BUCK, Joshua; dwlg hse

CLARK, George; dwlg hse

BOND, James; 83A (4A sold for taxes - 1805)

BOND, Barnet of Thos.; 78A (4A sold for taxes - 1805)

CARROL, Charles; dwlg hse

COURTNEY, Hercules; Hensey GRIFFITH; dwlg hse

COURTNEY, Hercules; Sarah GRIFFITH; dwlg hse
COLLINS, George; dwlg hse
CROOK, James; dwlg hse
CARROL, Nicholas; Richard GRAY; dwlg hse
CHASE, Jeremiah T.; 333A (20A sold for taxes - 1805)
DAY, John; dwlg hse
DEMMITT, Moses; dwlg hse
GREGORY, James; dwlg hse
GOTT, Richard; James HUGES; dwlg hse
GROVER, Tabitha; 80A (50A sold for taxes - 1805)
GOUGH, Harry D.; dwlg hse
HUTTON, Thomas; dwlg hse
HAMMOND, Abr.; Henry SCHOTE; dwlg hse, 464A (310A sold for taxes - 1805)
HARRYMAN, Geo.; dwlg hse
HUGHES, Hugh; 83A (20A sold for taxes - 1805)
MILES, Thomas; dwlg hse
MORRIS, Elnor; dwlg hse
MACMECHEN, David; Occupant: Barnet ASHER; dwlg hse
PRION Simon; dwlg hse
PRESBURY, George G.; dwlg hse
PRESBURY, Walter G.; dwlg hse
PRESBURY, Walter G.; Occupant: Wm. STEWART; dwlg hse
RIDGLEY, Gen. Charles; Occupant: Charles JESSOP; dwlg hse
RIDGLEY, Gen. Charles; Occupant: Solomon DISNEY; dwlg hse
RIDGLEY, Gen. Charles; Occupant: James McCLASKEY; dwlg hse
RIDGLEY, Gen. Charles; Occupant: Wm. GWYNN; dwlg hse
REES, Daniel; 83A (20A sold for taxes - 1805)
RAVIN, Luke; dwlg hse
RISTEAU, Capt. John; dwlg hse
SMITSEN David; dwlg hse
STEWART, David, Jr. (Balto.); Occupant: James ENSOR; dwlg hse
SKINNER, John; dwlg hse
SEDDON, James; dwlg hse
STEWART, Robert; Occupant: James BARTON; dwlg hse
STANSBURY, Abraham; dwlg hse
TALLY, James; dwlg hse
WILSON, Given; 25A (8A sold for taxes - 1805)
WEYLEY, Vincent; dwlg hse
WORTHINGTON, Vachael; dwlg hse
WEBSTER, James; dwlg hse

"General List of Lands, Lots &c. Continued," including dwelling houses and out houses of a value not exceeding $100.

ARMITAGE, William; 98A
ASHER, Abraham; 109A
ALLENDER, Sophia;
    Occupant: Thomas LEDDARD; 614A
ARNOLD, Joshua; 255A
BOSLEY, William; 45A
BRITON, Richard;
    Occupant: William HENDERSON; 270A
BRITON, Richard;
    Occupant: James COO; 862A
BURNET, Joseph; 156A
BURNET, Joseph;
    Occupant: Geo. GROVER; 156A
BRYAN, Nicholas;
    Occupant: William GILMORE; 325A
BOND, Thomas;
    Occupant: Archibald DAVIS; 83A
BOND, James; 83A
BOND, Barnet of Thos.; Occupant: John
    TARMAN; 78A
BUCK, Joshua; 124A
BOYCE, Eleanor, widow of Jno.;
    Occupant: James RICHARDSON; 156A
BOYCE, Eleanor, widow of Jno.;
    Occupant: John BISHOP; 156A
CLARKE, George; 98A
CARROLL, Charles; 50A
COURTNEY, Hercules; 536A
COURTNEY, Robert; 750A
COLLINS, George; 104A
CHASE, Jeremiah T.;
    Occupant: John WILKISON; 333A
CROOK, James;
    Occupant: William CARBACK; 288A
CARROLL Nicholas;
    Occupant: Richard GRAY; 1145A
CROMBEE, John Abee; 98A
DAY, John; 748A
DEMMITT, Moses; 198A
DENTON, William; 80A
DEMMITT, Birch; 180A
DULANY, Elizabeth; 10A
GREGORY, James, for the heirs of
    Thos. BOND; 333A
GOTT, Richard of Sam'l;
    Occupant: James HUGHES; 106A
GROVER, Tabitha; 80A
GALLOWAY, William; 668A+

GALLOWAY, William;
    Occupant: Joseph GRIFFEN
GALLOWAY, William;
    Occupant: Joseph GRIFFEN; 91A
GIBSON, Wm., Esqr,, Balto;
    Occupant: William BANE; 607A
GIBSON, Wm., Esqr., Balto;
    Occupant: Nath'l HARRIMAN
HAMBLETON, James; 110A
HATTON, Thomas; 77A
HATTON, Chaney; 165A
HAMMOND, Abraham G.;
    Occupant: Wm. H. ANDREWS; 448A
HAMMOND, Abraham G.;
    Occupant: Arnold ORAM
HAMMOND, Abraham G.;
    Occupant: Elizabeth BURY; 112A+
HATTON, Aquila;
    Occupant: Joseph BEVENS; 320A
HART, Henry; 40A+
HUGHES, Hugh; 83A
HUGHES, Christopher;
    Occupant: Basil WALLER;
HUGHES, Christopher;
    Occupant: Wm. WALLER; 461A
HUGHES, Christopher;
    Occupant: Wm. HUNT;
HILTON, Abraham; 32A
HATTON, Jno. of Chaney;
    Occupant: Wm. WOOD; 100A
HOLLINGSWORTH, Zebulon;
    Occupant: Wm. MARRIS
HOLLINGSWORTH, Zebulon;
    Occupant: John HAYS; 333A
HOLLINGSWORTH, Zebulon;
    Occupant: Abraham PARKS
JARMAN, Mary (Govanes Town); 100A
LEAUGE, Aquila; 45A
MILES, Thomas; 142A
MESSERSMITH, George; 62A
MEAD, Martha; 200A
MORRIS, Elnor; 359A
MULLY, John; 120A
MYERS, Benjamin;
    Occupant: William PRICE; 47A
McMECHEN, David;
    Occupant: Banet ASHER; 388A
O'DONNEL, Col. John;
    Occupant: Luke GRIFFIN; 300A

O'DONNEL, Col. John;
  Occupant: John LAUDER
OWINGS, Caleb;
  Occupant: Aquila HATTON; 80A
PRION, Simon; 98A
PRESBURY, George G., Junr; 512A
PRESBURY, George G., Senr; 229A
PRESBURY, George G., Senr;
  Occupant: John MULLY
PEARCE, Charles (Balt); 157A+
PRESBURY, Walter G.; 231A
PRESBURY, Walter G.;
  Occupant: William STEWART; 86A
POTTER, John; 2A
PARKER, Sarah; 176A
RISTON, John;
  Occupant: Thos. COTRELL; 100A
RISTEAU, Capt. John; 105A
RICKETTS, Samuel;
  Occupant: Benj. FRENCH; 75A
REES, Daniel;
  Occupant: Barnett BOND of Wm.; 83A
RIDGLEY, Gen'l Charles;
  Occupant: Jessop CHARLES; 198A
RIDGLEY, Gen'l Charles;
  Occupant: Solomon DISNEY; 693A
RIDGLEY, Gen'l Charles;
  Occupant: William GUYNN; 401A
RIDGLEY, Gen'l Charles;
  Occupant: Robert PEAK; 2448A
RIDGLEY, Gen'l Charles;
  Occupant: Benj. LIGGET
RIDGLEY, Gen'l Charles;
  Occupant: John LITTLE
RIDGLEY, Gen'l Charles;
  Occupant: John LUDLEY, Junr; 1000A
RIDGLEY, Gen'l Charles;
  Occupant: James HAWKINS
RIDGLEY, Gen'l Charles;
  Occupant: Geo. HAWKINS
RIDGLEY, Gen'l Charles;
  Occupant: Cealea BAKER
RIDGLEY, Gen'l Charles;
  Occupant: Henry FLETCHER
RIDGLEY, Gen'l Charles;
  Occupant: John LUDLEY, senr
RIDGLEY, Gen'l Charles;
  Occupant: John LIGHT; 4076A
RIDGLEY, Gen'l Charles;
  Occupant: Geo. VARNEL
RIDGLEY, Gen'l Charles;
  Occupant: Isaac WALTERS

RIDGLEY, Gen'l Charles; 946A+
RIDGLEY, Gen'l Charles; 585A
RIDGLEY, Gen'l Charles; 765A+
RIDGLEY, Gen'l Charles; 395A
SKINNER, John; 348A
SPEAR, George, Junr; 16A
SEDDON, James; 522A
SMITSON, David; 4A
STEWARTS, David, Junr;
  Occupant: James ENSOR; 258A
STANSBURY, Abraham; 198A
SIMPSON, Dr. John;
  Occupant: Joseph MARRIS
SIMPSON, Dr. John;
  Occupant: John JONES; 520A
SIMPSON, Dr. John;
  Occupant: Jubel MAHONY
SIMPSON, Dr. John;
  Occupant: Drusila CURBY; 410A
SIMPSON, Dr. John;
  Occupant: Mary THOMPSON
SIMPSON, Dr. John;
  Occupant: Henry BELL
SIMPSON, Dr. John;
  Occupant: James TAYLOR; 267A
SIMPSON, Dr. John;
  Occupant: William WILSON
STEWART, Robert;
  Occupant: James BARTON; 148A
SINCLAIR, Moses;
  Occupant: William ENGLE; 101A
SINCLAIR, Moses;
  Occupant: Joshua BEVENS
SINCLAIR, Moses;
  Occupant: Nathan ROBERTS; 100A
SINCLAIR, Moses;
  Occupant: Casandra RIMMER
SINCLAIR, Moses;
  Occupant: George BURY; 100A
SUTTON, Joseph, senr;
  Occupant: John HILTON; 488A
SUTTON, Joseph, senr;
  Occupant: Resin GRIMES
TALLY, James;
  Occupant: John MacCUBBIN; 750A
VAN BIBBER, Andrew; 107A
WEBSTER, James; 198A
WORTHINGTON, Vachael;
  Occupant: Rich'd BENNET; 601A
WORTHINGTON, Vachael;
  Occupant: John LEAUGE
WILLIAMS, Enock; 31A

WRIGHT, William, Junr;
Occupant: Wm. WRIGHT, senr; 30A
WRIGHT, Joseph;
Occupant: Geo. WRIGHT; 30A
WALSH, Robert (Balto); 337A
WORTHINGTON, Samuel;
Occupant: Wm. TERMAIN

WORTHINGTON, Samuel;
Occupant: John WILSON; 276A+
WORTHINGTON, Samuel;
Occupant: James WALLADGE
WILSON, Giving; 25A
YOUNG, John T.; 33A

Middle River Lower Hundred

General List of Slaves owned, or superintended on the 1st day of October,
1798, within the 8th Assessment District in the State of Maryland

ALLENDER, Sophia; 5 slaves
ARNOLD, Joshua; 6 slaves
ASHER, Barnet; 5 slaves
ANDREW, William H.; 6 slaves
BOSLEY, William; 1 slave
BURNET, Joseph; 16 slaves
BRYAN, Nicholas; 6 slaves
CLARK, George; 5 slaves
CARROL, Charles; 4 slaves
COURTNEY, Robert; 5 slaves
COLLINS, George; 4 slaves
COURTNEY, Hercules;
sup: Henry GRIFFITH; 6 slaves
CROOK, James; 3 slaves
CROMBIE, John Abbe; 4 slaves
CARROL, Nicholas;
sup: Richard GRAY; 12 slaves
DAY, John; 16 slaves
DEMMITT, Moses; 2 slaves
DAY, Nicholas;
sup: Wm. STEWART; 1 slave
FULLER, Samuel; 4 slaves
FRENCH, Benjamin; 5 slaves
GREGORY, James; 4 slaves
GRIFFITH, Sarah; 4 slaves
GRAY, Richard; 7 slaves
GALLOWAY, William; 15 slaves
GALLOWAY, Robert C.; 1 slave
GALLOWAY, Moses exr of Pamela & Wm.
GALLOWAY: 12 slaves

GALLOWAY, Pamela; 9 slaves
GOUGH, Harry Dorsey; 40 slaves
HAMBLETON, James; 6 slaves
HATTEN Aquila; 1 slave
HATTEN, Chaney; 1 slave
HATTEN, Thos. of Thos.; 1 slave
HUNT, William; 3 slaves
JARMAIN, Mary; 2 slaves
LAWSON, Elizabeth;
sup: James ENSOR; 2 slaves
McCUBBIN, John; 1 slave
MANIS, Joseph; 2 slaves
PRESBURY, George G., Junr; 14 slaves
PRESBURY, Walter G.; 12 slaves
PARKS, Abraham; 1 slave
PARKS Aquila; 6 slaves
RISTEAU, Capt. John; 8 slaves
RIDGLEY, Gen'l Charles;
sup: Charles JESSOP; 68 slaves
RIDGLEY, Gen'l Charles;
sup: Solomon DISNEY; 14 slaves
RAVIN, Luke; 8 slaves
SKINNER, John; 20 slaves
SEDDEN, James; 1 slave
WEYLEY, Vincent; 2 slaves
WEBSTER, James; 14 slaves
WALLER, William; 3 slaves
WALLER, Basil; 4 slaves
WORTHINGTON, Vachael; 7 slaves

ALLEN, Richard (1 slave); Occupant: Stephen WHALLEN; 194A; pt Amsterdam; hewd log dwlg hse *, 1 stry, 22x20; round log stble 14x12; round log hse 14x12; round log barn, 1 stry, 32x20

ALLEN, Solomon (3 slaves); 661A; (Mill Seat 23A; Mill Dam 21A; Saplin Ridge 84A; pt Watsons Trust 19A; pt New London 70A; Live Well 60A; pt Carline Felix 171A; pt Canaan 188A; Mt. Pleasant 25A); stone mill, 2 stry, 50x30; fr cooper shop, 2 stry, 20x15; saw mill 38x12; fr stble 1 1/2 stry, 66x14; old round log stble 20x16; round log barn 24x14; fr barn 24x14; old log hse, 1 stry, 22x16

ASQUE, Joshua; 44A+; pt East Lothan, 4A+; Manor Hambleton 25A+; Williamson Trouble 8A+; pt Addition to Gardeners Garden 11A+; mill hse, 2 stry, 1 of stone, other fr, 26x26; stone fulling hse, 1 stry, 30x26; old log hse, 1 stry, 18x12, round log stble, 1 stry, 18x16; round log hse, 1 stry, 12x10

ABRAHAM, Jacob; 40P; pt Chance; round log dwlg hse, 1 stry, 12x12

BRUFF, William; Occupant: Benjamin BOND; 677A; pt sundry tracts; stone dwlg hse, 1 stry, 20x16; old log poultry hse, 1 stry, 24x18; stone milk hse, 1 stry, 12x12; barn, 2 stry, 1 of stone, and other logs, 72x24; round hse log, 1 stry, 16x16

BROWN, John; Occupant: Joseph KNIGHT; 50A; Chattam; round log dwlg hse, 1 stry, 16x16

BAILEY, Thomas; 50A; Jack's Delight; round log dwlg hse, 1 stry, 16x16; log stble, 1 stry, 14x12

BARDEL, Charles; 70A; Peters second Adventure, 50A; Addition to same, 20A; hewd log dwlg hse, 1 stry, 18x16, by add. of stone 20x10; hewd log milk hse, 1 stry, 8x6; log stble, 1 stry, 32x16; hewd log barn, 1 stry, 20x16

BAISEMAN, William (9 slaves); Occupant: George BAISEMAN; Wm's Luck & Wm's Neglect 574A+, pt London 20A+, William's Neglect 13A+; round log dwlg hse, 1 stry, 16x14; round log stble, 2 stry, 24x24; round log barn, 2 stry, 45x20, log shed add., 1 stry, 45x16; fr dwlg hse *, 1 stry, 38x16 with piazza, 1 stry, 28x8; round log kn, 1 stry, 14x14; round log smoke hse, 1 stry, 14x10; round milk hse, 1 stry, 10x8; round log negro quarter, 1 stry, 16x14

BANKS, John and BANKS, Andrew; 40P; pt Spring Garden; hewd log dwlg hse *, weatherboarded, 2 stry, 29x16; brk hse, 1 stry, 18x16

BRAMWELL, Henry (10 slaves); 557A; pt Scribners Folly 474A+; Lains Desire 83A; hewd log dwlg hse, 1 stry, 24x16; round log hse, 1 stry, 16x16; round log smoke hse, 1 stry, 12x8; round log barn, 1 stry, thatcht, 46x20

BOND, Samuel; pt Scribners Folly, 125A+; Lains Bottoms & Hills 120A, Lains Neglect & Crosses Lot 12A; hewd log dwlg hse, 1 stry, 20x16; round log hse, 1 stry, 20x16; round log smoke hse, 1 stry, 14x12; round log barn, 1 stry, 36x16; round log stble, 1 stry, 32x16; round log corn hse, 14x10

BECKLEY, John; Occupant: Christian WEAVER; 60P; pt Philips Desire; hewd log dwlg hse, 1 stry, 24x16; brk smiths shop, 1 stry, 24x18; hewd log stble, 1 stry, 20x18; brk dwlg hse *, 2 stry, 29x24; brk kn, 1 stry, 15x15; brk milk hse, 1 stry, 10x10

BOWERS, Daniel; Wm. BERRYMAN; 68A; pt Chase & Spring Garden; stone dwlg hse, 2 stry, 24x18; 2 hewd log stbles, each 16x16; old log barn, 1 stry, 40x20; fr dwlg hse *, 1 stry, hip roof, 40x20, by add. of fr 1 stry sq. roof, 22x20 with piazza

BAUGHMAN, Henry; 170A; Clarks Lot 50A, Good Will 60A, pt Soldiers Delight 60A; hewd log dwlg hse, 1 stry, 24x20; hewd log barn, 1 stry, 56x26; round log stble, 1 stry, 16x14

BOWERS, Daniel and MORGAN, James; 922A; pt Chase 250A, pt Graziers Delight 500A, Bowers Chance 128A; Gratitude 44A

BUTLER, Amon (4 slaves); pt sundry tracts 200A, pt Good Will 39A; log barn, 1 stry, 40x22; log corn hse, 1 stry, 22x12; fr dwlg hse *, 1 stry, 24x17; fr shed add., 1 stry, 24x9; log shed add., 1 stry, 17x12

BOWEN, Jehue (8 slaves); 142A; pt Musgroves Forest, Martins Nest & pt Fells Forrest

CORRICK, George; Occupant: Maurice BAKER; 76A; pt Musgroves Forest; log dwlg hse, 1 stry, 16x13; hewd log hse, 1 stry, 16x13; log barn, 1 stry, 40x20

CROSS, William; Occupant: John CROSS; 49A+; pt Gosnells Camp; round log hse, 1 stry, 15x15; round log hse, 1 stry, 18x14

CROXALL, Eleanor (27 slaves); Occupant: Jeremiah CULLISON; 955A; fr carriage hse, 1 stry, 14x14; old hewd log corn hse, 1 stry, 45x16; old fr stble, 1 stry, 80x22; old log stble, 1 stry, 20x12; old log barn, 1 stry, 46x22; log cider hse, 1 stry, 22x16; store hse, 1 stry, 14x12; 2 old fr hses, 1 stry, 14x12 & 20x12; fr barn 40x20; fr dwlg hse 24x20; log corn hse 12x10

COUNCILMAN, Eliz'th; 68A+; pt Soldiers Delight & pt Reisters Enlargment; hewd log currying shop, 2 stry, 28x18; brk bark shed, 1 stry, 100x16; old log hse, 1 stry, 18x16; old fr hse, 1 stry, fit for fuel, 16x14; hewd log barn, 1 stry, 40x20

CREADOCK(CRADOCK), Thos. (15 slaves); 738A+; pt Georges Beginning and pt Addition to Rich Level 170A, The Spot 10A; Simkon's Repose 100A, pt Addition to Simkons Repose 29A, pt Ashmans Delight 202A, pt Bedford Resurveyed 62A+, pt Garrison 3A+, pt Counter Search 20A, Murry's Gift to his daughter 130A, Cradocks Grove 11A+, log barn, 1 stry, 20x14; fr add. 30x14; old stble with shed 30x26; Occupant: Wm. COWARD; stone dwlg hse, 1 stry, 20x20; round log stble, 1 stry, 18x14; horse shed, 1 stry, 48x9; Occupant: George DEEMS: log dwlg hse, 1 stry, 34x18

CHINOWITH, Arthur (12 slaves); 163A; pt Arthurs Lot & sundry other tracts; stone mill hse, 1 stry, 26x26, hip roof; fr barn, 1 stry, 40x34; log stble, 27x818; old log stble, 1 stry, 27x11; old log hse, 1 stry, 16x14; old log poultry hse, 1 stry, 10x8; log corn crib, 1 stry, 14x8

CHINOWITH, Rich'd; 100A; pt Gilead

CHAPMAN, Nathan (2 slaves); 216A; pt sundry tracts; old log hse 16x14; round log barn, 1 stry, 36x10

CROSS, Nicholas; 71A; pt Graziers Delight; round log dwlg hse, 1 stry, 16x14; old log stble, 1 stry, 18x12

CLARK, Henry (4 slaves); 102A; pt Soldiers Delight; round log barn, 1 stry, 30x20, with shed at each end 20x10

CREAMER, Henry; 20A; pt Soldiers Delight; hewd log dwlg hse, 1 1/2 stry, 22x18 with piazza 22x6; hewd log milk hse, 1 stry, 12x10; log barn 26x20

CHOAT (CHOATE), Richard (2 slaves); 252A; pt Soldiers Delight, pt Clarks Park; round log barn, 1 stry, 46x22; round log stble, 1 stry, 18x10; round log shop 20x16; round log hse, 2 stry, 18x16

CHOAT (CHOATE), Auston (3 slaves); 248A; pt Clark's Park, pt Soldiers Delight; round log barn, 1 stry, 20x20; old log stble, 1 stry, 20x10

COUNSILMAN, John; 9A; pt Soldiers Delight; hewd log dwlg hse, 1 stry, 24x18; old round log still hse, 1 stry, 22x20

CROMWELL, John (8 slaves); 195A+; pt of sundry tracts; old log hse, 1 stry, 20x12; hewd log barn, 1 stry, 46x16 with open shed round 46x10

CLARK, John; 135A; pt Clark's Park; old hewd log dwlg hse, 1 stry, 32x16

CLARK, Richard; 254A+; pt sundry tracts; hewd log dwlg hse, 1 stry, 20x16; old round log 18x16, with shed 16x12; hewd log milk hse, 8x8; round log barn 50x20

CLARK, James; 445A; pt Miners Adventure; hewd log dwlg hse, 1 stry, 22x18

CARNAN, Robert North (22 slaves); 502A; Ristues Garrison; hewd log smith shop, 1 stry, 36x16; old coal hse, 1 stry, 18x14; round log shop 18x16; old log stble, 1 stry, 56x22; old log stble 30x14; fr barn, 1 stry, 42x22; fr granary, 1 stry, 26x20

CONAWAY, Richard; 83A; pt Sents (Scotts) Level; hewd log dwlg hse, 1 stry, 18x16; old log hse, 1 stry, 16x16

CHOAT (CHOATE), Edward (2 slaves); 200A; pt Soldiers Delight; round log dwlg hse, 1 stry, 16x12; round log poultry hse, 1 stry, 20x16; round log smoke hse, 1 stry, 10x10; round log barn, 1 stry, 30x16

COOK, William; 159A; pt Porters Desire; hewd log dwlg hse, 1 stry, 24x18; hewd log kn, 1 stry, 20x18; old round log barn, 1 stry, 36x18; round log stble, 1 stry, 24x18

COCKEY, Thomas; 221A; pt Pleasant Meadows, 48A; pt Joshua's Gift, 17A; pt Molly habitation, 12A; Howards Straits, 23A; Mill Lot, 21A; Cornelius & Mary's Lot, 100A; stone dwlg hse *, 2 stry, 36x22, stone kn add., 1 stry, 18x14; log smoke hse, 1 stry, 14x12; log poultry hse, 1 stry, 12x10; fr negroe hse, 1 stry, 14x12; stone mill hse, 3 stry, much out of repair, 30x30; fr barn, 1 stry, 30x30 with three open shed

CARROLL, Henry H.; Occupant: Michael MASON; 230A; pt Ely O Carroll; old log dwlg hse, 1 stry, 16x12; old fr hse, 1 stry, 20x16, with add. shed 16x10; old log barn, 1 stry, 40x20; log stble, 1 stry, 16x12

CARROLL, Henry H.; Occupant: Thomas HARVEY; 323A; pt Ely O Carroll; 1 hewd log dwlg hse, 1 stry, 20x18; shed add., 1 stry, 20x10; 1 log kn, 1 stry, 18x16; 1 hewd log smoke hse, 1 stry, 12x12; 1 fr tobacco hse 32x22; 1 old tobacco hse 12sx16

CARROLL, Henry H.; Occupant: Henry CRAINER; 100A; pt Ely O Carroll

CARROLL, Henry H.; Occupant: John LEEF; 134A; pt Ely O Carroll; hewd log dwlg hse *, 1 1/2 stry, 20x18; hewd log kn, 1 stry, 20x16; log barn 32x16

CARROLL, Henry H.; 416A; pt Ely O Carroll; Occupants: Nicholas HARVEY; old log dwlg hse, 1 stry, 40x16;' old log kn, 1 stry, 16x16; log stble, 1 stry, 20x10; old log barn, 1 stry, 20x14; old log hse, 1 stry, 14x12; Nicholas HARVEY, Jr.; old log dwlg hse, 1 stry, 20x16; old log barn 26x18; old log stble 12x12

CARROLL, Henry H.; Occupant: Robert North CARNAN; 116A; pt Ely O Carroll

CRAINER, Michael; Henry CRAINER; 107A; pt Angels Fortune; round log hse, 1 stry, 14x10; round log barn, 1 stry, 32x20; log dwlg hse *, 1 stry, 20x16; round log kn, 1 stry, 18x16; round log smoke hse, 1 stry, 12x10; fr milk hse, 1 stry, 12x8

DAVIS, Robert; 194A+; pt of sundry tracts; Occupant: James DAVIS: (pt of Cornelius & Mary's Lot); stone dwlg hse *, 2 stry, 30x16; fr dwlg hse, 1 stry, 24x18; log kn, 1 stry, 16x14; log milk hse, 1 stry, 10x8; round log stble, 1 stry, 20x10

DORSEY, Bassel (Basil) John; 100A; pt Scotchmans Desire; old hewd log dwlg hse, 1 stry, 16x16; log stble, 1 stry, 15x12

DUNKIN, Benj.; 75A; pt Soldiers Delight; log dwlg hse, 1 stry, 16x16; round log shop, 1 stry, 16x12; round log stble, 28x15

DECKER, Jacob (1 slave); pt Isinglass Glade, 14A+; pt Sinkins Repose, 3A+; fr dwlg hse *, 2 stry, 46x20; fr kn, 2 stry, 20x16, on Isinglass Glade;

hewd log stble, 1 stry, 20x16; Occupant: John DEEMS: pt Sinkins Repose;
hewd log dwlg hse, 2 stry, 20x15; hewd log kn, 1 stry, 10x10; fr smoke
hse, 15x14; old log, 1 stry, 18x16

DICKSON, Isaac; pt Spring Garden 80P, pt Mathews Forest and Mornings
Delight; 107A, pt Nicholson Manor 177A; Occupant: Thomas CLINGERS: hewd
log dwlg hse, 2 stry, 24x16; round log stble 12x12; hewd log dwlg hse, 1
1/2 stry, 20x16; Occupant: William GRIFFIN: hewd log hse, 1 stry, 18x16;
round log still hse 16x16

DIMMETT, William (5 slaves); 236A; Benjamins Lot 98A; Cross Wells Adventure
50A, pt Soldiers Delight 88A; hewd log dwlg hse *, 1 stry, 22x18; old log
kn, 1 stry, 20x16; round log smoke hse, 1 stry, 12x8; round log poultry
hse, 1 stry, 16x12, on Benjamin's Lot; Occupant: William GRIFFIN: round
log dwlg hse, 1 stry, 16x16; log poultry hse, 1 stry, 12x10; round log
barn, 1 stry, 22x20; 2 old log stbles, each 19x13

DEMMITT, Henry; 100A; pt Dividend; old log dwlg hse, 1 stry, 20x16; log kn,
1 stry, 16x12

DORSEY, Beal (12 slaves); 457A+; pt of sundry tracts 363A+, pt Soldiers
Delight 94A+; hewd log dwl hse *, 2 stry, 28x24; round log kn, 1 stry,
14x14; round log smoke hse, 1 stry, 14x12; round log milk hse, 1 stry,
10x8; round log poultry hse, 1 stry, 16x16, on sundry tracts; log stble,
1 stry, 16x14; log hse, 1 stry, 18x10; log barn 20x16; log poultry hse
12x10; 2 log tobacco hses each 28x24

DAVEY, Alexander; Rich'd WATTS; 114 A; pt Quebeck &c.; old log dwlg hse, 1
stry, 20x16; old log barn, 1 stry, 16x14

DEMONNIS, Dorothy; 10A; pt Randals Good Intent, pt Georges Park; hewd log
dwlg hse, 1 stry, 20x16; old log kn, 1 stry, 20x16; old log stble, 1
stry, 12x10

DICKSON, Thomas; 164A; pt Carline Felix; old round log barn, 1 stry, 30x20;
old round log stble, 1 stry, 16x16; horse shed 60x12; Occupant: Thos.
SACKS: stone dwlg hse, 2 stry, 42x21 1/2; hewd log smoke hse, 1 stry,
20x18; stone milk hse, 1 stry, 14x12, unfinished; Occupant: George
WORMAN: hewd log dwlg hse, 2 stry, 20x16; hewd log smoke hse, 1 stry,
20x16

EVANS, Joseph; Occcupant: Jonathan HAYWITH; 185A; pt Stinchcombs Hills 135A,
pt Jones Adventure 30A, pt Evan's Addition 20A; old log dwlg hse, 1 stry,
16x16; barn, pt fr & pt logs, 40x18; dwlg hse *, 2 stry, 1 of fr and
other of stone, 31x23; log smoke hse, 1 stry, 10x10 on Stinchcombs Hills

EBERT, John; Occupant: Catharine GIRTY; 271A; pt Plains of Paran; hewd log
dwlg *, 1 stry, 30x25; hewd log kn, 1 stry, 16x12; stone milk hse, 1
stry, 16x12; stone barn, 1 stry, 50x30; old log hse, 1 stry, 30x22; old
hse, log, 20x16; old log hse 16x16; round log kn, 1 stry, 12x12

EKELBERGER, Jacob; 1908A; pt of sundry tracts; fr dwlg hse *, 1 stry, 24x18,
with piazza, 24x5; hewd log kn, 1 stry, 33x16; log smoke hse, 1 stry,
10x8; barn, 2 stry, 1 of stone, other fr, 38x32; round log stble 26x12;
old fr hse 10x8; round log smith shop 18x16; old coal shop 15x14; old log
hse 10x8

FRESH, Francis (4 slaves); 128A; pt sundry tracts; log dwlg hse *, 1 stry,
26x20; round log smoke hse, 1 stry, 16x12; log poultry hse, 1 stry,
10x10; old log barn, 1 stry, 36x20

FORD, Samuel; 108A; pt Soldiers Delight

FORD, Thomas (1 slave); 111A; pt Fords Range; fr dwlg hse, 1 stry, 20x16, by
add. of ·log shed 20x8; old log kn, 1 stry, 16x12; log milk hse, 1 stry,

10x10; log smoke hse, 1 stry, 12x10; log poultry hse, 1 stry, 14x12; log barn, 1 stry, 40x20; log stble, 1 stry, 16x14

FORT, Samuel; 80P; pt Soldiers Delight; round log dwlg hse, 1 stry

FORD, Thomas; Occupants: Elizabeth BAKER, Ephraim BAKER, John ROOLES; 300A; Sewels Contrivance, 100A; Fools Folly, 50A; Sewels Hope, 150A; old round log dwlg hse, 1 stry, 20x18, old log barn, 1 stry, 16x16; old log stble, 1 stry, 10x8; round log dwlg hse, 1 stry, 20x16; old log dwlg hse, 1 stry, 28x16; old log kn, 1 stry, 16x14

FENTON, Charles; 219A; pt Bells Park; round log dwlg hse, 1 stry, 22x18, by add. of log shed, 1 stry, 22x10; log smoke hse, 1 stry, 24x20; round log barn, 2 stry, 48x24

FISHER, George; 2A; pt Chase & Spring Garden; brk dwlg hse *; 2 stry, 28x18, by add. of brk, 1 stry, 28x16; hewd log kn, 1 stry, 16x12; round log stble, 2 stry, 22x18, by add. of fr 18x12; round log stble, 1 stry, 22x20; waggon shed, 1 stry, 176x10; Occupant: John SCHULL: hewd log hse, 2 stry, 20x16, with fr add. 16x12; fr kn, 1 stry, 16x12

FORNEY, Daniel (1 slave) 23A; pt Chase & Spring Garden; brk dwlg hse *, 2 stry, 50x18; hewd log kn, 1 stry, 32x14; fr hatters shop, 1 stry, 22x17; fr horse shed, 1 stry, 88x10; double brk horse shed, 1 stry, 55x20; hewd log stble, 1 stry, 20x16

FRIZZELL, Hannah (7 slaves); 198A; pt of Carline Felix; hewd log dwlg hse *, 2 stry, 28x18; old round log kn, 1 stry, 16x15; old log stble, 1 stry, 16x14; old log stble, 1 stry, 14x12

GLADMAN, Thos. (1 slave); 128A;1 pt Plains of Parran; round log dwlg hse, 1 stry, 22x18, by add. of stone shed, 22x10; hewd log barn, 1 stry, 38x22 with stble beneath

GLADMAN, Mich'l; 180A; pt Gillchreth Discovery 108A, Hackel Pole 50A, Stocksdale 22A; hewd log dwlg hse, 1 1/2 stry, 22x12; old log stble, 1 stry, 20x18

GREEN, Henry; 171A; pt Mount Pleasant 112A, pt Raffo (or Rappo) 59A; hewd log dwlg hse, 2 stry, unfinished

GOSNELL, Charles; 360A+; pt Willmotts Chance and Watson Trust 163A, pt of resurvey on Willmotts Chance 199A; stone dwlg hse *, 2 stry, 24x20; hewd log kn, 1 stry, 20x16; log smoke hse, 1 stry, 8x8 on Willmots Chance & Watsons Trust; round log barn, 1 stry, 28x16; log stble, 1 stry, 14x12

GOSNELL, Peter; 234A; pt Gosnell's Camp 150A; pt Graziers Delight 84A; old fr dwlg hse, 1 stry, 24x16; old log kn, 1 stry, 12x10; old log barn, 1 stry, 24x16

GRUNDY, George; Thos. PORTER; 119A; pt McClains Hills; round log dwlg hse, 1 stry, 30x14; old log barn, fit for fuel, 40x18; old log stble, fit for fuel, 16x12

GORE, George and H. John GORE; Spring Garden; Occupant: Caleb WORRELL; 185A; pt Soldiers Delight; hewd log dwlg hse, 1 1/2 stry, 20x16; round log kn, 20x16; log barn, 1 stry, 40x18; round log stble, 1 stry, 16x16; hewd log dwlg hse *, 2 stry, 29x17; hewd log kn, 1 stry, 1 1/2 stry, 17x14; log smoke hse, 1 stry, 16x16

GANTZ, Adam; 198A; pt Harrisons Plains; hewd log barn, 1 stry, 40x23; old log hse, 1 stry, 23x9; log hse, 1 stry, 12x8; round log stble, 1 stry, 16x11; hewd log dwlg hse *, 1 1/2 stry, 27x24, with piazza, 1 stry, 27x7; round log smoke hse, 1 stry, 12x10; round log milk hse, 1 stry, 12x10

GOSNELL, Philip 244A; pt Three Sisters &c.; round log dwlg hse, 1 stry, 18x16; hewd log smoke hse 18x18; round log stble, 1 stry, 14x12

49

GRIFFITH, Abednego (1 slave); 100A; pt of sundry tracts; fr dwlg hse, 1 stry, 22x16; log shed add. 22x6; old log kn, 1 stry, 16x16; old log barn 24x16

GRIFFITH, Benjamin; 58A; pt of sundry tracts; stone dwlg hse *, 1 stry, 22x16; stone kn, 1 stry, 16x16; log barn, 1 stry, 24x16

GARREY, James; 100A; pt Soldiers Delight; round log dwlg hse, 1 stry, 18x16; round log smoke hse, 1 stry, 10x10; 3 old log tobacco hses, covered with straw 20x16 each

GOSNELL, William; 26A; Addition to Pleasant Pastures

GOSNELL, Greenberry; 81A; pt Wilmott's Chance; hewd log dwlg hse, 1 stry, 20x16; round log barn, 1 stry, 40x18

GOSNELL, Zebediah; 228A; pt Gosnells Pleasant Pasture, 104A; Williams Folly, 81A; pt Willmotts Chance, 43A; hewd log dwlg hse, 1 stry, 20x14; hewd log hse, 1 stry, 20x18; hewd log smoke hse, 1 stry, 12x8; hewd log barn, 1 stry, 30x20; log stble, 1 stry, 16x10

GIST, Thomas (4 slaves); 412A+; Norris's Chance and Choats Contrivance, 200A; pt Adventure, 191A; Gists Desire, 25A+; Occupant: Joshua HUTSON; fr dwlg hse *, 1 stry, 34x16; hewd log kn, 1 stry, 20x16; fr smoke hse, 1 stry, 12x10; log poultry, 1 stry, 20x16; hewd log stble, 1 stry, 22x18; log shed add., 18x8; log barn, 1 stry, 44x28; log corn hse 14x12; Occupant: Susanna GIST (7 slaves): fr dwlg hse *, 1 stry, 22x16, by add. of shed, 1 stry, 22x18; log kn, 1 stry, 14x12; log hse, 1 stry, 22x16; log smoke hse, 1 stry, 12x12; stone milk hse, 1 stry, 10x8; log poultry hse, 1 stry, 12x12

HAMBLETON, George; 133A; pt East Lothan; round log dwlg hse, 1 stry, 16x?; round log hse, 1 stry, 24x16; log stble 16x12

HAMBLETON, James; 128A; pt East Lothan; fr dwlg hse, 1 stry, 24x20; round log kn, 1 stry, 20x16; round log barn, 1 stry, 40x20

HAMBLETON, Samuel; 240A; pt East Lothan; round log dwlg hse, 1 stry, 20x16; round log stble, 1 stry, 12x10

HAMBLETON, Edward (3 slaves); 287A+; pt East Lothan; Occupant: Daniel HANES; round log dwlg hse, 1 stry, 20x14; round log hse, 1 stry, 20x16; round log stble, 20x12; log barn 16x16; log stble 20x16; fr dwlg hse *, 1 stry, 28x16; log kn, 1 stry, 20x16; log smoke hse, 1 stry, 12x8; log poultry hse, 1 stry, 12x8

HAINS, Catharine; 40A; pt Murry's Desire; round log dwlg hse, 1 stry, 20x16

HOWARD, Sarah (7 slaves) 308A; pt Bells Park & Soldiers Delight; hewd log dwlg hse, 1 stry, 22x16; round log hse, 1 stry, 16x16; round log kn, 1 stry, 20x18; round log smoke hse, 1 stry, 14x12; log stble 22x20; round log barn, 1 stry, 36x22

HOLLIS, Mary; 1A; pt Soldiers Delight; round log dwlg hse, 1 stry, 20x18

HOWARD, Samuel (4 slaves); 198A; Howard's Fancy; log barn, 1 stry, 22x18; stone dwlg hse *, 1 stry, 20x18; hewd log hse, 1 stry, 24x18; log smoke hse, 1 stry, 14x12; stone milk hse, 1 stry, 12x12

HOWARD, James; 343A; Howards Camp 98A, Howard Square 159A, Howard Organ 6A, Security Organ 62A, pt Ashman Delight 18A; old stone dwlg hse *, 1 stry, 40x21, with piazza, 1 stry, 40x6; hewd log kn, 1 stry, 32x14; hewd log smoke hse, 12x12; log milk hse, 1 stry, 12x12; log negroe hse, 1 stry, 20x14 on Howard Camp; hewd log barn, 1 stry with open shed round 54x20

HINKEL, John; 282A; pt Plains Parran; hewd log dwlg hse, 1 stry, 30x18; hewd log barn, 2 stry, 30x20; hewd log stble, 1 stry, 26x12; log stble, 1 sdtry, 24x10

HAMMON, Philip (2 slaves); 478A; Benjamins Prospect 98A, pt Rusturs Enlargement 50A, Saint Georges Plains 100A, Stevensons Plains 120A, Nathans Forest 95A, pt Murrys Plains Regulated 15A; Occupant: Mary BROTHERS; hewd log dwlg hse, weatherboarded, 1 stry, 28x18 *; hewd log kn, 1 stry, 22x18; hewd log smoke hse, 1 stry, 18x12; lo milk hse, 1 stry, 12x10; hewd log dwlg hse, 1 stry, 20x17; round log kn, 1 stry, 17x10; round log hse, 13x10; fr barn, 1 stry, 30x20; log stble 32x17; log stble 20x17

HOWARD, Cornelius (2 slaves); 527A; pt of sundry tracts; Occupant: brk dwlg hse *, 2 stry, 30x20, by add. of kn, 2 stry, 20x20; stone milk hse, 1 stry, 16x16; stone smoke hse, 1 stry, 20x16; log shop, 1 stry, 24x17; round log barn, 1 stry, 40x20; round log stble 24x20; round log stble 28x14; log dwlg hse, 1 stry, 18x16; fr milk hse 10x8; stone mill hse, 2 stry, 60x25; round log barn, 1 stry, 24x16; old fr dwlg hse, 1 stry, 36x16; Occupant: Joseph WEST: hewd log dwlg hse *, 2 stry, 28x20; hewd log kn, 1 stry, 20x20; stone smoke hse, 1 stry, 10x10; log poultry hse, 1 stry, 10x10; Occupant Moses BLACK: hewd log dwlg hse, 1 1/2 stry, 24x20

ISRAEL, Gilbert; 220A+; Taylor's Farm, 98A; Lonnon, 11A; pt Clark Park, 100A; pt Porters Desire, 11A+; round log dwlg hse *, 1 stry, 18x18, with piazza 14x5; fr kn, 1 stry, 12x12; stone milk hse, 1 stry, 10x8; round smoke log hse, 1 stry, 10x10 on Taylors Farm; log stble, 1 stry, 18x16; log stble 16x10; log barn, 1 stry, 30x20

ISRAEL, Ely; 230A; pt Clark Park, 140A; pt Soldiers Delight, 90A; hewd log dwlg hse, 1 stry, 20x16; round log barn 30x20

IGOE, Elizabeth; 99A; pt Cornelius & Mary's Lot; hewd log dwlg hse, 1 stry, 36x16; old log kn 16x16; round log barn, 1 stry, 30x18

JUDY, John; 128A; Springs Folly; round log dwlg hse, 1 stry, 30x15; round log milk hse, 12x12; round log barn, 1 stry, 40x22

JONES, Henry (4 slaves); 468A; pt Plains of Parran; stone dwlg hse *, 2 stry, 20x20, hewd log add., 30x20 with piazza, 54x7; hewd log barn, 2 stry, 54x26; round log stble, 1 stry, 16x13; hewd log smoke hse, 1 stry, 16x14; hewd log milk hse, 1 stry, 12x12; old hewd log hse, 1 1/2 stry, 28x18

JONES, Elis; 365A; pt Timber Grove 250A, pt Soldiers Delight 115A; round log dwlg hse *, 2 stry, 40x16, log shed add., 1 stry, 40x12; log smoke hse, 12x8; log milk hse, 1 stry, 10x8, on Timber Grover; Occupant: Adam REANY; round log dwlg hse, 1 stry, 20x16; round log barn 40x20; round log stble 10x8; round log smith shop, 1 stry, 20x16

JONES, Isaac; 80P; pt Spring Garden; hewd log dwlg hse, 2 stry, 24x14; round log stble 12x12; hewd log stble, 1 stry, 10x10

JACOBS Wm., heirs; 40A; pt Angels Fortune

JANE, Ruth (1 slave); 170A; pt sundry tracts; round log dwlg hse, 1 stry, 16x16; round log hse 16x16; stone cider, 1 stry, 20x12; log barn, 1 stry, 44x16; round log hse 14x12; round log stble 24x12

JONES, Thomas (8 slaves); 833A; Jones' Contrivance 248A, pt McClains Hills 128A, Stocksdale Abode Res. 204A, The Folly 150A; Addition to Gosnells Camp 75A, Wilmott's Chance Res. 28A; Occupant: John GORE; stone dwlg *, 2 stry, 26x21; hewd log kn, 1 stry, 24x16 on Jones Contrivance; Occupant: Robert CROSS; hewd log dwlg hse, 1 stry, 24x18; barn, 2 stry, 1 stry stone, other fr, 70x30; Occupant: Isaac DYKES: log dwlg hse, 1 stry, 16x16

KILLEY, Joseph; 198A; pt Adventure, 98A; pt Green Spring Punch, 100A; stone dwlg hse *, 1 stry, 24x20, by log add., 1 stry, 20x16; hewd log kn, 1 stry, 16x12 on Adventure; fr barn, 1 stry, 40x18; old log stble 24x12; old log stble 20x20

LYNCH, William (1 slave); 58A; pt Mount Organ 48A, pt Ashmans Delight 10A; fr dwlg hse *, 1 stry, 30x24 with piazza 30x6; stone kn, 1 stry, 16x16, by add. of stone shed 9x8; stone milk hse, 1 stry, 10x8, on Mount Organ; fr barn with stone stble beneath, 30x24; old fr hse, 12x10

LONAS, John; pt Brotherly Love;; brk dwlg hse, 2 stry, unfinished, 50x24

LITTLE, John; 1A+; pt Simkens Repose; hewd log dwlg hse, 1 stry, 16x15; round log store hse, 1 stry, 22x16; round log stble 12x12

LARSH, Abraham; 259A; Occupant: Joseph BUTLER; pt Sundry tracts, 109A; pt Beef Hall, 150A; round log dwlg hse, 1 1/2 stry, 23x18

LANE, Margaret (2 slaves); 140A; pt Hails Adventure, 100A; Williams Resurvey, 40A; fr dwlg hse, 1 stry; 24x20, by add. of shed 24x12; old log barn 42x22; old log hse 10x8

LOW, Nicholas (2 slaves); 124A; pt Soldiers Delight; log barn, 1 stry, 40x10; log stble, 1 stry, 22x12

LOW, John (1 slave); 192A; pt Soldiers Delight and Food Plenty; round log dwlg hse *; 1 1/2 stry, 24x20; round log kn, 1 stry, 14x14; round log smoke hse, 1 stry, 12x8 on Soldiers Delight; Occupants: David LOW, Florah LOW (2 slaves); hewd log dwlg hse, 1 stry, 20x16; round log smoke hse, 1 stry, 12x12; log stble 16x12; log stble 18x12

LOW, David (1 slave); 45A; pt Soldiers Delight

LUKESS, Priscilla; 63A; pt Fells Forest; hewd log dwlg hse, 1 stry, 24x18, by add. of hewd log shed 24x18; log milk hse, 8x8; log poultry 10x8; old log barn 24x15; round log stble 14x10

LYNCH, Hugh; 3A; pt Fells Forrest; old log dwlg hse, 1 stry, 16x16

LEWIS, Ephraim; 77A; Worthington's Neglect; log dwlg hse, 1 stry, 16x16

LYON, Robert (26 slaves); 1485A+; pt Mount Organ & other tracts; fr dwlg hse *, 1 stry, 62x20 with piazza, 52x9; fr, unfinished, 1 stry, 15x15; old fr, 1 stry, 16x16; log hse, 1 stry, 14x14; stone smoke hse, 1 stry, 16x16; stone milk hse, 1 stry, 12x12; log hse, 1 stry, 16x14; old log barn, 1 stry, 80x22; old log stble 40x14; old log corn hse, 22x16, by add. of shed 22x12; stone mill hse, 2 stry, 85x35; log cooper shop 16x16; hewd log hse, 1 stry, 16x14; hewd log stble 16x14; stone smith shop 46x24; old fr stble, 1 stry, 22x12; old log stble, 1 stry, 36x26; Occupant: Joshua WRIGHT (mill place); fr dwlg hse, 1 stry, 16x16, by add. of stone, 1 stry, 16x16; stone kn, 1 stry, 16x14; hewd log dwlg hse, 2 stry, 34x16; hewd log kn, 1 stry, 24x14; old stone store hse, 1 stry, 32x24

MAXFIELD, Rachel; Occupant: Daniel McKENSY; 116A; pt East Lothan; hewd log dwlg hse *, 2 stry, the lower stry of stone, 24x20; hewd log dwlg hse, 1 stry, 24x16; old round log smith shop, 1 stry, 26x16

McMACHIN, David; Occupant: Thomas FORD; 100A; pt Soldiers Delight; old fr dwlg hse, 1 stry, 26x24; old log barn 36x18

MABURY, Catharine; Occupant: Jacob WEAST; 1A; pt Brotherly Love; round log stble, 1 stry, 16x14; hewd log dwly hse *, 2 stry, 22x20, by add. of log shed, 1 stry, 12x10; log store hse, 1 stry, 16x16

MANING, Samuel; 357A; pt White Oak Bottom 208A, pt Hickory Bottom 90A, pt Cherry Tree Bottom 9A, pt Manings Delight 50A; old log barn, 1 stry, 32x20

MORGAN, James; Occupant: Rich'd HISER; 480A; pt Spring Garden; round log dwlg hse, 1 stry, 20x16; old hewd log hse, 2 stry, 24x18

MOALE, Eleanor (6 slaves); 741A; pt Green Spring Punch; fr dwlg hse *, 1 stry, hip roof, 31x18, by add. of log 1 stry, 28x17; old fr hse, 1 stry, 24x24; old log negroe hse, 1 stry, 20x12; stone barn, 1 stry, 62x25, by add. of stone shed 46x12; log hse 10x10; hewd log hse 14x9; log stble 20x12

MALLETT, William; 50A; Airs's Desire; old log dwlg hse, 1 stry, 18x16; log hse 18x16; log coopers shop 12x12

MACKARD, Joseph (2 slaves); 66A; pt Level Union; new fr dwlg hse, unfinished *, 1 stry, 48x25 with 2 wings, 25x14; old log stble 24x16; log cider hse 18x16; log hse 12x10; round log barn, 1 stry, 44x22; Occupant: John ISGRIG; hewd log dwlg hse, 1 stry, 24x16, by add. of log 1 stry, 24x6, by add. of log shed, 1 stry, 16x10; hewd log shed, 1 stry, 10x8

MADARY, Jacob; pt Spring Garden; brk dwlg hse *, 2 stry, 38x34; brk kn, 2 stry, 18x15; hewd log hse, 2 stry, weatherboarded, 28x18; old log hse, 1 stry, 38x18; hewd log granary 1 1/2 stry, 20x16; hewd & fr stble, 1 stry, 40x34

OWINGS, Thomas; Occupant: Isaac OWINGS; 446A; pt Timber Level & Sundry other tracts; 1 stone barn, 1 stry, 40x30; stone work hse, 1 stry, 26x16; 1 stble, 2 stry, 1 stone, the other logs, 44x20; 1 log hse 24x16; 1 stone mill hse 64x26; log stble 12x10

ORSLER, John; 120A; pt Long Look't For; 1 round log dwlg hse, 1 stry, 18x14; old log hse 20x16

ODLE, Walter; 60A; Minto, and Roole's Chance; 1 fr dwlg hse, 1 stry, 24x20; round log smoke hse 12x10; stone milk hse 10x8; barn, 2 stry, 1 of stone, the other hewd logs, 30x20; fr shed add. 30x9

OWINGS, Nicholas; Occupant: Wm. MORGAN; Bachelors Hall 60A, pt Sents Level 48A+, pt Harrisons Meddow 175A, pt Roboram 227A; 1 fr dwlg hse, 1 stry, 26x24

OWINGS, Benjamin; Harp Well; 50A

OWINGS, Catharine; Occupant: Benj. OWINGS; 100A; 1 log dwlg hse, 1 stry, 18x16; log barn 40x20; log stble 16x14; 1 fr dwlg hse, 1 stry, 20x20; round log kn, 14x12; log smoke hse 18x16; log milk hse 12x10

ODEL, John; Occupant: Wm. ODEL: Arnalls Chance 50A, Odels Addition 50A, Rooles's chance Resurveyed 148A+, pt Plains Barran 38A, Batchelors Choice 100A, Up and Down 75A, Philips Lot 38A, Old Mans Folly 50, pt Mount Pleasant 5A+; 1 old log barn, 1 stry, 20x14; log corn hse, 22x12; log stble 25x20; stone mill hse, 2 stry, 40x30; log smith shop 20x15, log barn 48x24

OWINGS, Samuel; 1775A; Timber Level, Lewis's Fancy, pt Harrisons Meadow, and pt of sundry other tracts; brk store hse, 1 stry, 24x20; brk & stone barn, 80x33; 2 log stbles each 16x12; 2 log shops each 20x20; waggon shed 34x16; brk mill hse, 2 stry, 50x44; brk mill hse 3 stry 45x45; brk mill hse, 3 stry 60x50; fr barn 60x24; round log dwlg hse, 2 stry, 16x14; hewd log dwlg hse, 1 stry 16x14; hewd log dwlg hse, 2 stry 16x14; round log dwlg hse, 2 stry, 26x20; hewd log dwlg hse, 2 stry, 26x18; log stble 16x14; log dwlg hse 24x16; log stble 14x12; brk dwlg hse, 2 stry, 28x17; log stble 20x16; log stble 24x24; 2 waggon sheds 80x10; hewd log store hse 16x14; log dwlg hse, 2 stry, 26x20

PENNY, Alexander; 106A; pt Soldiers Delight

PEDICORD, Adam; 46A; pt Fell Forest; hewd log dwlg hse, 1 stry, 16x14; log
hse 12x10; hewd log milk hse 10x10; round log corn hse 12x12; round log
tobacco hse 20x16; round log hse 20x16
PARKER, William; 132A; pt sundry tracts; hewd log dwlg hse, 1 stry, 22x18;
round log kn 14x12; round log barn 18x16; stone milk hse 10x8
PARRISH, Eliz'th; 65A; Stocksdale Neighbour; old log dwlg hse, 1 stry, 36x16
PARRISH, Edward; 90A; pt Clark's Park; round log dwlg hse, 1 stry, 20x16;
round log kn 16x12
PORTER, Philip; 50A; Porters Hall; 1 hewd log dwlg hse, 1 stry, 16x16
PATTERSON, William; pt Williams Resurvey & pt other tracts; 1 round log barn
20x20
PINDALL, John; Carline Forrest 98A, pt Wells Dividend 980A, pt Harrisons
Meadows 20A, Addition to Carline Forrest 1A+; 1 round log barn, 2 stry,
38x16; log stble 34x16; log stble 14x10
PORTER, Mury; 100A; pt McClains Hills &c.; 1 round log dwlg hse, 1 stry,
26x14; round log barn 26x16; round log stble 16x12
PEMBERTON, Wm. 80P; pt Level Union; hewd log dwlg hse, 2 stry, 26x24
PEMBERTON, Joshua; 122A; pt Level Union; round log dwlg hse, 1 stry, 28x18;
log hse 14x12; log smoke hse 10x10; log barn 24x16; log stble 18x10
PICKETT, George; 2A; pt Fells Forest; hewd log dwlg hse *, 2 stry, 22x16
with piazza 22x6, by add. shed 14x12; old still hse, 1 stry, 18x16; log
stble 18x10; old log hse 20x16
ROBERSON, William 15A; pt Carlisle Felix 5A, Stairs Field 10A; hewd log dwlg
hse, 1 stry, 20x18; old log hse, fit for fuel, 12x10
ROOLES, Ely (2 slaves); 356A; pt Jones Adventure 158A, William the Conquerer
91A, pt Stinchcombs Hills 43A, Rooles Care 25A; on Jones Adventure: fr
dwlg hse *, 1 stry, 28x24; log kn, 1 stry, 16x16; fr milk hse, 1 stry,
8x8; log barn, 1 stry, 36x20; round log stble 24x12
REED, Nelson; 199A; pt sundry tracts; round log dwlg hse *, 1 stry, 35x16;
old hewd log kn, 1 stry, 20x16 with add. of shed, 1 stry, 20x12; log
stble, 1 stry, 20x18; log hse 12x10; old round log barn 40x20; log corn
16x8; log stble 12x12; old log hse 16x12; log smoke hse, 1 stry, 12x12;
log poultry hse, 1 stry, 10x10
RISTER, Eve (2 slaves); ; 38A+; pt Chase, pt Three Sisters and pt Brotherly
Love; hewd log dwlg hse *, 2 stry, 28x18; hewd log kn, 1 stry, 22x15,
with add. of shed 22x9; log stble; 1 stry, 20x4; Occupant: Abraham LARSH:
old log dwlg hse *, 1 stry, 56x18, shed add. 1 stry, 56x6; log hse, 1
stry, 20x14
RISTER (REISTER), John, Sr.; Occupant: Catharine MABURY; 30A; pt Reisters
Desire & others tracts; on Reisters Desire: hewd dwlg hse *, 2 stry,
52x24, by brk add. 1 stry, 28x15; hewd log smoke hse, 1 stry, 10x10; fr
stble 18x12; horse shed 60x10
REISTER, John, Jr.; Occupant: John Reister , Sr; 63A; pt Reisters Desire; pt
of other tracts; on Reisters Deisre: round log dwlg hse *, 1 stry, 28x22;
log kn, 1 stry, 20x16; log poultry hse, 1 stry, 16x16; fr dwlg hse, 1
stry, 30x18; round log barn 70x28; log hse 26x18
RANDALL, Beal (2 slaves); 750A; pt Wells Manor 36A, pt Level Union 3A+, pt
North Hampton 100A, pt of sundry tracts 610A+; barn, 2 stry, 1 of stone,
other hewd logs 72x24; log stble 12x12; on Wells Manor: hewd log dwlg hse
*, 1 stry, 34x18; stone kn, 1 stry, 18x16; round log smoke hse, 1 stry,
18x16; Occupant: Michael ELDER: on Wells Manor: hewd log dwlg hse, 2

stry, 42x18; log poultry hse, 1 stry, 12 x12; Occupant: Mary GOSNELL: old
log dwlg hse, 1 stry, 22x18
RANDALL, Beal Thomas/RANDALL, Beal; 383A; Little Monster and pt of other
tracts; Occupants: John ALEXANDER, Tourance DUNAGAM, Geo. WHALEN (3
slaves); round log dwlg hse, 1 stry, 16x16; hewd log dwlg hse, 1 stry,
16x14; fr barn, 1 stry, 42x24, by add. of sheds 42x10; hewd log hse
16x12; fr hse 16x12; old fr stble 20x10; log hse 12x10; log hse 10x10; fr
dwlg hse *, 1 stry, 20x16, by add. of stone shed 20x12; hewd log kn, 1
stry, 18x14; round log negro hse, 1 stry, 20x16
RUTTER, Thomas; 15A; pt Beef's Hall
STOCKSDALE, John; Occupant: Joshua NORRIS; 2A; pt Simkins Repose; hewd log
dwlg hse, 1 stry, 20x16
STANSBURY, Caleb (2 slaves); 273A; pt of sundry tracts; hewd log dwlg hse, 1
stry, 16x16; round log kn 14x12; round log smoke hse 12x12; round log
barn 18x16; round log stble 16x10
STOCKSDALE, John (2 slaves); 236A; pt of sundry tracts; hewd log dwlg hse *,
1 stry, 22x20, stone shed add. 22x12; round log kn, 1 stry, 18x 15; log
smoke hse, 1 stry, 12x10; log milk hse, 1 stry, 8x6; log poultry hse, 1
stry, 10x8; log stble 24x10; log barn 36x20, shed add. 36x8
SATHERLEN, David (9 slaves); 50A; pt Soldiers Delight
STINCHCOMB, John; 47A; pt Stinchcombs Hill; round log dwlg hse, 1 stry,
20x16; round log kn 12x12
SCOTT, John; 298A; Powels Green Spring; round log dwlg hse *, 1 stry, 24x20;
round log kn, 1 stry, 24x20; round log smoke hse, 1 stry, 12x12; log
stble, 1 stry, 25x18
STOCKSDALE, Thomas; 240A; pt Additon to McClains Hills, 190A; pt Porters
Desire, 50A; hewd log dwlg hse, 1 stry, 20x16; round log barn 40x20
STOCKSDALE, Edward (8 slaves) 235A; Edward Industry 33A, Gosnells Range 50A,
Stocksdale Forrest 50A, Addition to Stocksdale Forrest 75A, pt Clarks
Park 16A, pt Addition to Stocksdale Forrest 11A; on Edwards Industry:
stone dwlg hse *, 1 stry, 28x25; hewd log kn, 1 stry, 20x16; hewd log
hse, 1 stry, 28x16; round log smoke hse, 1 stry, 24x12; round log corn
hse 16x10; round log barn 48x20; old log hse 24x16;
STONE, William (3 slaves); Occupant: Dennis HUTSON; 412A; Jones Prevention,
286A; pt New Tavern, 126A; on Jones Prevention: hewd log dwlg hse *, 1
stry, 32x22; stone smoke hse, 1 stry, 24x16; stone milk hse, 1 stry,
14x12; hewd log corn hse 20x18; hewd log barn 50x26; round log tobacco
hse 26x24
SUMMERS, John (4 slaves); 18A+; pt Two Tracts; hewd log dwlg hse *, 1 1/2
stry, 48x18, by add. of log shed, 1 stry, 20x12; brk milk hse, 1 stry,
12x10; fr hse, 1 stry, 10x8; round log smith shop 24x20; log stble 22x18;
log coal hse 26x12
STEWARD, Archibald and Co.; 1501A; pt Ridgely's Ambition, pt Gillead, pt
Cumber Chance and pt of sundry other tracts; Occupant: Robert CAMPBELL:
hewd log dwlg hse, 1 stry, 21x16; round log smoke hse 12x10; round log
milk hse 12x10; log barn 20x14; log corn 14x12; log stble 18x16; log
stble 18x16; Occupant: Matthew HARSNICK: on Ridgely's Addition; fr dwlg
hse *, 1 stry, 32x24; round log smoke hse, 1 stry, 10x10; Occupant:
Benjamin WILLIAMS: log dwlg hse, 1 stry, 16x14; log barn, 1 stry, 60x24;
saw mill, 2 stry, 1 of stone, other hewd logs, 38x24; saw mill 38x12; log
hse 18x16; log barn 40x26; Occupant: Jonathan DEAN: on Ridgely's
Ambition; stone dwlg hse *, 3 stry, 30x18; Occupant: Patrick KILLEY

(HILLEY): hewd log dwlg hse, 1 stry, 16x16; Occupant: John FROGG; hewd log dwlg hse, 1 stry, 22x20 with piazza 20x5; log kn, 14x12; fr hse 12x12; fr stble 32x12; fr barn 32x30

STINCHCOMB (1 slave); 215A; Addition to Bachelors hope and pt Absaloms Resolution; hewd log dwlg hse, 1 stry, 20x18; log barn 22x20; log stble 24x12

TUCKWORTH, Robert (1 slave); 1A; pt Soldiers Delight; hewd log dwlg hse, 1 stry, 18x16

THOMPSON, James; 550A; Orricks Return; Ocupant: George GUNNETT; round log dwlg hse, 1 stry, 18x16; log barn 42x24 with sheds at each end 24x12; log stble 36x12; Occupant: Jacob BARNHART; brk dwlg hse *, 2 stry, 42x22, by add. of stone shed, 1 stry, 16x14; hewd log kn, 1 stry, 18x16

TOWSON, Elizabeth; Willmotts Meadow 25A, Sheep Fold 12A

WALTERS, Eleanor (8 slaves); 186A; pt of sundry tracts; old log hse, 1 stry, 16x12; log hse 12x10; round log barn, 34x20; round log stble 26x20; fr dwlg hse *, 1 stry, 22x20 with piazza, 22x18, by add. of shed 22x10; round log kn, 1 stry, 36x14; stone smoke hse, 1 stry, 12x12

WARE, William (3 slaves); 127A; pt Jack's Delight and pt Mount Pleasant; log barn, 1 stry, 30x20; log hse 10x8; on Jacks Delight: old round log dwlg hse *, 1 stry, 20x17; round log kn, 1 stry 20x17; round log smoke hse, 1 stry 14x12; round log poultry hse, 1 stry, 16x14

WEARE, Thomas (11 slaves); Occupant: Robert WEARE; 459A; pt Jack's Delight, 130A; Fountain of Friendship, 40A; pt Gillcreist Discovery, 61A+; pt Raffo & Raffo Resurvey, 228A; hew log barn, 40x20; round log tobacco hse 24x18; hewd log dwlg hse, 1 stry, 20x18; round log kn 16x16; on Jack's Delight: stone dwlg hse *, 1 1/2 stry, 22x18, add. of logs, 1 stry, 20x16

WALTERS, Alexander of Samuel; 401A; pt of sundry tracts

WORTHINGTON, John Tolly; 103A; pt Spring Garden, 3A; pt Wells Manor, 100A

WALKER, Thomas Craddock Occupant: James THOMPSON; 153A+; pt Nicholson Manor; old log hse

WARD, John; Occupant: George MATTOX; 653A; pt New Tavern; pt Eagles Next; round log dwlg hse, 1 stry, 16x16; fr barn 36x25; log stble 18x12; log stble 14x12; fr hse, unfinished 24x18; on New Tavern: fr dwlg hse *, 1 stry, hip roof, 27x24; round log kn, 1 stry, 18x18; hewd log smoke hse, 1 stry, 12x12; stone milk hse, 1 stry, 12x10; hewd log hse, 1 stry, 20x16

WILLSON, Nicholas; 125A; Willsons's Adventure and pt Watson's Trust and others; hewd log dwlg hse, 1 stry, 24x15; log kn 14x14; log barn 20x20

WELLS, Thomas (10 slaves) 195A; Rogers Ridge & others; stone dwlg hse *, 1 stry, 40x20; round log kn, 1 stry, 20x16; round log smoke hse, 1 stry, 12x12; round log milk hse, 1 stry, 10x10; fr hse, 1 stry, 12x12; round log hse 16x12; log stble 20x10; log stble 22x17; log hse 12x10;

WEANT, Henry and LETTICK, George; 191A; pt Parrishes's Forrest; Edwards' Delight; pt Soldiers Delight; pt Brotherly Love; on pt Brotherly Love: stone dwlg hse *, 2 stry, with brk add. 40x27, by stone add., 1 stry, 17x17; stone smoke hse, 1 stry, 11x11; Occupants: John SWITSER, Jacob ROASE, George AYLOR; round log dwlg hse, 1 stry, 20x18; hewd log hse 20x16; stone mill hse, 2 stry, 40x28; log hse 14x14; hewd log dwlg hse, 1 stry, 24x16; round log barn 50x24; hewd log hse 16x16; round log hse 20x15; round log hse with add. of fr 40x20; brk dwlg hse 22x16; still hse, 2 stry, 1 of brk, other hewd logs 20x16; stble 20x16; log dwlg, 2 hses, 20x18

WALTERS, Jacob (18 slaves); 478A; pt Plains of Parran Res.; hewd log dwlg hse *, 1 stry, hip roof, 21x18 with piaza 21x12, by add. of shed 21x12; hewd log kn, 1 stry, 18x18; hewd log smoke hse, 12x10; round log negro hse, 1 stry, 20x16; round log corn hse, 1 stry, 16x12; round log barn, 1 stry, 40x18, by add. of shed 30x10; old log stble 24x12

WELLS, Charles; 198A; pt Good Will & William's Resurveyed; hewd log dwlg hse, 2 stry, 24x18, by add. of shed 24x10; round log smiths shop 18x18

WILLIAMS, Ann; 93A; hewd log dwlg hse, 1 stry, 20x16; by add. of shed 20x10; round log kn 14x12

WELLS, Benjamin; 424A; pt Airy Hills & Pleasant Springs; log stble, hewd log dwlg hse, 1 stry, weatherboarded, 24x18; log kn 20x16; old log barn 46x20; log stble 18x12; log hse 12x10

WEAVER, Christian; Occupant: Michael ELDER; 10A; pt Fells Forrest; hewd log dwlg hse *, 2 stry, 24x16, by add. of hewd log shed 24x10; log stble 24x12; horse shed 40x10

WON, Edward; 100A; pt Wons Chance Res. & pt of other tracts; round log dwlg hse, 1 stry, 22x16; round log kn 16x14; round log stble 16x12

WRIGHT, Jacob (2 slaves); 114A; Carters Choice & pt Wester Ogle; log dwlg hse, 1 stry, 16x16

WALKER, Charles; 522A; pt Harrisons Meadows & Tom's Choice; on Harrisons Meadows: old fr dwlg hse *, 1 stry, 30x18, log kn, 1 stry, 22x18; log barn thatched, 60x24; log stble 24x12; log poultry hse, 10x10

WORTHINGTON, Thomas (52 slaves); 5058A; pt East Lothan and pt of sundry other tracts; round log hse 20x12; log hse 40x24; log stble 28x25; log stble 50x16; stone dwlg hse *, 2 stry, 39x33, by add. of stone, 1 stry, 33x30; stone smoke hse, 1 stry, 16x15; stone milk hse, 1 stry, 18x14; log poultry hse, 1 stry, 18x12; log poultry hse, 1 stry, 12x10; Occupant: John WORTHINGTON: hewd log dwlg hse, 1 stry, 28x25; round log smoke hse, 1 stry, 14x12; round log kn, 1 stry, 28x14; Occupants: Baptist KNIGHT, John CARY, Boston FROG, Daniel BAILEY, Robert LYE, Richard DIVAUL; fr hse 32x16; hewd log barn 32x20; log hse 20x10 with fr shed 20x12; round log tobacco hse, 30x20; fr barn 30x20; round log tobacco hse 28x24; round log tobacco 24x20; log stble 30x10; round log dwlg hse, 1 stry, 24x20; round log dwlg hse 18x16; hewd log dwlg hse 20x16; round log kn 18x14; Occupant: John LEE: fr dwlg hse 20x18; Occupants: John LIDGET, Charles LEWIS, William HEMINGS, John LEE; round log dwlg hse 30x16; log barn 40x20; log hse 24x12; log dwlg hse 18x16; fr dwlg hse 24x20; Occupant John ROBERTSON: hewd log hse 16x16; log stble 14x12; Occupants: Ann BAILEY, Joseph WHISSEN, Joseph DAW; hewd log dwlg hse 16x16; round log dwlg hse 16x16; hewd log dwlg hse 22x18; round log dwlg hse 16x16; log hse 16x16; round log dwlg 16x16; log barn 24x20; log dwlg hse 20x16; log dwlg hse 16x14

ARMSTRONG, Joshua; 11A-93P; pt Hope, Tom's Choice; log dwlg hse 24x18, 1 stry, unfinished; log kn, 18x14, 1 stry; log cooper's shop 15x14, 1 stry; log & fr hse 20x14, 1 stry, unfinished

BAKER, Matthias; 10A; Pt Nemington; brk dwlg, 40x35, 2 stry; fr kn 20x14, 1 stry; old log stble, 16x12, 1 stry

BOONE, Elizabeth or heirs; 101A; Occupants: Solomon HARRIS;pt Parishes Range; log dwlg 22x16, 1 stry; add. fr 22x12, 1 stry; old log kn 18x16, 1 stry; old log hse 20x16, fit for fuel; old log stble 20x16; Occupant: John SHURER; pt Coles Adventure; fr dwlg 24x16, 1 stry

BURKHEAD, Solomon; 101A; Mount Royal; stone dwlg, 2 stry, 54x23, stone add. 2 stry, 31x18; round milk hse, 1 stry, 10 ft, fr smoke hse, 12x12, 1 stry; old log hse, 1 stry, 20x18; old fr 32x32, 1 stry; barns, 2 stry; 1 stone and other fr, 46x24, old brk hse; stone mill hse, 2 stry, 51x41

BLUFFORD, Wm.; 16A-120P; pt Parishes Range; log dwlg, 1 1/2 stry, 23x17 log add. 1 stry, 7x10; log stble, 1 stry, 18x14, add. 2 log shed 18x12, 1 stry

BOHANAN, James; 12A; pt Parishes Fear; fr dwlg, 2 stry, 30x22; piazza 30x8; add. fr 24x8, 1 stry, add. fr 2 stry 22x14, add fr 2 stry, 22x16, brk milk hse, 1 stry; garden hse 1 stry, 22x16; log stble 18x14

BUCKLER, Wm.; 10A; pt Parishes Fear; brk dwlg, 2 stry, 38x20; piazza 38x9; fr kn 1 stry, 13x11 1/2; fr, 1 stry, 8x8

BROWN, Dixon; dwlg; 60A-80P, pt Parish's Range; fr dwlg, 28x18 2 stry; fr add. 16x12; fr kn, 12x10, 1 stry; old log dwlg hse; log add. 20x15, 1 stry; fr stble, 18x14, 1 stry; fr hse 12x10, 1 stry; old log stble; old log barn, 20x10, 1 stry

BROOKS, Humphry; dwlg; 100A; pt Darbyshire; log dwlg hse, 18x18, 1 stry; log add., 14x16, 1 stry; log hse, 12x8; log hse, 16x16, 1 stry; log hse, 12x12, 1 stry

BARGER, Deter; dwlg; 3A; pt Tom's Choice, pt Coles Adventure; old log dwlg, 28x22, 1 stry; log shop, 24x18, 1 stry; log 12x10

BOWEN, Benj.; dwlg; 51A-2P; pt Bare Hills, pt Labrinth; log dwlg, 36x16, 1 stry; old log kn, 26x10, 1 stry; fr barn, 30x20; fr shed, 30x12, 1 stry

BARNET, Andrew; 164A (85 acres sold for taxes - 1805); pt Bonds Garrison, pt Cocks Pews Bullian; log dwlg, 40x20, 1 stry; piazza 40x6; log hse, 16x12, 1 stry & milk hse, 12x10, 1 stry; log hse, 22x14, 1 stry; old fr shed, 26x10, 1 stry; old log 28x18, 1 stry; log barn, 36x18, 1 stry

BOWLEY, Daniel; Occupant: John LONGLY; 50A; pt North Carolina

BROOKS, Joseph & Thos. BUCKINGHAM; dwlg; 100A; pt Hawkins Desire; log dwlg, 32x16, 1 stry; log meat hse, 12x12, 1 stry; log corn hse, 14x18; log 16x8, 1 stry; old log barn 30x16; log 12x12, 1 stry

BEAMS, Geo.; 213A; pt Darbishire; log dwlg, 52x22, 2 stry, fr add. 52x15, 1 stry, log add. 16x16, 1 stry; brk milk hse, 12x10, 1 stry; smoke hse, 12x12, 1 stry; log stble and some fr 32x16, 2 stry, 4 fr sheds; old log barn, 72x12, fit for fuel

BOONE, Sarah; 64A; pt Edward and Wills Valley & Hills; old fr dwlg, 32x28, 1 stry; old log kn, 20x16, 1 stry; old fr smoke hse, 12x12, 1 stry; fr milk hse, 12x88, 1 stry

BOONE, John; dwlg; 132A; pt Edward and Wills Valley & Hills; old fr dwlg, 24x16, 1 stry, 1/2 the roof off; log kn, 20x12, 1 stry; fr smoke hse, 18x12, 1 stry; old log stble, 24x12,1 1/2 stry, roof along off; old log hse, 16x9, 1 stry

BUCHANAN, Andrew; 9A+; pt Octontorly
BARTHOLOMEW, Joseph; 92A; pt Pimblico; log dwlg, 28x15, 2 stry; log add. 20x15, 1 stry; piazza, 48x7, add. fr 24x16, 1 stry; still hse, 43x23, 1 1/2 stry, stone, log add. fr. 12x10, 1 stry; log stble, 32x20, 1 stry
CARROLL, Henry; Occupant: Rudolph HOOK; dwlg; 100A; pt Littalony; old log dwlg, 24x18, 1 stry, stone add. 18x16, 1 stry; stone milk hse, 15x14, 1 stry; old log 1 1/2 stry, 18x14
CARROLL, Henry; Occupant: Michael KRANER; 110A; pt Littalony
CARROLL, Henry; Occupant: Robert ALDER; dwlg; 127A; pt Littalony; old log dwlg, 20x16, 1 stry; old log hse, 20x16, 1 stry; 2 old log bldgs, 14x12, 1 stry
CARROLL, Henry; Occupant: Thomas RITTER; dwlg; 100A, pt Littalony; log dwlg, 1 stry, hip roof, 20x16; log hse, 11x11, 1 stry; log stble, 18x14, 1 stry; stone meat hse, 14x11; old log barn, 36x20, 1 stry; old log barn, 18x15, 1 stry
CARROLL, Henry; Occupant: John BELL; dwlg; 100A; pt Littalony; old log dwlg, 44x16, 1 stry; log barn, 36x16, 1 stry; add. shed, 24x10
CARROLL, James, Esq.; Occupant: Edward TOOGOOD; 60A; pt Howard's Discovery, Georgia, Newtown, and Forge Land; old stone dwlg, 40x30, 1 stry; old fr not enclosed, 60x35, old log & old fr 24x18, 1 stry, fit for fuel; old log hse, 20x15
CARROLL, Margaret; Georgia; old log hse, fit for fuel, 30x24, 1 stry; old stone hse, 16x14, 1 stry; old fr 15x15, 1 stry; old fr 47x20, 1 stry; old fr barn, 38x22, 1 stry; old stone stble, 45x24, 1 stry; old log hse, 32x22, 1 stry; old fr stble, 24x16, 2 stry; old stone potato hse, 15x12, 1/2 stry; old log hse, 28x16, 1 stry; old log hse, 18x16, 1 stry; stone ice hse, 25 ft deep & 16 ft diam.; stone stble, 43x26, 1 stry, 25x25; stone corn hse, 18x16, 1 1/2 stry; stone press hse, 45x34, 1 stry; fr hse, 16x11, 1 stry; old fr corn hse, 21x16, 1 stry; millers hse, old fr 44x16, 1 stry, add. brk shed, 44x16, 1 stry; old stone blacksmith shop, 58x24, 1 stry; old cooper shop, brk, 16x13, 1 stry; brk mill hse, 26x26, 2 stry, pair of stones; stone mill hse, 50x46, 3 stry, 3 pairs of stones
CHAMBERLAIN, Sam.; Occupant: John FISHPAUGH; dwlg; 3A-93P; pt Hope, pt Toms Choice; fr dwlg, 24x12, 1 stry, log add., 12x12, 1 stry
CHAMBERLAIN, Sam. and CHAMBERLAIN, Robins; Occupant: John ORAM; dwlg; 1A; pt Tom's Choice; old log dwlg, 20x15, 1 stry; old log hse, 20x16, 1 stry (Oram); fr barn, 2 stry, 40x18; fr pourter, 1 stry, 16x12
CARROLL, Margaret; 848A; pt Georgia; brk dwlg, 2 stry, 46x36; piazza, 18x8; brk add., 1 stry, 34x18; add. brk & stone 51x21, 1 stry; add. brk shed 28x8, 1 stry; green hse 26x26, 1 stry; brk shed, 39x24, 1 stry; brk wash hse, 26x26; stone smoke & milk hse
COOPER, Stephen; dwlg; 8A-112P; pt Hope, pt Tom's Choice; fr dwlg, 36x12, 1 stry, posts in the ground, unfinished; fr stble, 15x14, 1 stry, posts in ground, unfinished
CLEM, Wm.; 70A; 40A pt Rogers Enlargments, 30A pt Parishes Fear; fr dwlg, 26x19, 2 stry; piazza, 26x6; stone add., 22x19, 1 stry; fr smoke hse, 15x12, 1 stry; stone milk hse, 12x12, 1 stry; summer hse, 15x15; fr 10x10, 1 stry; log stble, 15x14, 1 stry
CONNOR, Wm.; dwlg; 1A; pt Newtown; fr dwlg, 18x16, 1 stry, unfinished
COCKEY, John; 135A; pt Blunder; Occupant: Benj. LEMMON; fr dwlg, 2 stry, 48x48, unfinished; 2 log hses, 12x14, 1 stry; log barn, 48x18, 1 stry; Occupant: James BROOKS: old log hse, 24x18, 1 stry; stone shed, 18x10

CARSON, Henry; dwlg; 120P; pt Newington; fr dwlg, 1 stry, 16x12
COLTER, Alex.; 20A (2 acres sold for taxes - 1805); pt Parishes Range
CHANY, Zephaniah; 2A; pt Newington; fr dwlg, 28x16, 1 1/2 stry, fr add.
16x12, 1 stry; 1/2 add. piazza, 20x5; log stble, 36x11, 1 stry
DONLEY, Thos. and SEEKAMP Co.; 98A; pt Milford; fr dwlg, 32x20, 2 stry; fr
add. 16x12, 1 1/2 stry; stone milk hse, 12x12, 1 stry; old log hse 30x20,
1 1/2 stry; old shed, 100x12, 1 stry; old mill hse, 34x24, 2 stry; hip
roof old saw mill, 50x12, 1 stry
DAVIS, Jacob; dwlg; 79A; pt Darbishire; log dwlg, 48x12, 1 stry; old log
30x20, fit for fuel
DEMMITT, John; dwlg; 2A; pt Coles Adventure; old log dwlg, 14x12, 1 stry,
fit for fuel; old fr dwlg, 14x12, fit for fuel
DIXON, John; 2A, pt Chatsworth; fr dwlg, 22x16; 2 stry fr add., 18x12, 1
stry; piazza, 22x7; fr 18x14, 1 1/2 stry
DORSEY, Col. John; 219A; pt Chatsworth, Bonds Plesant Hills, Parrishes Fear,
and Georgia; fr dwlg, 48x22, 2 stry piazza each side 8x7; stone add.,
40x16, 1 stry; add. stone smoke hse, 20x18; milk hse, 14x14, 1 stry
DORSEY, Col. John; Oakly, being pt Chatsworth; fr hse, 18x12, 1 stry; old fr
10x10, 1 stry; ice hse, 16 ft diam.; stone & brk 16x14, stone & brk
entry, 18x6; fr barn, 1 stry, 58x30; fr carriage hse, 1 stry, 16x16; nail
manufactory of stone, 1 stry, 72x30,; fr add., 1 stry, 50x26; stone hse,
1 stry, 24x20; old log hse, 20x20, 1 stry; log hse, 14x12, 1 stry; stone
hse, 16x16, 1 stry; log hse, 26x16, 1 stry
DUNKLE, Geo.; 3A; pt Parishes Range
DAWSON, Philemon; 11A; pt Newington; log dwlg, 26x24, 1 stry, hip roof,
piazza 54x8; fr add., 18x16, 1 stry; fr add. 50x15, 1 stry; brk add.
26x14; log hse 15x12, 1 stry
DICHAUBIN, Lewis; Occupant: John BALEY; dwlg; 331A; pt Cromwells Deer Park;
brk dwlg, 1 stry, 28x26; add. brk, 1 stry, 14x14; add. logs, 1 stry,
24x18; brk milk hse 10x10; fr poultry, 1 stry, 24x16, 1 stry; log dwlg, 1
stry, 20x16; old log, 1 stry, 16x16; fr barn, 1 stry, 36x28, add. fr
shed, 1 stry, 18x8; log stble
EVANS, Walter; 24A+; pt Hope, pt Pimblico; fr dwlg, 20x16, unfinished, 2
stry; log hse, 13x10, 1 stry; fr stble, 2 stry, 24x18
ETTING, Solomon; 150A; pt Parrishes Fear; fr dwlg, 26x17, 2 stry; add. fr
28x24, 1 stry; piazza, 54x10; piazza 27x7; sm fr 1 stry 14x12; brk milk
hse 12x9, 1 stry; fr gardener hse, 10x10, 1 stry
ELLICOTT & Co.; dwlg; 170A; pt Helms Rich Newtown and other tracts; log
dwlg, 16x16, 1 stry; add old fr shed; plank 24x16; piazza 16x8 old log
kn, 13x12, 1 stry; old fr for blacksmith shop, 16x14, 1 stry; brk mill
hse, 80x40, 4 stry, 4 pair of stone; mill hse, 3 stry, 1 of stone and 2
of fr, 33x26, unfinished
ECLEBURGAR, Martin; Occupant: John WARD; dwlg; 9A; pt Octon Torley
(Auchenteroly); dwlg, 1 stry, 15x15, add. fr 1 stry, 12x10; log milk hse,
1 stry, 9x9; log barn, 1 stry, 21x17
ETTING, Reuben; pt Octontorly (Auchenteroly); fr dwlg, 2 stry, 24x20; add.
fr 20x18, 1 stry,; piazza, 44x6; fr stble, 1 stry, 20x16 add. fr 1 stry,
16x9
FITE, Peter; Occupant: Geo. RISTINE; dwlg; 103A; Jones's Farm, Oragnams
Choice; stone dwlg, 20x18, 1 stry; log kn, 22x20, 1 stry; log dwlg,
32x14, 1 stry; brk mill hse, 34x32, 2 stry; saw mill fr, 40x10, 1 stry;
stone barn, 46x30, 2 stry; old log hse, 1 stry, 26x16

FALLS, Dr. Moses; 45A; pt Parrishes Fear; fr dwlg, 2 stry, 32x20; piazza, 32x10; add. fr 10x6, 1 stry; add. fr 24x19, 2 stry; piazza 24x19, unfinished; fr stble, 49x16, 1 stry

GARDNER, Hannah, widow; Occupant: Dennis PEARE; dwlg; 83A; pt North Caroline; dwlg hse, 28x18, 2 stry,; a wing at each end, 1 stry, 18x14; shed 1 stry, 14x14, add. frame 14x14; log hse, 1 stry, 20x20; 7 log hses; old log dwlg, 36x16, 1 stry

GOUGH, Henry; Occupant: Thomas WHITE; dwlg; 133A; pt Hope; old log dwlg, 22x18, 1 stry; log hse, 14x12, 1 stry

GRANT, John, dwlg; 40P; pt Coles Adventure; log dwlg, 18x14, 1 stry

GITTINGS, James; 150A; pt Parishes Range

GREEN, Isaac; dwlg; 150A+; pt Merrymans Pasture; log dwlg, 1 stry, 18x16, add. logs 1 stry, 18x8; log kn, 1 stry, 16x12; add. fr shed, 1 stry, 12x12; stone milk, 1 stry 14x12; fr stble, 1 stry, 30x25; saw mill, fr, 1 stry, 54x14

GRIFFITH, Osborn; pt Parrishes Range; fr dwlg, 2 stry, 24x19; piazza, 24x7 1/2; add. fr, 1 stry, 20x16; log hse, 14x12, 1 stry; fr 1 stry, 10x8

GRIVE, Geo.; dwlg; 99A; pt Ensigns Grove; log dwlg hse, 1 stry, 18x14

HALL, Caleb; 50A; pt Constitution Hills; brk dwlg, 1 stry, hip roof, 18x17; old fr stble, 1 stry, 30x16; old log hse, 1 stry, 18x14, fit for fuel; fr hse, 1 stry, 20x16; log hse, 14x12

HOLLINGSWORTH, Sam. & Thos.; Occupant: Robt. ALEXANDER; 110A; pt Rogers Enlargement; fr dwlg, 1 1/2 stry, 24x20; add. fr 1 stry, 24x20; piazza, 24x6; log hse, 1 stry; stone mill hse, 2 stry, 48x32; stone stble, 1 1/2 stry, 1 of stone, 1/2 of logs, 31x22; add. stone 17 1/2x14

HOFFMAN, Adam; Occupant: Geo. COLDWELL; dwlg; 7A+; pt Coles Adventure, pt Hope; fr dwlg, 2 stry, 31x16; add. 14x12, 1 stry fr; stble, 18x16; 1 stry 16x16; old fr dwlg, 1 stry, 28x24; fr dwlg, 16x14, 1 stry; fr smith shop, 1 stry, 18x10; log stble, 14x12

HOOK, Rudolph; 23A+; pt Labrinth

HOOK, Jacob of Rudolph; 47A+; pt Labrinth

HOOK, Frederick; 15A; pt Cockpin Choice, Miller's Choice; log dwlg hse, 2 stry, 22x16; Occupant: Roger CORD; log dwlg, 16x12, 1 stry

HOOK, Jacob of Jacob; dwlg; 66A (10 acres sold for taxes - 1805); pt Enlargement; log dwlg hse, 1 stry, 20x17; old log kn, 20x18, 1 stry; log smoke hse, 1 stry, 12x12, old log stble, 16x14, 1 stry

HOOK, Jacob of Joseph; dwlg; 1A; pt Coles Adventure; log dwlg, 2 stry, 28x20, add. logs, 1 stry, 20x20; old log hse, 24x18, 1 stry;

HOOD, Thomas; dwlg; 50A; pt Edward & Wills Valleys and Hills; log dwlg hse, 1 stry, 20x16; add. fr 1 stry, 13x13; fr smoke hse, 1 stry, 12x11; old log stble, 1 stry, 16x12; mill hse, 2 stry, 36x30, 1 of stone the other fr; saw mill, 1 stry, 45x12

HAMBLETON, Nathaniel; 80P; pt Newtown

HENNICK, Christopher; dwlg; 1A-80P; pt Coles Adventure; old log dwlg, 2 stry, 25x20; add. fr, 1 stry, 25x12

HOOK, Dr. Jacob, Sr.; 19A; pt Coles Adventure; fr dwlg, 2 stry, 30x20; fr add., 1 stry, 30x10; piazza, 18x7; old stble, 1 stry, 19x18; add. logs, 1 stry, 30x18

HUSSELBOOK, John; 184A+; pt Coles Adventure, pt Constitution Hill and Nicholson Delight; brk dwlg, 2 stry, 40x35; add. brk, 1 stry, 45x16, brk milk hse, 9x9, 1 stry; fr barn, 1 1/2 stry, 40x28; log still hse, 36x22, 1 1/2 stry; log stble, 2 stry, 22x16; log hse, 17x10, 1 stry

HOLLINGSWORTH, Zebulon, Esq.; 108A; pt Parrishes Range; fr, 1 stry, 14x11; stone hog hse, 1 stry, 17x9, fr only enclosed in 2 stry 26x18

HOLLINGSWORTH, Zebulon, Esq.; Occupant: Geo. REED; dwlg; 62A; Mt. Pleasant & Norwoods Chance; old log dwlg, 1 stry, 20x18

HOLLINGSWORTH, Zebulon; 82A; pt Constitution Hill & pt Labrinth

JOHNSON, Dr. Edw.; Occupant: Harmanus ALDRICK; 20A; pt Coles Adventure; log dwlg, 2 stry, 24x14; piazza on each side, 24x8; add. fr 1 stry, 16x16; brk smoke hse, 2 stry, 12x12

JOHNSON, Dr. Edw.; Occupant: Geo. GARDNER; 146A+; pt Coles Adventure, pt Pimblico; fr dwlg, 2 stry, 32x22; fr kn, 2 stry, 18x14; brk milk hse, 1 stry, 14x14; log hse, 1 stry, 18x11; poultry hse, 1 stry, 10x10

HART, Philip; pt Newington; fr dwlg, 2 stry, 42x14; add. fr 22x14; add. fr 12x10, 1 stry each

JOHNSON, Thomas; 330A; Turkey Cock-Hall, pt Poor Jamaicaman's Plague and Beals Discovery; fr dwlg, 1 stry, 44x22, piazza on both sides, 44x8; log hse, 1 stry, 16x14; log hse, 1 stry, 15x12; log hse, 1 stry, 12x8; log barn, 2 stry, 34x32

JEFFRY, Richard; dwlg; 1A; pt Tom's Choice; log dwlg, 1 stry, 24x16; old log hse, 1 stry, 18x14

JONES, Thomas; Occupant: Joshua LINDSEY; 498A; pt Gallypots Level; old log dwlg, 1 1/2 stry, 26x20; old log kn, 1 stry, 16x16; old log hse, 1 stry, 18x14; log stble, 1 1/2 stry, 26x14

JONES, Richard; 7A+ (4 acres sold for taxes - 1805); pt Chatsworth; fr dwlg, 2 stry, 30x16; add. fr 1 stry, 32x16; piazza, 72x5; summer hse, fr, 2 stry; 20x20, other 10x10; fr poultry hse, 1 stry, 10x10; fr stble, 1 stry, 30x18

JOHNSON, Ann, widow; and heirs; Occupant: Mead JARVIS; pt Turners Hall 100A; log dwlg, 2 stry, 20x10; add. logs 20x10, 1 stry; Wm. MOLES; pt Turners Hall 50 A; log dwlg, 20x16, 1 stry

JOHNSON, Ann, widow; and heirs; Occupant: Michael ARMSTRONG; 48A; pt Turners Hall; dwlg log, 1 stry, 44x20; old log hse, 1 stry, 20x16; stone hse, 15x13, 1 stry

JOHNSON, Ann, widow or heirs; 197A; Pleasant Green; fr dwlg, 1 stry, 28x24; old log kn, 1 stry, 20x20; old log smoke hse, 1 stry, 16x14; old log milk hse, 12x8, 1 stry

KRAMER, Michael; dwlg; 98A; pt Angels Fortune, pt Germany, pt Cooks Adventure; log dwlg, 1 stry, 20x16; log hse, 1 stry, 36x16, 2 log hses each 1 stry, 16x20; 2 log hses, 1 stry each, 14x12

KEENER, Christian; 7A+, pt Chatsworth; fr dwlg, 2 stry, 24x16; piazza, 24x7; add. fr 1 stry, 24x14; add. fr 1 stry 34x12; brk smoke hse, 1 stry, 10x8; fr barn, 2 stry, 26x16; fr carriage hse, 1 stry, 14x14; fr 1 stry 12x12

LESTOR, Wm.; 1A+, pt Newtown; brk dwlg, 1 stry, unfinished, 33x23; add. log 1 stry, 9x8

LALAOURAUDAIS, Auguste Joseph; 71A; pt Laberinth; log dwlg, 1 stry, 40x16; piazza, 20x6; log barn, 1 1/2 stry, 38x18

LEE, George; 1A; pt North Carolina; log dwlg, 2 stry, 26x20; fr 1 stry, 10x10

LONGLEY, Elizabeth, widow, and heirs; dwlg; 50A; pt North Carolina; log dwlg, 1 stry, 20x15; add. logs, 20x15, 1 stry; piazza, 20x6; log barn, 1 stry, 50x18; old log hse, 1 stry, 20x14; old log 1 stry, 20x14; old log 1 stry, 10x8

LANDAIS, Francis; 27A+; pt Pimblico; log dwlg, 1 stry, 18x15; add. logs; log kn, 1 stry, 15x12; log poultry hse, 1 stry, 15x12; 1 stry 34x15; piazza, 32x8; add. fr, 1 stry, 20x8; piazza, 52x8; log barn, 1 stry, 36x17
LOWE, Barbara; Occupant: Wm. PRINE; dwlg; 2A; pt Coles Adventure; log dwlg, 2 stry, 22x16; add. logs, 1 stry, 22x16
LEWIS, Henry; dwlg; 45A (1 acre sold for taxes - 1805); Lewis's Purchase; log dwlg, 1 stry, 20x16; log, 1 stry, 12x8; log barn, 1 stry, 30x16
LEEF, John; Occupant: Geo. ROADS; dwlg; 36A+
JUDEA, Nicholas; Occupant: Thos. FLAGG; pt Coles Adventure; old log dwlg, 2 stry, 26x20; add. fr 1 stry, 16x12; old log and fr 1 stry, 20x20;; add. shed, 1 stry, 28x10
LEVY Thomas, dwlg; 2A+; pt Hope; log dwlg, 1 stry, 16x16; log stble, 1 stry, 16x10
LONGLEY, Sam.; dwlg; 121A; pt Constitution Hills; log dwlg, 1 1/2 stry, 14x12
LAWSON, Sarah, widow; 300A; pt Newington
MUCKLEVANE, Alexander; dwlg; 120P; pt Newington; fr dwlg, 1 stry, 36x12
MUCKLEVANE, Alex., Jr.; Occupant: Henry FRANKLEBERRY; dwlg; 7A (1 acre sold for taxes - 1805); pt Parishes Fear; fr dwlg, 1 stry, 16x16
MERRYMAN John of John; Occupant: Richard WATTS; dwlg; 264A; pt North Carolina; old log dwlg, 1 1/2 stry, 34x24; add. logs, 16x14; old log 1 stry, 20x16; old log barn, 1 stry, 30x20; old log stble, 1 stry, 20x17; old log 1 1/2 stry, 22x16
McCOLLASTER, Jehue; dwlg; 71A; pt Darbishire
McCLELLAN, John; dwlg; 122A; pt Parishes Fear, pt Venture; fr dwlg, 1 stry, 26x26; piazza, 26 x 7 1/2; old fr kn, 1 stry, 24x16; stone smoke hse, 1 stry, 14x13; fr milk hse, 1 stry, 10x10; old log dwlg, 1 stry, 43x16; add. logs, 1 stry, 14x11; log stble, 2 stry, 22x18
McKINLEYS, Robert & brothers; 80A (3 acres sold for taxes - 1805); pt Ensigns Grove
McKAIN, John; Occupant: John SWITESER; dwlg; 8A (1 acre sold for taxes - 1805); pt Parishes Fear
MINSHIRE, John; dwlg; 9A+; pt Rogers Enlargement
MOONNER, Kneffy; dwlg; 4A+; pt Tom's Choice; log dwlg, 1 stry, 18x12
MUMMEY, John; Occupant: Henry INLOC; dwlg; 37A; pt Toms Choice; pt Hope and Pimblico; log dwlg, 1 stry, 24x20; add. fr,1 stry, 20x16; add. fr 2 stry, 20x16; piazza add. fr kn,1 stry, 12x10; stone milk hse, 1 stry, 10x8; log smoke hse, 1 stry, 10x10
MERRYMAN, John of Samuel; Occupant: Benj. ORAM; dwlg; 64A; Merryman's Neighbour, Sams Meadows
MERRYMAN, Sam., Sr.; 177A; pt Cromwells Chance; pt Organs Forrest; log dwlg, 1 stry, 24x18; add. fr, 1 stry; 18x12; log kn, 1 stry, 36x17; stone smoke hse, 1 1/2 stry, 18x16; stone milk hse, 1 stry, 8x8
MERRYMAN, Caleb; 231A; pt Pay My Debts, pt Peace & Good Neighbourhood, pt Tom's Choice, pt Organs Forest, pt Nicholsons Delight; fr barn, 1 stry, 30x24; log stble, 1 stry, 60x16; log corn hse, 1 stry, 18x14; John GOLDSBOROUGH: fr dwlg hse, 1 stry, 18X14; Richard HULL: log coopers shop, 18x14; log dwlg hse; Luke MERRYMAN; 1 stry 18x14; old log hse fit for fUel, 14x12; Michael HORN; log dwlg hse, 1 stry, 18x14/Assessed Samuel MERRYMAN
McCLELLAN, John; 148A+; pt Parishes Fear

KIMMEL, Anthony; pt Newington; fr dwlg, 2 stry, 48x16; add. fr, 1 stry, 20x12; piazza, 12x7; pt Newington; fr dwlg, hip roof, 18x12; add. fr 1 stry, 12x10

McKAIN, John, and Leonard HELMS's heirs; Occupants: Joseph BURTON/James TOBIT/Wm. MORRIS; dwlgs: 1/1/1; 117A (4 acres sold for taxes - 1805); pt Parishes Range, Prospect Hills; log dwlg hse, 1 stry, 20x16; old log dwlg hse, 1 stry, 18x16; old log dwlg hse, 1 stry, 16x16

NORWOOD, Elijah; dwlg; 3A+; pt Tom's Choice; log dwlg hse, 1 stry, 20x14, log add. 1 stry, 18x12; old log shop 20x16

OLER, Philip; 1A; pt Newington; fr dwlg, 2 stry, 30x12

PEREGOY Joseph; dwlg; 20A; pt Parishes Range, pt Nicholsons Delight; log dwlg, 1 1/2 stry, 18x16, add. shed, 1 stry, 18x8; piazza 18x8; log hse 1 1/2 stry 18x16; shed 1 stry 16x10; log shop, 1 stry, 24x18; log stble 1 stry, 18x16

PRATT, Frederick; 2A; pt Chatsworth, pt Newington; fr dwlg, 1 stry, 30x16; piazza, 30x7 add. fr 1 stry, 14x12; fr 1 stry, 16x12

PEREGOY, Joseph; dwlg; 2A; pt Tom's Choice; log dwlg, 1 1/2 stry, 18x14; add. fr, 1 stry, 18x12

PIERCE, Humphry; 14A; pt Parishes Fear; fr dwlg, 2 stry, 27x20; piazza 20x4, 2 stry, add. fr 1 stry 18x16, add. fr 1 stry 20x16, add. fr 1 stry, 2x16; entry 16x12 and piazza 20x6; fr kn, 1 stry, 24x16; brk milk hse, 1 stry, 14x13; 2 poultry fr, 1 stry each 10x10; fr barn 1 stry, 20x16 add. fr shed 1 stry, 26x9

PRINGLE, Mark; Occupant: Henry WILLIS; 212A; pt Cromwells Park, pt Laberinth; fr dwlg, 2 stry 48x18, add. logs 24x18, 1 stry, add. stone, 1 stry, 30x18; brk milk hse, 1 stry, 11x11, smoke hse, 1 stry 24x12; log barn, 1 stry, 40x18; log corn hse, 1 stry, 16x12; stble, 1 stry 32x10; log smoke hse, 1 stry, 14x12

PRICE, Martha, widow; Occupants: Jesse WALKER and Rich. PRICE; 203A; pt Toms Choice, Cromwells Chance, Absoloms Meadows; old log and fr dwlg, 1 stry, 36x26; old log kn, 1 stry, 16x12, add. logs 1 stry, 16x12; log smoke hse, 1 stry, 12x10; log milk hse, 1 stry, 7x6; log dwlg, 1 stry, 18x12; fr dwlg, 1 stry, hip roof, 27x18; log shop, 1 stry; old log barn 12x8; corn hse 20x16

PHILIP, Conley; 80P; Newtown

PECK, Charles; 60A; pt Parishes Range

PRICE, Richard; 5A; pt Hope

PRICE, John; dwlg; 25A; pt Tom's Choice; log dwlg, 1 stry, 16x12

PRICE, Amon; Occupants: Jacob FRUSTY and Adam AMOS; 72A; pt Tom's Choice; fr dwlg, 1 stry, 25x16; log kn, 1 stry, 14x13; log barn, 1 stry, 36x20; log dwlg, 1 stry, 16x14; log dwlg, 1 stry, 20x16

PUNTNEY, Sarah & Lydia; Occupant: Thos. WEFFIN; dwlg; 29A+ (1 acre sold for taxes - 1805); Punteney's Chance; old log dwlg hse 1 1/2 stry, 15x13; old log stble, 1 stry, 10x9

TAGART and PENNINGTON; 33A; pt Ensigns Grove

ROGERS, Philip; Occupants: Joseph WRIGHT; pt Bonds Garrison & Pleasant Hills; stone dwlg, 1 stry, 30x16, log kn, 1 stry, 16x12; log stble, 1 stry, 12x10; Rich. BROWN; pt Bonds Garrison; brk dwlg, 2 stry, 52x40; add. brk, 1 stry, 20x14; brk barn, 2 stry, 80x32

READ, John; Occupant: Philip CONLEY; dwlg; 1A; pt Newtown; fr dwlg, not finished, 1 stry, 18x14; log cooper shop, 1 stry, 28x16

JOHNSON, Sam., Esq.; Andrew ALBRIGHT; 100A(?); pt Coles Adventure; fr dwlg, 1 stry, 19x19 add. logs 1 stry, 26x7; old fr 1 stry, 16x16; old log bank hse, 1 stry, 20x20

RUTTER, Thos., Jr.; Peter PECKINS and Wm. SYBERRY; 179A; pt Laberinth, pt Shoemakers Hall, pt Bare Hills; log dwlg, 1 1/2 stry, 24 x18; log dwlg, 1 stry, 20x16; old log 1 stry, 14x12

RUTTER, Thos. Sr.; 326A+; Timber Ridge, Short Leg Tom, Washington & Ritters Addition; Occupants: Jacob HOOK, son of Rudolph, John PARISH; log dwlg, 1 stry, hip roof, 24x18, add. stone, 1 stry, 34x17; log smoke hse, 1 stry, 12x12; log kn, 1 stry, 16x16; log poultry 1 stry, 12x10; log dwlg, 1 stry, 30x14; fr barn, 1 stry, 40x37, fit for fuel; old log 1 stry, 20x12; old log 1 stry, 20x12, fit for fuel; log corn hse, 1 stry, 20x12

RYNECKER, Geo.; 125A; pt Bonds Garrison; pt Darbyshire; fr dwlg, 1 stry, 32x16; add. logs 1 stry, 20x16; fr 1 stry, 12x12; log barn 1 1/2 stry, 38x20, has one pt fr

RUTTER, Henry; dwlg; 19A (1 acre sold for taxes - 1805); Monks Discoverys; fr dwlg, 2 stry, 22x18; log hse, 2 stry, 24x20

RITTER, Thomas; 23A+ (1 acre sold for taxes - 1805); pt Laberinth

OWINGS & ROGERS Co.; Occupant: John WOODYARD; dwlg; 321A; pt Pimblicoe; log dwlg, 1 stry, 18x14

RIDGELY, John, Esq.; Occupant: Jacob WILDERMAN and Joshua ORAM; 2 dwlgs; 448A; pt Pay My Debts; log dwlg, 1 stry, 32x14; fr barn, 1 1/2 stry, 40x22; fr stble, 1 stry, 30x22; Log corn hse, 1 stry, 20x16; old log 1 stry, 20x16; old log stble, 1 stry, 20x12, fit for fuel; log dwlg, 1 stry, 16x14

RIDGELY, John, Esq.; Occupant: Geo. WHITE; dwlg; 2A; pt Tom's Choice; log dwlg, 1 stry, 22x16

ROGERS, Nicholas; 2 dwlgs; 624A; Octin Torely (Auchtneterely); Occupant: David INLOC; Log dwlg, 1 stry, 20x18; log shed, 1 stry, 20x12; old log 1 stry, 10x8; old shed 1 stry, 36x12, fit for fuel; Occupant: Patience FLIN; log dwlg, 1 stry, 18x16; barn 2 1/2 stry; brk & fr; log stble 1 1/2, 24x18; old fr barn, 1 stry, 32x24

STEWART, David; Occupant: Anthony CONLEY; dwlg; 100A; pt Jackson Chance; log dwlg, hip roof, 22x16; log kn, 1 stry, 32x16; old log, 1 stry, 12x10; old log 1 stry, 10x8

STEVENSON, John; dwlg; 147A; pt Laberinth, pt Edward and Wills Valleys & Hills; dwlg, 1/2 fr, 1/2 logs, hip roof, 1 stry, 34x16; log smoke hse, 1 stry, 8x8; stone milk hse, 1 stry, 10x10, old log 1 stry, 22x20, fit for fuel; barn, 2 stry, 32x30, 1 stry fr & the other stone

STEVENSON, Mordecai; 185A+ (110 acres sold for taxes - 1805); pt Laberinth, pt Enlargement; log dwlg, 1 stry, 20x16; log poultry, 1 stry, 18x12; log stble, 1 stry, 16x12; log barn 1 stry, 36x24; Occupant: John Ed. WILLIAMS: log dwlg, 1 stry, 18x16

SMITH, John; 69A; pt Constitution Hills

SPICER, Valentine; 50A; Spicer Stoney Hill

STAUFFER, Henry; 4A; pt Newington; brk dwlg, 2 stry, 40x18; piazza, 1 stry, 14x7, add. fr 1 stry, 20x16; fr stble, 1 stry, 20x16

SCROGGS, Ann, widow; 80P; pt Newtown

ROGERS Nicholas; Occupant: Thos. BROTHERTON; Octin Torely (Auchenteroly); fr dwlg, 1 stry, 38x18 add. fr shed, 1 stry, 38x18; fr kn, 1 stry, 22x20; log smoke hse, 1 stry, 16x16; fr milk hse, 1 stry, 10x8

Middlesex Hundred

SMITH, Job; 6A; pt Parishes Range; fr dwlg, 2 stry, 18x16; stone milk hse, 1 stry, 8x8
SMITH, Rob., Esq., 38A, pt Parishes Fear; fr dwlg, 2 stry, 22x18, add. piazza, 1 stry, 22x6, add. fr, 1 stry, 20x9, add. fr 1 stry, 48x16, add. fr 2 stry, 20x16; brk milk hse, 1 stry, 12x9; fr bath hse, 1 stry, 14x14; fr bath hse, 10x10, 1 stry, 16x12
SLOAN, James; Occupant: Hugh RANKIN; 18A; pt Parishes Fear; fr dwlg, 1 stry, 50x21; steeple and room 12x12,; add. fr, 1 stry, 20x12; fr kn, 1 stry, 33x12; fr poultry, 1 stry, 10x10; fr milk hse, 1 stry, 16x12, stone add. 1 stry, 12x12; fr barn, 3 stry, 1 brk & 2 fr, 32x18, add. fr; fr hogg hse, 1 stry, 21x12
STENSON, Wm.; 110A; pt Rogers Enlargement; fr dwlg, 2 stry, 38x16, add. fr, 1 stry, 15x15, add. fr 1 stry, 27x15; log kn, 1 stry, 25x18,; add. shed 28x12; fr smoke hse, 1 stry, 20x14; sone milk hse, 1 stry, 12x12; fr 1 stry, 8x6; old log 1 stry, 15x11; log barn, 1 stry, 43x24; add. shed, 62x12, 1 stry; log stble, 1 stry, 25x15; stone potato hse, 62x14, 6 ft high; fr 1 stry, 29x12; fr shed, 1 stry, 62x16
STEWART Archibald; dwlg; 27A+; pt Parishes Range; fr dwlg, 1 stry, 14x12; log 1 stry, 13x13; old log, 1 stry, 20x16; stone milk hse, 1 stry, 12x12; fr barn, 2 stry, 36x18; add. shed, 1 stry, 36x24
SMITH, Sarah, widow; Occupant: John WOODEN; 12A; pt Parishes Range
SMITH, Nicholas; dwlg; 53A; pt Ensigns Grove; old log dwlg, 1 stry, 20x18; new stone hse, 2 stry, unfinished, 24x18; log barn, 1 stry, 30x16
TYSON, Elisha; Occupants: John STEEGAR and Sam COX; 2 dwlgs; 200A; Woodberry; fr 2 stry dwlg, 18x14; fr add., 1 stry, 16x14; log stble, 1 stry, 16x14; old log 1 stry, dwlg, 16x12; fr barn 1 1/2 stry, 50x20; brk mill hse, 2 stry, 43x43; log 1 stry, 38x18
TROMBO, Adam; 80P; pt Newtown
TAYLOR, Robert; 12A; pt Newington; fr dwlg, 2 stry, 42x18; brk kn, 1 1/2 stry, 24x12; brk smoke hse, 12x10 and brk milk hse, 12x10, each 1 stry; fr barn; posts in the ground, 1 stry, 54x26
VAN BIBBER, Abraham; Occupant: James WILLSON; dwlg; 66A; pt Pimblicoe; log dwlg, 1 stry, 32x16; log kn, 1 stry, 22x16; log smoke hse, 1 stry, 12x12; log milk hse, 1 stry, 12x10; old log, 1 stry, fit for fuel, 22x16; fr barn, 1 stry, 30x20, add. logs, 1 stry, 52x20; log corn hse, 1 stry, 20x14
VANBIBBER, Abraham; Occupant: John GRAMBURG; 51A; pt Coles Adventure, pt Peace & Good Neighbourhood; log dwlg, 2 stry, 26x20, by. add. logs, 1 stry, 20x12,; piazza 26x6; log stble, 1 1/2 stry, 22x19; shed, 1 stry 60x10
WELCH, John of James; Occupant: Joseph TAYLOR; dwlg; 180A; pt Traymore; log dwlg, 1 stry, 30x26 fr & brk gable ends
WILLEBY, Wm.; dwlg; 80P; pt Toms Choice; log dwlg, 1 stry, 22x12
WELCH, Robert; dwlg; 50A; pt Pimblecoe
WILLIS, Henry; Occupants: Eve BELT, Henry BISHOP; 2 DWLGS; 153A; pt Leterloney; fr dwlg, 1 stry, 20x20; add. logs, 1 stry, 18x12; old log barn, 1 stry, 36x16; old log, 1 stry, 14x10; log dwlg, 1 stry, 20x16
WILLIAMSON, David; 63A; pt North Carolina; fr & log dwlg, 2 stry 40x34, add. fr; stone ends, 1 stry, 20x20; fr 1 1/2 stry, 20x16, add. fr 1 stry, 20x12; stone smoke hse, 1 stry, 22x12; fr milk hse, 1 stry, 16x10; 4 fr 1 stry: 12x10, 12x8, 18x14 & 18x14

66

WOODWARD, Wm.; dwlg; 80A; pt North Carolina; log dwlg, 2 stry, 23x21; log kn, 1 stry, 18x16; fr & log 1 stry, 20x20; log barn, 1 stry, 30x18, hip roof, fr, 1 stry, 18x18; fr, 1 stry, 21x10

WOODEN, Thomas; 98A; pt Parishes Range; fr dwlg, 1 stry, 24x18,; add. shed 24x8, and piazza 24x7; log kn, 1 stry, 16x12; log smoke hse, 1 stry, 12x10; stone milk hse, 1 stry, 10x10; old fr barn, 1 stry, 40x20; log stble, stry, 16x12

WOODEN, Francis of Stephen; Occupant: Dixon BROWN, guardian; 60A; pt Parishes Range

WHITELY Wm.; Occupant: John DOWNEY; dwlg; 2A+; pt Hope, pt Toms Choice; fr dwlg, 1 stry, 16x12, add, fr shed, 1 stry, 12x11

WELCH, Robert; 106A; pt Parishes Range; log dwlg, 1 stry, 25x18; old fr, 1 stry, 8x8; log shed, 1 stry, 12x10. "The above houses almost fit for fuel. on 50 Ac."

WILLIS, Henry; Occupants: Wm. HOOPER, Nicholas TRACY, Geo. GRIFFITH; 3 dwlgs; 588A; pt Labrinith, pt Pimblicoe, pt Brothers Choice; old log dwlg, 1 stry, 22x16; log kn, 1 stry, 14x12; log milk hse, 1 stry, 10x10; log barn, 1 stry, 38x18, add. logs, 1 stry, 48x14; old log 1 stry, 18x12; log dwlg, 1 stry, 20x18; dwlg 2 stry, the one stry stone and the other logs, 18x16, add. logs, 1 stry, 16x16; old log 1 stry, 16x14, fit for fuel

YOUNG, Joseph; 70A (70 acres sold for taxes - 1805); pt Newington

YOUNG, Michael; dwlg; 250A; pt Hop Yard; fr & log dwlg, 1 stry, 40x15; log kn, 1 stry, 20x18; old log, 1 stry, 20x12; log stble, 1 stry, 20x12; old log, 1 stry, 20x18

ROGERS, Nich's; Occupant: Nich's ROGERS; Octin Torely (Auchenteroly); log dwlg, 1 1/2 stry, 50x18,; add. fr, 1 stry, 14x12; fr smoke hse, 1 stry, 12x12; brk milk hse, 1 stry, 13x13

RIDGELY, John, Esq.; Occupant: John Ridgely, Esq.; pt Pay My Debts; fr dwlg, 1 stry, 20x16, add. fr shed, 1 stry, 20x12, add. logs, 1 stry, 32x15; log kn, 1 sty, 30x15; log poultry, 1 stry, 26x10

TYSON, Elisha; Occupant: ALTHARE; Woodberry; fr dwlg, 2 stry, 32x20, add. fr 20x18; fr add. 1 stry, 27x14, piazza 27x6; stone smoke hse, 1 stry, 12x12

"General List of all Dwelling Houses which, with the Out houses appurtenant thereto, and the Lots on which the same are erected, not exceeding two acres in any case, were owned, possessed or occupied on the 1st day of October 1798, within the 8th assessment District in the State of Maryland exceeding in value the sum of one hundred dollars."

ATKIN, Dr. Andrew (Balto); dwlg hse
ARMITAGE, William; 102A (75A sold for taxes - 1805)
BOWEN, Sarah; dwlg hse
BATTEE, John; Occupant: Gray LYNCH; dwlg hse
BATTEE, John and Elizabeth SOLLERS; Occupant: John BATTEE; dwlg hse
BARRICKMAN, Anthony; dwlg hse, 21A (4A sold for taxes - 1805)
BAXTER, Nicholas; dwlg hse
BUCHANAN, Wm., Commissary; dwlg hse
BUTTEN Wm.; dwlg hse
BOWEN, John; dwlg hse
BARRY, James (Balto.); dwlg hse
BARRY, James (Balto.); Occupant: James WALKER; dwlg hse
COLEGATE, Elizabeth; dwlg hse
CLARKE, Wm.; Occupant: Bryan O'LAUGHLIN; dwlg hse
CARRERE, Jno. (Balto.); dwlg hse
CAMPBELL, Arch. (Balto.); dwlg hse
CHILDS, Benj.; dwlg hse; hse & lot; (hse and lot sold for taxes - 1805)
COUSTADE, Charles; 8A (1A sold for taxes - 1805)
DeBENSE, Marie Piere; dwlg hse; 37A (1A sold for taxes - 1805)
DEWIS, Ezekiel; 50A (8A sold for taxes - 1805)
CROOKSHANKS, Charles, heirs; 36A (18A sold for taxes - 1805)
DONALDSON, Eliz. (London); Occupant: Thomas BAILEY; dwlg hse
DULANY, Rebecca; dwlg hse
DEW, Philip (Buten); 37A (1A sold for taxes - 1805)
DILLON, Capt. John; dwlg hse
DILLON, Capt. John; Occupant: Mr. DYSART; dwlg hse
DILLON, Capt. John; Occupant: Daniel DILLON; dwlg hse
DILLON, Capt. John; vacant; dwlg hse
DOSH's, Michael, heirs; dwlg hse

DAVEY, Alex'd WOODROF: 127A (50A sold for taxes - 1805)
EVANS, Daniel; dwlg hse
DELUSORO, William; 20A (1A sold for taxes - 1805)
EGGLESTON, Abraham; Occupant: John REDDY; dwlg hse; 248A (50A sold for taxes - 1805)
EGGLESTON, John; Occupant: Eleanor EGGLESTON; dwlg hse
ELLICOTT, Benjamin; dwlg hse
FARMER, John; dlwg hse
FLAX, John; dwlg hse
GILL, Gabriel; 2A+ (2A sold for taxes - 1805)
GREEN, Solomon; dwlg hse
GREEN Josias; dwlg hse
GREEN, Vincent; dwlg hse
GORSUCH, Jno. of Rob.; Occupant: John GORSUCH; dwlg hse
GOODWIN, Wm.; Occupant: Edw. SWEETING; dwlg hse
GOODWIN, Wm.; Occupant: Ab'r. CARTWRIGHT; dwlg hse
HARRIS, Davis; dwlg hse
HUYSLER, Maximilian; dwlg hse
HACKET, John; dwlg hse
HOPKINS, Hopkin; dwlg hse
HOLLINGSWORTH, Sam. & Thos.; dwlg hse
HOLLINS, John; dwlg hse
HOLBROOK, Jacob; dwlg hse
HOWARD, James Q.; 58A (58A sold for taxes - 1805)
HETTINGER, Michael; dwlg hse
HUTTEN, Thomas; dwlg hse
JOIEE, Thomas; 85A (15A sold for taxes - 1805)
JONES, Maj. Thomas; dwlg hse
JONES, Charles; 25A (4A sold for taxes - 1805)
JESSOP, Charles; dwlg hse
KONICKE, Nicholas; dwlg hse
KINGSMORE, John Stone; dwlg hse
KING, Benjamin; dwlg hse
LONEY, Amos; dwlg hse

LYNCH Wm. of Roebuck; dwlg hse
LUTTIG, John C.; dwlg hse
LAWSON, Eliz. (widow of Alex.);
vacant dwlg hse
LAWSON, Eliz. (widow of Alex.);
Occupant: Geo. COLEHOUSE; dwlg hse
MINCHEN, John; dwlg hse, 98A (98A
sold for taxes - 1805)
MANN, Doct. Anthony; dwlg hse
MERRICK, Joseph; 82A (10A sold for
taxes - 1805)
MacKIM, Alex. (Balto.); dwlg hse
MADEWELL, James, Sr.; Occupant: James
MADEWELL, Jr.; dwlg hse
MacGRUE, Andrew; dwlg hse
MURRAY, James (Inn Keeper); dwlg hse
MARTIN, Luther; dwlg hse
MARTIN, Luther; Occupant: Benj.
PORTER; dwlg hse
MERRYMAN, Joseph; dwlg hse
MACCUBBIN, Wm.; dwlg hse
O'DONNELL, Col. John; dwlg hse
O'DONNELL, Col. John; Occupant: Mons.
TRULETT; dwlg hse
O'DONNELL, Col. John; Occupant: Mons.
STUPUY; dwlg hse
O'DONNELL, Col. John; Occupant: Geo.
PIPER; dwlg hse
OYSTEN, Lawrence; dwlg hse, 95A (3A
sold for taxes - 1805)
PARTRIDGE, John; dwlg hse
PARTRIDGE, John & Job; vacant; dwlg
hse
PERRIGO, Joseph; dwlg hse
PETERS, Thomas (Brewer); dwlg hse
POCOCK, James (near Fraey); dwlg hse
RUSK, Thomas, heirs; Occupant: Joshua
TURNER; dwlg hse, 38A (16A sold
for taxes - 1805)
ROGERS, Philip; dwlg hse
ROGERS, Philip; Occupant: Absalom
BOWEN; dwlg hse
ROGERS, Charles; dwlg hse
REYNOLDS, Nicholas; dwlg hse
RICHARDS, John; dwlg hse
ROGERS & OWINGS; Occupant: Nicholas
OWINGS; dwlg hse
STEEL, ---line; 18A (9A sold for
taxes- 1805)
STEELE, Capt. John (Fells Point);
dwlg hse

SMITH, Wm., Esq.; Occupant: Richard
PARKINSON; dwlg hse
SMITH, Job, Esq.; Occupants: ARNOLD &
GREEN; dwlg hse
SOLLARS, Elisha; dwlg hse
SOLLARS, Thomas; dwlg hse
STANSBURY, ---ad, heirs; 115A (7A
sold for taxes - 1805)
STANSBURY, Nathaniel; dwlg hse
STANSBURY, George; dwlg hse
SMITH, Samuel (Farmer); dwlg hse
SAMPEORE, ---; 137A (100A sold for
taxes - 1805)
SEVELL, ---, heirs; 50A (15A sold for
taxes - 1805)
STEWART, Dr. James; dwlg hse
STEWART, Dr. James; Occupant:
Ferdinand BATTEE; dwlg hse
SHAW, Sarah (widow of Nat.); dwlg hse
SHAW, Thomas; dwlg hse
STEVENSON, Sater; dwlg hse
STEVENSON, George; dwlg hse
STEVENSON, Wm.; dwlg hse
SMITH, Wm. R.; Occupant: Dr. Wm. P.
MATHEWS; dwlg hse
SHAW, Archibald (F. Point); dwlg hse
SMALLWOOD, Wm.; dwlg hse
SARGEANT, Sam. (York Rd.); dwlg hse
SLATER, Wm. (Balto.); dwlg hse
STERRETT, S. & COLE, T., Trustees for
heirs of John STERETT; Occupant:
Benj. WATTS; dwlg hse
SMITH, Gen. Samuel; dwlg hse
TINKER, Wm.; 50A (1A sold for taxes -
1805)
TRACY, Benj.; dwlg hse
THOMPSON, Hugh (Balto.); dwlg hse
THOMPSONS ---, 94A (5A sold for taxes
- 1805)
TOON, John; dwlg hse
TOON, John; Occupant: John WILSON;
dwlg hse
TURNER, Robert; dwlg hse
TODD, Thomas, heirs; dwlg hse
TROTTEN, Dr. John; dwlg hse
TYSON, Elisha; Occupant: Joseph
SCOTT; dwlg hse
VAN BIBBER, Abraham; dwlg hse
VAN BIBBER, Andrew; Occupant: Wm. Lee
FORMAN; dwlg hse
WORTHINGTON, Thomas; dwlg hse
WALSH, Jacob; dwlg hse

WALSH, Adam (Tobacconist); dwlg hse
WALKER, Christopher, Innkeeper; dwlg
  hse
WAUNTE, Stephen; dwlg hse
WEARY, Joseph; dwlg hse
WETHERBY, William; 90A (5A sold for
  taxes - 1805)
WOODEN, John; dwlg hse
WOOLRICH, Philip; dwlg hse, 98A (5A
  sold for taxes - 1805)
WINEMAN, Henry; dwlg hse
WILCOX, Wm.; dwlg hse
WEITER, Susannah, widow (Balto.);
  Occupant: Richard LAWSON; dwlg hse
WALKER, Thomas; dwlg hse

WISE, --- (Alexandria); 150A (100A
  sold for taxes - 1805)
WATTS, Sarah (the Elder)
WATTS, Sarah (the Younger)
WELLS, Rosanna, widow; Occupant: Geo.
  WILPART
WEAVER, Capt. John (Fells Point);
  vacant
WEEKS, William, cooper
WHEELER, John
WALLACE, Charles (Annapolis); vacant
WOOD, Peter; Occupant: Sam'l SMITH,
  farmer
YATES, Maj. Thomas; dwlg hse

General List of Lands, Lots &c. Continued, including dwelling houses and out
houses of a value not exceeding $100.

ARNEST, Caleb (Balto); dlwg hse
AITKIN, Dr. Andrew; 7A
AUNSPAUGH, Frederick;
  Occupant: Abraham KAUFFMAN; 6A
ARMITAGE, William; dwlg hse; 4A
BRYAN, James; dwlg hse; 600A
BOWEN, Sarah; dwlg hse; 526A
BOWEN, Sarah;
  Occupant: Peter ARNOLD
BROCK, Rachael; dwlg hse; 8A+
BOWEN, Absalom; vacant; 38A
BATEE, John & Elizabeth SOLLERS; 225A
BATEE, John;
  Occupant Lynch GRAY; 126A
BAKER, Benjamin; 6A
BURRELL, Thomas; 3A
BARRICKMAN, Anthony; 21A
BAXTER, Nicholas; 118A
BOWLEY, Daniel;
  Occupant: CROULE; 474A
BOWLEY, Daniel;
  Occupant: R. HALE
BIAYS, James; 9A+
BUCHANAN, Wm. (Register); 149A
BROWN, Jesse (Balto);2A+
BUTTEN, William; 13A
BAILEY, Thomas; 24A
BOWEN, John; 194A
BARRY, James (Balto); 138A
BARRY Lavelin, Junr (Balto);
  vacant; 33A
CURTAIN, James, butcher; 60A
COLEGATE, Elizabeth; 183A
COX, John (near G. WALKER); 2A

CONSTABLE, Charles (do); 8A
COCKEY, Thomas Dye; 4A+
CLARKE, William;
  Occupant Bryan OLAUGHLIN; 3A
CARRERE, John (Balto); 14
CAMPBELL, Archibald (Balto); 88A
COLVIN, John; 4A
COLE, William (Gough's road); 1A
COALE, George (do); 1A
CATON, Rich'd & C. CARROLL;
  Occupant: Abraham CORD; 192A
CATON, Rich'd & C. CARROLL;
  Occupant: Jno. CORAM
CROOKSHANKS, Charles, heirs;
  vacant; 36A
DAVIS, Ezekiel; 50A
DeBENSE Pierre Marie; 24A
DEAVER, John (Govane Town); 5A
DEW, Philip (butcher, Balto);
  Occupant: Greenbury COE; 27A
DEAVER, John (schoolmaster);
  Occupant: James GRAY; 125A
DULANY, Rebecca; 54A
DILLON, Capt. John; 4A
DOSH, Michael, heirs; 490A
DAVEY, Alexr. Woodrop; 13A
DELASERE, William; vacant; 20A
EGGLESTON, John;
  Occupant: Elenor EGGLESTON; 148A
EGGLESTON, Abraham;
  Occupant: John READY; 248A
ELLICOTT, Benjamin; 14A
EVANS, Daniel; 138A
EDWARDS, Jas. (Balto); 55A

FORNER, John; vacant; 9A
FORNER, Christian; 4A
FARMER, John, tavern keeper; 4A
FLEMING Elizabeth; 8A
FOOSE, William (near Bowley's);
   Occupants: Negroes; 7A
FOSS, John (Balto);
   Occupants: Quarriers; 1A+
GREEN, Solomon; 46A
GREEN, Josias; 172A
GRIFFITH, Nathan (Balto);
   vacant; 200A
GRAY, Ephraim; 115A
GODDARD, Capt. Lemuel; 5A
GILL, Gabriel; 2A+
GREEN, Vincent; 498A
GASH, Nicholas; 102A
GORSUCH, Robert;
   Occupant: John GORSUCH; 16A
GORSUCH, Jno. & Robert;
   Occupant: John GORSUCH; 156A
GOULDEN, Aquilla; 5A
GRUNDY, George (Balto);
   Occupant: William TRAPNALL; 8A
GRAY, James (Neck); vacant; 6A
GOUGH, Harry Dorsey;
   Occupant: Josias WATTS; 521A
GOODWIN, Wm. (Balt); vacant; 67A
GOODWIN, Wm. (Balt);
   Occupant: Edward SWEETING; 566A
GREEN, Joel;
   Occupant: Josias GREEN; 50A
HARRIS, David (Balto); 240A
HUYSLER, Maximilian; 40A
HACKETT, John (Balto); 12A
HYRE, John (Quarrier); 1A+
HOLLINGSWORTH, Thos. & Sam'l; 62A+
HOOPER, Nicho. (at Job SMITH's,
   Balto); 200A
HOLLINS, John (Balto); 92A
HOLBROOK, Jacob; 1A
HETTINGER, Michael; 3A
HUTTEN, Thomas; 10A
HALL, William; 80P
HOLTZ, Peter; 3A
HALFPENNY, Patrick;
   Occupant: William SAUNDERS; 80P
HOPKINS, Joseph; Occupant: negro; 60A
HOWARD, James Govane;
   Occupant: Alexander WALKER
HOWARD, James Govane; Occupant:
   Jos. CORPORAL (negro); 58A

HOWARD, James Govane;
   Occupant: David WALKER
HOWARD, Jno. Eager; vacant; 280A
JOYCE, Thomas; 85A
JOYCE, Basil;
   Occupant: Mrs. CARTWRIGHT; 50A
JONES, Thomas, Majr; 174A
JOYCE, Edward Bowen; 230A
JOSEPH (a black man at Ellicotts);
   40P
JARMAN, Mary (Govane Town); 1A
JESSOP, Charles, Capt;
   Occupant: mulatto AQUILA; 121A
JONES, Charles (Balto); 25A
KONIKE, Nicholas; 60A
KELSO, Jno & Geo. (butchers);
   Occupant: James HAYES; 4A
KAMINSKY, Alexr. (Balto);
   Occupants: Negroes; 12A
KINGSMORE, John S.; 550A
KEPLINGER, John (Quarrier); 1A
KING, Benj. (Fells Point); 2A
LONEY, Amos; 98A
LYNCH, William (of Robuck); 224A
LYNCH, Patrick; Occupant: John Meeks
LYNCH, Patrick;
   Occupant: Mrs. JONES; 351A
LYNCH, Patrick;
   Occupant: DALE (blacksmith)
LUTTIG, John C.; 23A+
LUX, Rachel;
   Occupant: Thos. D. COCKEY; 610A
LEAKIN, Robert;
   Occupant: Catharine POPE; 80P
LAWSON, Richard (Balto); 12A
LAWSON, Elizabeth, widow of Alexr.;
   Occupants: Sundries; 166A
MINCHEN, John; 98A
MANN, Dr. Anthony; 27A
McKIM Alexr. (Balto); 10A
MADEWELL, James, senr; Occupant:
   Alexr. MADEWELL, Junr; 38A
McGRUE, Andrew; 98A
MURRAY, Jno., tavern keeper; 4A
MARTIN Luther; 269A
MIRLE, Joseph (neck); 82A
MOALE, Ellen (widow of Jno.) & Sam'l
   JOHNSON (lawyer); 231A
MERRYMAN, Joseph; 154A
MERRYMAN, Job; 73A+
McCUBBIN, William; 695A

71

NORWOOD, Edward;
   Occupant: William SMITH; 400A
NICKEL, William; 8A
O'DONNEL, Col. John;
   Occupant: John Point MURRY; 380A
O'DONNEL, Col. John; 1606A
OYSTEN, Lawrence; 95A
OWINGS, Sam'l & Nicho.; vacant; 40A
PARTRIDGE, John; 336A
PARTRIDGE, John & Job;
   Occupant: Capt WILSON; 272A
PERRIGO, Joseph; 98A
PANNEL, John, heirs;
   Occupant: Dennis REILEY; 7A+
PERIAN, Peter;
   Occupant: Timothy COLLINS; 82A
PETERS, Thomas (Brewer); 97A
PENNINGTON, Josias; vacant; 5A
RUSK, Thomas, heir; 38A
ROGERS, Col. Nicholas;
   Occupant: Rosanna WELLS; 470A
ROSS, David;
   Occupant: Peter ARNOLD, senr; 294A
ROGERS, Philip; 176A
ROGERS, Philip;
   Occupant: Absalom BOWEN; 548A
ROGERS, Charles; 157A
REYNOLDS, Nicholas; 2A
RUTTER, Thomas, Junr; vacant; 37A
RICHARDS, John; 85A
RUNT, Christopher; 1A
RYLAND, William
   (Innkeeper, Fred Road); vacant; 7A
ROGERS & OWINGS;
   Occupant: Joseph SCOTT; 50A
ROGERS & OWINGS;
   Occupant: James ELLICOTT; 157A
RIDGLEY, Rebecca; vacant; 150A
RICHARDS, Jona. (Balto);
   Occupant: Joshua RICHARDS; 43A
RICHARDS, Joshua; 40A
RUTTER, John
   (guardian to Jno. SPICER; 25A
STERLING, James (Balto); vacant; 100A
STEEL, Capt. John (Fells Point); 13A
SMITH, Robert (Lawyer);
   Occupant: Daniel SAPP; 68A
SMITH, William, Esqr.;
   Occupant: Richard PARKINSON; 333A
SMITH, Job, Esqr.;
   Occupants: ARNOLD & GREENE; 5A
SOLLERS, Elisha; 282A

SOLLERS, Thomas; 392A
STANSBURY, Nathaniel; 238A
STANSBURY, George; 200A
STANSBURY, Daniel, Senr; 230A
STANSBURY, Daniel, Senr;
   Occupant: Daniel STANSBURY, Junr
STANSBURY, Richard, heirs;
   Occupant: Sarah STANSBURY; 115A
STANSBURY, Richard, heirs;
   Occupant: Sarah STANSBURY
STANSBURY, Elijah (Balto);
   Occupant: Schoolmaster; 33A
SWEETING, Edward;
   Occupant: Robert Sweeting; 75A
SMITH, Samuel (farmer); 206A
STEWART, Dr. James; 34A
STEWART, Dr. James;
   Occupant: Ferdinand BATTEE; 916A
STOPP, John; 16A
SAMPSON, Jacob; 137A
SMITH, John, heirs;
   Occupant: Mr. CORAM; 47A
SMALL, Jacob, heirs; vacant; 100A
SHAW, Sarah, widow of Nat.; 82A
SHAW, Thomas; 188A
SHAW, William; 115A
SCOTT, Rossiter;
   Occupant: John HARKER; 15A
STEVENSON, Sater; 164A
STEVENSON, William; 107A
STEVENSON, George; 130A
SMITH, William R.;
   Occupant: Dr. Wm. P. MATHEWS; 248A
SHAW, Archa. (wharf builder); 3A
STODDARD, David
   (ship builder); vacant; 18A
SHRACK, Dietrick; 120P
SMITH, George (Labourer); 4A
SMALLWOOD, Wm.; 10A
SLADESMAN, Michael (Balto);
   Occupant: Thomas DONOVAN; 33P
SMITH, James (butcher); 8A
STERRETT, John (heirs);
   Occupant: Benja. WATTS; 118A
SMITH, Genr. Sam'l; 516A
SPEAR, Wm. (heirs, Balto);
   vacant; 90A
SWAN, Joseph (Balto); 7A
SMITH, John (wheelwright); 40P
TRACY, Benjamin; 301A
THOMPSON, Hugh (Balto); 31A
TOON, John; 10A

TURNER, Robert; 38A
TROTTEN, Dr. John; 219A
TODD, Thomas (heirs);
  Occupant: Wm. TODD; 808A
TINKER, Wm. (butcher, Fells Point);
  Occupant: Rich'd EDEN; 50A
TYSON, Elisha;
  Occupant: Joseph SCOTT; 148A
TALBOTT, Benjamin (heirs);
  Occupant: James ARCHIBOLD; 125A
THOMPSON, Andrew; 94A
VAN BIBBER, Abraham; 228A
VAN BIBBER, Andrew;
  Occupant: Alexr. MADEWELL; 133A
WORTHINGTON, Thomas; 198A
WALSH, Jacob; 3A
WALSH, Adam (Tobacconist);
  Occupant: the Gardner; 4A.
WALKER, Christian (Innkeeper); 75A
WAUNTE, Stephen; 74A
WEARY, Joseph; 98A

WELLS, Rosanna (widow);
  Occupant: Geo. WILPART; 10A
WATTS, Sarah (The Elder); 20A
WATTS, Sarah (The Younger); 40A
WEATHERBY, William; 90A
WOODEN, John; 20A
WOOLRICH, Philip; 98A
WEAVER, Capt. John
  (Fells Point); vacant; 14A
WEEKS, William (Cooper); 40P
WINEMAN, Henry; 22A
WHEELER, John; 50A
WALLACE, Charles (Annapolis);
  vacant; 176A
WISE, --- (Alexandria); vacant; 150A
WOOD, Susannah (widow);
  Occupant: Richa. LAWSON; 12A
WEITER, Susannah (widow);
  Occupant: Richa. LAWSON; 12A
YATES, Majr. Thomas; 199A

General List of Slaves owned, or superintended on the 1st day of October, 1798, within the 8th Assessment District in the State of Maryland

ARNEST, Caleb; 2 slaves
BOWEN, Sarah; 9 slaves
BROCK, Rachael; 1 slave
BATTEE, John; 7 slaves
BRYAN, James; 8 slaves
BUCHANAN, Will'm, Register; 6 slaves
BUCHANAN, Capt. George;
  sup: Wm. BUCHANAN; 1 slave
BAILEY, Thomas; 7 slaves
BOWEN, John; 4 slaves
BOYCE, Eleanor;
  sup: Job MERRYMAN; 1 slave
BOND, Thos., Harford County;
  sup: Benjamin TRACY; 1 slave
CURTAIN, James; Fells Point; 1 slave
CARTWRIGHT, Abraham; 5 slaves
COLEGATE, Elizabeth; 2 slaves
COCKEY, Thos. Dye; 8 slaves

De BENSE Pierre Marie; 2 slaves
DULANY, Rebecca; 2 slaves
DILLON, Capt. John; 8 slaves
DEW, Ann, (widow of Thos.);
  sup: Nicho. GASH; 2 slaves
EGGLESTON, Eleanor; sup: John
  EGGLESTON; 4 slaves
EDWARDS, James; 4 slaves
FORMAN, Joseph; sup: Anthony
  BARRICKMAN; 1 slave
GREEN, Josias; 6 slaves
GRAY, Lynch; 2 slaves
GREEN, Vincent; 10 slaves
GORSUCH, Jno. & Robt;
  sup: John GORSUCH; 6 slaves
GASH, Basil (Fells Point);
  sup: Joseph PERRIGO; 1 slave

GIDDISON, John; sup: Anthony
   BARRICKMAN; 1 slave
HARRIS, David; 6 slaves
HART, William; 3 slaves
HACKET, John (Balto); 4 slaves
HARKER, JOHN (miller); 1 slave
HOLLINGSWORTH, Thos & Sam'l; 1 slave
HOLLINS, John (Balto); 6 slaves
HUTTEN, Thomas; 1 slave
HERRINGTON, Mrs.;
   sup: Anthony BARRICKMAN; 1 slave
HITCHCOCK, Mrs.;
   sup: Benjamin TRACY; 1 slave
JOYCE, Thomas; 4 slaves
JONES, Thomas; 8 slaves
JOYCE, Edward Bowen; 5 slaves
JESSOP, Capt. Charles;
   sup: Mulatto AQUILA; 4 slaves
KONECKE, Nicholas; 9 slaves
KING, Benj., Fells Point; 1 slave
LONEY, Amos; 5 slaves
LYNCH, Wm. of Roebuck; 10 slaves
LYNCH, Patrick; John MEEKS; 6 slaves
LUTTIG, John C.; 1 slave
LUTTIG, John C.;
   sup: Madame La COMB; 1 slave
MINCHEN, John; 3 slaves
MANN, Dr. Anthony; 3 slaves
MURRAY, DTss (?) John; 1 slave
MARTIN, Luther; 4 slaves
MARTIN, Luther;
   sup: Irenius MARTIN; 10 slaves
MERRYMAN, Joseph; 2 slaves
MERRYMAN, Job; 1 slave
McCUBBIN, William; 23 slaves
O'DONNEL, Col. John; 26 slaves
OYSTEN, Lawrence; 2 slaves
OWINGS, Nicholas; 10 slaves
OWINGS, Caleb;
   sup: Wm. SMALLWOOD; 1 slave
PARTRIDGE, John; 9 slaves
PETERS, Thomas (brewer); 10 slaves
READY, John; 5 slaves
ROGERS, Philip;
   sup: Absalom BOWEN; 5 slaves
ROGERS, Charles; 6 slaves
REYNOLDS, Nicholas; 5 slaves
REED, Edward;
   sup: Anthony BARRICKMAN; 1 slave
SOLLERS, Elizabeth; 1
SOLLERS, Basil;
   sup: Thomas SOLLERS; 1

SOLLERS, Elisha; 6 slaves
SOLLERS, Thomas; 5 slaves
STANSBURY, Nathaniel; 7 slaves
STANSBURY, George; 5 slaves
STANSBURY, Tobias; 7 slaves
STANSBURY, Dan'l, senr; 10 slaves
STANSBURY, Dan'l Junr; 1 slave
STANSBURY, Isaac; 1 slave
SWEETING, Edward; 17 slaves
SMITH, Sam'l (farmer); 10 slaves
STEWART, Dr. James; 3 slaves
STEWART, Dr. James;
   sup: Ferdinand BATTEE; 16 slaves
SAMPSON, Jacob; 4 slaves
SHAW, Sarah, widow of Nat.; 2 slaves
SHAW, Thomas; 7 slaves
STEVENSON, George; 1 slave
STEVENSON, William; 1 slave
SHAW, Alexander; 1 slave
STUPEY, Peter; 7 slaves
SMITH, Genr. Sam'l; 4 slaves
SLADE, Mrs.;
   sup: Anthony BARRICKMAN; 1 slave
SOLLERS, Miss Polly;
   sup: Dr. John TROTTEN; 1 slave
TURNBULL, Sarah;
   sup: Anthony BARRICKMAN; 1 slave
TRACEY, Benjamin; 3 slaves
TOON, John; 4 slaves
TODD, Thomas (heirs); 30 slaves
TROTTEN, Dr. John; 12 slaves
WORTHINGTON, Thomas; 8 slaves
WALKER, Christopher; 5 slaves
WAUNTE, Stephen; 5 slaves
WEARY, Joseph; 5 slaves
WATTS, Josias; 6 slaves
WATTS, Sarah, the Elder; 5 slaves
WEATHERBY, William; 1 slave
WOODEN, John; 8 slaves
WOOLRICK, Philip;
   sup: Benjamin CHILDS; 1 slave
WINEMAN, Henry; 4 slave
YATES, Thomas; 10 slaves

"General List of all Dwelling Houses which, with the Out houses appurtenant thereto, and the Lots on which the same are erected, not exceeding two acres in any case, were owned, possessed or occupied on the 1st day of October 1798, within the 8th assessment District in the State of Maryland exceeding in value the sum of one hundred dollars."

BARTON, Greenbury
BIDDISON Meshach
BIDDISON, Jeremiah
BIDDISON, Jeremiah Occupant:
WILLIAMS, Tobias (Free Negro)
BIDDISON, Shadrach
BOWLEY, Daniel
BOWLEY, Daniel
    Occupant: PARKE, Aquila
BROWN, Abraham
    Occupant: LAUGE, William
BUCK Benjamin, Sr
BUCK, Benjamin, Jr
BUCK, Christopher
BUCK, John of Benjamin
BURGAIN, Thomas
BURGAIN, Thomas
    Occupant: THOMPSON, Lewis
CARTER, Joseph
CARTER, Solomon
CHAMBELIN, John
CHRISTOPHER, John
CLARKE, William
COAL, Richard
COFFMAN, Abr'a
COLE Thomas
    Occupant: DOWNS, Joseph
CROMWELL, Joseph
DALLAS, Walter Riddle
DAUGHERTY, John
DAVIS, William
DELAPORT, Frances
FITCH, Robert
FITCH, William, Jr, of Henry
FITCH, William, Sr
FLOYD, Joseph
FOOS, William
FOWLER, Richard, Jr
FOWLER, Richard, Sr
GARRETSON, Cornelius
    Occupant: GARRETSON, Job
GARRETSON, Job, Jr Occupant:
GARRETSON, Job, Sr
GASH, Benjamin
GREEN, Catharine, ex. of Jos.
    Green, decd

GREEN, Joel
GREEN, Vincent
HAMM, Thomas
HARRISSON, William
HILLEN, Solomon
HILLEN, Solomon
    Occupant: RAWLIN, Isaac
HISS, Jacob
JARMAN, Benjamin, Jr.
JARMAN, Benjamin, Sr.
JOHNSON, William
LANE, Prudence
LANGDON, Joseph
LEMMON, Alexis
LITZINGER, George
LITZINGER, William
LONEY, Amos
    Occupant: CORD, Amos
LONG, John
LUCUS, Thomas
LYNCH, Joshua
LYNCH, William Kid
MORRIS, Mark
MUMMY, Christian
NORWOOD, Ruth
ORAM, Henry
OSBORN, Michael
PARLETT, David
PARLETT, William
PORTER, Augustine
PORTER, Robert
RICHARDS, Samuel
SCARF, William
SENDAL, Philip
SENDAL, Sam., Sr.
SENDAL, William
SMITH, Gen. Samuel
    Occupant: FORMAN, William Lee
SMITH, Sarah
    Occupant: STONE, Henry
SMITH, William, Esq.
    Occupant: IRONS, Thomas
STANSBURY, Charles
STANSBURY, Daniel
STANSBURY, Ephraim
STANSBURY, ex of Joseph

STANSBURY, James
STANSBURY, John D.
STANSBURY, John Ensor
STANSBURY, Tobias E.
STEMMER, Uredrec B.
STINCHICOMB, Catharine E.

TAYLOR, Isaac
TAYLOR, Joseph
TAYLOR, Richard, Jr.
TAYLOR, Richard, Sr.
TAYLOR, Samuel
TAYLOR, Thomas

General List of Lands, Lots &c. Continued, including dwelling houses and out houses of a value not exceeding $100.

ASKEW, Jonathan; 122A
BOWLEY, Daniel; 768A+
BOWLEY, Daniel;
    Occupant: Aquila PARKS; 380A
BARRY, Larallen;
    Occupant: Thomas HINTON; 50A+
BROWN, Francis; 61A+
BUCK Christopher; 187A+
BUCK, Benjamin, Junr; 280A+
BUCK, John of Benj.; 272A
BUCK, Benjamin, Senr; 369A
BIDDISON, Mishach; 239A+
BIDDISON, Thomas; 50A
BOWEN, Nathan; 105A+
BIDDISON Shadrack; 76A
BROWN, Abraham; 91A
BIDDISON, Jerimia; 454A
BARTON, Greenbury; 98A
BAKER, James;
    Occupant: Emanuel DEAN; 345A
BURGAIN, Thomas;
    Occupant: John BURGAIN;
BURGAIN, Thomas;
    Occupant: Garet FRANKLIN; 321A
BURGAIN, Thomas;
    Occupant: Joseph RICHARDS
CLARKE, William; 199A
CHAMBERLIN, John; 138A
CHRISTOPHER, John, Senr; 49A
CARTER, Solomon; 70A
CARTER, Joseph; 180A
COLE, Richard; 67A
COLE, Thomas; 99A
COX, James; 196A
CARBACK, John; 50A
CONTEE, Alexander;
    Occupant: Andrew BOYCE; 417A
CROMWELL, Joseph; 92A
COFFMAN, Abraham;
    Occupant: Joseph HARRIS; 298A

COFFMAN, Abraham;
    Occupant: Ambrose FIELD;
COUNCILMAN, George; 113A
COUNCILMAN, George
DELEPORT, Francis; 10A
DAUGHERTY, Thomas;
    Occupant: James CUNNINGHAM; 50A
DAUGHERTY, John; 48A
DAVIS, William; 22A
DUNKEN, Thomas;
    Occupant: Geo. SCHARF; 50A
DUNKEN, Thomas;
    Occupant: Nicho. WILSON
DALLAS, Walter Riddle; 257A
DALLAS, Walter Riddle;
    Occupant: William MATTAN; 100A
DALLAS, Walter Riddle;
    Occupant: Jesse BEVENS; 100A
DUKE, Charles;
    Occupant: Thomas STONE; 83A
DUGAN, Cumberland; 557A
FOSS, William;
    Occupant: John FOSS; 60A
FLOYD, Joseph; 188A
FITCH, Robert; 246A
FITCH, Robert; Occupant:
    Richard FOWLER, Junr; 100A
FITCH, Robert;
    Occupant: William WIREL; 70A
FITCH, Wm. of Henry; 85A+
FITCH, William, Junr; 208A+
FRANKLIN, Charles; 10A
FITCH, Thomas; 66A+
FOWLER, Richard, Senr; 96+
FOWLER, Richard, Junr; 14A+
FOWLER, John; 133A
FOWLER, Tammer; 147A+

GREEN, Vincent; 148A
GOUGH, Dorsey Harry; 1332A
GOUGH, Dorsey Harry
GASH, Benjamin; 245A+
GREEN, Catharine,
    Exer. of Jos. GREEN; 228A
GREEN, Nathaniel; 52A
GREEN, Joel; 168A
GRIMES, Mary; 133A+
GALLOWAY, Thomas;
    Occupant: Emanuel JONES; 78A
GOULDSBOROUGH, Robert (heirs);
    Occupant: Thos. FRANKLIN; 111A
GREEN, Isaac; 20A
GARRETSON, Job, Junr; Occupant:
    Job GARRETSON, Senr; 91A+
GARRETSON, Cornelius; Occupant:
    Job Garretson, Senr; 239A
GARRETSON, Job, Senr;
    Occupant: George DUBLIN; 320+
GARRETSON, Job, Senr;
    Occupant: Raria HOLBROOK; 32A+
GARRETSON, Job, Senr;
    Occupant: Mary AWL; 400A
GARRETSON, Job , Senr;
    Occupant: John STONE; 132A
HICKMAN, Elizabeth; 7A
HILLEN, Solomon; 253A
HILLEN, Solomon;
    Occupant: Isaac RAWLENS; 529A
HISS, Jacob; 201A+
HILLEN, Thomas; 100A
HAMMON, Joshua; 48A
HAMMON, Ann; 24A
HARRIMON, William; 274A
HAMM, Thomas; 59A+
HENDERSON, William;
    Occupant: Thos. CARBACK; 91A
HAWLET, JOHN; 74A
HARRIS, Edward; 106A
HUDSON, Margaret; 117A
JOHNSON, William; 98A
JOHNSON, Joseph; 74A
JOHNSON, William, Junr; 50A
JOHNSON, John; 40A
JOHNSON, Christopher; 165A
JARMAN, William;
    Occupant: Thos. JARMAN; 1A
JARMAN, Benj. Senr; 98A
JARMAN, Benj. Junr; 121A
LONEY, Amos;
    Occupant: Amos CORD; 328A

LEWIS, James; 12A
LITZINGER, William; 44A+
LITZINGER, George; 20A+
LANGDON, Joseph; 243A
LUCUS, Thomas; 99A
LANE, Providence;1 98A
LEMMON, Elexis; 164A+
LONG, John; 385A+
LONG, John;
    Occupant: Isaac WIGLEY; 135A
LONG, John; 118A
LONG, John; 119A+
LYNCH, William Kid; 198A
LYNCH, Joshua; 180A
MUMMY, Christian; 10A
MERRYMAN, Michajar;
    Occupant: Philip PINDELL; 332A
MERRYMAN, Nicholas;
    Occupant: James GRIMES; 280A
MOALE, Samuel (Balto); 334A
MORRIS, Mark; 20A
NORWOOD, Ruth; 98A
OLDHAM, Edwd. (heirs); 464A
ORAM, Henry; 111A+
OSBORN, Michael; 45A
PARLETT, David; 64A+
PARLETT, Martin;
    Occupant: William JARMAN; 50A
PARLETT, William; 48A
PASCAULT, Lewis;
    Occupant: Robt. PAWLIN; 93A
PORTER, Augustine; 98A
PORTER, Peregrine; 132A+
PORTER, Robert; 120A
RAVIN, Isaac; 100A
RAWLINS, William; 42A+
RAWLINS, Isaac;
    Occupant: Thos. MURRY; 26A
ROBINSON, James; 88A
RUSSELL, Thos. (heirs); 175A+
STERLING, James (Balto); vacant;
SMITH, William, Esqr.; 274A+
SMITH, William, Esqr.;
    Occupant: Thomas IRONS; 347A+
SMITH, Genr Sam'l;
    Occupant: Wm. Lee FORMAN; 739A+
STANSBURY, Daniel; Senr; 260A
SENDAL, Philip; 88A
SENDAL, Sam'l, Senr; 98A
SENDLE, William; 108A
SENDLE, William; 1A
STANSBURY, John D. 180A

STANSBURY, James (heirs); 134A+
STANSBURY, Charles; 180A
STANSBURY, Francis; 314A
STANSBURY, John Ensor; 172A
STANSBURY, Jacob; 132A
STANSBURY, Ephraim; 99A
STANSBURY, Tobias E.;
   Occupant: James BUSK; 718A
STANSBURY, Dixon;
   Occupant: William SHAW; 103A
STINCHCOMB, Catharine E.;
STINCHCOMB, Catharine E.;
   Occupant: Valentine CARBACK; 422A+
STINCHCOMB, Catharine E.;
   Occupant: Joshua ANNIS
SMITH, Sarah;
   Occupant: Henry STONE; 374A
STONE, Henry; 119A+
SCARLF, William; 2A
STIMMER, Barnard U.; 663A
STIMMER, Barnard U.

THOMAS, Richard;
   Occupant: Luke DEMSEY; 636A
TAYLOR, Joseph; 111A+
TAYLOR, Joseph;
   Occupant: Thomas TODD; 115A+
TAYLOR, Jos. for Elijah TAYLOR);
   Occupant: Thomas TODD; 114A+
TAYLOR, Isaac;
   Occupant: Thomas TODD; 112A
TAYLOR, Richard, Senr;
   Occupant: Thomas TODD; 594A
TAYLOR, Samuel;
   Occupant: Thomas TODD; 112A+
WATTS, Sarah (for heirs of Jno.
   WATTS) 80A
WHITE, Mary; 62A
WILLIAMS, Genr. Otho H.
   (heirs); 530A+
WHEELER, Solomon; 25A
WALSH, William; 91A

General List of Slaves owned, or superintended on the 1st day of October, 1798, within the 8th Assessment District in the State of Maryland

BOWLEY, Daniel; 39 slaves
BARTON, Greenbury; 6 slaves
BUCK, Benjamin, Senr; 5 slaves
BUCK, Christopher; 5 slaves
BUCK, John; 2 slaves
BIDDISON, Jeremiah; 2 slaves
CHAMBERLAIN, John; 8 slaves
CARTER, Joseph; 3 slaves
COLE, Richard; 1 slave
COFFMAN, Abraham; 2 slaves
DEMSEY, Luke; 1 slave
DAUGHERTY, John; 1 slave
DALLAS, Walter R.; 10 slaves
DUKE, Charles; 2 slaves
FLOYD, Joseph; 3 slaves
FITCH, Robert; 3 slaves
FITCH, William; 7 slaves
FOWLER, Tamer; 3 slaves
FORMAN, William Lee; 4 slaves
GREGORY, Mc Francis; 1 slave
GREEN, Joel; 3 slaves
GARRETSON, Job, Senr; 1 slave
GARRETSON, Cornelius & Garret; 4
   slaves
GASH, Benjamin; 3 slaves

GREEN, Catharine, exr of
   Jos. GREEN; 4 slaves
GREGORY, John; 1 slave
HOWLETT, John; 3 slaves
HILLEN, Solomon; 8 slaves
HILLEN, Solomon;
   sup: Isaac RAWLINS; 6 slaves
HARRIMAN, Joshua; 3 slaves
HARRIMAN, William; 1 slave
HAMM, Thomas; 4 slaves
JARMAN, Benj., Senr; 5 slaves
JOHNSON, John; 3 slaves
LONEY, Amos;
   sup: Amos CORD; 2 slaves
LITZINGER, William; 3 slaves
LANGDON, Joseph; 3 slaves
LYNCH, Wm. Kid; 6 slaves
LYNCH, Joshua; 2 slaves
LUCAS, Thomas; 3 slaves
LANE, Providence; 2 slaves
LEMMON, Alexis; 2 slaves
LONG, John; 12 slaves
NORWOOD, Ruth; 12 slaves
PARLETT, David; 1 slave
PORTER, Robert; 9 slaves

ROBERTSON, James; 2 slaves
SENDAL, Samuel; 4 slaves
SENDAL, Philip; 1 slave
SENDAL, William; 1 slave
STANSBURY, Jno. Ensor; 9 slaves
SCARLF, William; 4 slaves
STANSBURY, Tobias E.; 11 slaves
SMITH, Wm., Esqr. (Balto);
  sup: Thomas IRONS; 9 slaves
STANSBURY, Jno. Dixon; 5 slaves
STANSBURY, Charles; 8 slaves

STANSBURY, Daniel; 7 slaves
STANSBURY, Francis; 7 slaves
STANSBURY, Ephraim; 2 slaves
STIMMER, Udrick Barnard; 1 slave
TAYLOR, Joseph; 6 slaves
TAYLOR, Samuel; 4 slaves
TAYLOR, Thomas; 1 slave
TAYLOR, Richard, Senr; 18 slaves
TODD, Thomas; 1 slave
WHEELER, Thomas; 6 slaves

Patapsco Upper Hundred

ATKINSON, Joseph; 68A+; Shoemaker's Chance
BAILEY McClen; 80A; pt Athol; hewd log dwlg hse, 2 stry, 20x16; log kn, 1 stry, 16x14
BAILEY, George; 692A; pt Murry's Desire, pt Athol; fr dwl hse, 1 stry, 32x16 *; fr kn, 1 stry, 32x16; stone milk hse, 1 stry, 14x14; log barn 46x22
BAILEY, Elam (8 slaves); Occupant: Charles LEWIS; 295A+; pt Maidens Choice & other tracts; log dwlg hse, 1 stry, 24x16
BAILEY, Elam & NORWOOD, Edw.; 805A; pt Islington & pt of other tracts
BARNETT, Peter; 98A; pt Wells Manor; hewd log dwlg hse, 1 stry, 36x16 *; log barn 40x20; log hse 14x12, add. log add. 1 stry, 14x12
BARTON, James; Occupant: Robert ELLITT; 100A; Robins Camp; hewd log dwlg hse, 1 stry, 20x16; log hse 20x16; log barn 16x12; fr dwlg hse, 1 stry, 32x16
BRAKELY, Mathias; 50A; Level Union; log dwlg hse, 1 stry, 36x14; log barn 32x20
BARTON, John; Occupant: George LEWIS; 10A+; pt Stout; round log dwlg hse, 1 stry, 20x16; round log dwlg hse, 1 stry, 14x14
BAKER, Nicholas; 100A (16 acres sold for taxes - 1805); pt Tan Yard; round log dwlg hse, 1 stry, 20x16; log hse 36x16
BALTIMORE Company; 16,557A; Georgia, Brunswick, Parish's Range and pt of sundry tracts; brk hse, 2 stry, 52x22; fr hse, 1 stry, 40x20; fr hse 18x16; fr hse 26x16; fr hse 40x12; log stble 12x12; fr coal hse 50x20; stone coal hse 76x30; pt stone furnace 35x32; pt furnace 30x16; pt furnace, 2 stry, 27x25; fr hses, 16x14 and 32x14; fr hse 48x18; hewd log poultry hse 10x8; log stble 10x10; fr hse 16x10; stone smith shop 20x15; fr hse 12x10; stone hse 14x10; stone stble 48x26, add. shed 48x10; fr cow stble 44x22; log hse 20x16; hewd log hse 20x16; hewd log hse 20x16; log hse 20x16; fr hse 12x12; fr saddlers shop 14x12; fr hse 40x24; log poultry hse 10x10; round log stble 36x14; hewd log dwlg hse, 1 stry, 28x18; log barn 30x18; log barn 32x18; log barn thatched with straw, 50x20; hewd log dwlg hse, 1 stry, 20x12; round log dwlg hse, 22x16; log stble 20x12; hewd log dwlg hse, 1 stry, 20x16; round log dwlg 20x16; round log dwlg hse, 24x16; log stble 20x16; log stble 16x12; log barn 20x16; log dwlg hse, 20x16; log dwlg hse 20x16; log dwlg hse 18x16; log dwlg hse 18x16; Occupant: Charles DEAL: fr dwlg hse, 1 stry, 54x18, add. brk shed, 1 stry, 18x9 *; stone kn, 1 stry, 30x22; brk hse hip roof, 1 stry, 16x14; brk hse 22x16; fr milk hse 15x15; fr meat hse 22x19; stone smoke hse 22x14; fr milk hse 10x10; Occupant: Osborne GRIFFITH; on pt Parishes Range; fr dwl hse, 2 stry, 24x19, with piazza 24x 7 1/2, by add. fr 20x16; log hse 14x12; fr hse 10x8; Occupant: Henry OWINGS: log dwlg hse, 1 stry, 40x16; log kn, 1 stry, 14x12; Occupant: Charles GRIFFIN: on Brown's Adventure; fr dwlg hse, 2 stry, 24x18; log kn, 1 stry, 14x12; log smoke hse, 1 stry, 12x10; Occupant: Wm. KRAUFT: hewd log dwlg hse, 1 stry, 24x21, add. shed, 1 stry, 21x12 *; Occupant: Ezekiel KENADY: fr dwlg hse, 1 stry, 28x16; round log kn,

1 stry, 20x16; round log smoke hse, 18x16; fr milk hse, 1 stry, 12x12;
Occupants: James FLIN, Wm. LEMMON, Jr., Wm. LEMMON, Sr., Rich'd WILLMAN,
Rich'd MORRIS, Thos. SPICER, Widow SMITH, Francis McDONEL, Joseph JENKINS,
Nich's LEWIS
BALTIMORE Company; 117A; pt Parish's Range; Occupants: Joseph BARTON; old
log dwlg hse, 20x16; James TOBIT; log dwlg 18x16; Wm. MORRIS; log dwlg hse
16x16
BARNETT, George; 153A; pt Ambros's Lot Augmented; hewd log dwlg hse, 1 stry,
20x18; log kn 16x14; log barn 40x22; log stble 22x14
BARNETT, Jacob; 97A+; pt Millford Enlarged; hewd log dwlg hse, 2 stry,
22x19; log smith shop 22x16
BLACK, Eliz'th; Occupant: Jacob PEACOCK; 90A; pt Hammons Rich Land; hewd log
dwlg hse, 1 stry, 22x18; log dwlg hse 14x16; round log barn 20x18
COUNSILMAN, George; 3A+; pt Cordwainers Hall; hewd log dwlg hse, 1 stry,
24x16; log milk hse 10x8; log 20x16; log hse 14x12
CHAMBERLIN, Robins; 357A; pt Cordwainers Hall; log dwlg hse, weather
boarded; 1 stry, 30x18, add. shed, 1 stry, 20x12, piazza, 1 stry, 30x8 *;
log kn, 1 stry, weatherbd, 20x16; log barn 40x22; log hse 18x44; log hse
16x12; fr hse 22x12; log stble 22x12; log stble 24x12; brk milk hse
12x12; hewd log smoke hse 14x12; fr cow shed 90x10
CROOKS, John; 133A; Ambros's Lot Augmented; hewd log dwlg hse, 1 stry,
24x22 *; round log kn, 1 stry, 18x16; round log smoke hse, 1 stry, 12x12;
log barn sheded 40x20;
CARROLL, Daniel (20 slaves); 164A+; pt Cordwainers Hall; Occupant: Rich'd
DUFFELL; hewd log dwlg hse, 1 stry, 38x30; fr dwlg hse, 1 stry, 20x14;
log hse, 24x18; log hse 16x12; log stble 16x14; Occupant: Barick STRONG;
hewd log dwlg hse, weather-boarded, 2 stry, 40x18, add. shed 14x12; log
kn, 1 stry, 24x18
CARNAHAM, Thos.; 6A; pt Smith's Forest; hewd log dwlg hse, 1 stry, 18x16;
hewd log kn, 20x16
CROUSE, Henry; 50A (20 acres sold for taxes - 1805); pt The Pavement; old fr
dwlg, 1 stry, 30x18
COOPER, Wm.; 109A; pt Frederickstadt; log dwlg hse, 1 stry, 34x16
CROMWELL, Jacob (1 slave); 112A+; pt Maidens Choice; hewd log dwlg hse, 1
stry, 16x16; log kn 14x14; log barn 24x16
CROMWELL, John; 88A; pt Maidens Choice; fr dwlg hse, 1 stry, 24x22; log kn
16x16; log stble 20x14
CORREY, James; 50A+ (40 acres sold for taxes - 1805); pt Maiden Choice; hewd
log dwlg hse, 1 stry, 24x20; log hse 14x14; log hse 14x12
CHAMBERLIN, Sam'l; 1A+; pt Stout; hewd log dwlg hse, 1 stry, 20x16
CROSS, Robert; 7A+; pt Parkers Palace; round log dwlg hse, 1 stry, 16x16
CLEM, William; 350A; pt Ashmans Hope; hewd log dwlg hse, 1 stry, 22x16
CROXALL, Sam'l and Thomas; Occupant: Joseph JENKINS; 252A (160 acres sold
for taxes - 1805); pt of sundry tracts; round log dwlg hse, 1 stry,
18x16; log kn 18x16; log stble 12x10
CROXALL, James; Occupant: John CROXALL; 264A; pt Brothers Inheritance; fr
barn 40x20; log stble 20x14
CONWAY, American; 85A+; pt Bear Thicket; hewd log dwlg hse, 1 stry, 20x18;
log barn 18x16; log stble 16x14
DUFFET, Richard; 5A; pt Cordwainer's Hall; hewd log dwlg hse, 1 stry, 20x16;
log hse 16x14
DILWORTH, Joseph; 2A; pt Gillboa; hewd log dwlg hse, 1 stry, 16x14

DORSEY, Allen; 100A; Long Acre; fr dwlg hse, 1 stry, 24x18; fr kn 20x16
DUN, Samuel & Arthur; 40A; pt Wells's Manor; hewd log dwlg hse, 2 stry, 22x18
DORSEY; Ezekiel Jno. and Ezikiel, Sr.; Occupant: Ed. DORSEY of Edw'd; 948A+; pt Parkers Palace and others; round log hse 20x16; log corn hse 30x12; log barn 50x24; log tobacco hse 24x24; log tobacco hse 24x24; fr dwlg hse, 2 stry, 24x24*; fr kn, 1 stry, 16x12; fr milk hse, 1 stry, 12x12; stone dwlg hse, 2 stry, 40x34 *; round log kn, 1 stry, 20x16; round log negroe hse, 1 stry, 20x16; stone pantry, 1 stry, 12x12; fr smoke hse, 1 stry, 12x12; stone milk hse 12x12
DORSEY, Edward; Occupant: Allen DORSEY; 2012A+; pt Taylor's Forrest and others; fr dwlg hse *, 1 stry, 24x18; stone forge 70x45; fr mill hse 20x20; stone smiths shop 18x14; stone kn, 1 stry, 34x16; stone milk hse, 1 stry, 10x10; stone smoke hse, 1 stry, 12x12; fr negroe hse, 1 stry, 24x18; fr hse, 1 stry, 24x18; stone coal hse, 60x30; hewd log stble 24x16; fr hse 16x16; saw mill 60x18; fr hse 24x18; hewd log hse 16x14; fr slitting mill hse 40x30; fr granary 40x14; open shed 50x14
EMMART, Wm.; 171A+; pt Wells Manor; hewd log dwlg hse, 1 stry, 20x14
EMMART, Michael; 171A+; pt Wells Manor; hewd log dwlg hse, 1 stry, 18x16; hewd log kn 16x16; log hse 12x8; fr barn 32x18
ELY, Maylon, 178A; pt Murphy's Delight; round log dwlg hse, 1 stry, 20x16; log kn 20x16; log barn 36x20
ELLICOTT, Judath; 91A; pt Hoods Haven
ERLACHER, Mich'l; 2A; pt Cordwainers Hall; hewd log dwlg hse, 1 stry, 24x18, add. shed 24x10 *; log stble 18x14
ENGLAND, Jacob; 2A; pt Cordwainers Hall; round log dwlg hse, 1 stry, 18x16
ELLICOTT & CO.; 778A+; pt Mount Unity and pt of other tracts; Occupant: Henry MILLER; fr dwl hse, 2 stry, 20x16; stone stble 62x38; stone shop 34x24; fr coal hse 24x20; stone shop, 2 stry, 15x15; saw mill 60x14; stone mill hse 100x36; stone store hse with cellars 53x33; fr stble 60x14; stone hse 16x14; fr stble 16x12; stone shop 33x18; Occupant: John ELLICOTT; stone dwlg hse, 2 stry, 32x26 *; stone kn; 18x18; Occupant: George ELLICOTT; stone dwlg hse *, 2 stry, 44x24; stone kn, 1 stry, 25x16; Occupant: Jonathan. ELLICOTT; stone dwlg hse *, 2 stry, 32x25; stone kn, 1 stry, 24x16; Occupant: Benfor RICH; dwlg hse, 2 stry, 1 of stone and other fr, 25x25*
FORMAN, Isaac; 1A; pt Cordwainers Hall; hewd log dwlg hse, 1 stry, 18x16
FITE, Peter; 147A; pt Wells's Manor
FORD, John Howard; Occupant: Wm. BEACHAM; 151A; pt Reserve; round log dwlg hse, 1 stry, 36x16; log kn 16x12; log barn 20x16; log dwlg hse 20x16
FITE, Andrew, Heirs; 130A; name of land not known; hewd log dwlg hse, 1 stry, 18x16; log kn 12x10; log stble 18x16
GODFERRY, Samuel; Occupant: Henry ELSON; 320A; pt Food Plenty; round log dwlg hse, 1 stry, 20x16; log barn 30x20; pt Mount Unity; stone dwlg hse, 2 stry, 34x20, add. fr 13x7 *; fr kn, 1 stry, 21x14
GIBENS, Thomas; Occupants: Conrod TEMPLER, Thos. SHAD; 57A+; pt Teels Search; log dwlg hse, 1 stry, 16x16; log dwlg hse, 1 stry, 16x16; stone cooper shop 30x20; stone barn 30x20; stone dwlg hse *, 1 stry, 30x20; log hse 1 stry, 14x12
GITMORE, Robt. & Co.; 190A; pt Crowleys Adventure and Woodens Venture; dwlg hse, 3 stry, 1 of stone and 2 of fr, 44x18 *; brk milk hse, 2 stry, 12x12; 4 stone powder mill hses, 2 stry, 30x22; hse, 1 stry, 36x32; hse

40x36; hse, 1 stry, 26x24; hse 22x18; hse 24x18; fr hse 20x16; log hse 14x14

GROUND, Adam; 24A+; pt Canans Lot; hewd log dwlg hse, 1 stry, 26x16; log hse 20x16; log smiths shop 16x14

GARDNER, John; 25A (4 acres sold for taxes - 1805); pt Islington; round log dwlg hse, 1 stry, 18x16; log hse 18x16; log barn, 30x20

HISSEY, Charles; 43A+; pt Chance; hewd log dwlg hse, 1 stry, 16x16; log hse 16x14; log hse 16x13

HIPSEY, Charles, Jr.; 19A; Addition to Hipsy's Chance; hewd log dwlg hse, 1 stry, 20x16; log stble 14x12

HUSH, John, Sr.; 3A+; pt Croxalls Addition; hewd log dwlg hse, 1 stry, 35x16; log hse 26x18; log hse 14x12

HUSH, John, Jr.; 100A; Johnsons Interest; hewd log dwlg hse, 1 stry, 20x18; log kn, 20x18; log stble 18x12

HANCOCK, Wm. 27A+; pt Teals Choice; round log dwlg hse, 1 stry; 20x14; log barn 23x12

HAGARTHA, John; 30A; pt Stout; fr hse, 2 stry, 34x16 *; stone kn, 1 stry, 24x16; hewd log hse, 1 stry, 20x16; stone hse 16x12; log stble 18x18; stone paper mill hse, 3 stry, 110x38

HIPSEY, William 25A; pt of sundry tracts; round log dwlg hse, 1 stry, 18x16; log kn 14x12; log stble 14x12

HIPSEY, Action; Occupant: Edward BEIL; 147A; Hipseys Adventure; hewd log dwlg hse, 1 stry, 24x16; log kn 12x10; log hse 24x12

JESSOP, Abraham; 3A; pt Smiths Forrest; fr dwlg hse *, 2 stry, 30x24 with piazza 30x8; round log kn 18x14; log stble 24x12;

KISER, Derrick; 33A; pt White Hall; fr dwlg hse, 1 stry, 16x14

KILLAMIRE, Lawrence; 50A+; pt Wells's; hewd log dwlg hse, 1 stry, 16x16; log hse 20x16

KRAUFT, William; Occupant: Jacob FRECKER; 14A+; pt Partner's Lot; hewd log dwlg hse *, 2 stry, 40x18; round log stble 40x16

LAUSON, Eliz'th; 167A; Lydias Pleasure Ground; fr dwlg hse *, 1 stry, hip roof, 42x16, add. fr, 2 stry, 20x16; stone kn, 2 stry, 20x16; fr hse, 2 stry, 20x20; fr smoke hse 16x12; Negro hse 14x14; fr hse 12x10; fr carriage hse 16x16; fr stble 34x24; log hse 14x14

LIMEBERGAR, And'w; 2A; pt Well's Manor; brk dwlg hse, 1 stry, 24x22

LIMBERGAR, Philip; 100A; pt Islington and pt Wells Manor; stone dwlg hse, 1 stry, 32x16; log kn, 22x14; log hse 16x14; log hse 26x22; log hse 22x20

LIMBERGAR, Wm.; 114A; pt Islington, & others; round log dwlg hse, 1 stry, 33x14; mill hse, 12x10; log barn 35x20; log shop 18x14

MOALE, Randall; 128A; pt Canaan

MITCHEL, John; 58A; pt White Hall & others; fr dwlg hse, 2 stry, 33x23 *; fr kn, 1 stry, 30x16; brk milk hse, 1 stry, 11x10

MILLAR, Rachel; 48A; pt Georges Park; log dwlg hse, 1 stry, 18x16

MALLET, Wiliam; 50A; Occupant: Eliz'th GINAVAN; Airs's Desire; round log dwlg hse, 1 stry, 18x16; round log dwlg hse, 1 stry, 18x16

MORTAN, Greenbury; 20A (20 acres sold for taxes - 1805); pt Stout; log dwlg hse, 1 stry, 16x14

McMACHIN, David; 250A; pt Parker's Palace; hewd log dwlg hse, 1 stry, 16x13; log kn 16x13

MILLER, Joseph; 212A; pt George's Park; hewd log dwlg hse, 1 stry, 28x16; add. shed 28x16; stone smoke hse, 16x10; log kn, 12x12; log barn, 32x20; log stble 15x12

LEWIS, Edward; 7A+; pt Parkers Palace; fr dwlg hse, 1 stry, 30x14

MACCUBIN, Zach'ah 765A; pt Ashmans hope, pt Bunkers Hill and pt other tracts; fr dwlg hse, 1 stry, hip roof, 20x16, with piazza 20x6, fr add. 18x12 with piazza 18x6 *; stone kn 24x18 with add. shed 16x8; hewd log hse 16x12; hewd log hse 18x18; brk milk hse 10x10; hewd log smoke hse 20x14; fr hse 18x12; old fr barn 40x20; log stble 20x12

MOAK, Henry; 68A; pt Nancy's Fancy; Occupant: Wm. KRAUFT: hewd log dwlg hse, 1 1/2 stry, 24x21; hewd log dwlg hse, 1 stry, 24x18; log stble 36x14; log barn 24x20; log hse 16x14; log stble 50x12; log hse 30x16; add. shed 21x12; Occupant: John MOAK: fr dwlg hse, 2 stry, 26x20; round log smoke hse, 1 stry, 16x16

MOALE, John; 406A; Job's Beginning

MOALE, Richard; 161A; pt Moale's Purchase

MOALE, Thomas; 107A; Huckleberry Forrest

NORWOOD, Edward; 449A; pt United Friendship; brk dwg hse, 2 stry, 48x28 *; brk kn, 1 stry, 22x16; brk hse, 1 stry, 22x16; brk meat hse 14x14; brk hse 14x14; brk barn 36x25, add. shed 36x11; stone cow shed 90x10; log stble 44x14; log stble 22x16

NORWOOD, Samuel; 423A; pt United Friendship; fr dwlg hse, 1 stry, 20x16 *, brk add. 26x16; brk kn, 1 stry, 18x16; stone smoke hse, 1 stry, 16x14; stone Negro hse, 1 stry, 36x20; hewd log hse 16x14; fr hse 14x12; stone hse 16x16; fr barn 38x24; log stble 40x30

OWINGS, Joshua; 200A; pt Scuts (Scott's) Level; hewd log dwlg hse, 1 stry, 24x22; log smoke hse 12x12; barn, 2 stry, 1 of stone, other of round logs, 50x24

OWINGS, Richard and Co.; 164A; pt of sundry tracts; stone dwlg hse, 2 stry, 30x18 *, fr add., 1 stry, 22x14; stone mill hse, 2 stry, 50x46; stone stble, 2 stry, 54x22; stone cooper shop 32x24; hewd log hse 16x16; stone hse 20x16

OWINGS, Caleb; 249A; pt Forrest and others; fr dwlg hse, 1 stry, 52x18 *; stone smoke hse, 1 stry, 14x10; fr barn 40x24; fr stble 30x14; log hse 28x24

POMMEAR, Peter; 98A (70 acres sold for taxes - 1805); pt Cromwells Range; stone dwlg hse, 2 stry, 28x18 *; log kn, 1 stry, 16x16; 2 old log hses, each 16x16; log barn 32x16

PIERPOINT, Walter; 98A; pt Pierpoint Friendship; fr dwlg hse, 1 stry, 20x14; fr kn 16x12; log barn 36x16

PIERPOINT, Joseph; 54A+; pt United Friendship; fr dwlg hse, 2stry, 16x14; 2 log hses each 15x13

PIERPOINT, Thos.; 100A; pt Friendship; round log dwlg hse, 1 stry, 16x12

PIERPOINT, Benad't; 54A+; pt Pierpoints United Friendship; round log dwlg hse, 1 stry, 20x16; log barn 30x15

PIERPOINT, Samuel; 20A; pt Pierpoint United Friendship; hewd log dwlg hse, 1 stry, 16x14; log kn 14x10; log stble 14x12

PIERPOINT, Mary; 80P; pt Georgia; fr dwlg hse, 1 stry, 24x15

PEN, Rizen; 36A+; pt Hopes Lot; fr dwlg hse, 1 stry, 24x20; log stble 12x10; log barn 20x16

PECK, Nicholas; 22A; pt Cromwells Range; hewd log dwlg hse, 1 stry, 22x18

PEN, Nathan; 36A+; pt Hopes Lot; round log dwlg hse, 1 stry, 16x14

PEN, William; 36A+; pt Hopes Lot

PEN, Caleb; 36A+; pt Hopes Lot; log dwlg hse, 20x16

PEN, Shadrach; 36A+; pt Hopes Lot

PEN, Carline; 6A; pt Hopes Lot

PEN, Maryam; 6A; pt Hopes Lot

POTTNEY, Thomas; 18A (4 acres sold for taxes for taxes - 1805); pt White Hall

PECK, John; 122A; pt Cromwell's Range; hewd log dwlg hse, 1 stry, 30x18; log hse 18x14; log barn 36x18; log hse 14x14

RANDAL, Johnze; 2A; pt Croxalls Addition; round log dwlg hse, 1 stry, 18x16; log hse 16x14

RIGHT, William; 3A; pt Croxall's Addition

RINEHEART, Joseph; 4A; pt Croxall's Additon; round log dwlg hse, 1 stry, 18x16

RUSH, Charles; 24A+; pt Nancy's Fancy; round log dwlg, 1 stry, 18x16; log stble 15x12

REESE, John; 18A; pt White Hall

RANDALLS, Nicholas; Occupant: Nich. WILLAMAY; 50A; pt Gilboa; round log dwlg hse, 1 stry, 16x16

REED, John; 14A; Millers Addition; hewd log dwlg hse, 1 stry, 24x20; fr stble 54x12; fr cooper shop 16x16; log hse 30x14

RIDGELY Charles of Wm.; 796A+; pt United Friendship; brk dwlg hse, 2 stry, unfinished, 50x26, add. fr, 1 stry, 26x20 *; brk Negro hse, 1 stry, 28x16; brk milk hse, 1 stry, 12x12; brk smoke hse, 1 stry, 16x14; fr barn 40x24; fr stble, 40x16; log hse 18x14; log hse 18x16

STINCHCOMB, Christ'r; 146A; pt Stinchcombs Park; round log dwlg hse, 1 stry, 16x14; log kn 12x10; log barn 35x20

SWAN, John; 691A+; Saits Morning Choice, and others; barn, 2 stry, 1 of stone, other fr, 36x24, add. shed 36x10; log stble 20x10; log hse 32x12; fr barn 24x20; log hse 10x10; fr dwlg hse, 2 stry, 22x16; kn 20x16; Occupant: Peter COHRAN: on Saits Morning Choice - stone dwlg hse, 2 stry, 40x30 *; stone kn, 1 stry, 22x20; stone milk hse, 1 stry, 16x16; fr hse, 1 stry, 20x16; log hse, 2 stry, 20x16; Occupant: Arthur McCLAIN: pt Tan Yard and other tracts - dwlg hse, 1 stry, 24x16, add. shed 24x10 *; log kn, 1 stry, 16x14

SHAMPAIN, Henry; 270A+; pt Tan Yard; brk dwlg hse, 2 stry, 40x18, add. brk 16x16 *; brk stble 50x30; log granary 18x16

SMITH, Samuel; 1A+; pt Mount Unity; stone dwlg hse, 2 stry, 30x20 *; stone kn, 1 stry, 20x14; stone currying shop 1 1/2 stry, 30x11; fr bark mill hse, 1 stry, 30x18

STOCKET, Wm. Thomas; 148A; pt Owings Adventure; fr dwlg hse *, 2 stry, 32x16; round log kn, 1 stry, 17x13

STIGAR, John; 110A; pt Maidens Dairy; fr dwlg hse *, 2 stry, 30x20, add. 20x15, add. 20x15; stone milk hse, 1 stry, 12x12; barn, 2 stry, 1 of stone, other fr, 36x24

STINCHCOMB, Wm.; 130A (90 acres sold for taxes - 1805); pt Stinchcomb Park; round log dwlg hse 18x16; log barn 35x20

STINCHCOMB, McClain; 134A; pt Wells Manor; hewd log dwlg hse, 1 stry; 21x16; log kn 16x15; log milk hse 10x8; log stble 16x10

STINCHCOMB, Enoch; 146A; pt Stinchcomb Park; fr dwlg hse, 1 stry, 20x16, add. shed 20x10; log kn, 15x10; log barn 32x18

SPENCER, Abel; 75A; pt Murphy's Delight; hewd log dwlg hse 21x14

STINCHCOMB, John; 112A; pt Mount ____; round log dwlg hse, 20x16

STRONG, Ludwick; 2A; pt Croxalls Addition; log dwlg hse, 1 stry, 16x14

STINCHCOMB, Thomas; 213A; pt Airy Hills & Pleasant Spring; small log hse

SMITH, Joshua; 14A; pt Pauls Meadows; hewd log dwlg hse, 1 stry, 20x16

STOCKSDALE, Edm'd; 125A; pt the Reserve
SHUGARS, Edw'd; 5a; pt Teals Search; log dwlg hse, 1 stry, 16x16
SMITH, Adam; 41A; pt Parkers Palace; hewd log dwlg hse, 1 stry, 18x16, add.
   shed 10x8; brk hse, unfinished, 15x15; log barn 30x16
THOMAS, Richard; 377A (110 acres sold for taxes - 1805); pt Wells Manor
TAYLOR, Solomon; 4A; pt Croxalls Addition; round log dwlg hse, 1 stry, 18x16
TAYLOR, Leven; 74A+ (74 acres sold for taxes - 1805); pt of sundry tracts;
   hewd log dwlg hse, 2 stry, 21x18; round log barn 36x20
TAYLOR, George; 6A; pt Smiths Forrest; round log dwlg hse, 1 stry, 20x16;
   log smith shop, 20x16; log stble 16x14
TALO, John; 362A (362 acres sold for taxes - 1805); fr dwlg hse, 1 stry,
   18x16; log kn 14x14; log hse 18x14; fr hse 25x18; fr hse 20x20; fr hse
   16x16
TOUZAC, Anthony; 124A (all 124 acres sold for taxes - 1805); pt Wells Manor;
   stone dwlg hse, 2 stry, 27x26; hewd log kn, 1 stry, 18x16; round log barn
   36x26
TSCHUDY, Martin; 58A; Sly's Venture; stone dwlg hse *, 2 stry, 34x22; stone
   kn, 1 stry, 17x14; stone milk hse, 1 stry, 17x14; barn, 2 stry, 1 of
   stone, other fr, 30x20, add. shed 20x10; stone cooper shop 20x14; mill
   hse, 2 stry, 1 of stone, other hewd logs, 30x24, add. stone 24x10
VANBIBER, Isaac; 69A; pt Georgia and Wells Chance; stone dwlg hse *, 3 stry,
   1 of stone, 2 of brk, 33x30, with piazza 33x8; fr hse, 2 stry, 20x16
WALTERS, Alexander; 346A; Occupant: Thos. MORGAN; 346A; Lucky's Adventure;
   hewd log dwlg hse *, 1 stry, 22x16, add. shed 22x9 with piazza 22x6;
   round log kn 16x12; round log smoke hse, 1 stry, 12x12; round log milk
   hse, 1 stry, 10x10; hewd log dwlg hse, 1 stry, 30x24; log stble 20x10; fr
   barn 22x2
WILDERMAN, Geo.; 77A; pt Wells Manor; hewd log dwlg hse, 1 stry, 26x16; log
   cooper shop 30x12; log barn 39x18
WILDERMAN, John; 50A; pt Wells Manor; round log dwlg hse, 1 stry, 24x18
WHITE, Charles; 3A; pt Croxall's Addition; fr dwlg hse, 1 stry, 26x16; log
   hse 16x14
WONT, John; 114A+ (25 acres sold for taxes - 1805); pt Croxall's Addition;
   hewd log dwlg hse, 1 stry, 20x16, add. hewd logs 20x16; log barn 24x16
WORDLE, ___; 2A; pt Gilboa; round log dwlg hse, 1 stry, 16x14
YOUNG, Jacob; 4A+; pt Cordwainers Hall; round log dwlg hse, 1 stry, 24x16
ZIMMERMAN, Geo.; 248A; pt McClains Friendship; hewd log dwlg hse *, 1 stry,
   20x16, by add. of logs 20x16, with piazza 20x7; hewd log milk hse, 18x10;
   round log dwlg hse, 1 stry, 24x20; log corn hse 16x12; log barn 40x22

ALGUIRE, John; 451A; pt Ribbles Folly; hewd log dwlg hse, 1 1/2 stry, 25x22, add. shed 22x10; log smoke hse, 14x12 *; log barn 36x22; log corn hse 22x12

ALESROAD (ELSEROAD), John; 150A; pt Hales Venture; hewd log dwlg hse, 1 1/2 stry; log milk hse 10x10; log barn 40x20

ALGUIRE, Jacob; 153A; Jacobs Beginning; hewd log dwlg hse, 1 1/2 stry, 25x20; log milk hse 12x8 *; log smoke hse 14x12; log barn 30x20

ECKLER Samuel; Occupant: Geo. BAKER; 125A; pt North Canton; hewd log dwlg hse, 1 stry, 24x20; log still hse 16x16; log barn 24x16

ALPAUGH, Zachar; 167A; pt Everything Needful; log dwlg hse, 1 stry, 20x18, add. log shed 20x9; log barn 40x20

ARMAGOSH, Peter; Occupant: Rich. SAMPSON; 150A; Hooker's Meadows Resurveyed; hewd log dwlg hse, 1 stry, 16x14; log still hse 14x12; log dwlg hse, 1 stry, 16x14; stone add. 16x12

AMBROSE, Welb.; 361A; Sapling Ridge; log dwlg hse, 1 stry, 20x16; log kn 16x10; log barn 30x18

BUTLER Amon; 144A; pt Butler's Farm; log dwlg hse, 1 stry, 20x16, log shed add. 28x8; log kn 20x16 *

BUTLER, Nicholes (1 slave); 137A; pt Butler's Farm; log dwlg hse, 1 stry, 20x18, log shed add., 12x18

BUSHY, Henry; 148A; Addition to William; hewd log dwlg hse, 2 stry, 29x22; hewd log kn, 16x14; log barn 16x14 *

BLIZARD, Wm.; 378A; Blizards Bottom; log dwlg, 1 stry, 24x18, add. 18x14; log kn 16x16 *; log barn 40x20

BUTLER, Absalom; 135A; pt Wm. Resurvey; hewd log dwlg hse, 2 stry, 24x18; hewd log kn, 16x16 *; log barn 36x18; hewd log store hse, 2 stry, 18x18

BROWN, John; 161A; pt Jermon Town; hewd log dwlg hse, 1 stry, 20x16, log add. 20x16; log barn 40x20; log milk hse 10x8; log smoke hse 12x12

BROWN, John R., Sr; 36A, name of tract unknown; mill hse, 2 stry, 1 of stone, the other logs, 30x26, saw mill

BAXTER, Samuel; 175A; Baxter's Choice; hewd log dwlg hse, 2 stry, 30x18 *; log barn 36x20; smoke hse 10x10

BUKER, Christian; 108A; Hooker's Meadow; log dwlg hse, 1 stry, 20x16

BROWN, Rich'd; 134A+; pt We Bit; hewd log dwlg hse, 1 1/2 stry, 22x16; log barn 25x20

BROWN, Matthias; 70A; Ludwickburgh; hewd log dwlg hse, 1 1/2 stry, 24x18; log kn, 16x14 *; log barn 40x24

BUKER, Jacob; 100A (50 acres sold for taxes - 1805); Newfound Land; hewd log dwlg hse, 1 stry, 18x14; log shop 16x14

BROWN, Henry; Occupant: Wm. BROWN; 186A; pt Flower Garden, pt Jacobs Beg.; hewd log dwl hse 1 1/2 stry, 24x20; log barn 40x20; log dwlg hse, 1 stry, 14x14

BROWN, Geo.; Occupant: Wm. BROWN; 160A+ (35 acres sold for taxes - 1805); Richards Delight; hewd log dwlg hse, 2 stry, 20x20; log kn, 19x14 *

BURNS, Adam and John; 585A+; pt Winchester Lot; Adam BURNS: hewd log dwlg hse, 2 stry, 26x24 *; John BURNS: hewd log dwl hse, 2 stry, 35x26 *; log barn 80x22; log milk hse 16x14; stone milk hse, 14x12; log smoke hse 12x10

BROWN, John, Jr.; 323A; John's Lot; log dwlg hse, 1 1/2 stry, 22x18; log barn 50x20

BAUGHMAN, Chris.; 248A; pt Everything Needful; hewd log dwlg hse, 1 1/2 stry, 22x18; log kn 18x18 *; log still hse 20x16; log barn 46x18

BUSH, Shadrack; 120A; Matthew's Friendship; hewd log dwlg hse, 1 1/2 stry, 20x16
BELT, Joseph; 173A; Huggemuggy; log dwlg hse, 1 stry, 18x16; log kn 14x12
BELT, Leonard; 239A; Three Times Survey'd; log dwlg hse, 1 stry, 16x14; log kn 14x12
BAXTER, Charity; 214A; Baxter Choice; fr dwlg hse, 1 stry, 30x20 *; log barn 50x24; log corn hse 16x8; log smoke hse 18x12
BLIZARD, John; 580A; pt Rochester; hewd log dwlg hse, 1 stry, 24x20; log barn 40x18; log stble 20x16
BLIZARD, Stephen; 148A; pt Hales Venture; hewd log dwlg hse, 1 stry, 18x16
CRAY, John; 122A; Addition to Elledges Farm; log dwlg hse, 1 stry, 20x16
CHENWORTH, Wm.; 102A; Helms Chance; hewd log dwlg hse, 2 stry, 26x16; log barn 56x24; log shop 16x12
CROMWELL, Conrad; 92A; pt Cromwell's Desire; hewd log dwlg hse, 1 1/2 stry, 20x14
CATEAR, Peter; 208A; pt Winchester Hope; hewd log dwlg hse, 2 stry, 30x24 *; log barn 44x24; log barn 46x26
CONROD, Henry; 1A; name of tract unknown; hewd log dwlg hse, 1 stry, 16x13
HIVELY, Christian; 80P; name of land unknown; hewd log dwlg hse, 1 stry, 26x22; log kn 16x14 *
CORBIN, Benjamin; 109A; pt Hickry Ridge; log dwlg hse, 1 stry, 20x16
CORBIN, Elijah; 105A+; pt Timber Bottom & others; log dwlg hse, 1 stry, 18x16; log shop 14x14; log still hse 16x16; log barn 20x16; log milk hse 10x9; Occupant: Wm. PARKS: log dwlg hse, 1 1/2 stry, 24x22
COX, Christopher; 14A; Hampstead; hewd log dwlg hse, 2 stry, 18x16, log shed add. 10x8
CULLISON, Joshua; 100A+; pt Sportsman Hall, log dwlg hse, 1 stry, 20x16; log kn 15x12
CHENWORTH, Rich'd; 39A+; pt Elledges Farm
CROMWELL, Nathan; 212A; Hooker's Ever Lasting Pasture; hewd log dwlg hse, 1 stry, 24x20; log kn 16x12; log corn hse 16x10; log stble 16x14; log barn 16x16
CHENWORTH, Arthur; 121A; Rions Ridge; log dwlg hse, 1 stry, 18x16
CRIDOR, John; 323A; pt Rochester
DITTO, Jacob; 273A; pt Iron Intention; hewd log dwlg hse, 2 stry, 24x18, stone add., 1 stry 14x14 *; stone mill hse, 1 stry, 24x20; saw mill 40x13; log barn 40x20
DAVIS, Wm.; 100A; pt Everything Needful; hewd log dwlg hse, 2 stry, 24x18; log kn 18x16 *
DEAL, John; 211A; Woodham & Philipsburgh; hewd log dwlg hse, 1 stry, 20x16; log add. 16x16; log smoke hse 16x10; log barn 64x24
DYE, Thos. Cockey; 175A; Dye's Adventure
EPAUGH, Henry; 371A+; pt Trouting Streams; log dwlg hse, 1 stry, 22x14; mill hse, 2 stry, 1 of stone, the other log, 30x30; saw mill 35x10; log fulling mill
EPAUGH, Catherine; 2A; pt Henry's Discovery; hewd log dwlg hse, 1 1/2 stry, 28x20; log barn 60x24
EPAUGH, John; 227A; Jacobs Lot Enlarged; log dwlg hse, 1 stry 16x16
EPAUGH, George; 124A; Epaugh's Hope; hewd log dwlg hse, 2 stry, 26x22 *; stone milk hse, 14x12; log barn 30x20; log shop 20x18

EVERHART, George; 312A+; pt Wells Care Enlarged; stone dwlg hse, 1 stry, 30x16, * stone add. 24x16; log milk hse 10x8; log barn 50x20; log barn 30x20; log shop 20x18

FRINGER, Michael; 32A; pt Baxter's Folly and Chesnut Level; hewd dwlg hse *, 2 stry, 20x16; log kn 20x16; log barn 20x14; log bark hse 12x10

FRAUNK, Eliz.; 68A; I Will and Will Not; hewd log dwlg hse *, 1 1/2 stry, 27x22, log shed add., 27x10; log barn 40x20

FISHER, John; 162A; Johns Pleasure; log dwlg hse, 1 stry, 16x15; log barn 20x15

FRANKFADER, Philip; 103A+; Good luck; log dwlg hse, 1 stry, 18x16; log barn 40x24

FISHER, Clarer; 308A; Clear A New Holland; hewd log dwlg hse, 1 stry, 20x_; log barn 40x24

FISHER Jno. of Geo.; 150A; Tyierary; dwlg hse *, 2 stry, 1 of stone, other log, 30x24; log barn 14x12; stone milk hse 14x12

FISHER, Leonard; 152A+; pt Friendship; hewd log dwlg hse, 1 1/2 stry, 24x20; barn, 2 stry, 1 of stone, other logs, 60x24

FISHER, Eliz.; 44A; Tyierary; brk dwlg hse, 2 stry, 26x20, log add. 26x20; log barn 40x20; log shop 18x16

FOUBLE, Michael; 198A; name of land not known; hewd log dwlg hse *, 2 stry, 24x20, log add. 20x10; log kn 16x14; log barn 40x16

FRAUNK, Peter; 80P; Hampstead; hewd log dwlg hse, 2 stry, 24x18

FOSTER, Thomas; 50A; name of land not known

FOUBLE, Melker; 277A; pt Stodards Delight; hewd log dwlg hse, 1 1/2 stry, 20x18, stone shed add., 20x18; log smoke hse 12x8; stone milk hse 12x10; log barn 30x18; Occupant: Thos. ALMACH; hewd log dwlg hse, 1 1/2 stry, 20x18; mill hse, 2 stry, 1 of stone, other logs, 26x24

FISHER, David; 64A; pt Rochester

FRINGER, Jacob; 100A; pt Rochester

FLUTTER, George; 103A; Staines Neglect; hewd log dwlg hse, 1 stry, 26x22; log still hse 16x16

GIST, Thos. of Wm.; 102A; Gist Good Contrivance; hewd log dwlg, 1 stry, 24x18, add. 18x12

GORE, Samuel & Philip; 180A; pt Nicholsons Manor; log dwlg hse, 1 stry, 16x16, log add. 16x10; stone milk hse 10x10

GILL, Thomas; 159A; Thomas Choice; log dwlg hse *, 2 stry, 23x17; log barn 40x20; log smoke hse 10x10

GILL, Urith; 66A; pt Tom's Choice; log dwlg hse, 1 stry, 20x16

GILL, Benjamin; 66A; pt Tom's Choice

GILL, Edward; 137A; pt Tom's Choice; hewd log dwlg hse *, 2 stry, 24x18; log barn 40x15

GRICE, Jacob; 2A; pt Richards Town; hewd log dwlg hse, 1 stry, 16x14

GROCE, John; 601A; Pleasant Hills; log dwlg hse, 1 stry, 20x18; log barn 30x18

GRAMMER, John; 762A; Abrahams Garden; hewd log dwlg hse *, 2 stry, 24x22; log barn 40x20; log still hse 20x18

GIST, Col. Thos.; Occupant: Joseph CORBIN; 408A; pt Frankford; log dwlg hse, 1 stry, 16x10

GILL, John (of Jno.); 124A; pt Butler's Farm; log dwlg hse, 1 stry, 20x16

GILL, Charles; 183A; Rogues Path's

GILL, Edw. of Jno.; Occupant: Jno. MALLONEE; 116A; pt Cray Enlarged; hewd log dwlg hse, 1 1/2 stry, 18x14

GILL, Jno., Jr., of Jno; Occupant: Thos. MURPHY; 406A; Buck Harbor Resurvey'd; log dwlg hse, 1 stry, 12x12
HELM, Daniel; 82A (15 acres sold for taxes - 1805); Imburgh
HOOFMAN, Henry; 98A; Addition to William; hewd log dwlg hse *, 2 stry, 17x17, hewd log add. 17x9
HOOFMAN, Michael; 160A; pt Wells Inheritance; hewd log dwlg hse, 2 stry, 24x18
HEDINGTON, Nicho's; 110A; pt Well's Inheritance
HILTERBRAND, Jacob; 66A; pt We Bit; log dwlg hse, 1 stry, 20x18; log barn 30x20
HOLMES, James; 234A; pt Rochester; log dwlg hse, 1 stry, 20x18; log shop 16x16; log barn 40x20
HOLMES, JOHN; 160A (10 acres sold for taxes - 1805); pt Rochester; log dwlg hse, 1 stry, 18x16
HAYS, Sarah; 323A (100 acres sold for taxes - 1805); hewd log dwlg hse, 1 1/2 stry, 25x20, log add. 20x16; log mill hse 20x20
HISER, Frederick; 113A; Cotom
HILEMAN, Conrod; 191A; Hogstead; hewd log dwlg hse *, 2 stry, 20x16; log shop 20x16; log barn 40x20
HARRIS, Alis; 50A; name of land not known; hewd log dwlg hse, 1 stry, 20x16; log still hse 16x16; log barn 40x20
HINKLE, Wm.; 36A; Friendship; hewd log dwlg hse *, 2 stry, 24x20; log barn 24x20
HENNISTOPHEL, Jacob; 225A; Merrymans Meadow; hewd log dwlg hse, 2 stry, 24x22; log barn 40x20
HENNISTOPHEL, John; 288A; pt Merrymans Meadow; log dwlg hse, 2 stry, 18x14; log shop 15x12; log barn 40x20
HENNISTOPHEL, Wm. and Barnet; 286A; Stophels Delight; log lumber hse, 16x16; stone dwlg hse *, 1 stry, 30x24; stone milk hse 12x10; log barn 30x25
HOOKER, Thomas; 448A; Point Lookout; stone dwlg *, 1 stry, 20x18, log add. 24x18; log smoke hse 10x8; log barn 44x24; corn hse 14x8
HORN, Adam; 177A; pt Frankford; hewd log dwlg hse *, 2 stry, 24x22; log barn 40x24
JONES, Charles; 126A; Addition to Elleges Farm; hewd log dwlg hse *, 2 stry, 24x18; log kn 18x16; log barn 50x20
JOHNSON, Hickman; 140A; pt Elleges Farm; stone dwlg hse *, 2 stry, 36x22; stone kn 20x16; stone barn 40x26; stone smoke hse 12x12
JOHNSON, Jeremiah; 216A; Share and Share Alike, Addition to Elleges Farm; fr dwlg hse *, 2 stry, 30x20; log kn 20x18; log barn 52x20; log smoke hse 12x12
JAMES, Thomas; 225A; pt Rochester; log dwlg hse, 1 stry, 16x16 log add. 16x10; log barn 30x20
JOHNS, Richard; 326A; pt Addition to Elleges Farm; stone dwlg hse *, 1 stry, 27x27; log kn 30x18; log quarter 30x18; log mill hse 40x36; fr lumber hse 18x14; log barn 78x18; log school hse 30x18; log granary 30x18; log stble 18x15; log hse 15x14
KELLY, Wm.; 124A; Good Contrivance; hewd log dwlg hse *, 1 1/2 stry, 20x18; log kn, 16x16; log barn 40x18; log corn hse 12x10
KING, William; 65A; What's Left
GITTINGER, Jacob; 233A; Bottle Hill; log shop 26x21; log barn 40x20
GITTINGER, Henry; 259A; pt Hookers Meadows; log barn 50x20; log barn 30x18
LOCKARD, Matthew; 95A; pt Rochester; log dwlg hse, 1 stry, 24x20

LEPPO, Jacob; 133A; Righ Bolts Meadows; hewd log dwlg hse *, 2 stry, 20x18; log milk hse 10x10; log barn 50x20

LOUDERSLAGLE, George; 141A+; Come By Chance; log dwlg hse, 1 stry, 16x14, log add. 14x14*

LOMMOT, Francis; 117A; Rope Warp (Ropewalk); hewd log dwlg hse, 2 stry, 60x30*; log barn 60x20; log shed 50x10

LITE, Jacob; 56A; Wells Inheritance; log dwlg hse, 1 1/2 stry, 18x14;

LANE, Rebecah; Occupant: Zale BUCKINGHAM; 184A; Millers Gain; log dwlg hse, 1 stry, 20x18

LOVEALL, David; 125A; Hickry Ridge; hewd log dwlg hse, 1 1/2 stry; 18x18, fr add. 14x14; fr shed 18x8; log still hse 16x16; log barn 37x17

LOVEALL, Wm.; 141A; Williams Luck; hewd log dwlg hse, 2 stry, 20x18; log kn 18x14*

LONG, Conrod; 138A (30 acres sold for taxes - 1805); Ann's Partion Enlarged; log dwlg hse 1 1/2 stry, 20x18, log add. 18x12*; log barn 30x20

LILLY, Samuel; 475A; pt Helms Chance and other tracts; Occupant: James MOORE, log dwlg hse, 1 stry, 16x16; Occupant: Joseph BUTLER; log dwlg hse, 1 stry, 20x18

LOVEALL, Luther; 165A; pt Iron Intention; log dwlg hse, 1 stry, 18x18

LISTER, Daniel; 158A; pt Jones Discovery; hewd log dwlg hse, 2 stry, 30x18; log milk hse 10x10*; log barn 58x25

LOVEALL, Henry; 248A+; Loveall Enlargment; hewd log dwlg hse, 1 1/2 stry, 21x17; log barn 46x18; log corn hse 14x10; smoke hse 12x12; milk hse 10x10

LOVEALL, Zachariah; 186A; Halefax; hewd log dwlg hse, 1 stry, 20x18; 186A+; log barn 20x20

LOVEALL, Susannah; 32A; name of land not known; log dwlg hse, 1 stry, 16x16; log barn 20x20

LANE, Abraham; 97A; pt Rochester; hewd log dwlg hse, 1 1/2 stry, 20x18; log kn 12x12

LAUDERSLAGLE; Solo'm; 53A; Hills Burgh; stone dwlg hse, 1 stry, 30x24*; log barn 40x20

LANE, Richard; 124A; pt Rochester; hewd log dwlg hse, 1 stry, 20x18

LOUDERSLAGLE, Adam; 55A; pt Hillsburgh

LOUDERSLAGLE, Francis; 25A; pt Hillsburgh

MILERON, Jacob; 45A; pt Williams Resurveyed; hewd log dwlg hse, 2 stry, 26x24; hewd log kn 20x16*; log barn 30x18

MURRY, Christopher; 428A; pt Addition to Elleges Farm; fr dwlg hse, 1 stry, 24x24; log kn 20x14*; log corn hse 12x12; log barn 40x22

MAJORS, John; 127A+; Bells Delight; log dwlg hse, 1 stry, 16x16

MAJORS, Jacob; 125A; pt We bit; hewd log dwlg hse, 1 1/2 stry, 26x20

MAJORS, Greenberry; Occupant: Mom BEACH; 315A (80 acres sold for taxes - 1805); pt Iron Intention; hewd log dwlg hse, 1 stry, 20x18; log barn 40x20

MATTHIAS, George; 28A; Goodneighbour; hewd log dwlg hse, 2 stry, 26x22; barn, 2 stry, 1 of stone, other logs, 42x28, add. of logs 38x28

MORTER, George; 226A; pt Winchesters Lot; log dwlg hse, 1 1/2 stry, 40x26; stone milk hse, 16x18*; log barn 50x24; log barn 40x24; log stble 20x16; log shop 16x16

MURRY, Rebeccah; 489A; pt Addition to Elleges Farm; hewd log dwlg hse, 2 stry, 26x18; log kn 20x18

MILLER, Jacob; 126A; pt We Bit; log dwlg hse, 1 stry, 20x18; log kn 16x14

MITTING, John; 158A; pt Rochester
NULL, Elizabeth; 82A; pt Smiths Spring; hewd log dwlg hse, 2 stry, 20x16
NULL, Jacob; 98A; pt Wells Inheritance; hewd log dwlg hse, 2 stry, 26x20; log milk hse, 12x10*; log barn 30x20
NULL, John; 110A; pt Wells Inheritance; log dwlg hse, 1 stry, 20x16; log kn 16x16
NOYER, Leonard; 102A; Decker's Plague; log dwlg hse 20x18; log barn 30x20
NACE, Geo., Jr.; 55A; pt Naces Tavern; hewd log dwlg hse, 2 stry, 30x26, log shed add. 30x15; brk kn 26x16; log barn 65x25; log stble 30x16
NACE, Peter; 106A; pt Every Thing Needful; hewd log dwlg hse, 2 stry, 24x18; log barn 52x22
OSBURN, Joseph, Sr.; 85A; Ellegies Folly; log dwlg hse, 1 stry, 18x14; log kn 16x16
OATS Peter; 426A; pt Winchesters Lot; hewd log dwlg, 1 1/2 stry, 33x24*; log kn 24x20; stone milk hse 22x18; stone barn 30x24, log add. 74x30; log still hse 22x18
OSBURN, Joseph, Jr; 225A; Buck and Doe Harbor
OWINGS, Samuel; 50A; pt Everything Needful
PRICHARD, John; 210A; Foxes Thicket; log dwlg hse, 1 stry, 20x18
PIXLER, Christian; 141A; pt Wisces (Wises) Mill; log dwlg hse, 1 stry, 16x16
PENNYBAKER, Wm.; 134A; New Germany; hewd log dwlg hse, 1 stry, 26x24*; log barn 40x20
PIXLER, Jacob; 355A; pt Wisces Mill, pt Well's Care; hewd log dwlg, 2 stry, 28x22*; log mill hse 29x20; log barn 40x20; log lumber hse 20x16
PLOWMAN, James; 150A; Jonathans Meadows; log dwlg hse, 1 stry, 20x16
PLOWMAN, Edw'd; 180A; White Oak Bottom; log dwlg hse, 1 stry, 28x16
PETERS Henry; Occupant: Geo. TRACEY; 50A; pt Manham Town; log dwlg hse, 1 stry, 18x16
PILOYER, Peter; Occupant: Frederick RHODES; 108A; pt Greens Goodwill; hewd log dwlg hse, 1 1/2 stry, 18x16, log add. 18x16*
PIERLY (BIERLY), Peter; Occupant: John HAGAR; 162A; Castle Hannah; log dwlg hse, 1 stry, 18x16; log barn 50x18
PORTS, Philip; 100A (30 acres sold for taxes - 1805); pt Manham Town
POPLETS, Jacob; 108A; Rinehearts Folly; log dwlg hse, 1 stry, 20x18; log barn 30x20
RICHARDS, Richard, Sr.; 1658A (total); Occupant: Moses CRAWFORD; Transylvania Resurveyed and sundry other tracts; brk dwlg hse, 2 stry, 23x20, log add. 18x16*
RICHARDS, Richard, Jr. and Sr.; Occupant: Rich'd SAMUEL; pt Corn Hill; stone dwlg hse, 2 1/2 stry, 44x26 *;log loom hse 26x16; stone lumber hse 17x17; log barn 64x26; log barn 33x26; log corn hse 20x10; stone mill hse, 2 stry, 46x26; saw mill 40x12; hewd log dwlg hse, 1 1/2 stry, 16x16; log barn 45x18
RUSSEL, Jacob; 36A; pt Flower Garden; stone dwlg hse, 1 stry; 44x19; stone milk hse 18x44*; log barn 40x20
RICHARDS, Richard, Jr.; 432A+; pt Corn Hill Resurveyd & others; hewd log dwlg hse, 1 1/2 stry, 36x18*; log smoke hse 15x18
RITTER, John; 288A; Novascotia; hewd log dwlg hse, 1 stry, 20x18; log lumber hse 16x16; log barn 40x20
REESE, George; 118A; Reese's Purchase; hewd log dwlg hse, 1 stry, 22x18; log kn 20x16; log milk hse 10x10; log barn 40x20

ROBERTS, Conrod; 300A; name of land not known; hewd log dwlg hse, 2 stry, 20x18; barn, 2 stry, 1 of stone, other of logs 50x20

RIGGLE, Henry; 152A; pt Everything Needful; hewd log dwlg hse, 1 stry, 18x14

RIDGELYS Heirs; 597A; Speculation

REESE, Jacob; 406A; pt Iron Intention

STULL, John; 82A; Smith's Spring; hewd log dwlg hse, 2 stry, 18x16

STANSBURY, Caleb; 449A; Oxmoore; log dwlg hse, 1 stry, 18x16; log kn 14x14; stone mill hse 28x28; log stble 14x12; log stble 16x16

SEGLAR, Peter; 100A; pt Manham Town; hewd log dwlg hse, 1 1/2 stry, 22x18

SHAVER, John; pt John's Hope & others; stone dwlg hse, 1 stry, 40x25; log kn 20x18 *; stone milk hse 16x14

SHAVER, Frederich; 47A; I Will & I Will Not

STOCKSDALE, Edw'd; 321A; Hookers Meadows; log dwlg hse, 20x18; log kn 15x15; log barn 50x24

SHAUK, John; 180A; name of land not known

STEVENS, Abraham; 404A; Stevens Defence; log dwlg hse, 1 stry, 24x20; log barn, 2 stry, 1 of stone, other logs, 64x25; stone milk hse 14x12

SWITZER, John; 180A+ (30 acres sold for taxes - 1805); pt Jacobs Beginning; log dwlg hse, 1 stry, 24x20

STORROP, Peter; 131A; pt Hickory Ridge; hewd log dwlg hse, 2 stry, 26x22; log barn 40x20

SIAS, Benjamin; 118A; Ann's Portion; log dwlg hse, 1 1/2 stry, 20x18

SYES, Joseph; 82A; Kellies Delight; log dwlg hse, 1 stry, 17x17

STEWART, Archibald & Co.; 200A; Ridgely's Ambition

SHAVER, John; 248A; pt John's Hope; barn, 2 stry, 1 of stone, other logs, 26x21

STEVER, Adam; 55A; pt Iron Intention; hewd log dwlg hse, 1 stry, 20x18; log barn 28x15

SAP, Peter; 133A; Stony Hill and others; hewd log dwlg hse, 2 stry, 30x25; log barn 40x20

SHOWERS, John; 933A+; Good Luck; hewd log dwlg hse, 2 stry, 30x26; log kn 16x14 *; log barn 26x16, log add. 18x16, log add. 50x24; stone shop 20x16; log shop 16x14; log barn 50x20; Occupant: John SELLERS; hewd log dwlg hse, 2 stry, 28x24 *

SENCE, Peter; 130A; Providence; hewd log dwlg hse, 2 stry, 24x18; log kn 20x16 *; log barn 25x14

SENCE, Christian; 110A; Mollys Delight; log dwlg hse, 1 stry, 20x16

SENCE, John; 84A; Prospect

SMITH, Christopher; 107A; pt Iron Intention; log dwlg hse, 1 stry, 18x16

SENCE, Peter of Peter; 100A; pt Iron Intention; log dwlg hse, 1 stry, 18x16

SHAVER, Jacob; 108A; pt John's Hope; hewd log dwlg hse, 2 stry, 24x22 *; log barn 40x20

SNYDER, Christopher; 200A; pt Iron Intention; hewd log dwlg hse, 2 stry, 26x22 *; log barn 40x20

STUMP, Mary; 24A; pt Iron Intention; hewd log dwlg hse, 2 stry, 24x20 *; log barn 30x18

STORM, Jacob; 400A; Jacobs Beginning; log dwlg hse, 1 1/2 stry, 18x14; log milk hse 12x9

STANSBURY, Wm.; 217A+; Mattergant; stone dwlg hse, 1 1/2 stry, 30x28 *; stone barn 42x40

SALBOOHER, Henry; 398A; Overland in Barren; hewd log dwlg hse, 1 stry, 33x15; stone milk hse 18x12*; barn, 2 stry, 1 of stone, other logs, 30x22

SHARRER, John; 319A; Stars Meadow; hewd log dwlg hse, 1 stry, 20x18; log kn 18x12; log milk hse 12x10; log barn 30x24

SELLERS, Paul; 217A; pt Everything Needful; hewd log dwlg hse, 1 1/2 stry, 26x22 *; log milk hse 10x9; log barn 40x20; log barn 50x24

SELLERS, Jacob; 100A; pt Everything Needful

SHUSTER, Joshua; 50A; name of land not known; hewd log dwlg hse, 1 1/2 stry, 20x16; log milk hse 11x11

SHUSTER, Catharine; 109A; Frances Houser; log dwlg hse, 1 stry, 16x16

SENCE, Peter of Christian; 200A; pt Iron Intention

SNYDER, Frederich; 132A; pt Petticoats Loose; hewd log dwlg hse, 1 1/2 stry, 22x18; log barn 40x20; log shop 16x16

STANSBURY, Tobias; Occupant: Wenson COLE; 250A; pt Greens Godwill; log dwlg hse, 1 stry, 16x16; log smoke hse 12x10

SHILLING, Murrey; 67A; name of land not known

SHINGLERY, Christop.; 50A; pt Castle Hannah; log dwlg hse, 1 1/2 stry, 20x18; log mill hse, 2 stry, 24x20

SNIDER, Martin; 146A; pt Petticoats Loose

TAYLOR, John; 181A (70 acres sold for taxes - 1805); pt Hales Venture; hewd log dwlg hse, 1 stry, 22x18

TROYER, George; 221A; Germantown; hewd log dwlg hse, 1 1/2 stry, 20x16; log barn 40x20

TOWSON, James; 88A; pt Jacobs Beginning; log dwlg hse, 1 stry, 16x16

TANNER, Philip; 50A; name of land not known

TANNER, George; 153A; pt Petticoats loose; hewd log dwlg hse, 2 stry, 20x18, log shed add. 12x10 *

VAUGHAN, Rich'd; 3A; name of land not known; log dwlg hse, 1 stry, 16x16

WILLIAMS, John; 230A; I Will and Will Not; log dwlg hse, 1 stry, 18x18; log kn 16x16; log corn hse 12x10

WORTHINGTON, Sam'l; 289A; Frogs Forrest and pt of other tracts

WORTHINGTON, John Tolly; 109A; pt Addition to Ellegies Farm

WAMPLER, Ludwick; 209A; Philips Retirement; log dwlg hse, 1 stry, 20x15; stone mill hse, 2 stry, 50x30; saw mill 40x13; barn, 2 stry, 1 of stone other fr, 55x22

WALKER, Hannah; Occupant: John ELRODE; 146A; Hehns Chance; log dwlg hse, 1 stry, 16x16; log barn 40x20

WALKER, Thomas; Occupant: Prudence WELCH; 101A; name of land not known; log dwlg hse, 1 stry, 16x16

WAREHAM, Henry, Jr.; 142A; pt Well's Care; hewd log dwlg hse, 1 stry, 28x24 *; log barn 38x26

WEAVER, Philip; 240A; pt Gothum and other tracts; Gumwell's Desire; hewd log dwlg hse, 2 stry, 26x20; log kn 18x16 *; log barn 44x25

WEAVER, Henry; 23A; name of land not known; hewd log dwlg hse, 2 stry, 26x20; log kn 20x16 *

WEAVER, John; 358A; Bets's Purchase; hewd log dwlg hse, 1 1/2 stry, 26x22 *; log kn 20x18; log milk hse 14x12; log barn 24x10; log shop 16x14

WATTS, Nathaniel; 114A+; pt Greens Good Will; hewd log dwlg hse, 1 1/2 stry, 19x18; log kn 16x12; log corn hse 20x18; log barn 20x18

WALSH, Robert; Occupant: Peter PIERLY (BIERLY); 295A; pt Castle Hannah; log dwlg hse, 1 stry, 16x14; log barn 20x14

WOODEN, Stephen; 256A+; pt Daniels Delight; hewd log dwlg hse, 2 stry, 22x18; log kn 14x12; log smoke hse 14x12; log barn 40x20

Pipe Creek Hundred

WHITELEATHER, A.; 161A; pt Ellegies Farm; hewd log dwl hse, 1 1/2 stry,
24x24; log barn 40x20
WALKER, Charles; 383A; pt Ellegiies Farm; log quarter, 20x18; fr dwlg hse, 1
stry, 30x30 *; stone milk hse 12x12; log poultry hse, 16x10; log corn hse
18x16; log stable and corn hse 65x25; fr barn 35x25
YINGLING, Christ.; 8A; pt Johns Pleasure; hewd log dwlg hse, 1 1/2 stry,
24x18 *; milk hse, 2 stry,1 of stone, other logs

Delaware Upper Hundred

All the lands above the original Liberty Road or Diggs Wagon Road are now
in Carroll county, part of Baltimore County until 1837.

ABBOUGH, Lawrence; 165A; pt Calidonia; log dwlg hse 16x16, 2 story; log kn
20x16, 1 stry; outhse 16x14, 1 stry, logs; old log hse 16x14, 1 stry
ARNOLD, Joseph; Occupant: James ARNOLD; 203A; pt Glandrick; log dwlg hse
18x16, 1 stry; log kn 20x18, 1 stry; smoke hse 14x10, 1 stry; barn 32x22,
2 stry; wood stble 16x10, 1 stry; log barn 32x22, 2 stry, log stble
16x10, 1 stry
ARNOLD, Joseph; Arnolds Harbour; 135A; log dwlg hse 16x12, 1 stry; log barn
32x20, 2 stry
ARNOLD, Benjamin; pt Rochester; 368A; log dwlg hse 18x14, 1 stry
BENNETT, Elisha; Gumfork; 178A; stone dwlg hse 38x22, 2 stry; log kn 18x14,
1 stry; smoke hse 15x14, 1 stry; log stble 18x16, 1 stry
BENNETT, Elisha; Occupant: Samuel BENNETT; 230A; pt Watsons Trust; pt
Bennetts Park; fr dwlg hse 26x24, 1 stry; log kn 18x14, 1 stry; moke hse
15x10; dairy 14x10, 1 stry; log barn 50x22, 2 stry; log stble 30x14, 1
stry; log barn 50x22, 2 stry; log stble 30x14, 1 stry
BENNETT, Elisha; Occupant: William BATTEY; 149A; pt White Oak Bottom; log
dwlg hse 20x18, 1 stry
BENNETT, Thomas; 244A; pt Wagerses Trust, Addition to Wagerses Trust,
Everritts Friendship, Marshals Discovery, Watsons Trust, Thos. Roadlog
dwlg hse 22x18, 1 stry; stone add. 14x12, 1 stry; log kn 18x18, 1 stry;
smoke hse14x10, 1 stry; outhses (all 1 stry): cornhse 18x12; stble 19x14;
stble 18x12; stble 16x16; dairy 8x8; stble 19x14, cornhse 18x12, cornhse
18x12, cornhse 16x16; dairy 8x8
BENNETT, Thos.; Occupant: Robert BENNETT; (all dwlgs, 1 stry); stone dwlg
hse 20x16; log kn 21x17; old kn 18x12; smoke hse 16x12; outhse 18x12,
logs
BENNETT, Thos. Occupant: Leven LAWRENCE; 273A; Tevesis Chance, Fathers Gift,
Costly, Stony Point, Bens Location, pt Fine Soil Forrest; old log hse
18x12, stry; fr tobaccohse 44x22, 1 stry, other old hse 18x16, 1 stry
BENNETT, Sam'l (1 slave); 285A; pt Sandy Bottom, Wageres Trust, Bennett's
Addition, Chance Luck; stone dwlg hse *, 30x22, 1 stry; log kn 15x14,
smoke hse 14x10; dairy 14x10, 1 stry each; out hse 16x12, 1 stry
BENNETT, Sam'l; Occupant: Lloyd BENNETT; 335A; pt Upper Molborough; log dwlg
hse, 18x16, 1 stry
BORING, Wm. (7 slaves); 122A; pt Escape, Logs Range, Tevises Park; log dwlg
hse *, 24x18, 1 stry; log kn 16x16; smoke hse 10x10; dairy 8x8, 1 stry;
log stble 20x12; log barn 18x18, 1 stry each
BARNES, Adam (2 slaves); 142A; Hopewell; log dwlg hse *, 22x18, 1 stry; log
kn, 20x16, 1 stry; smoke hse 8x8; out hse 10x8, 1 stry

94

BEVER, John; 479A; pt Rochester; log dwl hse 22x20, 1 stry; out hse 18x16, 1 stry

BAISEMAN, Joseph; 570A; Baisemans Discovery, Conaway Venture; log dwlg hse *, 52x18, 1 stry; log kn 12x12; smoke hse 8x8, 1 stry; log dairy 8x8, 1 stry; barn 48x22, 2 stry; log stble 20x16, 1 stry

BAISEMAN, Thos; 664A; Baeseman Discovery Corrected, Turks Range, Deerpark & Trouting Stream, Stepney Causway; log dwlg hse *, 28x16, 1 stry; log kn 20x16; log smoke hse 12x12; log dairy 12x12, 1 stry each; log barn 48x22; log stble 20x16; other hses 11x11 & 8x9, 1 stry each

BARNES, Dorsey; 132A; pt Morgan Tent; log dwlg hse 36x15, 1 stry, unfinished; log kn 16x12; dairy 10x8, 1 stry each

BARNES, John (1 slave); Occupant: Mathias POOL; 195A; pt Deerpark & Trouting Stream; log dwlg hse 16x16, 1 stry; log kn 18x10; smoke hse 12x10, 1 stry each

BAKER, Allen; 60A (18 acres sold for taxes - 1805); pt Flag Meadow; log dwlg hse 16x14, 1 stry

BUCKINGHAM, Obediah; 282A; Teagues Ramble, pt Edinborough; old log dwlg hse 20x16; log kn 16x16; stble 16x14; log stble 12x14, 1 stry each

BUCKINGHAM, Benj.; 191A; Buckinghams Goodwill, Smiths Fancy; old fr dwlg hse 20x16, 1 stry

BORING Ezekiel; 17A; pt Bucks Range; log dwlg hse *, 20x16, 2 stry; kn 16x16, 1 stry

BARNES, Elijah; 78A; pt Bucks Range; log dwlg hse 18x16, 1 stry

BUCKHANNAN, Wm.; Occupant: Ignatius HARDEN; 1900A; pt Windsor Forrest, Davis's Farm, Thos's Jolly; old log dwlg hse 40x20, 1 stry

BOND, Benj.; 130A; pt Rochester; log dwlg hse 16x14, 1 stry

BROTHERS, Joshua; 112A; pt Glendoick (or Glendoice); log dwlg hse 16x14, 1 stry

BARNHART, Davis; 78A; pt Lindsays Meadow; log dwlg hse *, 23x18; log shop 22x22, 1 stry

. BELL, Wm. of Phil'd; Occupant: Geo. GREAGRERY; 3977A; pt White Oak Bottom, Calidonia, Westphalia, Hookers Meadow, Isaac's Retirement, Hammonds Meadow, Bucks Forrest, Rochester, Mathews Forrest, Timber Neck; the mansion hse, brk 40x36, 2 stry; stone kn, 30x20, 1 1/2 stry; stone dairy 10x10, 1 stry - "The Elms"; stone barn 66x36, 2 stry; Occupant: Wm. GARDNER: stone dwlg hse 24x18, 2 stry

BEVER, John; 479A; pt Rochester; old log dwlg hse 16x14, 1 stry

BEVER, Adam; 100A (40 acres sold for taxes - 1805); pt Rochester; old log dwlg hse 18x16, 1 stry

BROOKS, Clement; Occupant Joshua BANKS; 1238A; Brooks New Adventure, Barbadoes, Daniels Delight, Duttans Desire, Castle Rising, Peters Choice, Friends Goodwill, Rogerses Bottom, Tricks & Things, Butlers Farm, Addition to Elijahs Farm; stone dwlg hse *, 30x18, 1 stry; add. fr 22x18, 1 stry; stone kn 30x18; stone kn 18x12, 1 stry; smoke hse 14x10; dairy 12x10, 1 stry each; stone barn 58x32, 1 stry; stone stble 24x20, 1 stry

COOK John; 108A; Watsons Trust, Escape; log dwlg hse 20x16, 1 stry; log kn 16x12, 1 stry

CONAWAY, Chas. (2 slaves); 498A; pt Baesemans Discovery, Willmott's Discovery,, pt Calidonia; log dwlg hse *, 38x14, 1 stry; log kn, 18x16, 1 stry; smoke hse 16x14; dairy 10x8, 1 stry each; out hse 10x8, 1 stry

CONAWAY, John (1 slave); 212A; Conaways Adventure, Baesemans Discovery; log dwlg hse, 20x16, 1 stry

COOK, Greenbury; 196A; pt Deerpark & Trouting Stream, Escape; log dwl hse *, 24x18, 1 stry; log kn 24x18, 1 stry; smoke hse 14x12; old log stble 12x12, one other 9x8, 1 stry each

COOK, Nicholas; 73A; pt Escape; old log hse 24x20, 1 stry; old log 16x14, 1 stry each, fit for fuel

CHRISMAN, Geo.; 237A; pt Buck's Forrest; old log dwlg hse, 24x24, 1 stry; old kn 20x14; stble 20x18, 1 stry each

CONNER, James (5 slaves); Occupant: MANRO, Jonathan (2 slaves); pt Bucks Park, Williams Neglect, Calidonia; log dwl hse *, 20x20, 1 stry; log kn, 20x20k, 20x14, 1 stry; smoke hse, 18x10, 1 stry; dairy 9x8; other hse 11x11, 1 stry; log barn 30x20; stbles 18x16, 10x12, 10x10, 1 stry each

CROSS, John; 75A; pt Carifagus; old log dwlg hse 18x16; old log kn 14x12, 1 stry each

CABLES (or CAPLES), Sam'l; 338A; pt Flagsmeadow, Bushey Hill, Cold Saturday; old log dwlg hse 16x14, 1 stry

COLE Wm., 18A; name of tract unknown; log dwl hse 15x14, 1 stry

CROMWELL, Wm. 180A (60 acres sold for taxes -1805); Hookers Meadow, Flag Meadow, Blindfold; log dwlg hse, 38x16, 1 1/2 stry; kn 16x12, barn 40x18, 1 stry each

CHRISWELL, Benj.; 150A (40 acres sold for taxes - 1805); name of land unknown; old log dwlg hse, 18x16, 1 stry

COOK, John of Thos.; 185A; pt Bakers Discovery, Welshes's Industry; log dwlg hse *, 32x18, 1 stry; smoke hse 16x10; log kn 18x16; out hse 12x10, 1 stry

COOK, Thomas; 100A; Chesnut Ridge; log dwlg hse 16x14, 1 stry

COCKEY, Thos.; 412A; Pleasant Meadow, Joshuas Gift, Molleys Habity, on which stand out hses built of stone 28x22, 1 stry

CONN, Daniel; 63A; pt Everretts Progress

CLARK, Elizabeth; Occupant: Nathan PHILLIPS; 24A; pt Marshals Desire; old log dwlg hse 16x14, 1 stry

DORSEY, Orlanda G.; 464A-40P; John's Park, Forrest Level, Long Forrest Resurveyed; log dwlg hse *, 20x16, 1 1/2 stry; log kn 30x16, 1 stry; smoke hse 20x12, 1 stry; log dairy 12x10, 1 stry; log out hse 20x16; 2 log stbles 20x16, 18x16, 1 stry each

DILLIN, James; 135A; pt Baker's Discovery; old log dwlg hse 24x18; log kn 16x16, 1 stry

DYE, Thos Cockey; 95A; pt Bonds Forrest Resurveyed; log dwlg hse 20x18, 1 stry; log smoke hse 12x10, 1 stry

DORSEY, Bazzel; Occupant: Sam'l STEVENSON; 213A; pt Rich Meadow; old log out hse, 18x16, 1 stry

EVANS, John of Job; 40A; Evans's Risk

ELEXANDER (ALEXANDER), Henry; 1402A; Monzie, Dunblane

FOWLLER, John (1 slave); 313A; pt Denmark; log dwlg hse *, 48x16, 1 stry; smoke hse 10x10, 1 stry

FRIZZELL, John; 115A; Hansons Choice; log dwlg hse 18x18, 1 stry; log kn 18x16, 1 stry

FRIZZELL, Absolam; 160A; pt Peach Brandy Forrest; log dwlg hse 22x16, 1 stry; log kn 12x10, 1 stry

FARVOUR, John; 98A; pt Bakers Discovery; log dwlg hse *, 22x18, 1 1/2 stry; log kn 18x18, 1 stry; dairy 12x10, 1 stry; log out hse, 18x16, 1 stry

FEID (FIST), George; 50A (40 acres sold for taxes - 1805); Occupant: Christopher LITTLE; Dorseys Discovery, Phillips Grove; log dwlg hse 18x16, 1 stry

GRIFFEE, Richard (1 slave); 23A-40P; Cross Chance; stone mill hse 45x38, 3 stry with 2 pairs of stones; fr stble 20x14, 10x10; dairy 8x10, 1 stry each

GORSUCH, Nathan; 309A; pt Bakers Discovery, Millfrog, The Dimer, Upermalborough, Rock Harborer; log dwlg hse *, 22x18, 2 stry; log kn, 18x16, 1 1/2 stry; log smoke hse 15x10; dairy 12x10, 1 stry each; log barn 36x20; log stble 18x16, 1 stry each

GIST, Joshua; 116A (75 acres sold for taxes - 1805); pt Fells Dale

GIST, Thos.; 298A; pt Surveyors Discovery, Good Luck

GORSUCH, Thomas; 218A; pt Morgans Tent, Plumtree Bottom, Grivan Friendship, Rabbits Pasture, Little Bit, The Woolf Trap; log dwlg hse *, 28x16, 1 1/2 stry; log kn 20x16; smoke hse 16x14; log dairy 12x11, 1 stry; other hse 9x9, 1 stry; log bar 42x22, 2 stry; log stble 20x13, 1 stry

GORSUCH, John (6 slaves); 157A; pt Morgans Tent, Plumtree Bottom; fr dwlg hse *, 20x16; log kn 22x16; smoke hse 16x10, 1 stry; dairy 8x10, 1 stry; log barn 38x18, 1 stry; log stble 20x18, 1 stry

GARDNER, Wm.; 175A; Edenborough

GOODWIN, Loyd; Occupant: George BUCKINGHAM; 210A; Shadrichs Last Shift; old log dwlg hse 16x16, 1 stry; log kn 12x12, 1 stry

GOODWIN, Loyd; Occupant: Will'm BUCKINGHAM; 210A; Shadricks Last Shift; log dwlg hse 20x18; log kn 14x12; log barn 30x20, 1 stry

GOODWIN, Wm.; 175A; Tevises Venture

GRIFFEE, Richard; 219A; pt Deerpark; loog dwlg hse 20x16, 1 stry; log barn 28x20, 1 stry

GARDNER, John; 175A; pt Edenborough; log dwlg hse 18x16, 1 stry

GORSUCH, Richard; 220A; Cock Pit, Robersons Beginning; one other tract, name unknown; log dwlg hse 18x16, 1 stry

HEWITT, Robert; 80A; pt Sandy Bottom; old log dwlg hse 24x18; log kn 22x12; smoke hse 14x14, 1 stry

HOOKE, Anthony; 180A; pt Carifagus; log dwlg hse *, 24x18, 1 stry; log kn 18x18, 1 stry; smoke hse 18x12, 1 stry; out hse 18x128, 1 stry

HOOKER, Jacob; 342A; pt Stevensons Folly, Long Medow, Blindfold, Simons Delight; stone dwlg hse *, 40x20, 1 stry; log kn 12x10, 1 stry

HOOKER, Rich'd; Occupant: Rich'd JORDAN; 260A; pt Flagmeadow, Hookers Medow; log dwlg hse 18x14, 1 stry

HOOKER, Sam'l and Richard; 440A; pt Hookers Meadows, Flagmeadow, Griffees Delight; log dwlg hse *, 20x16, 2 stry; log kn 16x13, 1 stry; smoke hse 12x10, 1 stry; log mill hse 28x20, 2 stry; 2 log stbles 20x18, 18x16, 1 stry each

HUNTER, Peter; 44A; pt Bonds Forrest Resurveyed; log dwlg hse *, 24x18, 2 stry; log kn 18x16, 1 1/2 stry; old log stble 12x10, 1 stry

HADEN, Wm.; 332A; pt Frienship Complete, Glendoice; log dwlg hse *, 18x16, 1 stry; log kn 16x15, 1 stry; smoke hse 12x14; other hse 16x14, 1 stry each; log barn 40x20; log stble 20x18, 1 stry each

HORN, Christopher, heirs; 60A; pt Rochester; log dwlg hse 16x12; kn 12x12, 1 stry each

HERRINGTON, Wm.; 70A; pt Glendoice

HAWKINS, Joseph; 258A (100 acres sold for taxes - 1805); pt Peach Barndy Forrest; log dwlg hse *, 24x16, 2 stry; log kn 18x16, 1 stry; log smoke hse 15x10, 1 stry; log barn 36x20; log stble 18x12; corn hse 14x12

HAINES, Michael; Occupant: George DIFFENDAFFER; 168A; pt Upper Malborough; log dwlg hse *, 18x14, 2 stry; fr Mill hse with 2 pairs of stones; 36x32, 2 stry; log barn 40x20, 2 stry; log still hse 28x24, 1 stry

HOWARD, Joshua and STONER in Co.; Occupant Anthony ARNOLD; 233A; Gistsylvania, Surplus, Strawberry patch; old log dwlg hse 20x10, 1 stry; kn 16x14, 1 stry

HUTSON (HUDSON), Robert; 250A; Hutsons Forrest; log dwlg hse *, 20x18, 1 stry; log kn 16x14, 1 stry; old log out hse 18x16, 1 stry

HALL, Jacob; Occupants: John and Nathan BUCKINGHAM; 325A (320 acres sold for taxes - 1805); Deep Valley Resurveyed; hse 32x16, unfinished, 1 stry; log dwlg 1 1/2 stry; out hse 18x16

HARDEN, Ignatius (2 slaves)Occupant: Grove SHIPLEY; 246A (land sold for taxes - 1805); pt Arabia Petre Enlarged; log dwlg hse 28x18, 1 stry; log smoke hse 12x10, 1 stry

HAMMOND, Nathan; fr dwlg hse 24x24, 1 stry; log kn 32x20, 1 stry; old stone store hse 20x18, 1 stry; smoke hse 12x12, 1 stry; dairy 12x10, 1 stry; log hses: 46x12, 20x12, 8x8, each 1 stry; stone hse 12x12, 1 stry

HOOD, James; log dwlg hse 40x20, 2 stry; log dwlg 16x12, 1 stry, well finished; log hse 48x18, 1 stry; old log hses 24x18, 12x12, 18x16, 24x12 and 8x8, 1 stry each

HARTIGAN, Wm.; 2A; Occupant: John McMURRUY (Supt.); log dwlg hse 28x20, 1 1/2 stry; log kn 12x12, 1 stry; smoke hse 8x8, 1 stry, on the publick road

JORDAN, Wm.; Occupant: Sam'l JORDAN; 361A; pt Buchingham Goodwill, Indian Town, Harryford, Sevensons Mannor, Bucks Forrest, Nathans Desire, Chance, Sandy Bottom; log dwlg hse 17x16; log barn 54x21, 1 1/2 stry; Occupant: Caleb JORDAN: old log dwlg hse *, 31x21, 1 1/2 stry; smoke hse 11x10; stone dairy 16x13

JORDAN, Thos; 2A; Duck Broad, Thos. Luck; old log dwlg hse 18x16; old log kn 16x12, 1 stry each

JAMES, Joseph; Occupant: Rich'd WHEELER; 77A; James Purchase; old log dwlg hse 16x11, 1 stry

JERVIS, Phillip; 153A; pt Edenborough, Arnold Choice; log dwlg hse 18x16, 1 stry

JACOBS, John (8 slaves); 1572A; pt Sevensons Mannor, Calidonia, Willmotts Mannor, Mattocks Folly, Barnes Level; stone dwlg *, 28x16, 1 stry; stone kn 20x15; stone smoke hse 12x10; stone corn hse 22x17, 1 stry; stone dairy 12x10, 1 stry; stone barn 56x32, 2 stry; stone hen hse, 10x8; old log hse 16x14; old log hse 18x14; old log hse 28x18; old log hse 18x16, 1 stry each

KNASH, John; 102A (75 acres sold for taxes - 1805); Slaineses Neglect; old log dwlg hse 20x16, 1 stry

KNEFF, Hannah; 56A; Rochester; log dwlg hse *, 24x20, 1 1/2 stry; log dairy 10x8, 1 stry; out hse 12x10, 1 stry

KNEFF, Henry 217A; pt Rochester, Friendship; old log dwlg hse, 20x18, 1 stry

LINTHACUM, Zachariah; 82A; pt Sandy Bottom; log dwlg hse 26x18, 1 stry, unfinished

LOGUE, Richard; 166A; pt Glendoice, Peggy's Choice, Rochester; log dwlg hse 18x16, 1 stry

LOGSDEN, Lawrence; 213A; pt Denmark, Peach Brandy Forrest; Samuels Neglect; log dwlg hse *, 32x16, 1 stry; smoke hse 8x8; log barn 28x20, 1 stry
LOGUE, Mathias; 90A; pt Glendoice; log dwlg hse 16x14, 1 stry
LOYD, Thos.; 255A; pt Hankins Fancy, Lawrence Industry, Fathers Gift; log dwlg hse *, 34x20, 1 1/2 stry
LAVELY, Christopher; 12A; pt Edenborough; old log dwlg hse 28x20, 1 stry
LITTLE, Ludwick (1 slave); 101A; pt Perseverance; log dwlg hse *, 48x20, 2 stry; log kn 16x12, 1 stry; smoke hse, 12x12, 1 stry; dairy 10x10, 1 stry; log stble 46x12, 1 stry
MASH, John; 20A; pt Sandy Bottom; log dwlg hse 16x16, 1 stry; log kn 12x8, 1 stry
McKLEFISH, David; 98A; pt Watsons Trust, New Tavern, Davids Hope; log dwlg hse *, 24x16; log kn 16x14, 1 stry; smoke hse 16x12; dairy 14x12, 1 stry each; old log barn 24x18; old stble 18x8, 1 stry each
MERRYMAN, Sam'l, Sr.; Occupant: Nicholas MERRYMAN (5 slaves); 172A; pt Cumberland; log dwlg hse 24x18; log kn 16x14, 1 stry; out hse 20x16, 1 stry
MERRYMAN, Sam'l; 110A; pt Cumberland log dwlg hse *, 20x18, 1 stry; kn 18x16, 1 stry; smoke hse 12x10; log out hse, 18x16, 1 stry; sawmill
MERRYMAN, Martico; Occupant: Manuel COOK; 166A; pt Cumberland; old log dwlg 18x16, 1 stry
MERRYMAN, John; Occupant: John BUCKINGHAM; 406A; pt Barbadoes, Charles Luck; old log dwlg hse 20x18, 1 stry
MALEN, Wm.; 160A; pt Flagmeadow; log dwlg hse 17x15, 1 stry
McMACHEN, David; Occupants: Edward and Nathan STOCKSDALE (2 Slaves); Adam SHIPLEY; 1935A; Deerpark and Trouting Stream, Willmoth's Meadows Resurveyed, Roberts Lot, Wartarice; stone dwlg hse *, 38x22, 1 stry; stone kn 39x17, unfinished; log dwlg hse 22x18; kn 14x12, 1 stry each
MANNAN, Abraham; 128A; pt Calidonia; log dwlg hse 18x16, 1 stry
MANNAN (MANNING), Richard; 100A; pt Bonds Forrest, Game Plenty
MERCER, Andrew; 155A; pt Peach Brandy Forrest
MASTER, Lee, heirs; Occupant: Thos HOLTAN; 633A; Warburrough Hills; old log dwlg hse 16x14, 1 stry
MITCHEL, Ann; 50A; pt Peach Brandy Forrest; old log dwlg hse, 18x16; kn 14x12; stble 16x14; dairy 8x8, 1 stry
MITCHEL, Gedion; 120A; pt Chesnut Ridge; log dwlg hse, 24x18, 1 stry
MONROE, Nathan; 441A; Upper Malborough; log dwlg hse *, 22x18, 2 stry; log barn 20x16, 2 stry
MANNAN (MANNING), Sam'l; 235A (235 acres sold for taxes - 1805); pt White Oak Bottom; log dwlg hse 18x16, 1 stry
MANNAN (MANNING), Joseph; 100A; pt Elizabeths Fancy
McALSTER, James; 19A; Schoolhouse Lot, Pleasant Meadow; log hse 18x16, 1 stry
NEWCOMER, John; 343A; pt Glendoice, Newcomers Delight
OGG, Benjamin (4 slaves) and Wm. OGG (8 slaves); 310A; Georges Lot, Bashan; fr dwlg hse *, 26x24, 1 stry; log kn 18x18, 1 stry; Negro quarter 20x20; dairy 10x10, 1 stry each; stble 16x16, 1 stry
OGG, George (5 slaves)/OGG, James (6 slaves); 200A; pt Carifaugus; log dwlg hse 20x14; kn 14x14, 1 stry
OUSLER, Ely; 224A; pt Bucks Range, Bucks Park, Adam Riders Industry; log dwlg 38x12, 2 stry; log kn 20x12; smoke hse 14x14; 2 log stbles, 16x12, 12x10;

OUSLER, Wm.; pt Bucks Range; 82A; log dwlg hse *, 38x12, 2 stry; log kn 25x19, 1 stry; add. to dwlg hse 16x12, 1 stry; old hse 18x16, 1 stry; old log milk hse 18x16, 1stry

ORR, John; 100A; pt Peach Brandy Forrest; old log dwlg hse 20x14, 1 stry

OWINGS, Christopher; 146A; pt Rich Meadow; log barn 50x22; log stble 14x12, 2 stry each

OWINGS, Leaven, heirs; 146A; pt Rich Meadow

OWINGS, Richard (15 slaves); Occupant: John GREEN (Supt.); 2277A; Owings Chance, Scheming Defeates, Timber Bottom, Rich Meadow, Stinchecombs Reserve, Browns Sharp, Amons Inheritance, Ruth's Gain, Ruth's Disappointment, Point Expritt, Surplus, Rochester; stone dwlg *, 30x20, 1 stry; 2 log kns 22x20, 1 stry and 22x15, 1 stry; smoke hse 15x12, 1 stry; log barn 72x24, 2 stry; 2 log stbles 40x20 and 22x16, 2 stry each

PHILLIPS, Thos, Sr. (7 slaves); 654A; pt Wageres Trust, Marshals Desire, Sandy Bottom, Bennetts Grievance, Dispute Ended, Conaways Venture, Basemans Discovery; mansion hse, wood, 24x18, add. 24x12, 1 stry; old log kn 18x12, 1 stry; smoke hse 16x12, 1 stry; log corn hse, 20x12; 1 old stble 24x20; other hse 28x20, 1 stry

PHILLIPS, Thos, Sr. (5 slaves); Occupant: Thos PHILLIPS, Jr.; 62A; pt Tevises Luck; old log dwlg hse 24x18; kn 16x12; old log corn hse 16x12; barn 20x18, 1 stry

PHILLIPS, Thos, Sr. (3 slaves); Occupants: John and Sam'l PHILLIPS; 276A; Willmoths Mountain, Willmoths Wilderness, Watsons Trust, Everretts Progress, Comforts Desire; log dwlg hse 20x18; out hse 18x12

POPHAM, Sam'l; 228A (225 acres sold for taxes - 1805); pt Wilsons Range, Long Trust; log dwlg hse 18x16; kn 16x14; stble 20x14

PARRISH, Jonathan; 125A; pt Flagmeadow, Parrishes Chance; log dwlg hse *, 20x18, 2 stry; log kn, 16x16, 1 stry; log barn 20x18, 1 1/2 stry

PARRISH, Wm.; 173A; pt Flagmeadow, Deerpark; log dwlg hse *, 18x16, 2 stry; log kn 16x12; smoke hse 14x10, 1 stry; out hse 8x8, 1 stry

PARRISH, Richard; 112A; pt Flagmeadow; old log dwlg hse 22x16, 1 stry

POOL, Henry; 278A; pt Georges Lott, Duncans Lott, Hooks Resurvey; log dwlg hse 24x18, 1 stry

PHILLIPS, James; 100A; pt Peach Brandy Forrest; log dwlg hse 18x16; log kn 14x12, 1 stry each; log barn 24x18, 2 stry

PHREN, Frederick; 148A; name of tract unknown; log barn, 28x20, 1 stry; log dwlg hse *, 30x22, 2 stry

RAUBOUGH, Henry; 175A; (100 acres sold for taxes - 1805); pt Glendoice; log dwlg hse 20x18, 1 stry

RANDAL, Christopher; 330A; pt Father's Gift; old log dwlg hse 20x18; log kn 16x14, 1 stry each

RINEHART, David; 197A; pt Upper Malborough

RIDGELEY, John, heirs; 150A; pt Bonds Meadow

SHIPLEY, Peter; 193A; pt Charles Luck; old log dwlg hse 20x188k 1 stry

SATER, Charles (5 slaves); 413A; pt Glendoick, pt Calidonia, Gay Meadows; log dwlg hse *, 16x16, 1 stry; log kn 20x16; smoke hse 10x10, 1 stry each; stble 16x12, 1 stry

SNITES, Ludwick; 60A; William Intent; log dwlg hse 20x16, 1 stry

STEVENSON, Edw.; 163A; pt Bucks Range, Canaan; log dwlg hse 20x16, 1 stry

SELMAN, Vachel (8 slaves); 148A; Neighbours Friendship; log dwlg hse *, 24x22, 2 stry; log kn 30x16, 1 stry; smoke hse 18x18; dairy 8x8, 1 stry each; log barn 26x18; stble 16x12; stble 16x14, 1 stry

SCOLES, John; 198A; pt Dowleys Range, Calidonia; log dwlg hse *, 26x18, 2 stry; old log hse 18x16, 1 stry

STEVENSON, Sam'l (5 slaves); 284A; pt Rich Meadow, Bite the Biter; log dwlg hse *, 22x18, 1 stry; log kn 12x12, 1 stry; stone dairy, 12x12, 1 1/2 stry; old log hse, 18x16, 1 stry

SMITH, Joshua (3 slaves); 561A; Surveyors Discovery, Rich Meadow, Surplus Land, Millplace, Strawberry Patch, Sidelin Hill; stone dwlg hse *, 32x24, 2 stry; stone kn, 20x20, 1 stry; log smoke hse 16x16; fr dairy, 12x12, 1 stry each; log barn 36x12, 1 1/2 stry

STRINNER, Richard (3 slaves); 325A; Lawrences Disappointment; log dwlg hse *, 28x20, 2 stry; log kn, 16x14, 1 1/2 stry; smoke hse 10x10, 1 stry; log sill hse, 32x24, 1 stry

SMITH, John (1 slave); 295A; pt Upper Malborough, Surveyors Discovery; log dwlg hse 20x16, 2 stry

STONER, John; Occupant: John HANNAH; 91a; pt Upper Malborough; log dwlg hse 24x20, 1 stry

STOCKSDALE, Edmond; 579A; Stocksdale Retirement; ; log dwlg *old log dwlg hse, 18x16;; old log kn 18x16 & smoke hse 18x16, 1 stry each; log corn hse 20x14; log stble 20x16; 2 old fr tobacco hses, 40x20, 1 stry each

STEEL, John; 30A; Hawkins Fancy, The Spike; log dwlg hse *, 20x18, 1 1/2 stry; log kn 12x10, 1 stry - A tavern; old log stble 18x16, 1 stry

SHARRAT, John; 22A; pt Rochester; log dwlg hse 16x14, 1 stry

TARMAN, Quillar; 4A; pt Hookers Meadow; log dwlg hse *, 42x18, 2 stry; log kn 16x12, 1 stry; smoke hse 10x10, 1 stry; stble 16x12, 1 stry

WORTHINGTON Thos (7 slaves); Occupant: Frederick HARPS; 496A; pt Perseverance, Abners Delight; log dwlg hse 18x16; out hses, 16x12, 12x12, 16x16, 30x24, 16x17, 48x22, 1 stry each, all of wood

WELSH, John; 98A; pt Ariabria Petre (called Comforts Delight in 1804); log dwlg *, 48x15, 1 stry; kn 30x18, smoke hse 12x10; dairy 9x8, 1 stry; old fr hse 18x16; log fr hse 18x16, 1 stry

WELSH, Mary; 398A; pt Arabia Enlarged; another tract, name unknown

WHEELER, Edw.; 40A; Vonsons Adventure

WOOLLERY, Christopher (4 slaves); 143A; pt Glendoice, Success; log dwlg hse *, 44x18, 2 stry; log kn 20x12; smoke hse 16x12; other hse 18x12, 1 1/2 stry each; log barn 74x22, 1 1/2 stry; 2 ware hses, 31x19, 28x13, 1 stry

WILLIAMS, Benj. (1 slave); 148A; pt Peach Brandy Forrest; log dwlg hse 26x18, 1 1/2 stry; log kn, 16x15; smoke hse 12x14; log barn 38x20, 1 1/2 stry; log stble 20x16, 1 stry

WAGERS, Luke; 79A; pt George's Lot; log dwlg hse 18x16, 1 stry

WILLIAMS, Robert; 177A; pt Flagmeadow; log dwlg hse 14x12; smoke hse 12x8; out hse, log, 18x16, 1 stry each

WINCHESTER, Stephen and William; 2026A; pt Edenborough

ALDRIDGE, Zachariah; 180A; name of tract unknown

ADAMS, Jacob; 1016A-80P; pt Chases Forrest

BARNES, Thomas; 50A; pt Charles Delight; log dwlg hse 14x14, 1 stry; old kn, 20x18, fit for fuel

BENVARD, Wm.; 60A; pt Shivers Integrety; log dwlg hse 16x14, 1 stry

BUZZARD, Daniel; 64A-84P; pt Shivers Integrety; log dwlg hse, 18x16, 1 stry; old outhse 20x18, 1 stry

BROWN, James, heirs; 135A; pt Tredways Quarter; old log dwlg hse, 20x18; old tobacco hse, 48x24, 1 stry

BROWN, Benj.; 191A; Favour and Ease; out hses; barn 36x20, 1 1/2 stry; log dwlg hse *, 24x20, 2 stry; log kn, 16x16, 1 stry; smoke hse 12x10; log dairy 10x10, 1 stry

BROWN, Abel of Jacob; 75A; Deavours Forrest; log dwlg hse, 16x14, 1 stry, unfinished; out hse 18x16; 8x8, 1 stry

BROWN, David (1 slave); 178A; Turkey Thicket; old tobacco hse 48x26; log dairy hse 10x8; log dwl hse *, 24x22, 2 stry; kn 16x16, 1 stry; smoke hse 14x14; other 12x12

BROWN, Abel, Sr (1 slave); Occupants: Joshua BROWN, Joseph GRAY; 300A; pt Hunters Chance; old log dwl hse, 20x16, 1 stry; log kn 16x16; smoke hse 14x10

BROWN, John, Sr (7 slaves); 198A; pt Hunters Chance; old tobacco hse, 48x24, 1 stry, fit for fuel; fr dwlg hse *, 24x24, 1 stry; log kn 16x12; stone dairy 10x10; smoke hse 12x12 & others

BOLEY, Daniel; Occupant: Nicholas DORSEY; 240A; Peticort Hope and others; old dwlg hse, 16x16, 1 stry; old kn, 16x12, 1 stry; smoke hse 8x8, 1 stry

BROWN, Elias (18 slaves); 1198A; Owenings Out Land Plains, Hammonds Fine Soile Forrest, Browns Independant Prospect, Browns Inheritance; log dwl hse *, 44x18, 1 stry; log kn, 20x18, 1 stry; smoke hse 14x12, 1 stry; hse 18x14, 1 stry; Occupant: John LEE: on Owenings Out Land Plains, 1 stble 30x14, 1 stry, 3 old out hses, 12x12, 1 stry; fr dwlg hse *, 40x20, 1 stry; stone kn 20x18; smoke hse 16x12; negro quarter 20x18, 1 stry; Occupant: John LINDSAY: on Brown's Independant Prospect; out hse 27x22, 1 stry; 16x12; 14x12; Occupants: Henry G. DORSEY and Andrew DEMMITT on Brown's Inheritance: dwlg hse 20x16, 1 stry; hse 16x14, 1 stry; smoke hse 8x8, 1 stry; out hses, 40x16, 1 stry; 36x12, 1 stry; 12x12, 1 stry; 16x12, 1 stry; 5 old tobacco hses, fit for fuel

BROWN, Mosses (6 slaves); 574A; pt Johns Chance, Fine Soil Forrest, Forrest Level & Owings Out Land Plains; log stble 20x18; hse 18x16; old tobacco hse; log dwlg hse *, 25x25, 2 stry; kn 20x18, 1 stry; smoke hse 15x12, 1 stry; hse 11x11, 1 stry

BUTCHER, John; 138A; pt Hoods Friendship; old log dwlg, 20x16, 1 stry

BERRY, Jerimiah; Occupant: Thos. DALEY; 250A; pt Belly Acke Thickett, pt Gardners Delight; old log dwlg hse, 16x14, 1 stry

BARNES, Nathan; 70A; pt Nathans Morsel; log dwlg hsew, 18x16, 1 stry

BROWN, Edward; 58A; Fine Soil Forrest; old stble, 16x14, 1 stry; log dwlg hse *, 24x18; log kn 18x12; smoke hse 12x10

BROOKSMITH, John; 300A; pt Hamton Cort

CHAPMAN, Joshua; 227A; pt Hood's Friendship; old fr dwlg hse 26x22, 1 stry; old smoke hse 12x12; dairy 8x8; stble 15x15; old tobacco hse 30x24

COLE, Sam'l, heirs; 670A; pt Dorseys Thicket; Thos. McMACKEN: log dwlg hse, 20x16, 1 stry; Occupant: Thos. JINKINS: old log dwlg hse, 24x24, 1 stry; old log kn 24x16, 1 stry

CROW, James, heirs (4 slaves); 138A; pt Johns Chance, Fine Soil Forrest; barn 24x22; stble 20x14; fr dwlg hse *, 24x24, 1 stry; log kn, 20x14, 1 stry; smoke hse 16x12; hse 12x10, 1 stry

COILE, Miheal; 149A-80P; pt Hoods Friendship; old dwlg hse, 16x14, 1 stry

CLARY, Elenor; 272A; Hobsons Choice & Molleys Choice, Valley of Strife; log barn 50x20, 1 stry, fit for fuel; log dwl hse *, 28x24, 1 stry; kn 18x12, 1 stry; hse 24x20, 1 stry

COMMINGS, James; 186A; pt Pars Ridge; 1 stry log hses, 20x22 & 20x16; log dwlg hse *, 30x18, 1 stry; kn 18x18, 1 stry

CONDAL, Richard (3 slaves); 48A; name of land unknown; out hse, 12x10, 1 stry; log dwlg hse *, 20x17, 1 stry; log kn 20x20; smoke hse 12x10; hse 13x13, 1 stry

CARROL, Charles of Carrollton; 6A; pt Elders Inheritance

DAVIS, Zachariah; 193A; pt The Valley of Strife; old log dwlg hse, 24x22, 1 stry

DORSEY, Robert; 125A; pt Hawksnest Rebuilt

DORSEY, Caleb of Th's. Beal DORSEY; 410A; pt Hamton Cort

DORSEY, Resau; 112A; pt Dorsey's Thicket; log dwlg hse, 14x12, 1 stry

DORSEY, Edw. of Edw.; 608A; pt Crambury Grove, Dorseys Delight, Progress; Occupant: Benj. McMACKEN: old fr dwlg hse, 20x16; log kn 18x12; old smoke hse 16x14, 1 stry each; Occupants: Sam'l McMACKEN, Hugh McMACKEN: log dwlg hse 16x14; log hse 20x18, 1 stry; 2 old tobacco hses 40x24 & 44x24, 1 stry

DORSEY, Johnsa (19 slaves); 617A; pt Dorseys Thicket; log barn, 42x18, 1 stry; log barn 52x22, 1 stry; old log hse 32x18, 1 stry; log dwlg hse *, 26x26, 2 stry; log kn 24x14, 1 stry; smoke hse 20x14, 1 stry; negro quarter 18x14, 1 stry; dairy 12x12, 1 stry

DORSEY, Ruth; Occupant: Johnsa DORSEY, guardian; 345A; Red Oak Ridge, Dorsey Industry

DORSEY, Ely (1 slave); 402A; pt Long Trusted Resurvey, Eleys Beginning, Eleys Folly, Addition to Eleys Folly, Dorseys Puzzel; old log dwlg hse, 16x12; log kn 12x8; old tobacco hse 44x22, 1 stry each

DORSEY, Leven; 370A; Polleys Habitation, Long Medow, Eliases Neglect; old mill hse 22x18, 1 stry, 1 pair of stones; stone dwlg hse *, 18x18, 1 1/2 stry; blacksmith's shop 18x16, 1 stry

DORSEY, Benj. (3 slaves); Occupant: Deborah DORSEY; 295A; Dorsey Thicket, Brothers Discovery, Kindals Delight; old fr dwlg hse, 14x14, 1 stry; fr kn, 16x14, 1 stry; smoke hse 12x10, 1 stry; 2 old log stbles 20x16, 16x10, 1 stry; tobacco hse 22x18, 1 stry

DORSEY, Mary; Occupants: Solomon WILSON and Charles WILSON; 186A; pt Dorsey Industry; old log dwlg hse, 18x16, 1 stry; smoke hse, 13x13, 1 stry; log dwlg hse *, 28x18, 1 1/2 stry; log kn 15x13, 1 stry; old negro quarter 33x15; log dairy 10x10, 1 stry

DORSEY, Edwd of Vachel (5 slaves); Occupant: Josias PERCE (or Pearce) (supt.); 1124A; pt Dexterety, Lawrence Plasant Valley, name of tract unknown; old out hse 22x16, 1 stry; log dwlg hse *, 20x18, 1 stry; log kn 20x16; dairy 8x8, 1 stry

DORSEY, Josias (6 slaves); 733A; pt Dorsey Thicket, Eleys Lot, Tricks & Things, Dorseys Choice; log barn 56x24, 1 stry; log dwlg hse *, 28x18, 1 stry; log kn 24x24, 1 stry; smoke hse 14x14, 1 stry

103

EVANS, Thos (4 slaves); 102A; pt Perseverance; log corn hse 14x12, 1 stry; log dwlg hse *, 28x28, 1 stry; log kn 16x12, 1 stry; smoke hse 12x12; dairy 9x9

ELDER, Owen (1 slave); 323A; pt Elders Inheritance; old out hse 12x10, 1 stry; stone dwlg hse *, 30x30, 1 stry; log kn, 18x12, 1 stry; smoke hse 8x8, 1 stry

ELDER, Sarah (2 slaves); 98A; pt Adams Garden; old tobacco hse 60x26, 1 stry, fit for fuel; log dwlg hse *, 28x28, 1 stry; log kn 12x8, 1 stry; stone smoke hse 12x12, 1 stry; old stone kn 22x14, 1 stry

EVANS, Daniel; 48A; pt Darlington, Evans Meadows; old stble 24x18; old barn 20x18, 1 stry each; log dwlg hse *, 40x18, 1 stry; log kn, 18x16, 1 stry; smoke hse 12x12, 1 stry

EVANS, John, Jr.; 56A; pt Darlington, Evanses Meadows; out hse 20x20, 1 stry; log dwlg hse *, 22x17,, 1 1/2 stry; log kn 17x12; dairy 8x8, 1 stry, each well finished

EVANS, David; 127A; pt Millfrog; old out hse 12x10, 1 stry; log dwlg hse *, 22x17, 1 1/2 stry; log kn 16x12; smoke hse 12x10; dairy 10x8, other 8x8

EVANS, John, Sr.; 127A; Evanses Venture; out hse 20x16, 1 stry; log dwlg hse *, 32x18, 1 stry; log kn 18x12, 1 stry; smoke hse 12x10, 1 stry; dairy 8x8, 1 stry, well finished

EVANS, John of Job; 40A; Evanses Risk

FRANKLIN, Rezin (3 slaves); 128A; Sherdines Range, Eppington Forest, name of tract unknown; 2 out hses, each 12x18, 1 stry; log dwlg hse *, 38x20, 1 stry; log kn 20x12, 1 stry; negro quarter 20x10; corn hse 20x18; dairy 10x10, 1 stry

FRANKLIN, Charles; 34A-80P; Charles's Last Choice; log dwlg hse 20x18, 1 stry, unfinished

FRIZZEL, Absolom; 35A; pt Wm's Purchase, Chaneys Stonye Meadow, Goodwill; old blacksmith shop, 20x18, 1 stry; log dwlg hse *, 26x18, 1 1/2 stry; log kn 16x12, 1 stry; smoke hse 12x10, 1 stry; dairy 10x10, 1 stry

FINLEY, John; Occupant: John COLE; log dwlg hse *, 36x22, 2 stry, with add. 21x14, 1 stry, at the end; kn 15x12, 1 stry

FRENCH, James; pt Greay Hound Forrest; 567A

FONDA, Abram; 100A; pt Forrest Level; old fr dwlg hse 42x16, 1 stry, cover off; old smoke hse 14x12, 1 stry; old dairy 3x8

GRIMES, James; 110A; pt Valley of Strife; old log dwlg hse 28x12, 1 stry; log dairy 10x18; smoke hse 12x8

GORE, Andrew & Cooper (2 slaves); 58A; Harmonds Valley & Elders Inheritance; stone mill hse 44x36, 2 stry, with 2 pairs of stones; stone sill hse 24x22, with add. 18x16, 1 stry each; stble 25x20, 1 stry; log dwl hse *, 24x20, 1 1/2 stry; log kn 18x16, 1 stry

GLOVER, John (7 slaves); Occupant: Joshua GLOVER (2 slaves); 356A; Johns Mistake, Johns Chance, Cramberry Grove, Glovers Addition; out hse 20x20, 1 stry; log dwlg hse 18x16, 1 stry; log dwlg hse *, 54x18, 1 stry; log kn 18x12; smoke hse 20x12, 1 stry

GOSNELL, Benj. 164A; pt Grayhound Forrest, another tract name unknown; old out hse 16x14, 1 stry; log dwlg hse *, 20x16, 1 stry; log kn 18x16, 1 stry; smoke hse 10x10; dairy 8x8, 1 stry, each

GILLIS, John (1 slave); 1670A; pt Dorseys Prospect, Bachelors Refuge, Late(?) Lad, The Back Branch, Cork to the Empty Bottle, Just in Sight; old fr dwlg hse 18x18, 1 stry; old kn 20x20, 1 stry; 2 old log stbles, 20x12, 18x16, 1 stry

HAMMOND, Nathan (27 slaves); 886A; Hammonds Pursuit, Tevis Adventure, Brunts Meadow, The Addition to Hammonds Pursuit, Additon to Brunts Meadow, Kingsale Resurvey, Gilchrists Meadow, Elders Inheritance, Labado, Edw. Discovery, Gilchrists Discovery, Johns Camp; 2 old tobacco hses, 28x22, 1 1/2 stry; old stble 46x12, 1 stry; 2 other out hses, 20x12, 8x8; stone store hse, 12x12, 1 stry; fr dwlg hse *, 24x24, 1 stry; log kn 32x20, 1 stry; old stone store hse, 20x18, 1 stry; smoke hse 12x12; dairy 12x10, 1 stry; Occupant: Peter BORING: log dwlg hse 20x16, 1 1/2 stry; old log kn 20x14, 1 stry; dairy 10x10

HOOD, Elizabeth (5 slaves); Occupant: Peter PORTER; 283A; pt Bachelors Refuge, Dorseys Prospect, Pole Cat; log dwlg hse, 24x16, unfinished, 1 stry; log kn 20x16; smoke hse 12x10, 1 stry each; out hse 16x14, 1 stry

HOOD, Hannah; Occupant: Orlando G. DORSEY, guardian; 283A; pt Bachelors Refuge, Dorseys Prospect, Pole Cat

HIPSLEY, John; pt Progress; 100A; log dwlg hse 18x16, 1 stry; smoke hse 10x8, 1 stry

HOOD, John, heirs; Occupant: James HOOD; 17A-80P; The Mill Lot, Hoods Fine; old stone dwlg hse 42x18, 1 stry, unfinished; stone mill hse 28x26, 2 stry, with 2 pairs of stones; saw mll hse 40x16, 1 stry

HOOD, James (9 slaves); 1553A; Sally Chance Resurveyed, Rich'd Third Chance, Dorseys Goodwill, Addition to Sally Chance Res., Bachelors Refuge; old log out hse 48x18, 1 stry; old negro hse 24x18; old smoke hse 12x12; 2 old stbles 18x16, 24x12; dairy 8x8, 1 stry each; log dwlg hse *, 40x20, 2 stry; log dwlg 16x12, well finished; log hse 48x18, 1 stry; 5 old log hses 24x18, 12x12, 18x16, 24x12, 8x8, 1 stry each

HOWARD, Joseph; 678A; Occupant: Benj. SHIPLEY; Wilks and Liberty, Pools Desire; old log dwlg hse 16x16, 1 stry; old stble 20x10; old tobacco hse 40x24

MOALE, John, heirs (2 slaves); 158A; Marys Promise, Darlington, another tract, name unknown; Occupants: John McMURRAY (supt.); old log stble 20x16, 1 stry, fit for fuel; log dwlg hse *, 28x20, 1 1/2 stry; log kn 12x12, 1 stry; smoke hse, 8x8, 1 stry (See footnote No. 1)

HOBBS, Wm.; Occupant: Wm. CONDAL; 616A; pt Chases Forrest, Shivers Integrity; old log dwlg hse 30x14, 1 stry; old fr tobacco hse 60x24, 1 stry

HAMMOND, Nathan; fr dwlg hse, 24x24, 1 stry; log kn 32x20, 1 stry; old stone store hse 20x18, 1 stry; smoke hse 12x12, 1 stry; dairy 12x10, 1 stry; out hses - log hse 46x12, 1 stry; log hse 20x12, 1 stry, log hse 8x8, 1 stry, stone hse 12x12, 1 stry

HOOD, James; log dwlg hse 40x20, 2 stry; log dwlg 16x12, 1 stry, well finished; out hses; log hse 48x18, 1 stry; old log hse 24x18, 12x12, 18x16, 24x12 and 8x8, 1 stry each

HARTIGAN, Wm.; Occupant: John McMURRAY; log dwlg hse 28x20, 1 1/2 stry; log kn 12x12, 1 stry; smoke hse 8x8, 1 stry, on the publick road

HOOD, Benjamin; 655A; pt Dorseys Industry, Marys Victory, Lawrences Pleasant Valey, Dorseys Industry; stone barn 50x20, 2 stry; log barn 24x20, 1 stry; stone dwlg hse *, 40x22, 2 stry; stone kn 18x16, 1 stry; log smoke hse, 14x12; dairy 10x8, 1 stry; hse 18x10, 1 stry

HOOD, Benjamin; Occupant: Joshua HIPSLEY; 627A; pt Johns Chance, Variation Breeds Contentions, Hoods Friendship, pt Mount Pleasant; old log dwlg hse 18x14, 1 stry; old log kn, 18x14, 1 stry; 2 log stbles 34x14, 14x10, 1 stry each

HAMMOND, Nathan; Occupant: Will'm THOMAS; 700A; pt Gilboa; old log dwlg hse, 18x18, 1 stry

HOOD, John; Occupant: Mosses BARNES; 732A; pt Concord Resurveyed; Hoods Fine Soil Forrest, Bucks Forest; old log dwlg hse 18x16, 1 stry; log kn, 18x14, 1 stry

LAWRENCE, Benj. 179A; Sidelin Hill, Addition to Progress, Improved Center; out hse 18x16, 1 stry; log dwlg hse *, 28x18, 1 stry; log kn 16x12, 1 stry; smoke hse 12x8, 1 stry

LONGSWORTH, Solomon; 284A; pt Valley of Strife; log dwlg hse, 16x16, 1 stry; log kn 14x12, 1 stry

MERCER, Richard (8 slaves); 263A; Mercers Trouble; log hses 26x10, 10x10, 1 stry each; fr dwlg hse *, 26x26, 2 stry; log kn 18x16, 1 stry; smoke hse 16x16, 1 stry; dairy 12x12, 1 stry

MERCER, Andrew; 178A; pt Hopsons Choice, Sally Chance; 2 log hses 14x20, 10x10, 1 stry each; log dwlg hse *, 24x16, 1 stry; log kn 16x16, 1 stry; smoke hse 14x14, 1 stry; dairy 8x8, 1 stry

MANEWEATHERS, Nicholas; 283A; pt Bachelors Refuge, Dorsey Prospect, Polecat; old log hse 16x14, 1 stry, fit for fuel

MANEWEATHERS, Nicholas; 331A; Occupants: John SOWERS, Jacob BOSLEY's heirs; 331A; pt Snowdens Cowpen, Addition to Snowdens Cowpen; Occupant: Eley BOSLEY: old log dwlg hse 18x16, 1 stry; old log dwlg hse 14x12; old log dwlg hse 18x16, 1 stry

MILLER, Daniel, heirs; Occupant: Sivley MILLER; 125A; pt Elders Inheritance, Johns Camp; log dwlg hse 14x12, 1 stry

OWENS, Bale (Beal OWINGS); 657A; pt Dexterity, Youngs Folley, Eleys Lot, Vachels Purchase, Addition to Vachels Purchase and tract of unknown name; log hse 16x12, log hse 12x12, 1 stry; log dwlg hse *, 20x16, 2 stry; log kn, 20x16, 1 1/2 stry; log smoke hse 12x12; 2 other hses 10x10 each

ODONNAL, John (Col. John O'DONNELL); Occupant: William ORT; 498A; pt Winsor Forrest, Good Neighbourhood; stone dairy, 12x12, 1 stry; old log stble 70x14, 1 stry; fr dwlg hse *, 27x16, 1 1/2 stry, with add. of 16x16 at one end, 1 1/2 stry; log kn 20x16, with add. 18x12, 2 stry; fr hse 14x12, 1 stry (well finished)

PATTERSON, Wm. (25 slaves); 1558A; pt Neighbours Goodwill, Chaneys Neglect, Progress, Johns Chance, Chaneys Neglect, Perseverance, Everetts Progress, Whipses Progress, Adams Garden, Charles Delight; log barn 54x24, 1 stry; 2 stbles 50x16, 1 stry, & 20x16; old negro quarter 24x18; old hse 40x12, 1 stry; log dwlg hse *, 54x25, 2 stry, well finished; log kn 24x24, 1 1/2 stry; smoke hse 10x10, 1 stry; Occupant: James CONNER (Supt.): log dwlg 50x20 *, 1 stry; log kn 20x12, 1 stry; log kn 18x16, 1 stry; smoke hse 12x12; stone dairy 12x12

PORTER, Joshua (2 slaves); 444A; Porter Pleasant Level; log barn 60x26, 2 stry; log barn 44x22, 1 stry; log dwl hse *, 24x18, 2 stry; log kn 29x18, 1 stry; smoke hse 14x12; dairy 10x8, 1 stry

PACAN, Henry, heirs; 500A; pt Eppington Forrest

PHILLIPS, Thos., Jr.; 164A; pt Malborough; old log dwlg hse 16x16, 1 stry; log stble 12x10, 1 stry

RANDAL, Nathan; 6A-120P; pt Tevis's Chance; stone dwlg hse 26x20, 1 stry

SCOT (SCOTT), John (16 slaves); Occupant: Tush HEARN (supt.); 308A; Peters Garden; outhse 24x12, 1 stry; log dwlg hse *, 18x16, 1 stry; log kn 20x16; log smokehse 12x10; dairy 8x8, 1 stry each

SPUIRER, Alpheas; 197A-80P; pt Valley of Strife, Pleasant Spring, Hobsons Choice; old log dwlg hse 38x16; 1 stry, kn 16x12, 1 stry; barn 38x20; old barn 16x14

SHIPLEY, Absolam, Sr. (6 slaves); Occupant: Absolam SHIPLEY, Jr. (1 slave); 308A; pt Everett's Progress, Kindal Delight, Good Neighbourhood; Perseverance, Addition to Everett's Progress; log dwlg hse 20x18, 1 1/2 stry; log dwlg hse 32x18, both unfinished; log dwlg hse 20x18, 1 1/2 stry; log kn 20x18; log smokehse 12x10, 1 stry each

SHIPLEY, Adam, Sr.; 171A; pt Everett's Progress; old log dwlg hse 20x16; smokehse 12x10; log stble 15x40; barn 36x20, 1 stry each

SNOWDEN, Francis; Occupants: John WIER, Miheal SCANTLIN, Mary SNOWDEN; 248A; Watsons Trust; old log dwlg 27x27, 1 1/2 stry; mill hse half stone and half wood 36x26, 2 stry, with 2 pairs of stones; dwlg, 16x14, 1 stry; dwlg hse 16x14, 1 stry; kn 10x10; log barn 52x26, 2 stry; old tobacco hse 38x20, 1 stry, fit for fuel; stone dwlg hse *, 36x24, 1 stry; stone quarter 30x18, 1 1/2 stry; stone cook kn, 16x10, 1 stry; stone smoke hse, 16x12, 1 stry; old wooden hse 16x10, 1 stry

SNOWDEN, Francis; Occupant: Thos. LOCKARD; 707A; pt Escape, Snowdens Chance, The Peapatch, The Spring Road, Snowdens Cockermouth, Tevis' Luck, Eagles Nest; old log dwlg hse 30x20, 1 stry

SHIPLEY, Wm.; Occupant: John CRATON; 65A; pt Hoods Friendship; old log dwlg hse 14x12, 1 stry

STEVENS, Rezin; Occupant: Joshua POOL; 386A; pt Cranberry Grove, Whipses Purchase, Johns Chance, Hoods Friendship; fr dwlg hse 20x20 *, 1 stry; log kn 20x18, 1 stry; out hse, log dwlg hse 26x16, 1 stry

SHIPLEY, Brice (1 slave); 180A; Long Reach; old log dwlg hse 20x18, 1 stry; old log hse 18x14, 1 stry

SHIPLEY, Duncan (1 slave); 221A (sold for taxes in 1805); Malones Resolution, Hard Ditching; log dwlg hse *, 24x20, 1 stry; log kn 18x10, 1 stry; smoke hse 10x10; dairy 8x8, 1 stry each; log barn 44x16; stble 20x16, 1 stry

SHIPLEY, Ezekiel; 114A (114 acres sold for taxes - 1805); pt Malones Resolution; old log dwlg hse 18x16; kn 16x14, 1 stry; old tobacco hse 40x22

SELBY, Nicholas; 169A; pt Absolams Chance; log dwlg hse, 22x17, 1 1/2 stry; log kn 16x12, 1 stry; smoke hse 16x14, 1 stry; dairy 10x10, other hse 11x11

SHIPLEY, Robert; 312A; pt Adams Garden, Charles Purchase, Williams Purchase, assd by Martice MERRYMAN

TENER, George; Occupant: Phillip TENER; 483A; pt Hawks Nest Rebuilt, Eppington Forrest; log dwlg hse *, 26x20, 2 stry; log dairy 23x15, 2 stry, finished; log barn 45x24, 2 stry

TENER, Jacob; 61A; pt Eppington Forrest; 61A; log dwlg hse 20x16, 1 1/2 stry; log kn 16x16, 1 stry   .

TEVIS, Benj. (6 slaves); 319A; pt Victory; Fine Soil Forrest; stone dwlg hse *, 28x24, 1 stry; log kn 24x18, 1 stry; smoke hse 16x12; stone dairy 12x12; log hse 10x10, 1 stry each; barn 20x20, 1 stry; old tobacco hse 40x22, 1 stry; old stble 20x12; old log stble 16x14, 1 stry each

TALBOT, Jerimiah, heirs; Bayley Income; 20A

VANBIBER, James; Occupant: Charles RIKETT; Empty Bottle, pt Bachelors Refuge; 251A; old log dwlg hse 16x14, 1 1/2 stry; 1 log barn 26x22, 2 stry

WHIGHT, Rich'd; 148A; pt Adams Garden; log dwlg hse 24x18, 2 stry; log dairy 10x10, 1 stry; outhse 34x17, 1 outhse 16x12, 1 stry; old log barn 34x17; stble 16x12, 1 stry

WORTHINGTON, John; Occupant: Zachariah CLARY; 2174A; pt Ebpington Forrest, pt Mansfields purchase; old log dwlg hse 16x16; kn 16x14, 1 stry; old fr tobacco hse 44x24, 1 stry; old log stble 22x14, 1 stry

WARFIELD, Seth; Occupant: James LUCAS; 190A; name of tract unknown; old dwlg hse 16x14, 1 stry

WALKER, James; 95A; tract, name unknown

ZEPT, Christopher; Occupant: Adam ZEPT; 116A; pt Cramberry Grove; old log dwlg hse 18x16,. 1 stry

Footnote No. 1.   A Tavern on 1794 map.   Related is case Samuel MOALE vs. Geo. ENSOR, Henry COVER, John McMURRAY, Samuel McMURRY, John LITTLE.   See also deed dated Aug 1805, W.G. 87-329 & W.G. 145-442, Randal Hulse MOALE of Balto. City to John McMURRAY of Balto. Co., Farmer, 40A - Marys Promise, 89A - pt Darlington

Taneytown & Piney Creek Hundred, District 6

ANGEL, Charles; pt Ohio & others as before, 166A

ANGEL, Michael; pt The Resurvey on Brothers Agreement, 100A, assd before Matthews SHROYER

ARMSTRONG, James; pt The Resurvey on Brothers Agreement, 150A

AISBERGER, John; pt Ross's Range, 30A - midling land, built log hse & stble, assd before in the other Hundred to Upton SCOTT

ADAMS, Thomas; pt Owings Chance & others, 100A, poor land, built a log barn, assd before to John STONER, Sr.

ADAM, Andrew; pt Resurvey on Lemmons Range, 198 3/4 A, addition to barn, assd before to Jno. LEMON's heirs

ALGREE, Rachel; pt Black Oak Level, 45 1/2 A

ARNOLD, John; pt Ohio & others, 95A, assd before to Christopher HASNLIN's heirs

BUFFENDEN, Jacob; pt Bedford, 220A, built a saw mill, 120 acres formerly assd to N. BRUCE

BROOKE, Raphail; Brothers Agreement, 306A

BRACK, Adam; pt the Resurvey on Brothers Agreement, 120A, 11 acres assd before to Adam GOOD

BRICE, Normand; pt Epping Forrest, error being assd to Robt DODS

BARRACK, John; pt Resurvey on Brothers Agreement, 245A, assd before to Andrew BOYD of Balto. Town

BLACK, Joseph (miller); pt Runney Mead, 192A, assd before to Catharine and to Joseph BLACK

BLACK, Frederick; pt Resurvey on Brothers Agreement, 360A

BEAMER, Philip; Frog Meadow, 96A, built a log hse

BALDWIN, Elijah; pt Brookes discovery & others, 197 1/4 A

BIEGLER, Israel; pt Hulls Choice & others, 160A, built a hse

BAKER, John; pt Patients Care & others, 150A

BANKARD, Abraham; pt Carolina & others, 169 1/2 A, assd formerly to Jacob BANKARD, Senr.

BANKARD, Jacob; pt Carolina, 125A
BEIGLER, Samuel; pt Big Meadow & others, 223A, built a small still hse
BOMGARDNER, Henry; pt Ohio, 130 1/2 A, built a log hse
BROWN, Daniel; Bell Choice & others, 125A
BEIGLER, Nicholas; pt High Germany & others, 21 1/4 A, built log hse and
    black smith shop, assd before to Henry KOONTZ & Nich. DICE
BOMGARDNER, Jacob; pt Chesnut Ridge, 98A
BOCKMAN, Frederick; pt Ohio, 100A, assd before to John LONG
BEALE, David; pt Mount Pleasant & others, 150A, midling land & improvements,
    assd before by mistake to David PEEL 54 acres before assd to Samuel
    OWINGS
BROWN, Peter; pt Ohio, 250A, built a log hse, 130 acres formerly assd to
    Margaret BROWN
BOWERSOCK, Geo. A.; pt Unity, 100A, log barn, assd last to Jno. NOWEL
BOOS, Peter; pt Unity, 118A (51 acres: name unknown, 67 acres not before
    assd); assd before to Henry SHOUG
BEAHLE, Christian; pt Ohio, 78A, assd before to George SINDORFF
BUSHMAN, Jacob; pt Ohio, 100A
BOWER, John; pt The Pines, 202 1/2 A, assd before to Mich. HORNER & 20 acres
    to Leon EKLEBERGER
BOWER, John - P.S.; pt the Pines and others, 89A, assd before to Jacob
    NESTOR
BISHOP, Peter - P. S.; pt Exchange, 35A - poor land, assd before
BUSHMAN, Andrew; pt Exchange, 50A, assd before to Michael MILLER
BUSHMAN, Henry; pt Exchange, 50A
BIGGS, Jacob; pt Six Brothers, 148 1/2 A, built a small stone hse, assd
    before to Wm. BIGGS, Sr.
BIGGS, Frederick; pt Six Brothers, pt Terra Rubra; 306A, from Jno. R. KEY
BIGGS, William, Jr.; pt Six Brothers, pt Trura (1A+), pt Terra Rubra (59
    1/3 A) from J. R. KEY; total: 245 1/3 A
BRACKENRIDGE, Robt. & Wm.; pt Epping Forrest, 280A, built 2 small log hses &
    barns, assd before to N. BRUCE
BEAMER, John; pt Brookes Discovery & others, 48A, assd before to Wm. HILL
BALDWIN, Daniel; pt of Brookes Discovery & others, 100A
BENTLY, Elie; pt Resurvey on Brothers Agreement, 10A
BOYLE, Daniel; pt Peggy's & Molleys Delight; 219 1/4 A, 27A assd before to
    Hugh THOMPSON & the rest to Henry LINN
BIGGS, Joseph; pt Six Brothers, pt Terra Rubra, 198A
CROUSE, John; pt Brooks Discovery & others, 153 1/2 A
COONSE, Abraham; pt Heads Industry, 162A
CROUSE, Valentine; pt Brookes Discovery, 158A
COONSE, Wm.; pt Heads Industry, 280A
COONSE, Henry; Red Island & others, 370A, built a new barn
COONSE, George; pt Dyers Mill Forrest, 154A, poor land, formerly assd to
    Ludwick MILLER
CONNELLY, John; pt Ligonier, 135A
CROMRILL, Conrod; pt Gothen, 10A
CASLERING, Ludwick; Trupe Robbin, Resurvey of the same; 475A, 315A assd
    before to Sam. NEWCOMER, 149A assd to SUISONS of St. Mary's County
CLUNT, Jacob; Holland Spring, 232A

CRISHER, Peter; pt Angels last Shift & others, 270A, log hse, 30A assd before to Sam. OWINGS, 25A assd to Steph. WINCHESTER, 215A to Frederick YINGLING

CROMRINE, John; pt Ohio, 200A

CALL, Matthew; pt Ohio, 6A - poor land, no improvements but a cabbin assd before to John JONES

COLE, Samuel, of Balto Co; pt Ohio, 423A, built a log hse & barn, 173A assd before to Acquilla TARMAN

COBLENTZ, John; pt Black Oak Level, 81 1/2 A, a small still hse

COBLENTZ, Philip; pt Ohio, 260A, 160A, formerly assd to Sam. OWINGS

CRAGLOE, George; pt Owings Chance & others, 220A, small stil hse, 20A to Yost RIFFLE, 100A assd before to Jacob & Geo. PIPER

COONSE, Paul; pt Brooks discovery, 287 1/4 A

COVER, Yost; pt Trueroe & others, 143 3/4

CROFF, Henry; pt Rich Level, 217A, assd before to Casper RICE

CRABBS, George; pt Brooks Discovery &c., 102A

CLABAUGH, Jno. of Jno; pt Brooks Discovery, 39A, assd before to Wm. & Hugh FERGUSON

CALF, Jacob; pt Brooks Discovery, 137A, assd before to OBERSON's heirs

CRABSTER, Rudoph; pt Brooks Discovery, 100A

CRAMER, Casper; pt Brooks Discovery, 60A

COURTS, Richard H.; pt The Resurvey on Brothers agreement, 1A assd before in the Town Book

DILL, Nicholas; pt Ohio &c, 351A, a small hse & stble, 65A assd before to Sam. OWINGS

DAYMAN, Frederick; pt Ohio, 217A

DERR, Abraham; pt Ohio, 125A, a log barn, 25A assd to S. OWINGS, the rest to Charles ANGLE

DERR, George Mich'l; Tarr Hills, 150A

DEAL, John; pt The Resurvey on Brothers Agreement, 1A, formerly assd to Leon DEAL

DODS, Robert; pt Epping Forrest, 142 3/4 A, assd before to N. BRUCE

DAVIDSON, Phinis; pt The Resurvey on Brothers Agreement, 5A, an out lot with a small hse - poor land

EICHER, Joseph; pt Rosses Range, &c., 199 1/2 A, stone mill

EICHERD, Michael; pt Carrolls Range &c., 226A

ERB, Christopher; Erbs Pleasure, 700A, 60A bought of Thomas DURBIN, 100A of Peter ERB

ERB, Peter of Christ.; pt Patients Care, 120A, assd before to Thos. DURBIN

ERB, Peter; pt James Fancy & other, 300A, built a large log hse, assd before to Peter & Jno. ERB

ERB, John; Patience Care, 460A, built a log grist mill, 2 pairs of stones, assd before to Jno. MARKER; pt High Germany &c., assd before to Peter & Jno. ERB

ESTERLINE, John; pt Ohio, 40A, assd before to Sam'l OWINGS

EARHART, Valentine; Empty Bottle &c., 100A, built a log hse & barn, 75A assd before to Geo. EARHART, Sr.

EARHART, George; pt Empty Bottle, 75A, assd before to Geo. EARHART, Sr

ETTINGER, Jacob; pt Ohio, 128A

EICHELBERGER, Leonard; ; pt The Pines, &c., 430A

ELDER, Joseph; pt Brooke Meadow &c., 126 1/2 A, assd before to Margaret FICKLE

ELDER Francis; pt Epping Forrest, 106 1/2 A
ELDER, Thomas; pt Epping Forrest, 130A
FERGUSON, Wm.; pt Brookes Discovery &c., 100A, assd before to Hugh & Wm. FERGUSON
FINFROCK, Henry; pt Resurvey on Brothers Agreement, 185A, 85A assd before to Sam. NEWCOMER
FAIR, Charles, heirs; pt Resurvey on Brothers Agreement, 59A, assd before to Mary FAIR
FEESER, Adam; pt Ohio, 180A
FEESER, Jacob; pt Ohio, 200A
FEESER, Nicholas; pt Ohio, 25A
FORNEY, Abraham; Wattles Fancy &c., 270A, built a stone hse, 130A assd before to W. KEY or W. BRUCE
FUSS, John; pt Escape &c., 177A, formerly assd to Thomas HARRIS
FICKLE, Rachel; pt Brooke Discovery, 25A, assd before to Margaret FICKLE
FICKLE, Matthias; Connected (Resurveyed by this name), 107A, 25A assd before to Wm. DORSEY
FERGUSON, Samuel; pt Brooke discovery, 80A
FINK, Adam; pt Brooke discovery, 30A
FRINGER, Nicholas, pt Brooke discovery, 3 1/2 A, assd before to Jno. HUGHES
GONGER, John; pt Resurvey on Brothers Agreement, 190A, assd before to Nich's MONSHOWER
GRIFFITH, David, heirs; pt Owings Chance, 114A, assd before to Wm. CORNELL
GORDON, Joseph; Contention Agreed, 122A
GROFF, John, Sr., heirs; pt Dyers Mill Forrest, 294 3/4 A, built a small stone kn and addition to the Mill
GROFF, John, Jr.; pt Dyers Mill Forrest, 100A, midling land & improvements
GRISE, Stephen; name unknown, 20A - poor land, no improvements
GLASS, George; pt Company, 127A, 32A assd before to Mich. EICHERS
GALT, John, Jr.; pt Resurvey on Brothers Agreement, 80A - midling good land, no improvements, assd before to Matthew GALT
GILLEYLAN, John; pt Epping Forrest, 202A, assd before to Ester GILLEYLAN
GWINN, John; pt Resurvey on Brothers Agreement, 260A, assd before to Mary BOYLAN
GALT, Matthew; pt Resurvey on Brothers Agreement, 277A
GOOD, Adam; pt Resurvey on Brothers Agreement, 325A
HAND, Henry; pt Bedford, 192A, built a stone still hse
HEINER, Christian; pt Owings Chance &c., 72A
HARRIS, Samuel; pt the Resurvey on Brothers Agreement, 340A, 214A assd to Jno. POTT, 126A assd to Jno. CHARTON
HAMMER, Francis; pt the Resurvey on Brothers Agreement, 120A
HERSH, Herman; pt Heads Industry, 251A, built a small hse & barn
HAYES, Joseph; pt Addition to Brookes discovery, 106A
HAWN, Jacob; pt Resurvey on Brothers Agreement, 220A
HAWN, John; pt Patience Care, 6 1/4 A, built a small log hse, assd before to Jacob YINGLING
HUBERT, Peter; Look about &c., 125A, built a large log hse
HUFFHOGER, Michael; pt Ohio, 40A - poor land, no improvements, assd before John ROGER & Sam. OWINGS
HORICK, Jacob; Hahnstadt, 175A, built a small log hse
HESSON, Wendle; pt Turkey Hill &c., 172A
HESSON, Batzer; pt Turkey Hill &c., 142 1/4 A

HULL, Andrew; pt Lemmons Range &c, 298A, Good Meadow, a small still hse, 28A assd before to Mich. ECKHARD

HUMBERT George; pt High Germany, 203A, assd before to Conrod SNIDER

HUMBERT, Adam; name unknown, 20A, poor, hilly land, no improvements, bought of Jno. LOW

HERNER, Jacob; pt Ohio, 35A

HAWN, Ludwick; pt Carroll's Range, 130A

HERNER, Michael, 99A, formerly assd @ 44.00, 15A appears to fall in Penna.

HEMLER, Joseph; name unknown, 20A, assd before to Jonas HAMMER

HARRIS, John; pt The Resurvey on Boxes Search &c, 140A

HARRIS, Thomas; pt The Resurvey on You Boxes Search &c, 350A

HILL, Isaac; pt Brookes discovery &c., 100A

HILL, Richard; pt Brookes discovery &c., 100A

HILL, Abraham, Jr., heirs; pt Brookes discovery, &c., 100A

HILL, Wm.; pt Brookes discovery, &c., 19A - poor cleared land

HESS, Charles; pt Brookes discovery, &c., 30A, built a log hse

HILL, Rich., Jr., heirs, pt Brookes discovery, &c., 50A

HOKE, Conrod; pt Resurvey on Brothers Agreement, 18A

HAUK, Peter; pt of Resurvey on Brothers Agreement, 175A

JONES, Wm.; pt Bedford, 102 1/2 A, assd before to Jno. EVANS

IRONS, John, Sr.; pt Bedford, 203 1/2 A

JONES, John, P. C.; pt Ohio, 374A, 180A assd before to Jacob TARR

JONES, Elisha; pt Ohio, 186A

JONES, John, Sr.; pt Brookes discovery &c., 117A

JAMISON, Robert; pt Watsons Delight &c., 300A

JONES, Thomas; pt Peggy & Molleys delight &c., 223 1/2 A

KEY, John Ross; pt Terrarubra, pt heads Industry, pt Trura Industry, 1800A, built a stone barn 100 ft long

KEIFER, Henry; pt Brookes discovery, 146A

KEPHART, David; pt Resurvey on Brothers Agreement &c., 218 3/4 A, 4 3/4 A where Mr. POPPLE formerly lived, the rest assd to Jno. POTT

KOONTZ, Henry, Sr.; pt High Germany &c, 199A, 4A assd before to Mich. DILL

KEMP, Peter, Sr.; pt Rosses Folly, 140A, built a log hse

KNOX, John; pt Owings Chance, 300A

KARR, James; pt Brookes discovery &c., 196 1/2 A, a small add. to the hse

LANEY, John; pt Bedford,102A, a small log hse, assd before to Norm. BRUCE

LEWIS, Sarah; pt Brookes Disocvery &c., 150A

LINN, Nicholas; York &c., 240A

LANE, John (miller); pt Logsdons Amendment &c., 64 1/4 A

LIPPY, George; pt Ohio, 200A, 100A assd before to John BOYER

LIPPY, Henry; pt Gotham, 80A

LINDERMAN, John; pt Ohio, 100A

LINGENFELTER, Daniel; pt Phillipsburgh &c., 190A, 50A assd before to Stephen NIPPLE

LINGENFELTER, Valentine; pt Boomgarden, 180A, built a small log hse

LEISTER, Conrod; pt Ohio, 100A

LOWE, John; pt Carrollsburg, 57 1/2 A, assd before to Thomas REESE

LONG, Mary; Bramberg, 200A - poor land & log barn, assd before to Leonard LONG

LEICH, James; pt Exchange, 100A

LEICH, Benj.; pt Brookes discovery &c., 100A

LOVE, Robert; pt Epping Forrest, 200A

LONG, Daniel, Jr.; pt Brookes discovery &c., 78A
LINN, Michael; pt Brookes discovery &c., 245A
MOCK, Peter; pt Resurvey on brothers Agreement, 350A, assd before to John THOMAS
MARTIN, Jacob, Sr.; pt Resurvey on Brothers Agreement &c., 153A
MESSINGHAMER, Jonas; pt Wm. Folly, 14A - poor land, small hse
MILLER, John; pt Rock Spring &c., 200A, 140A assd before to Sam. OWINGS
MATTHIAS, Joseph; pt Halls Range &c., 236A
MATTHIAS, Henry; pt Palendine &c., 171A, built a log hse, assd before to Jacob MATTHIAS
MATTHIAS, George; pt Palendine &c., 139A, 50A assd before to Jos. MATTHIAS, 89A to Chris. FREFOGLE
MICHSELL, Peter; pt Halmstadt, 150A, built a log hse
MARTIN, George; pt High Germany, 204A
MONTZ, Jacob; pt Ohio &c, 115, 75A assd before to Philip HUBBARD
MERTEL, Nicholas; pt Carrolls Range, 156A, 25A assd before to Ludwick KESSLING
MIDHOUR, John; pt High Germany, 120A
MUMMER, Adam; pt Ohio, 20A, built a stble
MILLER, Jacob, Sr.; pt Adams Delight &c., 240A, built a small log hse
MOALES, George, heirs; pt Ohio, 100A
MERKLE, John; pt Ohio, 136A, built a small log hse, 66A assd before to Sam. OWINGS
MARING, Wolfgang; pt Ohio, 100A
MANDON, Barbara; pt Unity, 30A, assd before to Rinehart MANDON
MARK, Peter; pt Resurvey on Brothers Agreement, 163A
MILLER, John (P.C.); pt Unity, 80A, assd before to Michael ECKHARD
MAJORS, Ann Eve; pt Addition to the Pines &c., 116A, assd before to James MAJORS
MILLER, Martin, heirs; pt Ohio, 100A
MILLER, George, (P.C.); pt Ohio, 160A
McALLISTER, Alexander; pt Exchange, 150A, built an end to the hse
MUMMY, William; pt Exchange, 100A, assd before to Valentine SHARD
MONSHOWER, Nicholas; pt Resurvey on Brothers agreement, 182A, assd before to Valentine CRESS
MOYER, John; pt Terrarubra, 400A, built a log hse
MILLER, John of John; pt Brookes discovery &c., 202A
McCUNE, Samuel; pt Carrolton &c., 106 1/2 A, built a saw mill
McCUNE, Thomas (P.S.); pt Carrolton &c., 70A
McGHIE, Thomas; pt Brooke discovery &c., 610A, built a log barn, assd before to James SUMMERVILLE of B.T.
McKALEB, John; pt Resurvey on Brothers Agreement, 42A - midling land, no improvements, 40 assd before to Mary BOYLAN, 2A assd before to Hugh THOMPSON
McCALEB, Joseph; pt Resurvey on Brothers Agreement, 141A
McSHERRY, Bernard, heirs; pt Resurvey on Brothers Agreement, 88A
NULL, Michael, Sr.; pt Resurvey on Brothers Agreement, 210A; built a small stone hse and log barn
NEICOMER, Samuel; pt Resurvey on Brothers Agreement, 107A, assd before to Lodwick HONEYWALT
NAIL, Jacob; pt High Germany &c., 125A
NAIL, Philip; pt Carolina, 255A, built a log hse

NIPPLE, Stephen; pt Gotham, 50A
NULL, Valentine; pt Brookes Discovery &c., 93 1/2 A
NOEL, Bloines; pt Landstool, 100A, built a barn, assd before to Geo. NIPPLE
NEALE, Magdalene; pt Rich Levels, 220A
NULL, Abraham; pt Brookes discovery &c., 50A, assd before to Valentine NULL
NULL, Michael, Jr.; pt Brookes discovery, 99A, assd before to Mary and Michael NULL, Jr.
OTTO, Peter; pt Bedford, 156A
OHARRA, Henry, Jr.; pt Long Acre, 150A, assd before to Henry OHARRA, Sr.
ORNDORFF, Peter, Jr.(?); Resurvey on Brothers Agreement, 130 1/2 A
ORNDORFF, Abraham; Resurvey on Brothers Agreement, 139 3/4 A
OHARRO, Henry, Sr.; Ohara's Ineritance, 77 1/2 A, built a log hse & stble
OLER, Peter; pt Piney Grove &c., 51A
PUTTINBERGER, Michael; pt Bedford, 180A, 108A assd before to Norm BRUCE
POTT, John; pt Resurvey on Brothers Agreement, 296A
PRICKER, Anthony; pt High Germany, 150A, assd before to Jacob KESSLER
PAXTON, Thomas, heirs; pt Brookes discovery &c., 170A
PHILIPS, Reese; pt Brookes discovery &c., 94A
RECK, Abraham; pt Bedford, 89 3/4 A
ROGERS, John; pt Resurvey on Brothers Agreement, 159A
REEVER, Ulrick; pt Brooks Discovery &c., 407A - land bought of OWINGS, midling land, built several small hses, 171A assd before to Sam'l OWINGS
ROADPOUCH, Frederick; pt Ohio, 99A
RUMMELL, David; pt Ohio &c., 164 3/4 A, built a small log hse & barn, 13 3/4 A assd before Jos MATHIAS, 42A to Geo. HECK, 14A to N. BRUCE
ROBB, Stephen; pt Palendine, 120A, 50A assd before to James HOLLIDAY of Balto. Co.
REED, Jacob; pt Florida &c., 237A
RINERMAN, Wm. (P.S.); name unknown, 100A
RINEDOLLAR, Sophia; Hoyle Home &c., 117A - poor land & improvements
RIGEL, John; pt Ohio &c., 180A, 55A assd before to Peter MICHAEL
RINEHART, George; pt Philipsburgh &c., 721A, built a large brk hse, has a large log hse, 100 assd before to Barbara RINEHART, 3 1/2 A to Elisha MAJORS, 143A to Leonard STUNG, 11A to Sam. SHADE
ROUTSONG, Conrod; pt Ohio &c, 67A, built a log hse
RINEDOLLAR, Henry; pt Ohio, 150A
REED, Jonas; pt Pines &c., 186A, assd before to Zadock NUTTER
RIFE, Christian; pt Brookes Discovery &c., 146A, 46A assd before to Hugh & Wm. FERGUSON
REESE, John; pt Brookes Discovery &c., 150A
ROSENPTAL, John; pt Resurvey Brothers Agreement, 8 1/2 A
RUDICILL, Tobias; pt Resurvey Brothers Agreement, 207A, 7A assd before to Adam GOOD
REED, Hugh; pt Resurvey Brothers Agreement, 10A, assd before to John Upton POWEL
STIMMEL, Jacob; pt Bedford &c., 197 1/4 A, built a stone hse
SIX, Henry; Buck Lodge, 200A
SPARKS, Joseph; pt Resurvey on Brothers Agreement, 146A
SANE, Philip, Sr.; pt Bedford &c., 101 1/4 A
STERLING, Sarah; pt Peggy & Molleys Delight &c., 80 1/2 A, assd before to John BOWDER

SHEELY, Andrew; pt Brookes discovery &c., 330A, assd before to Martin & Thomas ADAMS
SOANE, John; pt Resurvey on Brothers Agreement, 106A, built a stone hse, assd before to Jonathan ADGEY
SHOEMAKER, George; pt Resurvey on Brothers Agreement, 100A, built a small hse
SHEELY, Christian; pt Terrarubra, 160A, built a stone hse, 10A assd before to Geo. DIXON
SLIDER, Peter; pt The Resurvey on Brothers Agreement, 50A
STORM, John, Jr.; pt Troublesome Jobb, 180A
STORM, Joseph; pt Troublesome Jobb, 212A, built a new barn
SOWERS, Wm.; pt Resurvey on Brothers agreement, 100A, assd before to Augustine SHARROW
SHROYER, Matthias; pt Resurvey on Brothers Agreement, 100A
SCHRIVER, Philip, heirs; pt Resurvey on Brothers Agreement, 95 1/4 A, built a log hse
SCHRIVER, Philip & Geo.; pt Resurvey on Brothers Agreement, 130A, assd before to Raphail BROOKE
SANBRUN, John; pt Brookes Discovery &c., 150 1/2 A, built a log barn
SNIDER, Matthias; pt Patience Care, 50A
SHILLING, Conrod; pt Dyers Mill Forrest &c., 42A
SHEETS, Peter; pt High Germany, 109A, built a log barn, assd before to Dan'l OHARRA
SLIDER, Sunon; pt Jacobs Lott &c., 125A, built a log hse
SCHOLE, Stephen; pt Ohio, 257A
SHERMAN, Jacob; pt Colenline, 110A
SORICK, Henry; pt Gotham &c., 204A, 104A assd before to Jas. EASTEY, 100A to John HARNAN
SIPP, Peter of Balto. Co; pt Palendine, 63A
SNACH, Jacob, Jr.; pt Gotham, 50A, assd before to Nathan EASTEY
SNACH, John; pt Gotham, assd before to John SMEAK, 15A
SMEAK, John; pt High Germany, 185A
STAGNER, Peter; Trout Spring &c., 250A
SHILLING, John; pt Ohio &c., 67A, built a small log hse
SHAWL, John; pt Ohio &c., 462a, 80A assd before to Mich. WINTZ, 34A to N. BRUCE
STONECIPHER, Daniel; pt High Germany &c., 383A, 100A, assd before to Peter SHAFER, 100A formerly to And. CLUNT
STUDY, Martin; pt High Germany, 187A
STONECIPHER, Peter; Pt Johns Delight, 35A, built a small hse, assd before to Stephen WINCHESTER
SCHOLL, Philip; name unknown, 100A, built a small hse - poor land, formerly assd to widow GILBERT or heirs
SCHOLL, Michael; name unknown, 100A, built a small hse - poor land, assd to Philip KEEFER
STEINER, Christian; pt Ohio, 149A, made add. to the hse
STUMP, Geo.; pt Chesnut Ridge, 100A
SUMMER, John (P.S.); pt Ohio &c, 122A
SLATES, Frederick; pt Ohio, 130A
STONER, George; pt Ohio, 114A
SMITH, Jacob, P.C.; Mansinger &c., 280A
STONER, David; pt Truroe &c, 116A, assd before to Jno. COVER

115

SIX, Philip; pt Resurvey on Mary Fancy & c., 20A, assd before to Geo. DIXON
SHEETS, Jacob, Jr.; pt Brookes discovery, 111A, built a saw mill
SMITH, Jacob; Smiths Mount, 100A
SPALDING, Henry; pt The addition to Brookes Discovery, 545 3/4 A
SHELLHOUSE, Peter; pt Brookes Discovery, 36A
SHOEMAKER, John; pt Brookes Discovery, 158 1/2 A
SHEETS, John; pt Benjamins Inspection, 123 1/2 A
STEWART, Robert, P. T., 139A
SINGUE, George; pt Brookes Discovery &c., 142A, built a log hse
SWOPE, Henry; pt Resurvey on Brothers Agreement, 3A, assd before to John HUGHES
SCOTT, Upton; New London, 1460A
TANEY, Joseph; pt the Resurvey on Brothers Agreement &c., 142 1/2 A
THOMAS, Amos; pt Brookes Discovery &c., 139A
THOMPSON, Joseph; pt Resurvey on Brothers Agreement, 264A
TODD, Thomas of Balto. Co.; pt Resurvey on Brothers Agreement, 132A, assd before to Raphael BROOKE
THOMPSON, John & Sam.; pt Resurvey on Brothers Agreement, 221A
TRUMP, Casper; pt Ohio, 200A, made add. to the same
TUTTEROW, John; pt Ohio &c., 208A
TUTTEROW, Conrod; pt Truroe &c., 315A
TRUCKS, John; pt Brookes Discovery, 221A
UPJOHN, James; pt Robbit Harbour, 9A
WOLF, Eliz.; pt Resurvey on Brothers Agreement, 101A
WIMMER, Abraham; pt Brookes, Discovery &c., 225A
WIVIL, Joseph; Resurvey on Brothers Agreement, 250A
WINE, Henry; pt Ohio, 116A, built a log hse, assd before to Jacob CONROD
WILT, Geo. P. S.; name unknown, 50A
WINTZ, Philip, P. S.; name unknown, 200A - poor land, no improvements
WOLF, Michael; pt Ohio, 105A
WELSH, Adam; pt Pines &c., 10A
WHITEMAN, Geo.; pt Addition to the Pines, 30A, assd before to Robt. MAJORS
WEATLY, Bernard; pt The Pines &c., 2 3/4 A, assd before to Philip NILE
WEATLY, John, Sr.; pt the Resurvey on Pines, 125A, saw mill, gone to destruction
WEATLY, John, Jr., pt the Resurvey on Pines, 114 1/2 A, 47A assd before to Mich. REEL
WOLF, Philip; pt Brookes discovery &c., 59 1/2 A, assd before to Peter MILLER
WHITE, Andrew; pt Brookes discovery &c., 159A
WALKER, James; pt Brookes discovery &c., 110A, assd before to Wm. PAXTON
WOOD, James; pt Brookes discovery &c., 220A
YINGLING, John; pt Molley Delight &c., 150A
YINGLING, Jacob; pt Resurvey on Patience Care, 194A, built a log hse
YOUNG, Samuel; pt Ohio, 135A, assd before to Peter MICHAEL
YINGLING, Abraham; pt Ohio, 68A, 18A assd before to Thomas REESE
BROOKE, Roger; Assr. pt The Resurvey on Brothers Agreement &c., 496A

List of Lands in District 6 never before assessed - 1798

BOYLE, Daniel; pt Peggy & Molleys Delight, 3A - midling land about 1/2 meadow, bought of Wm. CORNELL

DILL, Nicholas; pt High Germany, 14A - poor land, no improvements, bought of Nich. CARROLL

FICKLE, Matthias; pt Connected, 5 1/2 A - poor land, taken up since last assessment

HERNER, Michael; pt Pines, 15A - poor land, laying within the Penna Line, bought from person in Penna.

KOONTZ, Henry; pt High Germany & Resurvey on High Germany, 23A - poor land, no improvements

LINGANFELTER, George; pt Resurvey on Brothers Agreement, 19A - midling wood land, bought of William DIGGS

WEMMER, Abraham; pt Brookes Discovery &c., 30A - midling wood land

ARNOLD, Benjamin; 1 lot; ground rent due to Stephen WINCHESTER, last assd to
Nicholas FURNEY

ADLESPARRY, Thomas; 1 lot; ground rent due to Jacob SHEARMAN

BARNOUOR, George; 1 lot

BETZ, Frederick; 1 lot; last assd to Jonathan BEAL

BORRING, Thomas, 1 lot; ground rent due to Stephen WINCHESTER; assd before,
small log cabbin

BROWN, Henry; 1 lot; rent paid by Peter LAYER, ground rent due to Jacob
SHEARMAN

CROMWELL, Stephen & Oliver; 4 1/2 lots, ground rent due to Stephen
WINCHESTER; 3 lots last assd to John CRAWFORD; 1 1/2 lots in new Addition

CROWS, Jacob; 6 lots; ground rent due to Stephen WINCHESTER; 2 lots last
assd to Nat. MYERS, 2 lots last assd to John SHARROTT, 2 lots in New
Addition

DELL, John; 5 lots; ground rent due to Stephen WINCHESTER; 3 lots assd to
Nicholas DELL; 2 lots in New Addition

DELL, Peter; 1 lot; rent paid by Job LOGSDON; last assd to Nicholas DELL

ECKLER, Ulrick; 1 lot; ground rent due to Stephen WINCHESTER; assmt to (too)
high - hse bad

FISHER, David; 3 lots; ground rent due to Stephen WINCHESTER

FRINGER, Jacob; 2 lots; ground rent due to Stephen WINCHESTER

GWYNN, John; 2 lots; ground rent due to Stephen WINCHESTER

GIST, Joshua; 3 1/2 lots; ground rent due to Stephen WINCHESTER; 2 lots last
assd to Geo. HAMMON, 1 1/2 lots in new Addition

HOOKS, Richard; 2 lots; ground rent due to Jacob SHERMAN; 2 lots last assd
to Andrew URLARF

LANE, Rebekah; 3 lots; rent paid by Elias UENBAUGH; ground rent due to Jacob
SHERMAN; last assd to John LANE, heirs, too high

LEOMMAN, Nicholas; 12 lots; ground rent due to Jacob SHERMAN; 5 lots last
assd to John SHOWER, 4 in last add. to Westminster

LEOMAN, Peter; 3 lots; ground rent due to Jacob SHEARMAN; last assd to
Martin HAINES

POWDER, Jacob; 13 lots; ground rent due to Jacob SHEARMAN; 12 lots in New
Add. to Westminster

POWDER, Andrew; 2 lots; ground rent due to Jacob SHEARMAN; not improved in
New Add. to Westminster

REESE, Andrew; 2 lots; rents paid by Jacob KESENDER & Jeremiah TARLTON;
ground rent due to Jacob SHEARMAN

SHEARMAN, Jacob; 2 1/4 lots; ground rent due to Jacob SHEARMAN

SYFORT, Henry, heirs; 1 lot; rent paid by Arehart WINTERS; ground rent due
to Jacob SHEARMAN

SAP, Leonard; 2 lots; ground rents are due to Stephen WINCHESTER

SHARROTS, John; 15 lots; rent paid by Wm. BRAYAN; ground rents due to
Stephen WINCHESTER; 10 lots in new Add. to Westminster

SWINNY, Hugh; 2 lots; rent paid by Harry LITESINGER; ground rent due to
Jacob SHERMAN; last assd to James WELLS

STEVENSON, Henry; 3 lots; ground rent due to Jacob SHERMAN; not improved

STEVENSON, Josias; 3 lots; ground rent due to Jacob SHERMAN; last assd to
Henry STEVENSON

TOLBERT, Ann & Eliz.; 1 lot; last assd to them, too high

UTZ, Jacob; 2 lots; ground rent due to Jacob SHEARMAN; last assd to George
ECKHARD

WINCHESTER, Lyda; 1 lot; ground rent due to Jacob SHERMAN; last assd to Peter WERKENER

WINCHESTER, Stephen; ground rent due to Jacob SHERMAN; last assd to Peter WERKENER

WELLS, Jennett; rents paid by Abraham RICHARDS & Paddy HINES; ground rent due to Jacob SHERMAN; last assd to her

WIGART, Andrew; 1 lot; ground rent due to Stephen WINCHESTER

WINTERVAT, Henry; 2 lots; ground rent due to Stephen WINCHESTER; last assd to Martin HAINES

WINTERS, John; 1 lot; last assd to Paul CRUSE

WAMPLER, Ludwick; 3 lots; ground rent due to Stephen WINCHESTER

YINGLING, John; 5 lots

Total am't of value of improvement in houses & lotts in Westminster town since last assessment is 149 pounds, 10 shillings - by Wm. DURBIN, Assessor -

- - - - -

Account of Land in District 3 containing Pipe Creek & West Minster Hundred, - Wm. DURBIN, Assessor

ALBAUGH, Zacharias; 150A; pt Red Land; log hse, barn

ANGEL, John; 77A; pt Ohio & Good Hope; log hse & barn - good

APLER, Jacob; 204 3/4 A; Jacob & Mary Bottle & Philips Range; brk hse, log barn, with other improvements - midling

ARTER, Michael (1 slave); 522 1/2 A; Fathers Care, pt Good Fellowship; brk hse, log barn, saw mill

ARNOLD, Joseph; 159A; pt Iron Intention; log hse, barn - poor; assd last to Nathan MAJORS

ARTER, Daniel; John Plague & Browns Vexation, 81A; Snake Den, pt Honours Delight, Bens Choice, tract of unknown name;136A; assd last to David MYERLY

ANGLE, Charles; 62A; Ground Oak Remnant; not improved

BOBLIN, Philip; pt Hard Grubbing & Christians Chance, 140A; log hse, barn - midling; pt of No Name, not improved, 25A; Assd last to William BELL

BURGOO, Jacob; pt of Three Springs, 172A - building poor; pt of three Springs, 10A, not improved, assd last to Valentine NICODEMUS

BISHOP, John (near M. Branch); pt Friendships Agreements, 100A, log hse, barn; pt new Locations, Errors Corrected, 12 1/2 A, not improved, assd last to J. SNIDER & BOST

BOST, Valentine; Errors Corrected Resurveyed, 289A, 2 log hses, barn

BEAM, Philip; pt Shear Spring, 148 3/4 A, 2 log hses, barn - midling; pt Shear Spring, 50A, log hse - small

BROWN, Joshua; pt Brown's Plague, 138A, log hse, barn

BROWN, Henry, Sr.; pt Brown's Plague, Molley Industry, 154A, log hse, barn - poor; pt Brown's Plauge, Spring Garden, 32A, not improved, Assd last to Valentine FLEGLE

BARNHART, Jacob; Pleasant Spring, 100A, log hse, barn, assd last to Anthony BARNHART, too low; pt Stephens Purchase, 122A, not improved, assd too high

BOWER, Stephen; pt Miery Spring, pt Retirement, pt Stephens purchase, 178A, 2 log hses, 2 barns

BROWN, Ann; pt Crags Harbour, pt Exchange, 125A, Buildings bad

BRICKER, John; Fathers Advice, pt Look about, 168 1/2 A; log hse, barn - good

BOYER, Mary; pt Lambs Choice, 149A, log hse, barn - poor; Addition to Choice, 16A, not improved,

BOWER, Christian; Smith's Lott, 150A, log hse, stbles, assd last to Ludwick SWITZER

BOWER, Jacob; pt Esters Industry, pt Legonier, 40A, log hse, stbles, not assd before

BUMGARDNER, Michael; Chance about, 178A, log hse, barn - midling; What Wednesday & Square, 30 A - not improved

BISHOP, John, near Westminster; Johns Luck, Peters Look, 110A, log hse, barn

BOWERS, John; Halls Range, 60A, log hse, barn, grist mill, last assd to Fornaca BOWERS

BURKESSER, George; Empty Bottle, pt Logonier, 73 1/2 A, log hse, barn - poor, last assd to John HEGNOR

BOYER, Catharine; pt Valleys & Hills, Cool Spring, pt Browns Vexation, 128 1/2 A, 2 log hses, barn, last assd to Casper BOYER; Jameses Choice, 50A, 2 log hses, 1 barn - bad, last assd to John BUMGARDNER

BOYER, Gabriel; pt Browns Vexationn, pt Stevensons Conclusion/52 3/4 A, log hse, barn - good

BROWN, George; pt Browns Plague, pt Browns Vexation, Snake Den/116 1/2 A, log hse, barn - midling

BRUCE, Upton; pt Good Intent, pt Addition to Good Hope, 1067 1/2 A, 2 dwlg hses, stone mill hse, last assd to Normond BRUCE

CROUSE, Philip; pt Locust Neck, Weavers Lott, and more that we thought, 151A, 2 dwlg hses, stone mill hse

CARVER, John; pt Markes Delight, pt Runny Mede, 129A, buildings poor

COVER, Daniel; pt Stephens Purchace, 16A, log hse, small barn, last assd to Jacob BARNHART

COVER, Arehart; pt Orchard, 130A, log hse, small barn - bad, last assd to Wm. BEALL

COONSE, George; pt Bedford, 145A, log hse, small barn - poor; pt Bedford, 63A - not improved, last assd to Normond BRUCE

COVER, Jacob; pt Markes Choice, pt Carmarks Trouble, 41A, log hse, barn, tanyard, last assd to And'w COTTEBOUGH & Evan CARMACK

CARMACK, Evan; pt Mackes Choice, pt Carmacks Trouble, Addition to Clarke discovery, 281A, log hse, barn - bad, last assd to himself

CORSSEE, George; Cooksons Hill, 13A, log cabbin - poor, not assd before

CASSEL, Jacob; Mill Lot Resurvey, pt Lambs Choice, 333A, 2 log hses, barn, grist mill

CASSEL, Henry; Taylors Delight, Free Gift, Sun Lott, pt Gills Range, 204A, 2 log hses, barn - middling, last assd to Paul CRUSE

COVE, Jessee; pt Green's Meadow, 116A, 2 log hses, barn - midling, last assd to John COVE, Sr.

COVE, John, Jr.; pt Green's Meadow, 116A; 2 log hses, barn - midling; pt Molleys Fancy, 5A, no improvement, last assd to John BROTHERS

COVER, John; Young's Purchase, 200A, log hse, barn - good, last assd to Davalt YOUNG

CROWEL, Michael; pt Kelly's Range, 67A, log hse and barn - good; Close Work and Daniels Den, 60A, log hse and barn - good, last assd to Eve COVER

CAUNADY, Mary; Molley's desert, pt Logonier, 70A, log hse and barn - bad

CHASD, Wm. pt Ligonier, 20 1/2 A, cabin - bad
COON, Mary; Good Rum, Addition to Good Rum, 97A, 2 log hses, barn
COCKEY, Joshua; pt Resurvey on Lime pits, 150A, log hse, barn - good, last
assd to David GIST
CLARK, James; Indian War, Jacks Purchase, pt Cobs Choice, pt Bonds Meadow,
Content, Narrow Bottom, pt Bottom & Top, pt Brown's pluge, pt Gabriels
Choice, pt Look about, Cool Evening, Long Valley, who would of thought
it, 2123A, log hse, barn, old grist mill, saw mill, last assd to Legh
MASTER
DURBIN, Thomas; pt Durbins Mistake, 238A, 2 log hses, barn
DERN, Frederick; Forrest, pt Long Snake, 154A, 2 log hses, barn, stone mill
hse
DEVENDALL, John; pt Addition to Clark's Discovery, 40A; log hse, barn, stone
mill hse raised to square, partly covered
DUDDERON, Conrod; pt Shelly Range, 188A, log hse, barn - poor, last assd to
John PAINTER
DEVERBAUGH, John; pt Bond's Meadow, Keesses Pasture, pt Hard Grubbing, Kemps
Luck, 185 1/2 A, log hse, barn - midling
DUDDEROW, Frederick; pt Iron Intention, 88A, log hse, barn
DURBIN, Benjamin; 72 1/2 A, Graveyard, pt Iron Intention, log hse - good
DURBIN, William; pt Cobs Choice, Goodfellowship, 100A, stone hse, log barn -
good
DURBIN, Mary; pt Cobs Choice, Goodfellowship (her 1/3 or dower right), 50A,
stone hse - poor
DILLOPLAIN, Joshua; pt Now or Never, pt Terra Rubra, 110 3/4 A - no
improvement, last assd to John R. KAY
ENGLAND, John, pt Liganier, 11 1/4 A, log hse, last assd to Mary LEPO
ECKLER, Ulrick, heirs; Water Oak Level, 70A - no improvements
ENGLAR, Philip; pt Miery Spring, Addition to Miery Spring, Lewis Forrest,
200A, log hse, barn - good
ENGLAR, Philip; Unity and pt Susan Fancy, 70A, no improvements
EMRICK, John; Spring Garden, Casselfin and Justice take place, 168 1/4 A,
small brk hse, log barn
ENGLEMAN, John; Neighbours Contention, 207A, log hse, barn - midling
EGG, Elizabeth; pt Logonier, 102A, log hse, barn - midling, last assd to
Jacob EGG
ENGLAR, Jacob; pt Goodfellowship, 184A, log hse, barn - midling
ECKHARD, George; Speal Bank, 243A, log hse, barn - poor, last assd to Edw'd
HODSKISS - too high
EARP, Joshua; pt Ellery, 125A, log hse, barn
FLEAGLE, Vallentine; pt Spring Garden, pt Browns Delight, 118A, log hse,
barn - midling
FROCK, Daniel; pt Ohio, 330A, log hse, barn; pt Keefers Range, 20A, no
improvements, last assd to Peter GEITSHALL
FROWNFILTER, Felix; pt Durbins Mistake, 6A, log hse - poor, last assd to
Thos. DURBIN
FLEAGLE, John; pt Locust Neck, 78A, log hse, barn, saw mill, last assd to
John REAGLE
FOUTZ, Solomon; Big Medow & Something, 326A, 2 log hses, stone barn; big
Meadow & Something, 16 1/2 A, fulling mill and saw mill, barn, log mill
hse

FARGUSON, John; pt Retirement Corrected, 500A, log hse, barn - poor; pt half
    Moon, pt Stoney hill, 123A, log hse, barn - poor, last assd to John
    PAPPLE & pt to himself
FEESS, Philip; pt Good hope, 1A, log hse, stble, sheds
FIRESPAUGH, Eve; pt Mackes, 100A, log hse, barn - poor
FARQUHAR, Moses; Mount Pleasant, Rock Land & Fancy, 306A, log hse, barn -
    poor
FOULLER, James; Winterses Lott, 60, cabbin - poor, last assd to Philip
    SCHRYNER's heirs
FULKER, Hyronimus; pt Stevensons Lott & Comby Chance, 55 1/2 A, log hse,
    stble, last assd to Edw'd STEVENSON
FARQUHAR, Allen; pt Wm. Defence & Rock Land, pt Forrest Need & Deer Park,
    327A, brk hse, stone barn; pt Retirement Corrected, 200A, log hse, barn,
    last assd to Hugh FURGUSON
FULKER, Christopher; pt Exchange & pt Crags harbour, 110A, log hse, barn
FLICHINGER, Jacob; pt Stockselsdale & Hill, 104A, log hse, barn - good, assd
    too low
FREEZE, Moddlenah; pt Molleys Fancy, 20A, log hse, last assd to her
FOGLESTONG, George, Sr.; Foglesong, Foglesong Lots, 155A, log hse, barn -
    poor
FOREMAN, Jacob, Sr.; pt Bare Meadow, 170A, log hse, barn - poor
FORMWALT, Lawrance; London, 62.9A, log hse, barn burnt and cattle(?); pt
    Brown's Plague, 38 3/4 A - no improvements, last assd to Jacob PAINTER;
    Beckeys fancy, 100A, log hse, last assd to Fred. REESE
FRYFOGLE, John; pt Bowers Struggle, 20A - no improvements, last assd to
    Greenberry MAJORS
FLICKINGER, Andrew; Fryers Delight Resurvey, 165A, log hse, barn - good,
    last assd to Adam STUMP; pt Ohio, 39A - no improvements, last assd to
    Normond BRUCE
FITTERLING, Jacob; pt Iron Intention, pt Powder Plot, pt Rochester &
    Williams Choice, 163A, log hse, barn
FISHER, David; pt Weedings Choice, pt Bonds Meadow, 104A, log hse, barn
FORNEY, Philip; Ground Oak Thickett, 39 1/2 A, cabbin - poor, last assd to
    Chas. ANGEL, if at all
GERTSHELL (GEETSHELL), Peter; pt Keefers range, 150A, stone hse, log barn
GROVEY, Francis; pt Good Fellowship, 26A, log hse, stbles, sheds, last assd
    to Jacob LYSTER
GIST, John; Lime Pitt, pt Resurvey on Rock Spring Limepitt, 400A, log hse,
    barn - poor
GRAMMER, Jacob; pt Bonds Meadow Enlarged, 117A, stone hse, log barn
GITTINGS, James, Jr.; pt Bonds Meadow, 99 1/4 A - not improved, not before
    assd
GRANDADAM, Francis; pt Bonds Meadow, pt Bedford, 24 1/2 A, log hse, barn -
    good, last assd to John SHARROTS
GRAMER, John; pt Friendship Completed, 1/2 A, log hse, barn - bad
GIST, Susannah; pt Limepitts, her 1/3 (dower), 80A, Oldfields
GROFF, Jacob; pt Dyers Mill Forrest, 105 1/4 A - no improvements, last assd
    to John GROFF, Sr.
HINES, Martain; pt Shoemakers, pt Ohio, 100A, log hse, barn
HULL, John; pt Durbins Mistake & Huckleberry Bottom, 297A, stone hse, log
    barn, stbles under
HAGER, Barbary; pt Red Land, 190A, log hse, barn - poor

HAHN, Andrew; pt Molleys Fancy, pt Clase Meadow, 325A, 2 log hses, barn
HARMON, John; Gead Spring, 60A, 2 log hses, barn - poor
HAHN, John; Crookabout, pt Retirement, 190A, stone hse, log barn, last assd
    to Jacob BROTHERS; pt hard Grubbing, pt Orchard, 62 3/4 A, no improve-
    ments, last assd to Wm. BELL; pt Stephens purchase, 12A, log hse, stbles,
    last assd to Jacob BARNHART
HITESHEW, Philip; pt Retirement Corrected, 250A, log hse, barn, last assd to
    Hugh FERGUSON
HYNOR, Harbett; pt Beford, pt Retirement Corrected, 591A; 2 log hses, barn;
    pt Beford, 250A - not improved
HITER, Stoffle; pt Bedford, 206A, log hse, barn
HANN, Matthias; pt Bedford, 167A, log hse, barn
HERSH, Harmon; pt Mackeys Choice, 217A, log hse, barn
HUSTON, John; pt Andess Choice, 1A, log hse, stbles, last assd to Conrod
    RYNECKER
HANN, Henry; pt Good Hope, 149A, log hse, barn - poor, last assd to Philip
    FEISS
HARTSOCK, Daniel; pt Resurvey on Rock Land, 91 3/4 A, stone hse, log barn
HETTLEBRECK, George; Log Cabbin Branch, 153A, log hse, barn - good
HITESHEW, Jacob, Sr.; Something, 153A, log hse, barn - good
HAINS, William; Woods Gain a Resurvey, 177A, log hse, brk barn; pt Susans
    Fancy, 100 1/2 A, not improved, last assd to Richard WOOD, too high
HARMON, Jacob; pt Look about, 80A, log hse, barn - midling
HAINS, Samuel; Hains Inheritance a Resurvey, 416A, brk hse, barn good; pt
    Rock land & Susans fancy, 56A, cabbin - poor, last assd to Richard WOOD
HIDE, Jonathan; pt Pork Hall, Black Oak Hill, pt new Insor, 170A, log hse,
    barn - poor
HIBBERT, Aaron; pt Pork Hall, 13A - no improvements, not assd before
HAINS, Mordecai, name of tract not known, 100A, stone & log hse, log barn
HAVNER, George; pt Browns delight, 137A, stone hse, log barn - good
HAUPTMAN, Henry, heirs; no name to be found, 40A, log hse, barn - good
JONES, William; pt Molley's Fancy, 52A, log hse - poor
JOHNSON, Thomas; pt Molley's Fancy, 88 1/2 A, log hse, new add't & barn
JACOBS, Mary; pt Bedford, 150A, building bad
JOHNSON, Christoph'r; pt Black Oak Hill, 110A, log hse, barn
KEPHART, David; No Spring, 140A, brk hse, barn, brk mill hse, bridge, saw
    mill, last assd to Solomon KEPHART
KITCHMILLER, Leonard; Good Spring, 193A, 2 log hses, barn; pt Molley Fancy,
    19 1/2 A - no improvements, last assd to Andrew HAHN
KEMP, Judith; pt Mackey's Choice, 1A, log hse - poor
KERBY, Joseph; pt Good Hope, 137A, log hse, barn - bad, assd too high
KEROUFT, Andrew; pt Good Intent, 11A, 2 log hses, barn small, last assd to
    HASSELLER
KEEFER, Frederick; pt Keefers range, 175A, log hse, barn - good
KEESE, Casse, pt Honours delight, pt Bens fancy, 93A, log hse, barn - poor,
    last assd to John KEESE
KLINE, Daniel K.; pt Bonds Meadow & Leather Bottle, pt Molley's Industry,
    150A, log hse, barn - midling
LONG, John; pt Ligonier, 86A, log hse, barn - midling
LONG, Jacob; pt Ligonier, 169A, log hse and barn, midling, last assd to him
LAYNARD, John; pt Ohio, pt Tryers Delight, 37A, new log hse, small, last
    assd to John ANGEL

LAMBERT, John; pt Black Oak Hill & Troublesome, 200A, log hse, barn; Point about, pt New Winsor, 48A - no improvements

LEIM, Henry; Good Intent, 212A, log hse, barn - good, last assd to Wm. KENWORTHY, Sr.

LYSTER, Nicholas; pt Good Fellowship, 190A, log hse, barn - midling

LAMBERT, George; pt Resurvey on Good Fellowship, Good Will, Bethel Recovered & unexpected, 208A, log hse, barn - poor

LANCET, George; Spring Hill and Unwilling, 227A, log hse, barn - good

LYSTER, John; pt Molleys fancy, Look about & Chance Luck, 243A, log hse, barn - midling; pt Locust neck, Surveyed since, 107 1/2 A, log hse, barn - midling, last assd to Henry KAUPTMAN

LAWYER, Casper; pt Iron Intention, 49 1/2 A, new log hse, barn, last assd to Stephen WINCHESTER or OWINGS

LAWYER, Philip; New Switzerland, pt North Canton, 157 1/2 A, log hse, barn - good

MILLER, Edward; pt Fells Dale, 2A, log hse - poor

MARTIN, Jacob; pt Ligonier, 178 1/2 A, log hse, barn, last assd to Philip SOUER

MAJORS, Greenberry; pt Ligonier, pt Browns Vexation, 148A, log hse, saw mill, grist mill, fr hse to mill, last assd to John MAJOR

MATTHIAS, John; pt Adventure, Browns Vexation, 107A, log hse, barn - midling; pt Adventure, Bonds Meadow Enlarged, 114A, log hse, barn - midling, last assd to Joseph ADAMS

MAJORS, Elias; pt Bonds Enlarged, 170A, log hse and barn midling

MILLER, John; Bare Meadow, pt Ligonier, 237 1/4 A, 2 log hses, barn; pt Ligonier, 26A, cabbin useless, last assd to Stephen FORD; pt Shoemakers Lott, 31 1/4 A - not improved

MIKESELE, John; pt dughill, 113A, log hse, barn, last assd to Henry KAUPTMAN

MYERS, Joseph, Sr.; pt Resurvey on Bare Meadow, 65A, log hse, barn - poor

MAXWELL, James, heirs; Harmony Hall, 529A, building - very bad

MILLAR, Abraham; Wills Forest, pt Molley Fancy, 175A, log hse, barn - good

MYERS, Daniel; High Spring, 185 1/2 a, log hse, barn - poor, last assd to John SCHRINER

McNEALY, John; pt Retirement Corrected, 250A, log hse, barn - poor, last assd to Hugh FERGUSON

MORLOCK, Michael; Michael's Farewell, 81A, log hse, barn - poor, last assd to Henry BEISHER; pt Arnold's Remnent, 8 3/4 A - no improvement, last assd to Archib. ARNOLD

MYERS, Peter; pt Ohio, 26A, small log hse

MYERS, John; pt Ohio, 133A, log hse, barn - midling

MEARING, Frederick; pt Patience's Care, 190A, log hse, barn - midling, last assd to Eve ERB

MYERS, George; pt Locust neck, pt Lamb's Choice, 151A, log hse, barn - midling

McKINSEY, Elie; pt Molley's Fancy, 70A, log hse - poor

MYERS, Barbara & John; Michaels Fancy & no name, 175A, log hse, stone barn, last assd to Daniel MYERS, DUNKER; pt Rosses Range Resurveyed, 120 1/4 A, log hse, barn, last assd to Andrew YOUNG

MOSER, Peter; New Haven & Resurvey, 294A, brk hse, log barn - good; last assd to himself

METCALFE, Thomas; Cool Spring, Shear Spring, brk hse, barn; pt Black Oak Hill, 275A, log mill hse, 2 other, last assd to Wm. BELL

MOSER, Michael; pt Molley Fancy, 2 1/4 A, log hse, stble, not assd last time
MOONEY, Richard; pt Molley Fancy, 45 3/4 A, log hse, barn, last assd to him
MYERLYA, George; pt Iron Intention, pt Broad Meadow, Cryders delight, 252, small stone hse, log barn, small log hse
MITTEN, John; pt Friendship Completed, 14A, log hse, slauter hse, stble; pt Friendship Completed, 13A - no improvements
NORRIS, Nathaniel; pt Resurvey on Retirement, pt Stephens purchase, 250A, log hse, barn, last assd to him
NOGGLE, Jacob; pt Resurvey on Errors Corrected, 110A, building bad, last assdd to Henry SELL and pt Valentine BOST
OTTO, Wm.; pt Bedford, 240A, log hse, barn - midling
OTTO, Wm.; pt Bedford, 226A, log hse, barn - midling, last assd to Normon BRUCE
OVELMAN, Henry; pt Black Flink, 54A, log hse & barn midling, last assd to him
OVELMAN, Henry; name not known, 16A, no improvements, last assd to SAILOR
OLLERY, Jacob; pt Adams Plague, 19A, log hse - poor
OLLERY, Elizabeth; pt Bonds Meadow, 87A, log hse, barn - midling, last assd to Jacob Ollery
POPPLE, John; pt Stoney Hills, 52A, log hse, barn - poor
PECHT, Jacob; pt Mollies Fancy, 57A, log hse, barn - good, last assd to Peter BEAM
PECHT, Philip; Addition to Stockstells Hills, 21 1/2 A, log hse, stbles - poor, last assd to Jacob BACH
POWELL, William; Will Restored, 50A, log hse, stbles - poor
PICKSTER, Peter; Deer Park & Bowers Struggle, 140A, log hse & barn midling, last assd to Christ'n BOWERS
PHEASENT, Samuel; pt Ligonier, pt Ohio, 93A, log hse, stble - poor
PETERS, Henry; no name, 110A, building - poor, last assd to Andrew REESE, Sr
POWDER, Jacob; pt Addition to Whites level, 4A - no improvement, last assd to him
RADOLPH, Daniel; Sweet Hanover, pt Ohio, 219 1/2 A; log hse, barn, last assd to Peter RODOLPH
RINECKER, Paul; Leonards Lott, Peters Lott, pt Ohio, 473A, 2 log hses, barn, oyl (oil) mill - poor
ROLSTON, John; Pleasant Meadow, 130A, log hse, barn - bad
ROOP, Christian; Levell Spring, Poplar Spring, pt Black Oak Hill, 240A, log hse, brick barn, last assd to John HARGRADER's heirs
ROOP, Joseph; White Gravel Spring, pt Black Oak Hill, 279 1/2 A, log hse & barn - poor, saw mill (since last?), last assd to Christian ROOP
ROBERTS, Wm., Jr.; Brier wood Resur'd, pt Good Will, 390A, log hse, stone sheds, new kn, barn
ROOP, John; pt Browns Delight; pt Gills Range, pt Free Gift, 203 1/2 A, log hse, barn, log & stone grist mill, last assd to Frederick CRISTMAN
RUSSEL, Jacob; Pleasant Meadow, pt Hazzard, 110A, log hse, stone spring hse
RINEHART, George; pt Ligonier, 240A, no improvements, last assd to Normond BRUCE
REESE, Andrew; Hollow Rock, 102A, new log hse, barn
REESE, Jacob; pt Mollies Industry, 2A, log hse, stble, sheds, last assd to Daniel KLINE

SHRIVER, And'w and David G.; pt Carolina, pt Hill Spring, pt Ground Oak Hill, pt Mill Lott, 104 1/2 A, log hse, brk mill, hse under roof, saw mill, do re(?), last assd to Abraham BANKER

SMITH, William (near gs. P. CREGH); Good Will, pt Durbins Mistake, 28A, log hse, barn - midling

SELL, Peter; pt Keefers Range, 25A, not improved, last assd to Frederick WINCE

STULLER, Olrick, Sr.; Empty Cupboard, Addition to Empty Cupboard, pt Locust Neck, 214A, log hse, barn

STULLER, Henry; pt Locust Neck,, pt Weavers Lot, Lyda's Home, 195A, log hse, barn, last assd to Ulrick STULLARS, Sr.

STULLAR, William; This or None, pt Friendship, 60A, log hse, barn - poor, last assd to Joseph MYERS, Jr.

SHERFIGG, Modelenah; pt Redland, 120A, log hse, barn - midling, last assd to herself

SNIDER, Jacob, Jr.; Pretty Improvements, 151 1/2 A, small stone hse, log barn - poor

SNIDER, Jacob, Sr.; pt Clare Meadow, pt Crooked round, 64A, log hse, barn - good, last assd to John FLEGLE, Ulrick STULLER

SCOTT, Upton; **Runy Meede Enlarged**, 2877 1/2 A, 21 improvements

SCOTT, Upton; Runnee Meede Enlarged, pt Durbins Mistake, 742A, log hse, barn

SHOEMAKER, Peter; pt Mollies Fancy, 87 1/2 A, log hse, barn add't fence last, Pretty Improvements, 9 1/4 A, pt Three Springs, 85A, log hse, barn, last assd to Valentine NICODEMUS and Jacob SNIDER, Jr.

SLICK, John; pt Bedford, 200A, hse log, barn

SPANGLER, George; pt Bedford, 300A, log hse, barn

STULTZ, Mary; pt Bedford, 200A, 2 log hses, barns

STULTZ, Conrod; pt Bedford, 125A, log hse, barn, pt Retirement Corrected, 50A - no improvements, last assd to Hugh F.ERGUSON

SHEPART, Solomon; pt Willimas Defence, 220A, log hse, barn - bad

SHRINER, Peter; pt Resurvey on Susans Fancy, 314A, brk hse, barn - poor

STERN, Mathias; Resurvey on Small beginning, 241A, log hse & barn - bad, spring hse - fine

SWITZER, Mathias; Saplen Hill, pt Stephen Purchace, 226 1/2A, log hse, barn - bad, spring hse

SWITZER, Rudy; pt Myers pleasure, Black Oak Hill, Michaels fancy, 125A, log hse, barn, Spring hse; pt Orchard - no improvements, last assd to Wm. BELL

STEWARD, Mathew; pt Friendship, 131A, buildings - poor; pt Bethel, 4A - not improved, last assd to George LAMBERT

SWIKERT, Adam; pt Waggoners fancy, pt Resurvey unexpected, pt 2 Resurveys on Brier Wood;226 1/2 A, log hse, barn - midling, last assd to George EISLER; pt Black Oak Hill, 61A - no improvements, last assd to Wm. BELL

SHEWY, Daniel; Myers Resurveyed, Black Oak Hill, 296A, log hse, barn - good

SENSNEY, John; pt Range, 200A, log hse, barn - midling, last assd to John HARMAN

SMELTSER, Michael; pt Black Oak Hill, 50A, log hse, brk mill hse, barn burnt; pt Stevensons Gardens, 112 1/2 A - not improved, last assd to Edw. STEVENSON (Burnt House Woods)

SMITH, Richard; pt good Will, Brier Wood Resurvey, 176A, stone hse, barn of logs, last assd to Joshua, Richard and Gellary SMITH

SMITH, William (near M. Branch); pt Mollies fancy, 73A, log hse, barn

STANSBURY, William; pt Brown's Vexation, pt Alcada, 280A, log hse, barn - midling, last assd to him

STEVENSON, Charles; Stevensons Conclusion a Res., pt Ligonier, 361 3/4 A, log hse, barn, last assd too low

SHRIVER, Conrod; Valley & Hills Toms & Will Vexation, 140A, log hse, barn - midling; pt Bond's Meadow, pt Hazzard, 222 1/4 A, log hse, barn - midling, last assd to Jacob LEMON

SNOWFER, John; Valleys & Hills, Kemps friend, 2nd Amendment, 138A, log hse, barn; Valleys & Hills, Toms & Wills, 2nd Amendment, 97A, log hse, barn - poor, last assd to William ESTUB

SNIDER, George; pt Honours Delight, pt Ligonier, 123A, log hse, barn, last assd to Ludwick WALTER; pt Ligonier, 25A - no improvements, last assd to Gideon BOSSLY

SNIDER, Michael; pt Brown's Vexation, 126A, log hse & barn, last assd to Gideon BOSSLY

SHULTZE, John; pt Bonds Meadow Enlarged, pt Browns Vexation, 114A, log hse, barn - midling, last assd to Francis GRANDADAM

STEVENSON, Henry; Resurvey on Deary, 250A, log hse, barn - midling

SWIKERT, Christian; pt Good Fellowship, 170A, log hse, barn - midling, last assd to Jacob SNIDER

SHRIVER, David, Sr.; Addition to Mistake, Wilsons Chance, pt Good Fellowship Content & Mistake, 260A, 2 log hses, log barn, stone mill, spring hse - poor; Magnetick Variation, entirely lost in Elder Survey

SHEARMAN, Jacob; pt Brown's plague, pt Hard Grubbing, Neglect, pt Timber ridge;143A, log hse, barn

TEATER, Jacob; pt Durbins Mistake, 89A, log hse, barn

TRIPOLETS Mary, heirs; Boons Content, 480A, 2 log hses, 2 barns

TAWNEY, Frederick; pt Good Fellowship, 175A, log hse, barn - good; pt Arnolds Remnant, 106A, log hse, barn - poor, last assd to Archibald ARNOLD

TURNBOW, Mary; pt Friendship Compleated, 10A, log hse, stble - good, last assd to Conrod DRUMBORE

WILLIAMS, William; pt Durbins Mistake, 20A, log hse, barn - poor

WAGGONER, Michael; pt Shear Spring, 150A, log hse, barn - midling; pt Lambs Choice, 40A, small log hse, last assd to Pierce LAMB

WOLF, Andrew; Small Hope, Good Spring, 113 1/2 A, log hse, barn - midling; pt Crook about, 6 3/4 A - no improvements, last assd to John HAHN

WOLF, Jacob; Welsh Cabbin, Toms Fancy, 114A,log hse, barn - midling, last assd to him

WILSON, Samuel; Wilsons Inheritance a Resurvey, 254A, log hse, barn - poor

WILSON, Thompson; pt Susans fancy, 100A, buildings - bad, last assd to Richard WOOD

WAGGONER, John; Mount Lofty, pt Boons Content, pt Waggoners Fansy, 150A, log hse, barn - midling, last assd to him

WARNER, John; pt Unwilling, pt Molly Fancy, pt Good Fellowship, 292A, brk hse, log barn - good, assd too high

WINTER, John; pt Bedford a resurvey, 59 1/4 A, log hse and barn midling, last assd to John HAVNER; Dry Work, 27A - no improvement, last assd to Paul CRUSE; Six Originals, Taylors Lott, Taylors Mistake, pt Pork Hall, 306 3/4 A, log hse, barn, last assd to Geo. WINTERS

WERBLE, Philip; pt Bonds Meadow Enlarged, The Resurvey on Deary, 257A, 2 log hses, barn - good

WAMPLER, David; Rich Spring, Red Bottom, 173A, log hse - good, log barn - poor

WHITE, Patience; pt Andess Choice (1/3, her dower), 6 3/4 A - no improvement, last assd to John DEVENDALL

WILLSON, Catharine; pt good Intent, 152 1/2 A, log hse, barn, last assd to Norman BRUCE

WRIGHT, Joseph; pt Williams Defence, 120A, log hse, log mill

WINCE, Frederick; pt Keefers Range, pt Locust neck, 127A, log hse, barn - midling

WEAVER, Ludwick; pt Adventure, 50A, log hse, barn - midling

WAMPLER, Ludwick; pt Bonds Meadow Enlarged, 2 1/2 A, no improvements

WHITE, John; pt Bonds Meadow, pt Fanneys Meadow, 150A, log hse, barn - poor, last assd to John LOGSDON, Sr.

WHITE, Ann; pt Bottom and Top, 11A, log hse, barn, last assd to her

WINCHESTER, Stephen; pt White Level, pt Bedford, pt Fells Dale, Timber Ridge, 276A, fr hse, barn, last assd to him

WINTERS, George; pt White Gravel Spring, Black Oak Hill, Stevenson Lott, 125A, log hse, barn, last assd to him

WOOLSEY, George, heirs; pt Locust Neck, pt Lamb's Choice, 515A, fr hse, log barn - midling, last assd to Catharine WOOLSEY

YOUNG, Davall; pt Locust Neck, 50A, log hse, barn

YAWN, John; pt Molley Fancy, 45A, log hse, barn, last assd to him; pt Molley Fancy, 20A - no improvements, last assd to Peter SHOEMAKER; pt Locust Neck, 37A, log hse, barn, last assd to Henry HOUPTMAN

YOUNG, Joshua; pt Molley Fancy, 93A, building bad

YAWN, Jacob; pt Big Meadow, 52 1/2 A, log hse, barn - poor, last assd to Solomon FOUTZ; pt Orchard, 7 1/2 A, - no improvements, last assd to Wm. BELL

YINGLING, Margret; pt Ligonier, pt Remnant, 50A, log hse, barn - sorry; last assd to her

YINGLING, Peter; pt Ligonier, Smith Lott, 50A, log hse, barn - midling, last assd to Margret YINGLING

YINGLING, John; pt Water Oak Level, 13 3/4 A - no improvements

ZACHARIAS, Daniel; Neighbourly Kindness, pt Bonds Meadow Enlarged, pt Browns Plague, Zacharias Thickett, Keesses Industry, 168A, log hse, barn - good, last assd to himself

Land not assessed before:

APLER, Jacob; pt of deeps, 4A

BAUMGARDNER, Michael, Wet Wednesday & Square, 30A

CORSSEE, George; Cooksons Hill, 13A

DEVENDALL, John; 7th Dividend, pt Carmacks Trouble, pt Andiss Choice, Truxes Discovery; 125A

DURBIN, Benjamin; Grave Yard or Iron Intention, 11 1/2 A

GIST, John; pt Resurvey on Limepitts, 12A

GIDDINGS, James, Jr.; pt Bonds Meadow Enlarged, 99 3/4 A

FORNEY, Philip; Ground Oak Thickett, 39 1/2 A

HITESHAW, Jacob, Sr.; Carmacks Chance, 30 1/2 A

KEEFER, Frederick; pt Keefers range, 10A

MILLAR, Abraham; pt Wills Forrest, pt Mollies Fancy, 25A

SHRIVER, Conrod, Sr.; pt Bonds Meadow, pt Hazzar, 22 1/4 A

SPANGLER, George; pt Bedford, 70A

Frederick County, District 1

Ephraim Gaither, assessor

ATLEE, Isaac; pt Porkhale & pt Five Daughters 190A, from Thomas LLOYD; pt Stevenson Garden 14 1/2 A, from Edw. STEVENSON; saw mill

ARNOLD, Wm.; Arnolds Inheritance 216A; Hollow Rock 15 1/2 A, from James WELLS; middling

AKERMAN, Jacob; pt Resurvey on Englands Chance from Martin WINTERS, pt Mulberry Bottom from Joshua HOWARD, 142 1/2A; log & stone barn

BAKER, John; pt Hammon Strife 115 1/2 A

BROWN, Emunel; 208A; Resurvey on Walnut Bottom, Black rock; 108A, middling

BAKER, Henry; Trouble enough 140A; pt Nicholas Chance 51A; Bakers delight 28 1/2 A; Quilling Frolick 36A; pt Charles Choice, last assd. to H. KISMAN, 4A

BOND, Nichodemus; pt of Five Daughters 204A; log kn

BOND, Thomas; pt of Five Daughters 204A, from Nichodemus Bond; log stble

BROWN, Emanuel, Jr.; pt Park Hall 1/4 A, last assd. to LLOYD, Thomas; log hse

BALE, Peter; The Resurvey of fancy 99A; The Res of Bales industry 340A; pt of five daughters 220A; pt York Co. Defence, from John SWADENOR (?), 10A

BIS___, Peter; pt Baker's Discovery, from Ezekiel EVANS, 127A

BECRAFT, Peter; pt Woods Lott 106A

BOYER, Philip; pt Chittems Castle 118A; pt Woods Grove 4 3/4 A

BARNES, Philemon; Dodsons Tent 256A; What you Please 21A

BARNES, Zachariah; pt Caleb's delight; from Wm. GOODWIN, 66 1/2 A; log dwlg; kn; out hse; pt of Caleb's delight and The Plug 86 1/2 A, never before assd

BENNETT, Benjamin; Halls Range, 240A; spring hse; pt Hard Bargain 115 1/4 A, from Wm. GOODWIN

BENNETT, Samuel; pt Hard Bargain 99 3/4 A, from Wm. GOODWIN

BUTLER, John; pt Caleb's delight 200A, from Michael PUE

BOYER, Peter; pt Cold Fryday 99 1/2 A, from Evan DORSEY

CRAPLE, John; pt Hammonds Strife 122A; stone dwlgs, not finished; Mill Stone Pick 24A

CRAPLE, Peter; pt Hammonds Strife 127A; pt Resurvey of Strife 83 1/4 A

CLEMSON, John; pt Bar garden 186A, from Gabriel ISENBURGH, Sr.; pt Pleasant field 21 3/4 A, from Henry MAYNARD; pt Maynards Lott 1 1/2 A, from Henry MAYNARD; pt Uenstards Inheritance 3 1/4 A, from Enoch UMPOTARD; pt Justices Delight 100A, from Emargrat JUSTICE; Swants fancy 100A, Widow WILSON's dower; pt Wm. Neglect 60A, from Eliz. JUSTICE

CEELY, Philip; pt Wm. Neglect, stone & spring hse, 119A, from Tobias GARDINER

SHRIVER, Martin, Jr.; Setesolop 140A, from Martin CARVER, Sr.

CENSENY, John; pt Mount pleasant, good land; 348A, from Samuel GODFREY; 2 log hses & others

CRUMBECKER, Abram; pt of the Deeps 280A, from Abram CRUMBECKER, Sr.

CRUMBECKER, Peter; pt of New Winsor 10 1/2 A, from John ROBERTS; pt Five Daughters 122 1/2 A, from Abram CRUMBERCKER, Sr.

CLINE, Adam; pt Galloway 100A, from John CROWEL

CAMPBELL, John, Jr.; pt friendship 200A, from Ann CUMMINGS

CAPLE, John E.; pt Stevenson Garden, very good, 100A, from Edward STEVENSON

CAMPBELL, Jno., Sr.; Good Luck 130A; saw mill, log hse; pt Request, 146A; pt Slip 14A; pt Friendship 76 1/2 A

CASSELBERRY, Benjamin; pt Mount Plesant 77 1/2 A, from A. MACKLEY, trustee of Jo. MURRY; pt York Companys defence 10A, from Richard OWINGS

CALIUS, Richard; pt Stevenson Garden 790 3/4 A, from Edw. STEVENSON

CRUMBECKER, David; Roberts Care 240A, from Cath. CRUMBECKER

CRUMBECKER, Jacob; Hunters forest; pt Resurvey on this or None; 61 3/4 A, shed to dwlg hse

CROOMER, Philip; pt Cold Friday 234A, from Jacob SMITH; stale hse

CLARY, Ellinor; pt Rich Forrest 37A, from Leven SPURRIER

CAMPBELL, Eliz.; pt Colodew Resurvey 222 1/2 A, from Nicholas HOBBS; pt Venus 98A, from Nicholas HOBBS; pt Dear bought 62A, from Nicholas HAY, saw and grist mill; pt Friendship & Coloden 6 1/2 A, from Edw'd DORSEY; pt Friendship & Coloden 250 1/4 A, from Nich. HOBBS

CLARY, Rachel; pt Moal, poor land, 150A, from Wm. CLARY

CLARY, Benjamin; pt Hickory Ridge 66 1/2 A; Garrison 50A; pt Pretty Sally 125A; pt Pretty Sally 98A, from Jos. WOODINGTON

CUMMINGS, James; pt Moab, poor land, 10A

CLARY, John; pt Moab 150A & pt Shivers Integrity 8A, from Henry WELCH

CLARY, David; pt long trustees 150A, improvements

CONDON, Sarah; pt Moab 180A, poor land; pt Molhine 50A

DELL, Nicholas; pt York Comp. defince Resurvey and now called Fathers Gift, 60A, from John FINBONE

DAVIS, Mary; Pleasant Grove 404A, from Amos DAVIS; log & corn hse

DICKENSHEETS, Wm.; Nicholas Chance 46 1/2 A; small log hse burnt down

DICUS, John; pt Wood's lot 4 1/2 A, good improvements

DORSEY, John; Timber Ridge 25A, sorry

DEVILBISS, Casper; pt Capers loss 554A, good; and pt Strips purchase 79 1/4, from Jacob STRIPE

DAGAN, John; pt Pork Hall 1/2 A, from Thos. LLOYD

DORSEY, C. Eliz'th; pt Walnut Ridge; pt the Resurvey on Walnut Ridge; pt Dukes Woods; pt the Resurvey of Dukes Woods; Luck; Sandy Spring; 282A; formerly too high (the previous assessment)

DORSEY, Wm. of Basil; pt Walnut Ridge, 250A; log hse burnt down

DEVILBISS, Cath.; pt dear bought, small log hse; pt Resurvey of dear bought, pt Ushers Freehold; 207A, from Adam DEVILBISS

DORSEY, Basil; pt Vinas, 102A, not improved

DORSEY, Evan, guardian for Upton LAWRENCE; pt Mount Pleasant 74A; Third Addition to Mount Pleasant 150A; pt Cold Friday 49A; Pleasant Forrest 120A; Malnixo chance 100A; Discord lately Resurveyed 35A; last assd to Martha LAWRENCE

DORSEY, Caleb; pt Hammonds Contrivance 280A; pt Long trusted Contrivance 300A, from Thos. HYDE

DUDROW, Conrod,Sr.; Mistake rectified 117 1/2A; pt Pleasant Field & pt ___ ridge 330A; Walnut Ridge 76A; Apple Orchard 23 1/2 A; pt Resurvey on Justices delight 100A, from Adam MARKLE; Good Pasture from 2 1/2 A, good improvements

DORSEY, Ely; pt Pleasent Fields 373 1/4 A; pt Charlies Choice 47 3/4 A; Anything 98 3/4 A, pt Pleasent Fields, 159 3/4 A from Thos. DORSEY; pt Nicholas Chance 58A, from Jos'a COCKS; pt Resurvey on Justices Delight 46A, from Jos''a COCKS; Quilting Frolick 69A, from Jas. PEARIA

DORSEY, Daniel; pt Pleasant Fields 350A; pt Woods Lott 150A; Prospect Hill 19 1/4 A; Resurvey on Hammond Strife 1 1/4 A, from Robt. ALCOCK

DORSEY, John, Jr.; pt Wm. Beginning 169 3/4 A, from Davis DORSEY

DORSEY, Sophia; pt Wm. Beginning 200A; pt Wm. Beginning 135 1/2 A; from Wm. DORSEY

EDSLER, John; pt Hammonds Strife 76A; stone addition to dwlg hse

ELGER, Joseph; pt Forrest of Need 3/4 A, from Wm. FARQUHAR; brk dwlg and others

ENGLE, David; pt Five Daughters 150A, stone add. to dwlg; pt Five Daughters 99A, from Adam CRUMBECKER

ENGLER, Jacob; Loss and gain 205 3/4 A

ENGLAND, Jacob; Englands Chance 93A; log hse burnt down

ENGLAND, John; pt Brothers Inheratance 102A; pt Resurvey on Ridgways Farm 13A

EVERLY, John; pt Spinning Wheel 137A; pt good fellowship 15A. widow dower in it

EVANS, Ezekial, for POWDER's heirs; pt Dorsey Mill Frog 110A, from Wm. GOODWIN; log dwlg, barn & others

ENGLE, Jesse; pt Strips Purchase 100A, from Jno. BOOSE; log hse

FARQUHAR, Samuel; pt Kile Faddy 173A

FOUTS, Jacob; pt small beginning 80A, from Mathew STEIN over Creek

FARQUHAR, Wm., Sr.; pt Forrest of Need 275 3/4 A, "3/4 to Elgar," log barn & log hse

FURNEY, Jno.; pt Strips purchase 36A, from Jacob STRIPE; log hse

FRANKLIN, Chas.; Resurvey on Sheridan Range 76A; Cabbin

GARDINER, Emagrell; pt Hard lodging 2A, from Tobias GARDINER; pt Umstards Inheritance 12 3/8; pt the Deep 124A, pt Lymberger 2 1/4 A

GILLINGHAM, James; pt Mount Pleasant 252A, last assd. as Priests lands; dwlg hse

GIGER, John; pt of the Range 70A; pt of the Deeps & pt Greenwood fancy 74 1/4 A, from Jacob HALL

GREENWOOD, Yost; pt of Deeps 300A; stone dwlg; Mount Pleasant 52A; Halls Neglect 3A; pt the Deeps 143A, from Jacob HALL

GIST, Joshua; Long Farm 468A, stone and farm barn

GREENWALT, Jacob; pt York Co. defence 108A, from John PONTER; pt York Co. defence 14A, from Rich OWINGS

GOODLANDER, Henry; pt Resurvey on Englands Chance, 83A from Geo. WINTER

GOUDY, Abram; pt Cold Friday 40A, from Geo. COAK

GAWSLIN, Amos; Whats left 109A, from Jacob BARNETT

GRIMES, Joshua; pt Value and Strife 304 1/2 A, from John T. WORTHINGTON

GILBERT, John; pt Cold Friday 149A

GLEASON, John; pt Frienship 269A, from Edw'd DORSEY; log barn & stone spring hse

GAITHER, Wm.; pt Pleasant Field 393A

GOUGH, Harry Dorsey; pt Roberts Delight 140A, poor land

HAINES, Nathan, Jr.; pt Bare Garden 232A, good improvements

HOSPLEHORN, George; pt Small beginning 100A, middling

HOSPLEHORN, Ludwick; pt Small beginning 100A

HOSS, Emagrat; pt Pork Hall 19 1/2 A, from Christian HOSS

HOCKMAN, John; pt Resurvey of Justices delight 20 3/4 A, good; pt brown delight 50A; pt Peach Orchard 13 1/2A; pt Quilting Frolick 195A, from James PEARIA; pt Browns Choice 45A, last assd. to Ann STOVER

HOCKMAN, Mary; pt Justices delight, pt Millers Den; middling, 258A

HALVERSTOD, Henry; pt resurvey on Justices Delight 10A; pt Quilting Frolick 5A, last assd.to James PEARIA

HALVERSTOD, Michael; pt Bone of Contention 2A, last assd. to Jacob TAGUN, log dwlg hse

HAMMOND, John; Hammond Chance 359 3/4 A, good improvement

HAMMOND, Nathan; pt Friendship 158 1/4 A; pt Gilboia 425A

HARTRUCK, Henry; pt Woods Lott 100A; pt Woods Lott 254 1/2 A, stone & log barn; pt Better than None 35 1/2 A

HOWARD, Ephraim; Paradice 578A

HAMMOND, Vachel; Hammond good Luck 488A; stone & meat hse, others improvements good; pt Gaths Chance 80 3/4 A

HANES, George; pt Calebs delight 200 3/4 A, log & barn & c.

HANES, Michael; pt five daughters 200A; 1 log, stone barn, log dwlg hse; pt Pork Hall 60A, from Joshua HOWARD

HANES, Jacob; pt Ridgeways Farm, pt brothers Inheritance, 170 1/2 A, small hse - good; pt Fells retirement & pt Englands Folly 78A

HARGRADER, Benjamin; I forgot the Name 8 A; last assd. to Cornelius SHAKAN

HOBBERT, Joseph; pt New Winsor 300A, fulling mill & log hse

HANES, Nathan, Sr.; pt Corn Wall 265A, brk bldg

HANES, Joseph; pt Corn Wall 134A, good; pt Stevensons Garden 123 1/2 A, from Edw. STEVENSON, good land

HELMN, Adam; The resurvey on Mount Pleasent 44 1/2 A, from Nich. HELMN

HANSEY, Eleanor; Coombers Inheritance 143A, for life

HOY, Nicholas, Jr.; pt Pleasant Field 119 1/4 A

HARMON, Michael; Markleys Discovery 14 1/2 A, from Adam MARKLEY

HALE, Benj.; Bite him softly 371A, poor land; Addition to Sparks delight 50A, poor land

HAMMOND, John of Nathan; pt Gilbsa 425A

HAMMOND, Ormond; Hammond Chance 192A, sorry

HAMMOND, John of Chas.; Favour and Ease 850A; Condon's good will 48A

HOBBS, Wm. of Chas; The Preparitary 562A, good improvement; pt Shiver's Integretory 206A, from Henry WELCH; pt Addition to Pars Range 100A, from Lucy ARNOLD

HOWARD, Joshua; Howard discovery 552A, brk grist mill, a saw mill and other improvements; Stringers Chance 6A, from Rich. STRINGER; pt resurvey on Cold Friday, poor, 85A; Tryangle 5 1/4 A; Mulbury bottom 2A; pt Mattinglay 40A; pt Pork Hall 20A; for Dennis WARFIELD - pt Conclusion and pt Quilting Frolick 161A; for Chas. WARFIELD - pt Conclusion and pt Quilting Frolick 161A; for David WARFIELD - Poor Mans Loss and pt Conclusion 153A

HARRIS, Nathan; Point Lookout 585A; Resurvey of Cold Friday 544A, good improvements; pt Resurvey on Cold Friday 20A; pt Calebs Delight 250A and pt Cold Friday 160A, 160A from Wm. GOODWIN; Long Snake 45A; Owings Choice 36A, from Rich. OWINGS; pt Joshua's Lott 11A, from Jos'a WRIGHT

ISENBURGHER, John; pt Resurvey on Small beginning; log

ISENBURGH, Gabrial, Sr.; pt Bone of Contention 107A, from Jacob TUGEN

JONES, Joshua; pt Stringers Chance 132A, from Rich'd STRINGER, Jr., log & stone and barn

ISRAEL, Robert, Jr.; pt Calebs delight enlarged 175A, poor; Land Gate 109 1/2 A; Bachelors Refuge 54A

ISRAEL, John Jr.; Two it if you can 102A

KEYS, Hooke or Henry COAKE; pt of the Deeps 100A

KIME, Jacob; pt Englands Chance 50A

KELER, Nancy; pt Mount pleasen, 68A, from Daniel KILER

KITZMILLER, John; pt Gators Chance, pt Howards Range 7 1/4 A
KELLER, Jacob; pt Friendship, pt Mount pleasent 50A, from Jacob WAMPLER,
    still hse, grist & saw mill
LANDIS, Henry; pt Resurvey on several lotts 125A; grist, saw & fulling mill
    & barn; pt Level Glade 50A, pt of Deeps 8 1/2A, from Jacob HALE; Tillers
    Mountain 16 1/2 A, from Jos. STEVESON; pt of the Deeps, from And'w
    HAVENOR, 9A; 4 Lotts on Sams Creek, 1A, rents at 12 pounds per year
LAWRENCE, Samuel; Mount Pleasant 80A, from Rich. OWINGS
LOOKENBEEL, Peter; Adam Fale 268A
LOOKENBEEL, John; pt Partnership 76A, good land, log spring hse; pt Stripes
    Purchase 250A, from Jacob STRIPE, log barn; pt Williams Beginning 20 1/4
    A, from Wm. DORSEY; pt Chartin Choice 1 1/4 A
LONG, Peter; Dorsey Mill Frog, log hse; pt Resurvey on this or None, spring
    hse, 102 1/2 A, from Wm. GOODWIN
LEATHERWOOD, Samuel; pt Calebs Delight 125 1/2 A, from Michael PUE
LEAKINS, Thomas; pt Calebs Delight 94A, from Michael PUE, log hse
LAWRENCE, John; pt Mount Pleasant 300A, from Martha LAWRENCE; pt Bite the
    Biter 144A, from Martha LAWRENCE; Poor Hill and Lovely Becky 45A
LAWRENCE, Richard; pt Cold Friday, Ararom Oye Resurvey now called Plate,
    507A
MAYNARD, John, Sr.; Hard fortune 176A, good land
MAYNARD, Henry, Jr.; pt Strawberry Plains 293 1/2 A, stone dwlg & kn & log
    barn; pt Pleasant Fields 150 1/2 A
MEREDITH, Lemon; pt Resurvey on Breackes 79A, widow dower; pt Timber Hill,
    64A
MOORE, Gehew; pt Round Spring 6 1/2 A, from John ORR, brk dwlg
MASSLER, Ulrick; pt Resurvey on Amendment 481 1/4 A, good land; pt the
    Agreement 24 1/2 A; pt Swants fancy 30A, from Samuel WILSON
MUMFRED, Mary; pt Woods Lott 592A, from James MUMFRED
McDANIEL, James; pt Chance 170A, small add. to barn; pt Joshuas Lott 222 1/2
    A, from Jas. WRIGHT
MYERS, Peter; pt Hawkings Chance 183 1/4 A; brk dwlg and add. to barn; pt
    Dear bought Neglected 10 1/4 A, from Edw. STEVENSON
MARKLEY, Gabrial; pt Good Range Rectified, pt Justices delight and pt Cold
    Friday, 225A, from Hester and Adam MARKLEY, improvements since
MASTERS, Lehaskins; Leigh Castle 2685A, pt York Companys defence 1125 3/4 A,
    pt Arnolds Chance 535 1/4 A, Neglect (2 old hses) 65A, Stoney Hollow 31A,
    Beauty Spott and Redbeed 48A, pt of Edward fancy 20 1/4 A, from Leigh
    MASTERS
MURRY, James; James Inheritance 183 1/2 A
MOORE, Tobias; James Inheritance 50 A; Mountain Stage 75A
MYERS Catherine; Henry Loss 170A, from Henry MYERS; pt Mount Pleasant 25A,
    from Henry MYERS; pt Bakers discovery 41A, from Ezekial EVANS
MARKLEY, Adam; pt good range 178A, saw mill; pt Cold Friday 50A, poor; pt
    Cold Friday 11A, last assd. to Jacob SMITH; pt Hall Side 50A
MILLER, George; this or nothing 85A, poor & stoney
McDANIEL, Wm.; pt of better than none 141A, from Joseph McDANIEL, small log
    hse
MULNIX, Thomas; pt Pretty Sally 267 1/2 A, last assd. to Joshua WADDINGTON
NORRIS, John, Sr.; pt Norriss Lott 186 1/2 A, saw mill; pt Williams Neglect,
    39 1/2 A, from Eliz'th JUSTICE; pt Ulmsterds Inheritance 116 3/4 A, last
    assd. to Nich. UMSTARD

NICHODEMUS, John; the Resurvey on Hawkin's Chance 105A, add. to barn; pt Fells Retirement 41A; Look at Last 3 1/2 A; Source glade 34A; pt Stevenson garden 88A, last assd. to Edw'd STEVENSON

NICHODEMUS, Philip; pt Stevensons Garden 6 3/4 A, from Edw'd STEVENSON

NICHODEMUS; Henry; pt York Companys defence 223A, grist & saw mill; pt Fells retirement 69A

NORRIS, John, Jr.; pt Timber Ridge 183A, stone dwlg & kn & log barn; pt Woods Lott 181 1/4 A

ORR, John; pt Forrest of Need 125A; pt Oliver 75A, and pt Round Spring 42A, good land

OLIVER, Thomas; pt Deeps 2A

OFF, Leonard; pt York Companys defence 65A, from John FINKBORN, log dwlg

OUSELTLER, Mary; pt Bacons discovery 50A

PLANE, David; pt Deeps 175A, good improvements

PUSEY, George; pt resolution 127 1/2 A, log hse

PILER, Joseph; pt deeps 100A, log hse

PROUGH, Conrad; pt brothers Inheritance 111A

PETERS, Henry; pt Stevenson Garden 100A, last assd. to E. STEVENSON, good land

POLSON, Cornelius, Sr.; Polson reserve 86 1/2A

POLSON, James; pt Stoney batter, Polson reserve, keep your wife at home, 105 1/2 A, from Rich. OWINGS

POLSON, Andrew; pt Polsons reserve 187 1/4 A, good improvements

POLSON, Cornelius, Jr.; pt Resurvey on Stoney Batter 102 1/2 A, from Rich. OWINGS

PEAREA, James; pt Pleasant Fields, pt Chitlam Castle; pt Partnership; 235A, from Wm. GAITHERS

PICKETT, Charles; pt Calebs delight 112A, from Mich. PUCE

POOL, Henry, Sr.; Seak & you shall find 36A, from Dan'l JAMES; Posles Polesy 7A

POOL, Wm.; pt Resurvey on long trusted 50 1/2 A, from Thomas DICKSTON

PUE (PUCE), Mary; pt Gilbsa 67A, from Michael PUCE

PARISH, Richard; long Snake

POOL, Henry, Sr.; Pooles Industry, 2 log dwlg hse & barn; pt Friendship, stone dwlg & kn

POOLE, Luke; pt Wm. beginning

POOLE, Brice; pt Wm. beginning

REG, Henry; pt Hammonds strife, stone dwlg & kn;

RAIL, John; pt friendship, add. to stone dwlg

RINEHART, David; pt Chance, pt round 109A, from JohnHOCKENAN, brk __ & barn; pt Caspers Loss 18 1/2 A

RIFFLE, Jacob; pt Browns delight 105A; pt Nicholas's Chance 44A

RIDENER, Andrew; pt Golloway 100A

ROGERS, Nicholas; pt Gabriels Choice 150A, from Philip ROGERS, cabbin

RANDALL, Christopher; Roberts chance 30A, from Rich. OWINGS

RIDGELY, Henry; pt Gilboa 500A, poor land

RUNKLES, Jacob; pt Cold Friday 88 1/2 A; pt Wm. beginning 20 3/4 A; from Wm. DORSEY

SIMPSON, Richard, Sr.; the Resurvey on Simpsons Chance 443A, log hse; Simpson Lott 10A, log hse & barn; pt the Grove 28A, fr hse; pt Hammonds chance 6 1/4 A

SMOUSE, Henry; High top Spring 30 5/8 A

SWEADNER, Eliz'th; pt bar garden 150A, left her by her husband for life; Copper Hill 16 1/2 A

SELMAN (or Zollman), Adam; Limeburgh 123 1/4 A; small beginning 130A

SPOON, Conrad; pt Williams neglect 150 1/2 A; Danners purchase 1 1/2 A

SHEPHERD, Solomon; pt Rich land 80A, fulling mill

STONER, John; pt hard bargain 125A, add. to brk dwlg; pt hard bargain 122A, from David STONER; pt Umstards Inheritance 31 3/4 A, last assd to Nich. Umstard; pt Caspers Loss 50A, from Cooper DEVILBISS

SAUM, Peter; Saum's Purchase 177 1/4 A (or 477 1/4 A), barn shed

STONER, Jacob; pt Hard lodging 124A

SHRIVER, Michael; pt Justices Delight & Browns choice 82 1/4 A, last assd to Ann STONER; Browns delight 4(?)A, from John HOCKMAN

STONER, Samuel; pt Justices delight & Browns choice, 132A, from Ann STONER, log & stone barn

SHRIVER, Peter; Kemp good Luck 173 3/4 A; pt Stripes purchase 79 1/4 A, from Jacob STRIPE; pt cold Friday 56A

SALLERS, Labrett; pt Howards Range 190A, last assd to Jacob WATERS

SALLERS, Basil; pt Howards Range 190A, last assd to Jacob WATERS

STRINGER, Richard, Sr.; Stringers Chance 150A, small barn

STROUSE, Nicholas; pt Charles Choice 3 1/2 A, cabbin

SNADER, Jacob; pt Mattingley 138 3/4 A, from Joshua HOWARD, log hse and stble; pt Pork Hall 16 1/4 A, from Joshua HOWARD

STEVENSON, Daniel; Good Will 150A; Owings Frolick 50A

STEVENSON, Joshua; pt Stevenson garden 418A, last assd to Edw'd STEVENSON

STONER, Daniel; pt Pork Hall 3/4 A, last assd to Thos. LLOYD, large fr hse & others; pt Stevenson garden 8 3/4 A, last assd to Edw. STEVENSON

STEVENSON, Richard; Good will 39A; Good will 112A; pt Come by Chance 4 1/2 A, from Tuker over Creek

SCHRIVER, Peter; pt Stoney Batter, Rich Meadow & keep your wife at home, 107 1/2 A, from Rich'd OWINGS

SILE, Conrod; pt Resurvey on Mount Plesant 25A; pt Goswick chance 50A

STEVENSON, John; pt Resurvey of Woods Lott 179A, from Jonathan WOOD, log & stone barn

SCHRIVER, John; pt Three brothers lott 67A, spring hse; Kemps good Luck 10 3/4 A, widow WOOD's dower in it; the Addition 30A; pt Stripes purchase 100A, from Jacob STRIPE

SCOLES, Thomas; pt Timber ridge 28A, poor land

SHIPLEY, Peter; hard Bargain 42 1/4 A, log dwlg

SHIPLEY Uriah; pt Horsepasture 71 1/4 A; pt Hard Bargain 77 1/2 A, from Wm. GOODWIN

SQUIRE, Michael; pt Joshuas Lott Rectified 100A

SHEREDINE, Upton; Resurvey on many tracts 551A, good improvements; pt Ushers fresh old 206 1/4 A, log dwlg hse

SPURRIER, Thomas; pt Long String 23A

STRIPE, Jacob; pt Stripe's purchase 110A

TODD, Alexander; pt favour and east 170A, poor land

TEANOR, John; pt Purs range 60A; pt Molkime 50A, from David CONDON

THOMPSON, Andrew; pt Cold Friday 102 3/4 A, from Robert LAWRENCE

UMPSTARD, Enoch; pt Umstards Inheritance 101 1/2 A, from Nich. UMPSTARD, 2 log hses; pt Joshua Lott & Wm. Neglect 48A, from Eliz. & Jesse JUSTISE; pt Bar Garden 3 1/4 A, from John CLEMSON

UPCRAFT, Robert; pt Joshua Lott 60A, poor land; pt Joshua Lott 40A, from Jos. WRIGHT

YARE, Isaac; pt Hammonds Stripe 90A, from Daniel ROOT

WOOD, Basil; pt Charles Choice & Borwn(?) Loss 100A, middling improvements

WEB, William; pt small beginning 50A, 2 small stone hses

WRIGHT, Isaac; Hazle Valley 100A; pt small beginning 200A

WRIGHT, Joel; pt Resurvey on Forrest of Need 249A

WILLIAMS, John; pt Resurvey on Breaches 159A, good improvements

WOLF, Martin; pt Chance, pt the Round, 138A, brk barn & add. to log dwlg

WORMAN, Jacob; pt the Range 150A, pt Pork Hall 222 1/2 A; good land

WAMPLER, Jacob; pt Level Glade 49 1/2 A, from Emegrat HASS; pt Deeps, pt Greenwoods Fancy, 82 1/2 A, from Jacob HALL

WORMAN, Henry; pt Resurvey on Justices delight 45A; pt Charlies Choice 107 1/2 A; Coornbers Inheritance 100A; pt Coornbers Inheritance 11A; pt Bakers delight 7 1/2 A; Addition to Male adventure 8A

WELLS, Thomas; Childrens Inheritance 428A, last assd to James WELLS, grist mill

WELLS, Joseph; pt Fells Dale 133A, good; pt Jacobs Well 105 3/4 A, add. to hse; Well's Industry 309A; hard Labour 4 1/2 A

WATERS, Michael; pt Mount Plesent 10A, from Henry MYERS, 2 log hses

WARFIELD, Alexander; Poor mans loss & brothers Generosity 181A, log hse; pt Conclusion 47A

WATERS, Ariasina; pt Howards Range 190A, last assd to Jacob WATERS; dead before returned

WORMAN, Andrus; Level Farm 248A, log milk hse, rents for 40 pounds per year; pt of Grove 160A, brk mill, 2 stry, stone, good stream of water; pt Cole Friday 137A; pt Charlies Choice 132A, from Rich. BRIGHTWELL, poor land

WRIGHT, Joseph; pt Mothers Segacity 110 1/2 A, from Philemon DAVIS

WOOD, Sarah; pt three brothers lott 212A, last assd. to John WOOD, log hse; pt three brothers lott, 24A

WODDINGTON, Joshua; Brandewine Spring enlarged 416A; the Addition 231A; pt Moab 292A; Mount Pleasant 52A; back 50 A called Brandy wine Springs 50A

WOLF, Peter; pt Moab 44 1/2 A, from Henry WOLF, grist mill, 2 stones

WRIGHT, Joshua; Joshua Lott 84 1/4

WARKER's heirs; pt Point Look out 585A

WOOD, Joseph; Woods Lott 265A, 2 log hses; Panes 11 1/4 A

WARNER, Adam; Second Best 60A, from Peter CAMP; first come first served, 5 A, from John REACH; name of tract unknown 10 1/2 A, from John REACH

YOUNG, Philip; Old Mans good Luck, pt small beginning; 44 3/4 A

YOUNG, Benard; Black Acre 5 3/4 A

Frederick County, District 1

Lands never before assessed

LOOKINGBEEL, John; pt Charles Choice
BARNES, Zadock; The Plug
FRANKLIN, Charles; The Resurvey on Sheridenes Range
POOLE, Henry, Jr.; Pools Policy
LAWRENCE, John; Poor Hill and Lovely Becky
DUDROW, Conrod, Sr.; Good Pasture
WARNER, Adam; Second Best
ARNOLD, William; Hollow Rock
DORSEY, Daniel; The Resurvey on Hammonds Strife

Showing names and amount to be paid in pounds/shillings/pence

Ann Nancey Allen 70
Hugh Allen 372/10
Geo. Alexander 101
John Allen 117
Doctr. And. Ailkin 771
Joseph Ager, living in Eitchelberg's
    house 78
Eve Abers 825
Sam'l Alburn 198/8/4
Fred. Atterbury 15
Henry Amy 150
Sarah Acklen 110
Nicholas Amy 185
Andrew Aupold 273
Barbary Alter 98
Henry Augustin 67
John Albright 713
Asquith Dalrymple, living in Miller's
    house 24
Fred. Amulung 98
John Brien 49
Wm. Burrage 33
Wm. Brant 70
John Brady 83
Bookman Barbary 85
Doctor Booze 60
Geo. Boos 38
Wm. Bowers 190
John Burton 65
Rebecca Burns 45
John Bowers 55
Joseph Barkman 79
John Bull 66/3/4
James Boxter 70
Chas. Brunt 40
Martin Bowers 830
Chas. Boon 40
Mary Bond 230
Benj. Bennet 65
John Bryson 122/3/4
Peter Bond 320
Wm. Bosley 22/10
Eales Buchanan 44
Robt. Buchanan 90
Jeremiah Brown 15
James Buttler 55
Clement Burk 140
Isaac Bennet 30
John Burk 90
Thomas Barley 165

Edw. Brown 85
John Brice 490/10
Geo. Bush 15
John Brewer 60
Geo. Buchanan 320
Abraham Both 95
Thomas Barkley, living in property of
    Priests 20
Valentine Bantz 101
Geo. Bailey 109
Elisha Bailey 166
John Brakin 71
Benj. Brown 15
Christian Baum 225
John Baxley, living in Hook's house
    31/6/8
Edw. Brightman 105
James Barton 63
James Barton, Jr 35
Dominick Bodar 134
Horatio Berry 482
W. John Berry 482
John H. Barnes, living in Berrys
    House 35
Judge Baker 50
Joseph Bowers 85
William Booth 281
Daniel Boley 875
Mary Barliry, widow 160
Gilbert Bigger 250
David Baxler 275
Jacob Brown 88
Elisha Burk 125
Peter Benson 125
John B. Bastion 100
William Burton 125
Peter Bankard 55
George & Nathan Bryson 235
Addison & Wm. Booth 106
Joseph G. Bend 113/6/8
B. Wm. Barney 110
Eliz. Brown, Sr. 170
Eliz. Brown, Jr. 165
Wm. Buchanan From land office
    doubtful if in precincts 55
Thomas Chisholm 99
John Constable 32/10
Conrod Crowl 90
Mary Crowl 35
Alex. Crook, living in John
    Patterson's house 28
John Church 249/8/4

Mr. Cross 415
John Canoles 90
Daniel Chambers 1326
John Campl 72
John Chalmers 1386/10
John Chalmers, Jr 455
James Chalmert 99/6/8
Isaac Cousy, Blackman living in John Lemmons house 17
Richard Colvin 70
Mary Churchman living in Jacob Stanbury's house 27
Simon Choppeas 128
Daniel Conn 85
Francis Crawford 15/8/4
W. Henson Cole 60
Robert Carter 1036
James Collins 100
John Crawford 60
Andrew Cunningham 53
Daniel Conn 187
Thomas Culverson 168
John Clackner 50
Thomas Curtain 90
Henry Cook 347
Samuel Cooper 84
John Clopper 335
Peter Carter 50
Thomas Cole 35
Jacob Covenhovin 23
Samuel Cook 102
Joseph Castle 40
Saml. Chamberlain 455
Mr. Conley 43
Keziah Cox, widow 33
Tomothy Connor 40
Wm. Cole 95
Ambrose Clark 414/10
Chritian Cappets 225
Philip Commer 43
William Clemm 277/10
Casper Cline living in Wilk's House 58
Joseph Cook 48
Ellen Cain 150
Wm. Cook 1020
Richard Cook 40/16/8
Thomas Cole 873
Patrick Crlortienly (Claherty?) 70
Hezekiah Clagett 691
Richard Constant 218
Saml. Chase 1190/16/8

Petter Cascaw 425
Lewis Calfoos 435
Danil Cromer 87
Val. Cahazel 145
---- Causten 283
Margret Carroll 435
Richard Culverwell 207/10
Jeremiah T. Chase 555
Michl. Carroll 35
James Clark 225
Henry Cable 35
Edmond Custus 140
Isaac Cousy (Blackman) 10
Peter Bormord Clary 1040
Edw. J. Cole living in Mosely's house 35
Cumberlane Dugan 820
Davis Gater living in Hook's house 42
John Dugby living in Mickle's house 18
James Deventure 310
Chr'n. Delcher 74
John Delcher 50
George Delcher 430
John Dobbin 265
Saml. Davis 60
Ann Dillon 44
Jack Dorsey (Blackman) 40
Mr. Duhurst 29
Saml. Davis 306/16/8
Henry Deal 152
Valentine Delcher 282
John Dodd 147/10
Elein Daugherty living in Ensor's house 120
James Donnally 91
Wm. Disney 105
Isaac Dixon 100
Thomas Donovan in the County 55
Barbary Ditmore 420
Wm. Dislance 44
Peter Davalt 172
Owen Dorsey 255
Eliza Dady 360
Henry Didier 738
Walter Dorsey 614
Patrick Dagan 1206/16/8
John E. Dorsey 816
John Donnell 2398/10
Lewis Delobert 220
Peter Dulany 40
John Durrow 50

Joseph Daugherty 40
Doctor Dunkil 70
Daniel Delozus 578/10
Margt. Dodds 43
Robert Doine 91
W. Dorsey & McMechen 500
Philip Deawalt 18
D. Peter Decandrey 378
Thomas Dempster 79
John Dorsey of O. 4548/10
Richard Daugherty 50
Ml. Diffenderffer 120
Dapheny Dickerson 22
Jacob Dell 220
John Diddigh 25
Jas. Lewis Delarue 812
Wm Dyer 91
Thos. De Roachbrune 145
John Dorson 28
Owne Duffey 59
Benj. Davis 35
Benj. Eaton 56
Luke & William Ensor 541
Martin Eichelberger 1566
Benj. Elliott 45
James Edwards 255
Jacob Everhart 66
Caleb Earnest 30
David Elphinson 226
James Elliott 523
Daniel Evans 95
John Elliott living in Taggerts house
  170/5
Concord Elfelin 1670
Mr. Elvers 165
George Eppard 395
Bassil L. Elder 195
Philip Entler 250
Ann Edwards, widow 430
Solomon Etting 420
Sarah Esclen, widow 81
Robert Edwards 353
Wm. Edwards 330
Fred. Ersler 230
Martin Eichelberger, Jr. in Mr.
  Jones's house 89/6/8
David Forney 249
Doctor Falls 265
John Fitzgerald 92
Joseph Fisher 144
Dorathy Foos 77/18/4
Henry Fisher 185

Stafford Forrister 61
Wm. Fisher 54
John Frail 77
Joshua Fort 35/10
Eliza. Fort 27/10
James Foster 100
Alexander Finletter 75
David Forman 55
David Forman, Jr. 40
George Foss 238
Alexander Forsyth 120
William Forsyth 53
Mark Forty 194
Valentine Forman 60
Benedict Funk 43
Chas. Floyd 126
Maria French 60
Thomas Florenty 63
Richard Fitzgerald 395
Derick Faune Stock 255
Ebenezer Finley 255
James Fulton livng in Myer's house 28
Peter Fowble 105
Joseph Fretts 61
Samuel French 66
Wm. Fiffe (or Fifer) 283
Mark Flemming 20
  Falls & Brown 70
John Gould 190
Benj, Garrison 75
Abbey Goodwin, widow of Doctor Loyd
  Goodwin 375
Golleham & Burk 85
Nicholas Gorsuch 230
Chas. Guy (B.man) 33
Mr. McGracey 65
A. Gunet (or A. Jno. Genett) 170
James Goodwin 66
Saml. Goodwin 43
John Glendy 50
Wm. Galloway, living in Evans House
  21
George Grundy 2082
William Gibson 2165
John Griffin 60
Josh. Goldsmith 55
Martin Griffin 43
John Glorhery 78
Wm. Gore 43
Cornelius H. Gist 330
Chas. Garts 909
Robt. Gilmore 580

Wm. Graham, Mercht. 50
John Graham 280
Absalom Gardner living in Amy's house
  13
Mr. Gwin, Lumberyard 250
Fred. Grapevine 250
Francis Gilmire 40
Thomas Griffin 155
Gabriel Gill 96
Anthony Groverman 43
John George 50
Wm. Goodwin 270
Alexander Gould living in Mickles
  house 38
Jacob Gillard 296
Freeborn Garretson 70
Guideman living in Bowley's house
  85/16/8
Joseph Gilis 46
Christopher Hughs 60
Edw. Haklon 500
Wm. Hodges 120
John Holland (paid) 93
H. John Hill 45
John Hague 21
Fredk. Hook 45
Wm. Hayward 240/8/4
Catherine Hersperger 60
George Henley 68
Ludwick Honeyworth 53
Wm. Harding living in the county on
  F. Town Rd. 65
Zachariah Hatton 105
Philip Hacket 38
John Hughs 24
John Harker 124
Wm. Howard 91
Wm. Hooper 79
Richard Harker 65
Bassil Hurst 27
Benedict Hurst 30
Wm. Hall 30
Girard Hopkins 140
Samuel House, living in Pennington
  house 12
David Harriman 105
Sam'l Harper 425
Alexander Haman 255
Joseph Harrison 445
Mrs. Hobbs 39
Sophia Hoburg 90/8/4
Hugh Hales 40

Benj. Henley 37
Susanna Hanson, living in Foster's
  house 14/10
Peter Horne 200
John Helm 66
Joshua Howard 81
Jacob Hannahwalt, living on Brown Lot
  108
John Hilt 90
John Hiplin 175
John Herrick, living in Keen's house
  18
Jacob Hamel 73
Sarah Harvey, ----- 50
Rezin Hammond 580/10
Wm. High 210
Thomas Hooper 60
Richard Hill 45
Arch'd Hawkins 35
John Herman 69
Philip Horn 175
John S. Horn 1035/13/4
Jacob Hay 140
Gideon Hughes 90
Littleton Holland 90
Joseph Hook 125
John Hammond 129
George Hyde 75
John Harris, Black man 45
Hugh Hambleton 70
Chr. Hutchings 82
Isaac Henderson (Black man) 70
Aaron Hogan 140
Robert Hicks 144
Isaac Henry 85
Fred'k Hoover 60
John Henry 126
John Hay 104
Wm. Hawkins 679
Wm. Hayward 270
David Hosetler 100
Peter Hodges 170
Moses Hand 270
Thomas Henning 75
John Haselton 90
Mich'l Hoover 63
James Headen 188
Mr. Hoskins 255
Caleb Hall 280
Thos. Hollingsworth 400
Benj. Hayward 64
George Hoffman 85

Henry Hoffman 147
Catherine Hoos 140
Wm. Hollins 80
Ignatius Hoover 142
Jesse Hollingsworth 660
Howard, Pennington & Ogleby 923/6/8
Howard & Pennington 155
John E. Howard 503/8/10
Zeb. Hollingsworth 140
John S. Horn 215
Hale (or Hall) Hugh 23/5
Robert Joyner 33
Moses Jerman 45
Benj. Jerman 53
Mich'l Jones 78
Wm. Jackson 60
James Jones 46
Mary Jarkin 78
Mary Jones, widow 505
Jacob Jones 96
Joseph Johnson 158
Solomon Johnson (Black man) 48
Ann Jarin 371
Henry Johnson (Black man) 32
Wm. Joyce 96
Wm. Isler 95
Thos. Johnson and Phil. Moore 510
Hosea Johns 720
Lewis Johntee 703
Jospeph Jemison 70
John Jagenfritz 343
Johns Talbot, living in Wm. Smith's
    house 55
Wm. Jackson 415
James Irwin 132
Beale Israel, living in George Hide's
    house 22
Capt. Iselen 15
Wm. Jones 245
Edw'd Ireland 1299
Fred. Johnson 65
James Jefferies 412
James Johnson, living in house 15
Mary Keiser 63
John Keplinger 195
Wm. Keplinger, living in Long's house
    88
Amasa King 68
Edw'd Kelly 175
John Kerby 68
John Potter Kelly 84/8/4
John Kennedy 30

Wm. Keen 180
Thomas King 81
James Kirby 162
Henry Kimble 70
John Kennedy 494
Doctor Hy Keerl 980
Chr. Keener 260
George Kentz 105
Thomas Kelbraith 597
Henry Keating 195
Jacob Kensbury 50
Elias King 65
Wm. Knebs 515
Philip Keys 300
John & Geo. Kelso 715
Mrs. Kelbraith 415
Martin Keaver 46
John Adam Knot 55
George Lindenberger 135
Caroline Lollecoffer (or Gollekoffer)
    160
Jane Luke, living in A. Riley's house
    12
John Lightner, living in Widow
    Wilson's house 15
Ferdinard Lawrance 60
Sam'l Long 510
John Luch 73
John Lemmon 45
George Lightner 680
Benj. Lynch 70/10
James Law, living in Bond's house 25
John Lucas 80
Jacob Lownslager, living in Cross's
    house 35/8/4
John Latour, living in house 37/10
John Lemmon, Jr, living in Tyson's
    house 76
John Lynch 25/16/8
Anthony Lewis 287/10
James Leslington 89
Anthony Lynch 42
Wm. Lanius 264
Robert Long, living in Raymond's
    house 330
Daniel Lammott 605/8/4
Andrew Leary 100
Peter Lingenfelter 420
George Legget 81
Kennedy Long 320
Wm. Lorman 562/10
John Librand 110

Nath'l Lock 175
Jacob Lock 65
Thomas Long 140
Wm. Lee 162
Nicholas Link 78
Peter Little 198
John Mickle 260
John Morgan, living in Baker's house 12
Chalres Moore 95
Lewis Miller 145
Arthur Mitchel 243
Will'm McMechen 212
Alex. McCalister 186
Wm. Mabile 66
John Maidwell 40
Wm. McClarey 410
David Mummy 479/5
Jacob Madinger 53
Wm. McCanley 50
Anthony Maim 440
Rebecca Morris, widow of Wm. 150
Mary McMahan 255
John Murray 137/10
Francis Murray, living in Wm. Murray's house 18
James Maidwell, Jr. 25
George Miller 135
Joseph Morancy 180
James Morriss 83
Clement Macatee 165
Wm. Macneer 44/8/4
James McColloch 150
John Melcod 35
John McCall 75
Robert McCool 165
Wm. Moor (Black man) 73
Thos. McCormick 35
Jesse Morgan 60
Luther Martin 1678
Thomas McElderry 3187/8/4
John Mycroft, living in Johnson's house 44/16/8
George Milbermon 440
Francis Maguire 66
M. McCausland & Co. 866
Nath'l Morton, living in William's house 40
Josiah (or Isaiah) Mankin 28
John McKim 95
Sam'l Maxwell 75

Jacob Medura, living at the Goal 121/5
Jacob Miller 50
Zachariah Miles 144/14/8
Benj. Mason 65
Kennedy Morrois 71
Benj'n Moul 420
David Muskberger, living in Widow Dutmar's house 30
John McFadon, mill stone maker, if not assessed in City 101
David Moore 492/10
George W. Moore 15
Henry Moore of David 95
Peter McDonogh 70
Hugh McCurdy 863
Margt. McAllister 100
Owen McKim 28
Roger McClane 43
Adam Moore 138
John Moale's heirs 1162/10
Jacob Moore 445
Widow Montalabore 112/10
Henry Myres 75
Louisa Meads 29
Richard Mathews 53
Wm. Matthews, living in Dady's house 18
Adam Miller 105
Jacob Miller 407
Wm. McCarty 90
John Marshall (Black man) 43
Moses Moore 43
James McCannan 481
James McHenry 4875
John McIntire 330/16/8
Henry Moore 260
Thomas Moore, living in Keener's house 50
Adam Moss 85
Sam'l Moale 25
Jacob Miller 75
Wm. Maxfield 75
Jacob Montcath 75
Wm. Murphy 33
Sam'l Merryman 140
Job Merryman 4/5
Jonathan Marsh 426
--- McKenzie 255
Job H. McCulloch 580/16/8
Alex. McCulloch 21
Conrod Miller 136

Francis Mitchell 70
James McCulloch 150
Jacob Milter (butcher) 28
Alex. McKim 180
Benj. Mason's heirs 35
Cap. Chas. Meyers 20
James Martin 45
Benj. May 31
Sam'l Nappet 43
George Nippard 875
James Norris (carpenter) 12
Henry Niccols 80
John Nail 25
James Nail 75
Henry Nicols (Qy.) 80
Mary Nicholson, widow 226/13/4
Wm. Neal 175
Patrick Nosn 60
Charlotte Nicols 930
Reynolds Nose 95
Henry Nange 384
Mr. Nox, living in Richmond, Va 495
Jacob Newman 73
James C. Nelson, living in Polk''s
    house 25
Daniel Obrien 25
Thos. Onion, living in a house of
    John Chabimer's 244/10
Brian OLoghlan 104
Sam'l Owings of Stephen 101/5
Jehu Otley 53
Thomas Obrian 63
John O'Donnel 260
Daniel Paul, living in Smith's house
    23
John Patterson 100
Daniel Powley 8
Joshua Pocock 15
James Piper 1168
Timothy Pritchards 33
Hezikiah Price 454
Sam'l Peters (Black man) 73
John Pritchards, living in the
    Country 40
Henry Pennington 373
John Pindal 98
John Powel 40
Isaiah Proctor 90
Wm. Patterson 1480
Wm. Price 130
Walter Patterson 193
Hy Peters 454/10

Isaac Philips, living in French
    Priests property 43
Jacob Penter 138
Lewis Pascault 1032/16/8
Walter Pierpoint 55
Arnos Pierpoint 55
Israel Pierce 70
Will'm Pan 250
James Poke 255
James Powers 288
Fred'k Pumphrey 145
Geo. Prestine 98
Elias Pollock 149/10
Wm. Paca's heirs 45
George Presstman 240
Josiah Pennington 1062
Geo. Parker 48
Wm. Paca 10
Patton & Jones 110
Elisha Perigo 68
Gige Presbury 360
Josias Pennington, from L. office
    33/15
Thomas Qyay 195
Adam Riley 86/5, paid Mar 5, 1805
Janet Ross 73
Mary Rice, widow 90
Joseph Robinson 42
Elisha Riggs 30
Conrod Riley 437
Jonathan Reitter 155
Henry Roberts 46
John Roberts 30
John Roger 40
Nicholas Roger 185
Charles Roger 360
John Rusk 738
Edw. Robinson 73
Thos. Rutter, Jr. 1388/4/2
John Rutter 843
James Riddlemoser 180
Hugh Ricketts 120
George Renicker 1045
Daniel Raymond 680
Geo. Roypold 603
Daniel Richardson 139
Alexander Robinson 621/6/8
Geo. Rosonstut 141
Geo. Rosenstut, Jr. 130
Nath. Ramsay, living in Doctor
    McHenry 244/6/8
Jno. & Paul Ruckle 70

Mary Roberts, living in Doctor McHenry's house 88
Jacob Rothrock 90
Mr. Riddlemoser 527
Geo. Reding 75
Isaac Reed 40
Wm. Randall 153
Wm. Roberts 25
Wm. Rollings, living in Lock's house 15
Russell & Pringle 90
Ch. Raymons 420
John Richards 38
Rose (Black woman) 128
Nich'l Ridgley 210
Robert Riddle 530
Josiah Rutter 255/16/8
Thos. & Jno. Rutter 790
James Randall 94
Joseph Ranise 65
Robert Sliver 2352
Wm. R. Smith 698/10
Cathrine Sly 188
John Sarer, living in Rosetter Scott's house 11/5
Rosetler Scott 235
Catherin Stegers 35
Wm. Suddon 116
Joshua Steepleton 32
Rob't Shaw 118
Wm. Scarf 116
Sam'l Sindall 110
Eliz. Shurman 24/10
John Sands 55
Josiah Stephenson 65
Dr. Hy Stephenson 1370/10
Dan'l Sprinkle 46
John Sinnard 56
Cath'n Smith, widow of Jno. Smith (butcher) 125
Jacob Stansbury 845
Henry Sigler 175
Fred'k Slremell 130
Jane Strobridge 60
Abigail Strobridge 198/8/4
Hezekiah Sarr, living in Wilson's house 15
Josh. Stansbury 20
Joshua Swan 103
Edw. Stone 90
John Simpson 263
Robt. Sellers 32

Chas. Settler 52
John Smith 32
James Summers 101
Darius Stansbury 117
David Shaw 285
James Sterling 4344
Catherin Swingle 187
Dr. Jacob Smull, at Hospital 23/8/4
Henry Star 112
Mark Shaw 55
Henry Shaw 75
Isaac Smiley 92
Smith and Jessop 1543
John Sinclair 145
Sarah Smith, living at the Alms house 440
Jno. (Brower) Sinclair 33
Charles R. Sterrel 240
Fred'k Sumwalt 350
Sam'l Smite 100
Mr. Stanfield 40
Sheets and Foss 340
Jacob Smith 298
Josh. Swartzman 75
Humphy Saunders 197
Jno. Stewart (Black man) 81
F. R. Sadler 75
James Stewert 80
Rob't Spence, living in Whitelock's house 30
Wm. Smith, Jr. 430
Rob't Sinclair 415
Jacob Stigers 297
Joseph Stall 50
Adam Sisnap 75
George Sanders 81
John Sherm 137
Beale Spurrier, living in Owen Dorsey's house 22/10
Mary Stephenson, widow of Josh. 70
Sam'l Shaw 30
Job Smith (baker) 479
Hy Shroder 1581
Geo. Steles 1667
John Steel 390
Jacob Shott 188
Peter Smith 128
Thomas Sharp 61
Nath'l Shroder 54
Nath'l Stune 90
John Scot 85
Geo. Selmon 185

Rob't Scott 58
John D. Summers 48
Nichols Strike 335
Eliz. Scek 44
Sam'l Smythe 240
Sam'l R. Smith 764
Rob't Smith 200
Harriman Snider 53
John Smith (cooper) 46
Edw'd Shipley 40
Arch'd Smith 15
Hy Shimburgh 70
George Sanders 55
Henry Sheaf of Philad. 72
Moses Sheppard 75
Philip Sisler 60
Mary Steven 90
Mich'l Shove 163
Philip Swatzer 361
V. John Sanders 147/10
H. Jno. Shriver, living in Shrs'
    house 25
Thomas Skipper 133
John Smith 205
Richard Smith 36
Barberry Tinges 29/10
Richard Taylor 1008/6/8
Isaac Taylor 90
Richard Taylor 30
Benj. Todd 40
Thomas Tague 55
--- Towson 30/10
Wm. Trimble 420
Philip Taylor 240
Gerrard Tipton 160
Catherine Talbot 130
John Tabot 160
John Twait 130
Rob't Thompson 185
Tagart and Pennington 2600
John Tagart 954
Elisha Tyson 410
Aquila Taylor 55
Alex. Thompson 81
James Temmon 140
Luke Tiernan 475
Nathan Tyson 140
Wm. Tarring 43
John Toob 40
Josins Thompson 210
Revd. John Tessier 3838/6/8

Gerrard Tipton, if not same property
    as above 160
Brune & Vonkapffe, Francis D. Blocks
    Est. 140
Abm. Vanbibber 910
Mary Underwood 40
John Valentine (waggoner) 63
Mr. Vice living near St. Jnos. Church
    415
Mrs. Underwood widow of Elisha 90
Henry Vickars 48
Wm. Urt 60
Felix Vice living in a lot of Col.
    Howards 25
Charles Williams (dyer) 15/8/4
Jacob Williams 150
Hannah Wilson (paid tax) 87
Henry Working living in V. Ducers
    house 12
Widow Williams 70
Thomas White 330
Cathr. Waters (blackwoman) 33
Mrs. Weisenthal 320
Saml. Webb 30/10
Edwd. Waters, living in Lory's house
    21
Edwd. Widler 40
Thomas Wheeler 38
Henry Willey 19
John Weathuhuburn 70
Wm. Wallace 150
John Wilson 100
Jno. Wilson if not the same 70
James Wilson 135
Saml. Wilson (Blackman) 27
James Wolf 75
Math'w. Walker in Williams house 27
Thos. Weaderstrand 76
Robt. Wheeler 50
Ezekiel Walker (cooper) 266
John Wright 415
Jonathan Whelan 163
Thomas Williamson 165
Joseph Watson 38
Chas. Whitelock 215
John Whitelock 60/8/4
Hugh Wilson 272/10
George Wuse 140
Bassil Whelan 51
James Whelan 55
Wm. Wistle 55
John Watson 20
Peter Whelan 82

John Wilson 77
John Winn 145
Peter Walter 270
Casper Weaver 283
Adam Welsh 1371/16/8
James Wignal 863
Chn. Wishahnple 90
Charles White 185
Regin White 175
Wm. Wilmer 100
James Wilks 130
Peter Walter 278
Willm. Wilkerson 43
Henry Webb 66
Mr. Whitelock 175
James Wilson living in Moale's house
    73
Elijah West 85
Michl. Waters 50
Philip Walter 328
James Winckle 350
Robt Welsh 375
George Wellen (Waller) 502
Jacob Warking 210
Hugh Westby 89
Daniel Wagones living in Captors
    house 30
Philip Walkey 50
Michl. Warner 721
Wm. Whipple 117
David Williamson 372/10
S. Joseph Woods 66
George Warner 1264
David Watson 98
Thomas Yates 2315
John Young 51
John Yuser 333/10
John Young, living in Sumwalts house
    62
Jermiah Yellott 2159
Ann Young 40
Larkin Young 188
Joseph Young 290
Samuel & Francis Young 67/10
Eve Zarnes (widow) 203/16/8
Christian Zell 288
Barnett Zell 553

BIGGS Frederick 109; Jacob 109;
Joseph 109; William 109
BINNIS Barney 29
BIS--- Peter 129
BISHOP Henry 66; John 42, 119, 120;
Peter 109
BISS George 40
BLACK Catharine 108; Elizabeth 80;
Frederick 108; Joseph 108; Moses
51
BLATCHLEY Thomas 32
BLIZARD John 87; Stephen 87; William
86
BLOCK Francis D. 138
BLUFFORD William 58
BOBLIN Philip 119
BOCKMAN Frederick 109
BODAR Dominick 138
BOHANAN James 58
BOLEY Daniel 102 ; 138

BOLINGER Joseph 19; Matthias 20
BOMGARDNER Henry 109; Jacob 109
BOND --- 142; Barnet 40, 42, 43;
Benjamin 32, 45, 95; Charles 2;
Denis 19; Edward 2, 12, 32; George
7, 8; James 40, 42; John 19, 32;
Mary 138; Nichodemus 129;
Nicodemus 32; Peter 138; Samuel
45; Solomon 32; Thomas 2, 9, 32,
40, 42, 73, 129; William 43
BOON Charles 138
BOONE Elizabeth 58; John 58; Sarah 58
BOOS George 138; Peter 109
BOOSE John 131
BOOTH Addison 138; Wm. 138
BOOZE Doctor 138
BORING Absolom 19; Absoslom 20;
Ezekiel 20, 95; James 20; Joshua
20; Peter 105; Pliles'r 20; Samuel
24; Thomas 20; William 94
BORRING Thomas 118
BOSLEY Ann 29, 32; Caleb 29; Eley
106; Elijah 1, 2, 13; Ezekiel 2,
3, 13; Greenbury 29; Jacob 106;
James 1, 3, 6; John 32; Joseph 32;
Mary 29; William 3, 32, 40, 42,
44, 138
BOSSLY Gideon 127
BOSSOM Charles 19
BOST Valentine 119, 125
BOTH Abraham 138

BOWDER John 114
BOWEN Absalom 69, 70, 72, 74;
Benjamin 58; Jehue 46; John 68,
70, 73; Josias 32; Nathan 76;
Nathaniel 32; Sarah 68, 70, 73;
Solomon 32; William 32
BOWER Christian 120; Jacob 120; John
109; Stephen 119
BOWERS Christian 125; Daniel 45, 46;
Fornaca 120; John 19, 120, 138;
Joseph 138; Martin 138; William
138
BOWERSOCK George 109
BOWLEY --- 141; Daniel 58, 70, 75,
76, 78
BOXTER james 138
BOYCE Andrew 76; Benjamin 1; Eleanor
42, 73; John 42
BOYD Andrew 108
BOYER Casper 120; Catharine 120;
Gabriel 120; Mary 120; Peter 129;
Philip 129
BOYLAN Mary 111, 113
BOYLE Daniel 109, 117
BRACK Adam 108
BRACKENRIDGE Robert 109; William 109
BRADFORD John 1, 7
BRADY John 138
BRAKELY Mathias 79
BRAKIN John 138
BRAMWELL Henry 45
BRANT William 138
BRANUMAN Samuel 19
BRAYAN WIlliam 118
BREWER John 138
BRICE John 138; Normand 108
BRICKER John 120
BRIEN John 138
BRIGHTMAN Edward 138
BRIGHTWELL Richard 136
BRITON Richard 42
BRITTAIN Richard 11
BRITTON Richard 3, 40
BROCK Rachael 70, 73
BROOKE Raphael 116; Raphail 108, 115;
Roger 116
BROOKS Charles 29; Clement 95;
Humphry 58; James 59; Joseph 58
BROOKSMITH John 102
BROTHER Joshua 95; Richard 20
BROTHERS Jacob 123; John 120
BROTHERTON Thomas 65

Stephen 118; Thomas 4, 33; William 4, 96
CROMWILL Conrod 109
CROOK Alexander 138; James 41, 42, 44
CROOKS John 80
CROOKSHANKS Charles 68, 70
CROOMER Philip 130
CROSS --- 142; Benjamin 21; John 21, 46, 96; Joshua 19; Mr. 139; Nicholas 46; Robert 51, 80; William 46
CROULE --- 70
CROUSE Christian 1, 3; Henry 80; John 109; Philip 120
CROW James 103
CROWEL John 129; Michael 120
CROWL Conrod 138; Mary 138
CROWS Jacob 118
CROXALL Eleanor 46; James 80; John 80; Samuel 80; Thomas 80
CRUMBECKER Abram 129; Adam 131; Catharine 130; David 130; Jacob 130; Peter 129
CRUSE Paul 119, 120, 127
CUDDY John 1
CULLASON William 21
CULLINGS Isaac 21; Jonathan 21; Thomas 21
CULLISON Jeremiah 46; Joshua 87
CULLUM Jeremiah 7
CULVERSON Thomas 139
CULVERWELL Richard 139
CUMMINGS Ann 129; James 130
CUNNINGHAM Andrew 139; James 76
CUNYER William 3
CUPPER Nicholas 3
CURBY Drusila 43
CURFMAN George 3, 13
CURTAIN James 70, 73; Thomas 139
CURTIS Joseph 3, 5; William 3
CUSTUS Edmond 139

DADY --- 143; Eliza 139
DAGAN John 130; Patrick 139
DALE --- 71
DALEY Jacob 1, 3; Thomas 102
DALLAS Walter R. 78; Walter Riddle 75, 76
DALRYMPLE Asquith 138
DANNALLY Cornelius 5, 7, 13
DARNELL Francis 4, 10, 11, 16, 18
DAUGHADY John 34; Richard 34

DAUGHERTY Elein 139; John 75, 76, 78; Joseph 140; Richard 140; Thomas 76
DAVALT Peter 139
DAVEY Alexander 48, 70; Alexander Woodrof 68
DAVIDSON Phinis 110
DAVIS Amos 130; Archibald 42; Benjamin 21, 140; Ezekiel 70; Francis 21; Jacob 60; James 21, 47; Mary 130; Philemon 136; Robert 47; Samuel 21, 139; William 75, 76, 87; Zachariah 103
DAW Joseph 57
DAWS Francis 4, 12
DAWSON Philemon 60
DAY John 41, 42, 44; Nicholas 44; William F. 5
DAYLEY Jacob 4
DAYMAN Frederick 110
DEAL Henry 139
DEAWALT Philip 140
De BENSE Pierre Marie 73
DEAHOOF John 22
DEAL Charles 79; John 87, 110; Leon 110
DEAN Emanuel 76; Jonathan 55
DEAVER John 70
DeBENSE Marie Piere 68; Pierre Marie 70
DECANDREY D. Peter 140
DECKER Jacob 47
DEEDS Philip 22
DEEMS George 46; John 48
DELAPORT Frances 75
DELARUE James Lewis 140
DELASERE William 70
DELAVET Peter 4
DELCHER Chr'n 139; George 139; John 139; Valentine 139
DELEPORT Francis 76
DELL Jacob 140; John 118; Nicholas 118, 130; Peter 118
DELOBERT Lewis 139
DELOZUS Daniel 140
DELUSORO William 68
DEMMITT Andrew 102; Burch 42; Henry 48; James 5; John 60; Moses 41, 42, 44; William 4, 5
DEMONNIS Dorothy 48
DEMPSTER Thmas 140
DEMSEY Luke 78
DENTON William 42

INDEX

FENTON Charles 49
FERGUSON Hugh 110, 111, 114, 123,
  124, 126; Samuel 111; William 110,
  111, 114
FICKLE Margaret 110, 111; Matthias
  111, 117; Rachel 111
FIFER William 140
FIFFE William 140
FINBONE John 130
FINFROCK Henry 111
FINK Adam 111
FINKBORN John 134
FINLETTER Alexander 140
FINLEY Ebenezer 140; John 104
FIRESPAUGH Eve 122
FISHER Christian 6; Clarer 88; David
  88, 118, 122; Elizabeth 88; George
  49; Henry 140; John 88; Joseph
  140; Leonard 88; William 140
FISHPAUGH John 34, 59
FIST George 97
FITCH Henry 76; Robert 75, 76, 78;
  Thomas 76; William 75, 76, 78
FITE Andrew 81; Peter 60, 81
FITTERLING Jacob 122
FITZ SIMMONS Pierce 26
FITZ Ulerich 22
FITZGERALD John 140; Richard 140
FITZHUGH George 6, 11, 12, 13
FLAGG Thomas 63
FLAX John 68
FLEAGLE John 121; Vallentine 121
FLEGLE John 126; Valentine 119
FLEMING Elizabeth 71; Mark 140
FLETCHER Henry 43
FLICHINGER Jacob 122
FLICKINGER Andrew 122
FLIN James 80; Patience 65
FLORENTY Thomas 140
FLOWERS Jonathan 5, 6; Solomon 5, 6
FLOYD Charles 140; Joseph 75, 76, 78
FLUTTER George 88
FOGLESTONG George 122
FONDA Abram 104
FOOS Dorathy 140; William 75
FOOSE William 71
FORD & PAXON 4
FORD & PAXTON 6
FORD Barney 22; Isaac 6; Jeremiah 6;
  John Howard 81; Joshua 22;
  Mordecai 22; Samuel 48; Stephen

124; Thomas 48, 49, 52; Thomas C.
  34
FOREMAN Jacob 122
FORMAN David 140; Isaac 81; Joseph
  73; Valentine 140; William Lee 69,
  75, 77, 78
FORMWALT Lawrence 122
FORNER Christian 71; John 71
FORNEY Abraham 111; Daniel 49; David
  140; Philip 122, 128
FORRISTER Stafford 140
FORSYTH Alexander 140; William 140
FORT Elizabeth 34, 140; John 34;
  Joshua 140; Samuel 49
FORTY Mark 140
FOSS George 140; John 71, 76; William
  76
FOSTER --- 141; Absolom 22; George 5,
  22; James 140; John 22, 29;
  Nicholas 22; Thomas 88
FOUBLE Melker 88; Michael 88; Peter
  22
FOULLER James 122
FOUTS Jacob 131
FOUTZ Solomon 121, 128
FOWBLE Peter 140
FOWLER John 76; Richard 75, 76; Tamer
  78; Tammer 76
FOWLLER John 96
FRAIL John 140
FRANCES Jonathan 5
FRANKFADER Philip 88
FRANKLEBERRY Henry 63
FRANKLIN Charles 76, 104, 131, 137;
  Garet 76; Rezin 104; Thomas 77
FRAUNK Elizabeth 88; Peter 22, 88
FRECKER Jacob 82
FREE John 5, 6
FREELAND John 5, 6; Moses 5, 6; Uriah
  22
FREEZE Moddlenah 122
FREFOGLE Chris. 113
FRENCH Benjamin 43, 44; James 104;
  Maria 140; Samuel 140
FRESH Francis 48
FRETTS Joseph 140
FREY Andrew 35
FRINGER Jacob 88, 118; Michael 88;
  Nicholas 111
FRIZZEL, Absolom 104
FRIZZELL, Absolam 104; Hannah 49

INDEX

FROCK Daniel 121
FROG Boston 57
FROGG John 56
FROWNFILTER Felix 121
FRUSTY Jacob 64
FRYFOGLE John 122
FUGATE Elizabeth 5; Martin 5
FULKER Christopher 122
FULKER Hyronimus 122
FULKS Jacob 9
FULLER Nicholas 2, 6, 16; Samuel 40,
    44
FULTON James 140
FUNK Benedict 140
FURGUSON Hugh 122
FURNEY John 131; Nicholas 118
FUSS John 111

GAIN William 23
GAITHER William 131
GAITHERS William 134
GALLOWAY Aquilla 8; Moses 44; Pamela
    44; Robert C. 44; Salathiel 6;
    Thomas 6, 9, 77; William 42, 44,
    140
GALT John 111; Matthew 111
GANTZ Adam 49
GARDINER Emagrell 131; Tobias 129,
    131
GARDNER Absalom 141George 62; Hannah
    61; John 82, 97; William 95, 97
GARRETSON Cornelius 75, 77, 78;
    Freeborn 141; Garret 78; Job 75,
    77, 78
GARREY James 50
GARRISON Benjamin 140
GARTS Charles 140
GASH Basil 73; Benjamin 75, 77, 78;
    Nicholas 71, 73
GATER Davis 139
GAUL Michael 23
GAWSLIN Amos 131
GEETSHELL Peter 122
GEITSHALL Peter 121
GENETT A. John 140
GENT Thomas 23, 35
GEORGE John 141
GERTSHELL Peter 122
GIBENS Thomas 81
GIBSON William 42, 140
GIDDINGS James 128
GIDDISON John 74

GIGER John 131
GILBERT Eleazer 7; John 131; widow
    115
GILL Benjamin 88; Charles 88; Edward
    23, 88; Elizabeth 23; Gabriel 68,
    71, 141; John 35, 88, 89; Joshua
    35; Stephen 22, 35; Stephen G. 35;
    Thomas 88; Urith 88
GILLARD Jacob 141
GILLEYLAN Ester 111
GILLEYMAN John 111
GILLINGHAM James 131; John 30
GILLIS John 104; Joseph 141; Robert
    6, 11
GILMIRE Francis 141
GILMORE Robeert 140; William 42
GINAVAN Elizabeth 82
GIRTY Catharine 48
GIST Cornelius H. 140; David 121;
    George 23; John 122, 128; Joshua
    6, 97, 118, 131; Susannah 122;
    Thomas 23, 35, 50, 88, 97; William
    88
GITMORE Robert 81
GITTINGER Henry 89; Jacob 89
GITTINGS --- 7; Benjamin 8; Hannah 8,
    9; James 3, 4, 6, 8, 10, 15, 18,
    61, 122; Samuel 15; Thomas 8, 16
GIVEN James 8
GIVENS James 7; John 6, 12
GLADMAN Michael 49; Thomas 49
GLASS George 111
GLEASON John 131
GLENDY John 140
GLORHERY John 140
GLOVER John 104; Joshua 104
GODDARD Lemuel 71
GODFERRY Samuel 81
GODFREY Samuel 129
GOLDSBOROUGH John 63
GOLDSMITH & WEATHEREL 18
GOLDSMITH Josh. 140
GOLLEHAM & BURK 140
GOLLEKOFFER 142
GONGER John 111
GOOD Adam 111, 114
GOODFELLOW William 23
GOODLANDER Henry 131
GOODWIN Abbey 140; James 140; Lloyd
    97, 140; Lyde 29; Rachael 7;
    Rachel 9; Samuel 140; William 3,

6, 7, 11, 12, 14, 15, 29, 68, 71,
97, 129, 131, 132, 133, 135, 141
GORDON Joseph 111
GORE Andrew 104; Christian 23; Cooper
104; George 35, 49; H. John 49;
John 51; Michael 35; Philip 88;
Samuel 88; William 140
GORSUCH Charles 2, 3, 7, 19, 29, 35;
David 6; Dickenson 29; Elisha 6;
Jeremiah 35; John 29, 38, 68, 71,
73, 97; Nathan 97; Nicholas 140;
Norman 32, 35; Richard 97; Robert
68, 71, 73; Thomas 29, 97
GOSNELL Benjamin 104; Charles 49;
Greenberry 50; Peter 49; Philip
49; William 50; Zebediah 50
GOTT Edward 35; Henrietta 7; Richard
35, 41, 42; Samuel 35, 42
GOUDY Abram 131
GOUGH Dorsey Harry 77; Harry 8; Harry
D. 41; Harry Dorsey 44, 71; Henry
61; Henry D. 9, 17, 19; Henry
Dorsey 8, 131
GOULD Alexander 141; John 140
GOULDEN Aquilla 71
GOULDSBOROUGH Robert 77
GRAHAM John 141; William 141
GRAMBURG John 66
GRAMER John 122
GRAMMER Jacob 122; John 88
GRANDADAM Francis 122, 127
GRANT John 61
GRAPEVINE Fred. 141
GRAY Ephraim 71; James 70, 71; Joseph
102; Lynch 70, 73; Richard 41, 42,
44; Thomas 7
GREAGRERY George 95
GREEN Abednego 6; Abraham 29;
Catharine 75, 77, 78; Clement 7,
8, 9, 13; Henry 49; Isaac 6, 7,
61, 77; Joel 71, 75, 77, 78; John
100; Joseph 75, 77, 78; Josias 68,
71, 73; Nathaniel 77; Shadrach 7,
14; Solomon 68, 71; Vincent 68,
71, 73, 75, 77
GREENFIELD Nathan 7
GREENWALT Jacob 131
GREENWOOD Yost 131
GREGORY James 41, 42, 44; John 78;
McFrancis 78
GRICE Henry 23; Jacob 88
GRIFFEE Richard 97

GRIFFEN Charles 79; Joseph 42
GRIFFIN John 140; Luke 42; Martin
140; Thomas 141; William 48
GRIFFITH Abednego 50; Abraham 29, 35;
Benjamin 50; David 111; George 67;
Henry 44; Hensey 40; James 38;
Nathan 71; Osborn 61; Osborne 79;
Sarah 44
GRIMES James 77, 104; Joshua 131;
Mary 77; Resin 43
GRISE Stephen 111
GRIVE George 61
GROCE John 88
GROFF Jacob 122; John 111, 122
GROG Jacob 23
GROUND Adam 82
GROVER George 42; Tabitha 41, 42;
William 1, 8
GROVERMAN Anthony 141
GROVEY Francis 122
GRUNDY George 49, 71, 140
GUDGEON Sutton 2, 7, 12
GUIDEMAN --- 141
GUITON Henry 7, 8; Underwood 1, 8, 9
GUNDY Peter 7, 9
GUNET A. 140
GUNNETT George 56
GUY Charles 140
GUYNN William 43
GUYTON Benjamin 7; Henry 7; John 7;
Underwood 10
GWINN John 111, 118
GWYNN William 4, 8, 12, 29, 41

HACKET John 68, 74; Philip 141
HACKETT John 71
HADEN William 97
HADLY John 23
HAGAR John 91
HAGARTHA John 82
HAGER Barbary 122
HAGUE John 141
HAHN Andrew 123; John 123, 127
HAIN Andrew 9
HAINES Isaac 30; Martin 118, 119;
Michael 98; Nathan 131
HAINS Catharine 50; Mordecai 123;
Samuel 123; William 123
HAIR Christopher 23
HAKLON Edward 141

INDEX

HENNISTOPHEL Barnet 89; Jacob 89;
    John 89; William 89
HENRY Isaac 141; John
HERMAN John 141
HERNER Jacob 112; Michael 112, 117
HERRICK John
HERRINGTON Mrs. 74; William 97
HERSH Harmon 123; Herman 111
HERSPERGER Catherine 141
HESS Charles 112
HESSON Baltzer 111; Wendle 111
HETTINGER Michael 68, 71
HETTLEBRECK George 123
HEWITT Robert 97
HIBBERT Aaron 123
HICKMAN Boston 23; Elizabeth 77
HICKS Abraham 29; Jacob 29, 30;
    Robert 141
HIDE George 142; Jonathan 123
HIGH William 141
HILEMAN Conrod 89
HILL Abraham 112; H. John 141; Isaac
    112; Richard 112 141; William 112
HILLEN Solomon 75, 77, 78; Thomas 77
HILLEY Patrick 56
HILT John 141
HILTERBRAND Jacob 89
HILTON Abraham 42; John 43
HINDLE Michael 9, 16
HINES Martain 122; Paddy 119
HINKEL John 50
HINKLE William 89
HINTON Thomas 76
HIPLIN John 141
HIPSEY Action 82; Charles 82; William
    82
HIPSLEY John 105; Joshua 105
HISER Frederick 89; Richard 53
HISS Jacob 75, 77
HISSEY Charles 82
HITCHCOCK Mrs. 74
HITER Stoffle 123
HITESHAW Jacob 128
HITESHEW Jacob 123; Philip 123
HIVELY Christian 87
HOBBERT Joseph 132
HOBBS Mrs. 141; Nicholas 130; William
    105
HOBURG Sophia 141
HOCKENAN John 134
HOCKMAN John 131, 135; Mary 131
HODGES Peter 141; William 141

HODSKISS Edward 121
HOFFMAN Adam 61; George 141; Henry
    142
HOGAN Aaron 141
HOKE Conrod 112
HOLBROOK Jacob 68, 71; Raria 77
HOLLAND George 1, 9; John 141;
    Littleton 141; Mary 1, 9
HOLLIDAY James 114; John R. 36
HOLLINGSWORTH Jesse 142; Samuel 61,
    68, 71, 74; Thomas 61, 68, 71, 74,
    141; Zebulon 42, 62, 142
HOLLINS John 68, 71, 74; William 142
HOLLIS Mary 50
HOLMES Gabriel 3, 7, 9; James 89;
    John 89
HOLTAN Thomas 99
HOLTZ Peter 71
HONEYWALT Lodwick 113
HONEYWORTH Ludwick 141
HOOD Benjamin 105; Elizabeth 105;
    Hannah 105; James 98, 105; John
    105, 106; Thomas 61
HOOFMAN Henry 89; Michael 89
HOOFMAN William 23
HOOK --- 138; Frederick 61, 141;
    Jacob 61, 65; Joseph 61, 141;
    Rudolph 59, 61, 65
HOOKE Anthony 97
HOOKER Benjamin 30; Jacob 97; Richard
    97; Samuel 97; Thomas 89
HOOKS Richard 118
HOOPER Nicholas 71; Thomas 141;
    William 67
HOOS Catherine 142
HOOVER Frederick 141; Ignatius 141;
    John 9; Michael 141
HOPKINS Ezekiel 9; Girard141; Hopkin
    68; John 36; Johnsy 36; Joseph 36,
    71; Nicholas 35
HORICK Jacob 111
HORN Adam 89; Christopher 97; John s.
    141, 142; Michael 63; Philip 141
HORNE Peter 141
HORNER Michael 109
HOSHEL Jesse 23
HOSETLER 141
HOSKINS Mr. 141
HOSPLEHORN George 131; Ludwick 131
HOSS Christian 131; Emagrat 131;
    Michael 36
HOUPTMAN Henry 128

161

LOVEALL David 90; Henry 90; Luther 90; Susannah 90; William 90; Zachariah 90
LOW David 52; Florah 52; Jesse 11; John 11, 18, 52, 112; Joshua 11; Nicholas 52
LOWE Barbara 63; Jesse 11; John 112; Joshua 16
LOWNSLAGER Jacob 142
LOYD Thomas 99
LUCAS James 108; John 142; Thomas 78
LUCH John 142
LUCUS Thomas 75, 77
LUDLEY John 43
LUKE Jane 142
LUKESS Priscilla 52
LUNEY John 15
LUTTIG John C. 69, 71, 74
LUX Darby 36; Rachel 36, 71; WIlliam 11, 14, 15
LYE Robert 57
LYNCH Anthony 142; Benjamin 142; Bernard 11; Cornelius 11; Gray 68; Hugh 52; John 142; Joshua 75, 77, 78; Patrick 11, 71, 74; Roebuck 36, 69; William 36, 52, 69, 71, 74; WIlliam Kid 75, 77, 78
LYNSEY John 11
LYON Robert 52
LYSTER Jacob 122; John 124; Nicholas 124
LYTLE James 11; Thomas 3, 9, 10, 11; William 11

M--- John 17
MABILE William 143
MABURY Catharine 52, 54
MACATEE Clement 143
MacCUBBIN John 43; William 69
MacCUBIN Zachariah 83
MacGRUE Andrew 69
MACKARD Joseph 53
MacKIM Alexander 69
MACKLEY A. 130
MacMECHEN David 41
MACNEER William 143
MADARY Jacob 53
MADEWELL Alexander 71, 73; James 69, 71
MADINGER Jacob 143
MAGUIRE Francis 143
MAHONY Jubel 43

MAIDWELL John 143
MAIM Anthony 143
MAJOR John 124
MAJORS Ann Eve 113; Elias 124; Elisha 114; Greenberry 90, 122, 124; Jacob 90; James 113; John 90; Nathan 119; Robert 116
MALEN William 99
MALES John 37
MALLET William 82
MALLETT William 53
MALONEE John 30; William 24
MANDON Barbara 113; Rinehart 113
MANEWEATHERS Nicholas 106
MANING Samuel 52
MANIS Joseph 44
MANKIN Josiah (or Isaiah) 143
MANN Anthony 69, 71, 74
MANNAN Abraham 99; Joseph 99; Richard 99; Samuel 99
MANNING Joseph 99; Richard 99; Samuel 99
MANRO Jonathan 96
MARING Wolfgang 113
MARK Peter 113
MARKE Jacob 25; Samuel 25
MARKEE Henry 25
MARKLE Adam 130
MARKLEY Adam 132, 133; Gabrial 133; Hester 133
MARRIS Joseph 43; William 42
MARSH James 25; John 37; Jonathan 143; Joshua 9, 12; Thomas 9, 12, 13; William 16
MARSHAL Thomas 2
MARSHALL Jacob 24; John 143; Thomas 24; William 24
MARSHEL Thomas 12
MARTIN George 113; Irenius 74; Jacob 113, 124; James 144; Luther 69, 71, 74, 143
MASH John 99
MASON Benjamin 143, 144; James 30; Michael 47
MASSLER Ulrick 133
MASTER Lee 99; Legh 121
MASTERS Lehaskins 133; Leigh 133
MATHEW Edward 13
MATHEWS Edward 13; Eli 30; John 36; Mordecai 30; Oliver 36; Rachel 30; Richard 143; Thomas 30; William 143; William P. 69, 72

INDEX

168

PAPPLE John 122
PARISH Edward 10, 14; John 65;
   Richard 134
PARKE Aquila 75
PARKER George 144; Sarah 43; William
   54
PARKINSON Richard 69, 72
PARKS Abraham 42, 44; Aquila 44, 76;
   Benjamin 37; David 37; William 37,
   87
PARLETT David 75, 77, 78; Martin 77;
   William 75, 77
PARRISH Aquila 25; Edward 14, 54;
   Elizabeth 54; Jonathan 100;
   Mordecai 25; Richard 100; William
   100
PARTRIDGE Job 69, 72; John 69, 72, 74
PASCAULT Lewis 77, 144
PATTERSON John 138, 144; Walter 144;
   William 54, 106
PATTON & JONES 144
PAUL Daniel 144; John 14; Thomas 15
PAWLIN Robert 77
PAXTON Thomas 114; William 116
PEACHY Martin 26
PEACOCK Jacob 80
PEAK Robert 43
PEARCE Charles 43; Josias 103; Thomas
   14; William 14
PEARE Dennis 61
PEAREA James 134
PEARIA James 130, 131
PECHT Jacob 125; Philip 125
PECK Charles 64 Nicholas 83
PECKINS Peter 65
PEDICORD Adam 54
PEEL David 109
PEIRCE Edward 18
PEMBERTON Joshua 54; William 54
PEN Caleb 83; Carline 83; Maryam 84;
   Nathan 83; Rizen 83; Shadrach 83;
   William 83
PENNINGTON --- 141; Henry 144; Howard
   142; Josiah 144; Josias 72
PENNY Alexander 53
PENNYBAKER William 91
PENTER Jacob 144
PERCE Josias 103
PERDUE Walter 1, 12, 14
PEREGOY Henry 25; John 26; Joseph 64
PERIAN Peter 72
PERIGO Elisha 144

PERKIPILE Jacob 26
PERRIGO Elisha 31; Joseph 69, 72, 73;
   William 31
PETERS Henry 91, 125, 134, 144; Jacob
   25; Samuel 144; Thomas 69, 72, 74
PHEASENT Samuel 125
PHILIP Conley 64
PHILIPS Isaac 144; Reese 114
PHILLIPS James 100; Nathan 96; Samuel
   100; Thomas 100, 106
PHILPOT Brian 37
PHREN Frederick 100
PICKETT Charles 134; George 54
PICKSTER Peter 125
PIERCE Edward 3, 8, 14, 18; Humphrey
   64; Israel 144
PIERLY Peter 91, 93
PIERPOINT Arnos 144; Benedict 83;
   Joseph 83; Mary 83; Samuel 83;
   Thomas 83; Walter 83, 144
PILER Joseph 134
PILOYER Peter 91
PINDAL John 144
PINDALL John 54
PINDELL Philip 77
PIPER George 69J, 110; Jacob 110;
   James 144
PIXLER Christian 91; Jacob 91
PLANE David 134
PLOWMAN Edward 91; James 91; Jonathan
   2, 10, 14
PLUCHOR Abraham 26
PLUCKER Jacob 26; John 26
POBLETS Charles 26; Christopher 26;
   Michael 26
POCOCK James 10, 11, 14, 69; Jesse 5,
   7, 12, 14; Joshua 144
POKE James 144
POLK --- 144
POLLOCK Elias 144
POLSON Andrew 134; Cornelius 134;
   James 134
POMMEAR Peter 83
PONTER John 131
POOL Henry 100, 134; Joshua 107;
   Mathias 95; WIlliam 134
POOLE Brice 134; Henry 137; Luke 134
POPE Catharine 71
POPHAM Samuel 100
POPLETS Charles 26; Jacob 91; Peter
   26
POPPLE John 125; Mr. 112

PORTER Augustine 75, 77; Benjamin 69; Joshua 106; Mury 54; Peregrine 77; Peter 105; Philip 54; Robert 75, 77, 78; Thomas 49
PORTS Philip 91
POTT John 111, 112, 114
POTTER John 43
POTTNEY Thomas 84
POWDER Andrew 118; Jacob 118, 125; Powder's Heirs 131
POWEL John 144; John Upton 114
POWELL William 125
POWERS James 144
POWLEY Daniel 144
PRATT Frederich 64
PRESBURY George G. 41, 43, 44; Gige 144; Walter G. 41, 43, 44
PRESSTMAN George 144
PRESTINE George 144
PRICE Amon 64; Benjamin 23, 38; Daniel 31; Hezikiah 144; James 31; John 25, 64; Joshua 25; Martha 64; Mordecai 38; Richard 64; Stephen 38; Thomas 14, 18, 25; William 25, 37, 42, 144
PRICHARD John 91
PRICKER Anthony 114
PRINE William 63
PRINGLE Mark 64
PRION Simon 41, 43
PRITCHARDS John 144; Timothy 144
PROCTOR Isaiah 144
PROSER Isaac 25
PROUGH Conrad 134
PUCE Mary 134; Michael 134
PUE Mary 134; Michael 129, 133
PUMPHREY Frederick 144
PUNTNEY Lydia 64; Sarah 64
PUSEY George 134
PUTTINBERGER Michael 114

Qyay Thomas 144

RADOLPH Daniel 125
RAIL John 134
RAMSAY Nathaniel 144
RANDAL Christopher 100; Johnze 84; Nathan 106
RANDALL Beal 54, 55; Beal Thomas 55; Charles 17; Christopher 26, 134; James 145; Nicholas Beal 26; William 145

RANDALLS Nicholas 84
RANISE Joseph 145
RANKIN Hugh 66
RAUBOUGH Henry 100
RAVIN Isaac 77; Luke 41, 44
RAWLENS Isaac 77
RAWLIN Isaac 75
RAWLINS Isaac 77, 78; William 77
RAYMOND --- 142; Daniel 144
RAYMONS Ch. 145
REACH John 136
READ John 64
READY John 70, 74
REAGLE John 121
REANY Adam 51
RECK Abraham 114
REDDY John 68
REDING George 145
REED Edward 74; George 62; Hugh 114; Isaac 145; Jacob 114; John 84; Jonas 114; Joseph 14; Nelson 54
REEL Michael 116
REES Daniel 41, 43
REESE Andrew 118, 125; Frederick 122; George 91; Jacob 92, 125; John 84, 114; Thomas 112, 116
REEVER Ulrick 114
REG Henry 134
REILEY Dennis 72
REISTER John 54
REITTER Jonathan 144
RENICKER George 144
REYNOLDS Nicholas 69, 72, 74
RHODES Frederick 91
RIBLE Nicholas 26
RICE James 15; Mary 144
RICH Benfor 81
RICHARD Richard 26; Samuel 26
RICHARDS Abraham 119; Job 18; John 69, 72, 145; Jonathan 72; Joseph 76; Joshua 72; Richard 91; Samuel 75
RICHARDSON Daniel 144; James 42; Thomas 14
RICKETTS Hugh 144; Samuel 43
RIDENER Andrew 134
RIDDLE Robert 145
RIDDLEMOSER James 144; Mr. 145
RIDGELEY Charles 38; John 100
RIDGELY --- 17; Charles 38, 84; Henry 134; John 65, 67; Rebecca 38; William 38, 84

INDEX

SHOEMAKER George 115; John 116; Peter
126, 128
SHOTT Jacob 145
SHOUG Henry 109
SHOVE Michael 146
SHOVER John 22
SHOWER John 118
SHOWERS John 92
SHRACK Dietrick 72
SHRINER Peter 126
SHRIVER Andrew 126; Conrod 127, 128;
David 127; David G. 126; H. John
146; Martin 129; Michael 135;
Peter 135
SHRODER Henry 145; Nathaniel 145
SHROYER Matthews 108; Matthias 115
SHRS --- 146
SHUGARS Edward 85
SHULS Philip 27
SHULTZE John 127
SHURER John 58
SHURMAN Elizabeth 145
SHUSTER Catharine 93; Joshua 93
SIAS Benjamin 92
SIGLER Henry 145
SILE Conrod 135
SIMMERMAN John 27
SIMPSON John 43, 145; Richard 134
SINCLAIR John 145; Moses 43; Robert
145; William 17
SINCLAR William 2
SINDALL Samuel 145
SINDORFF George 109
SINGARY Christopher 27
SINGUE George 116
SINNARD John 145
SIPLEY Peter 100
SIPP Peter 115
SISLER Philip 146
SISNAP Adam 145
SITH Samuel 77
SIX Henry 114; Philip 116
SKINNER John 17, 41, 43, 44
SKIPPER Elijah 22; John 19; Thomas
146
SLADE Abraham 3, 13, 15; Ezekiel 6,
9, 15; Josia 17; Josias 9, 16;
Mrs. 74; Thomas 15; William 9, 17
SLADESMAN Michael 72
SLATER William 69
SLATES Frederick 115
SLEE Joseph 8, 16

SLICK John 126
SLIDER Peter 115; Sunon 115
SLIVER Robert 145
SLOAN James 66
SLREMELL Frederick 145
SLY Cathrine 145
SMALLWOOD William 74
SMEAK John 115
SMELTSER Michael 126
SMILEY Isaac 145
SMITE Samuel 145
SMITH & JESSOP 145
SMITH Adam 26, 85; Archibald 146;
Catherine 145; Christopher 92;
Gellary 126; Jacob 115, 116, 130,
133, 145; Job 145; John 34, 101,
145, 146; Joshua 15, 27, 84, 101,
126; Larkin 13, 16; Peter 145;
Richard 126, 146; Robert 15, 146;
Samuel 74, 75, 84; Samuel R. 146;
Sarah 3, 13, 16, 19, 75, 78, 145;
Widow 80; William 75, 77, 79, 126,
142, 145; William R. 145
SMOUSE Henry 134
SMULL Jacob 145
SMYTHE Samuel 146
SNACH Jacob 115; John 115
SNADER Jacob 135
SNIDER Abraham 26; Conrod 112; George
127; Harriman 146; Jacob 126, 127;
Martin 93; Matthias 115; Michael
127
SNITES Ludwick 100
SNOWDEN Francis 107; Mary 107
SNOWFER John 127
SNYDER Christopher 92; Frederich 93
SOANE John 115
SOLLERS Basil 74; Elisha 74;
Elizabeth 74; Polly 74; Thomas 74
SORICK Henry 115
SOUER Philip 124
SOWERS John 1, 17, 106; William 115
SPALDING Henry 116
SPANGLER George 126, 128
SPARKS Elijah 11, 15; Francis 5, 14,
16; Joseph 114; Josias 15; Matthew
16; Matthews 16; Thomas 17
SPENCE Robert 145
SPENCER Abel 84
SPICER Thomas 80
SPINDLER George 26; Jacob 26; John
26; Nicholas 26

173

INDEX

WEBB Henry 147; Samuel 146
WEBLING Charles 28
WEBSTER James 41, 43, 44
WEEKS William 70, 73
WEFFLIN Thomas 64
WEISENTHAL Mrs. 146
WEITER Susannah 70, 73
WELCH Henry 130, 132; James 66; John
  66; Prudence 93; Robert 66, 67
WELLEN George 147
WELLS Benjamin 57; Charles 57; James
  118, 129, 136; Jennett 119; Joseph
  136; Rosanna 70, 72, 73; Thomas
  56, 136
WELSH Adam 116, 147; John 11, 101;
  Mary 101; Robert 147; William 31
WEMMER Abraham 117
WERBLE Philip 127
WERKENER Peter 119
WEST Elijah 147; Joseph 51
WESTBY Hugh 147
WETHERBY William 70
WEYLEY Vincent 41, 44
WHALEN George 55
WHALLEN Stephen 45
WHEELER Amelia 31; Benjamin 31; Brian
  28; Edward 101; Greenberry 28;
  James 31; John 70, 73; Joseph 40;
  Mordecai 28; Nat. 40; Richard 28,
  98; Robert 146; Solomon 40, 78;
  Stephen 31; Thomas 79, 146; Wasan
  18, 40; William 31
WHELAN Bassil 146; James 146;
  Jonathan 146; Joseph 31; Peter 146
WHIGHT Richard 108
WHIPPLE William 147
WHISNER Mathias 28
WHISSEN Joseph 57
WHITE Andrew 116; Ann 128; Charles
  85, 147; George 65; John 128; Mary
  78; Patience 128; Regin 147;
  Thomas 61, 146
WHITELEATHER A. 94
WHITELOCK --- 145; Charles 146; John
  146; Mr. 147
WHITELY William 67
WHITEMAN George 116
WHITFORD John 40
WIDENER Susannah 18
WIDLER Edward 146
WIER John 107
WIGART Andrew 119

WIGLEY Isaac 77
WIGNAL James 147
WILCOX William 70
WILDERMAN George 85; Jacob 65; John
  85
WILEY Greenbury 17; Vincent 17
WILKERSON William 147
WILKISON John 42
WILKS --- 139; James 147
WILLAMAY Nicholas 84
WILLEBY William 66
WILLEY Henry 146
WILLHELM Henry 28; John 28
WILLIAM --- 143; Forsyth 140
WILLIAMS --- 146; Ann 57; Benjamin
  55, 101; Charles 146; Enock 43;
  Jacob 146; John 93, 136; John
  Edward 65; Otho H. 78; Reese 18;
  Robert 101; Thomas 18; Tobias 75;
  Widow 146; William 18, 127
WILLIAMSON David 66, 147; Thomas 146
WILLIS Henry 64, 66, 67
WILLMAN Richard 80
WILLSON Catharine 128; James 66;
  Nicholas 56
WILMER William 147
WILMOT John 17; Ruth 17
WILMOTT John 4
WILSON --- 145; Andrew 18; Asael 4,
  19; Benj. 18; Capt. 72; Charles
  103; Gittings 18; Given 41; Giving
  44; Hannah 146; Henry 3, 16, 18;
  Hugh 146; James 146, 147; Jean 6,
  10, 18; John 12, 17, 18, 44, 69,
  146, 147; Kid 18; Nicholas 76;
  Robert 18; Samuel 127, 133, 146;
  Solomon 103; Thompson 127; Widow
  129, 142; William 43
WILT George 116
WIMMER Abraham 116
WINCE Frederick 126, 128
WINCHESTER James 40; Lydia 119;
  Stephen 101, 110, 115, 118, 119,
  124, 128; William 101
WINCKLE James 147
WINE Henry 116
WINEMAN Henry 70, 73, 74
WINN John 147
WINTER George 131; John 127
WINTERS Arehart 118; George 127, 128;
  John 119
WINTERVAT Henry 119

177

WINTZ Michael 115; Philip 116
WIREL William 76
WISE --- 70, 73
WISHAHNPLE Christian 147
WISTLE William 146
WIVIL Joseph 116
WODDINGTON Joshua 136
WOLF Andrew 127; Elizabeth 116; Henry
    136; Jacob 127; James 146Martin
    136; Michael 116; Peter 136;
    Philip 116
WOLFE James 18
WON Edward 57
WONT John 85
WOOD Basil 136; James 116; John 136;
    Jonathan 135; Joseph 136; Peter
    70; Richard 123, 127; Sarah 136;
    Susannah 73; Widow 135; William 42

WOODCOCK Robert 28, 31; Thomas 40
WOODEN Francis 67; John 66, 70, 73,
    74; Stephen 67, 93; Thomas 67
WOODING William 28
WOODINGTON Joseph 130
WOODS S. Joseph 147
WOODWARD William 67
WOODYARD John 65
WOOLF Valentine 28
WOOLLERY Christopher 101
WOOLRICH Philip 70, 73
WOOLRICK Philip 74
WOOLSEY Catharine 128; George 128
WORDLE --- 85
WORKING Henry 146
WORMAN Andrus 136; George 48; Henry
    136; Jacob 136
WORRELL Caleb 49
WORTHINGTON Charles 40; John 57, 108;
    John T. 40, 131; John Tolly 56,
    93; Samuel 39, 44, 93; Thomas 57,
    69, 73, 74, 101; Vachael 41, 43,
    44; William 40
WRIGHT George 44; Isaac 136; Jacob
    57; James 133; Joel 136; John 146;
    Jonathan 40; Joseph 44, 64, 128,
    136; Joshua 52, 132, 136; Solomon
    5, 18; William 44
WUSE George 146
WYMER Barnet 28

YARE Isaac 136
YATES Thomas 70, 73, 74, 147

YAWN Jacob 128; John 128
YEARLY William 17
YEISER Englehard 11, 19; Howard
    Englehard 4
YELLOTT Jermiah 147
YINGLING Abraham 116; Christ. 94;
    Frederick 110; Jacob 111, 116;
    John 116, 119, 128; Margret 128;
    Peter 128
YOUNG Andrew 124; Ann 147; Benard
    136; Davall 128; Davalt 120;
    Francis 147; Jacob 85; John 147;
    John T. 40, 44; Joseph 67, 147;
    Joshua 128; Larkin 147; Michael
    67; Philip 136; Rebecca 14, 19;
    Samuel 11, 116, 147
YOWN John 40
YUSOR John 147

ZACHARIAS Daniel 128
ZARNES Eve 147
ZELL Barnett 147; Christian 147
ZEPT Adam 108; Christopher 108
ZIMMERMAN George 85
ZOLLMAN Adam 135

www.ingramcontent.com/pod-product-compliance
Lightning Source LLC
Chambersburg PA
CBHW072237270326
41930CB00010B/2160